Middle Eastern Terrorism

Middle Eastern Terrorism

From Black September to September 11

MARK ENSALACO

PENN

University of Pennsylvania Press

Philadelphia

Published by
University of Pennsylvania Press
Philadelphia, Pennsylvania 19104-4112

Printed in the United States of America on acid-free paper

10 9 8 7 6 5 4 3 2 1

A Cataloging-in-Publication record is available from the Library of Congress
ISBN-13: 978-0-8122-4046-7
ISBN-10: 0-8122-4046-4

To Sofia, who was born to us just weeks before that terrible Tuesday in September—may we vanquish the scourge of terrorism in her lifetime

Contents

You are pregnant and shall bear a son;
you shall name him Ishmael,
For the Lord has heard you,
God has answered you.
He shall be a wild ass of a man,
his hand against everyone,
And everyone's hand against him;
In opposition to all his kin
Shall he encamp

—Genesis 16: 11–12

Introduction

In September 1970, a month that came to be known as Black September, terrorists belonging to the Popular Front for the Liberation of Palestine (PFLP) simultaneously hijacked three passenger jets bound for the United States in the skies over Europe. Alert air marshals prevented them from hijacking a fourth. Several days later, terrorists from the PFLP hijacked another jet. They flew the jets to a remote airfield in Jordan and held more than three hundred passengers hostage and issued a series of demands for the release of their comrades. The terrorists did not physically harm the hostages, or even threaten anyone. The incident dragged on for weeks. Then, in a spectacle to draw the world's attention to the plight of the Palestinian people, the terrorists blew up the empty jets as news cameras captured the images of exploding planes. That was 12 September 1970.

In September 2001, terrorists belonging to Al Qaeda simultaneously hijacked four American passenger jets in the skies over the United States. During the hijacking the terrorists stabbed and slashed passengers and flight attendants. They did not issue a single demand or statement of grievances. One hundred and eight minutes after the hijackings began, the terrorists crashed the jets into the World Trade Center's Twin Towers and the Pentagon as news cameras captured the images of exploding planes and collapsing buildings. The hijacking of the fourth jet was defeated by courageous passengers who sacrificed their own lives to prevent the destruction of the White House or the Capitol. In all, nearly three thousand perished. That was September 11, 2001.

In three decades the terrorism originating in the conflicts and geopolitics of the Arab and Muslim worlds had mutated from spectacle to atrocity.

On the morning of September 11, minutes after American Airlines flight 11 ripped through the World Trade Center's North Tower, the news director from the Dayton affiliate of ABC News summoned me to the newsroom. I had begun teaching courses on political violence and terrorism at the University of Dayton and for Air Force intelligence officers at Wright Patterson Air Force Base in 1989. The local news affiliate had called on me a number of times over the years: after the bombing of the World Trade Center in 1993, the attacks on military installations in Saudi Arabia in 1995 and 1996, the destruction of the U.S. embassies in Kenya and Tanzania in 1998, and the attack on the USS *Cole* in 2000.

I, like my colleagues who research or teach terrorism, knew enough about Osama bin Laden to be concerned about his organization. Al Qaeda was a clear and present danger to the United States. Bin Laden had issued a "declaration of war against the Americans who occupy the land of the two holy mosques" in 1996. In 1998 he issued a *fatwa* exhorting Muslims around the world to murder Americans anywhere they could find them. One had the disquieting sense that bin Laden could strike without warning. Al Qaeda terrorists had attacked and severely damaged the USS *Cole* just before the presidential elections in 2000. But as I watched the atrocity of September 11 unfold that morning, I was struck by its magnitude. I watched the towers collapse with the agonizing realization that thousands of human beings were dying before my eyes.

I returned to campus after the collapse of the towers and stood before a classroom of desperately frightened students. One student asked a question: "Where did this come from?"

As evening fell in the Midwest, my neighbors gathered in the commons behind our homes; an eerie silence hung over us because of the presidential order to halt all air traffic. The silence was broken by the sonic boom of two F-16 Falcons that roared out of Wright Patterson Air Force Base to rendezvous with Air Force One, which passed though Ohio airspace as the president returned to Washington from a Strategic Air Command Base in Nebraska. It was then that my wife persuaded me to write this book in an attempt to answer that student's question: "Where did this come from?"

The question can be taken to mean many things. Who was behind the attacks that Tuesday morning? What is the origin of the hostility? When did terrorists begin attacking Americans?

I remembered as a junior high school student watching the news coverage of terrorists destroying the empty passenger jets in the Jordanian desert in Black September 1970, and the spectacles that followed: the Lod Airport massacre, the Munich Olympic massacre, the destruction of Pan Am 103, and many other acts of terror. I could not think of a single book that covered the entire history of terror directed at Americans and American interests, so I decided to write one. This book narrates the evolution and transmutation of terrorism originating in the complex and conflictive politics and geopolitics of the Arab and Muslim worlds.

The contemporary era of terror began after Israel's victory in the Six Day War in 1967, an event that radicalized the Palestinian national liberation movement. It began with a campaign against civil aviation—hijackings, with the first hijacking of an El Al flight in the summer of

1968; automatic weapon and grenade attacks at airport terminals; the sabotage of passenger jets in the air. Richard Nixon was the first U.S. president compelled to confront the threat of Middle East terror. Americans were slaughtered in some of the early terror operations—twenty-nine U.S. Catholic pilgrims to the Holy Land died in the Lod Airport massacre in 1972, and others were held hostage aboard hijacked jets. The terrorists justified such assaults because, in the words of one of those involved in the Skyjack Sunday operation in September 1970, "No one heard our screams or our suffering."

In 1971, Yasser Arafat's Fatah faction of the PLO adopted the strategy of terror. This was the origin of the Black September organization. Its terror rampage lasted only three years, until the end of 1973. But in those three short years Black September conducted some of the most memorable operations: the murder of eleven Israeli Olympians in Munich in 1972 and of two U.S. diplomats a year later. The man behind Black September resorted to semantics in an attempt to distance himself from terrorism: "I do not confuse revolutionary violence, which is a political act," he said, "with terrorism, which is not."

The Israeli response to the atrocities by Black September, as well as the earlier ones by the PFLP, was guided by the biblical maxim of an eye for an eye: Israeli assassins hunted down and killed some of the men who were responsible, or thought to be responsible, for the terror directed against Israelis. The Nixon administration's response was more pragmatic. The CIA established a secret, back channel arrangement with the very men behind Black September. The arrangement was sealed with a warning. "The violence against us has got to stop," the acting director of the CIA told Fatah representatives, "or much blood will flow, and you may be sure that not all of it will be ours."

The end of Black September's terror rampage coincided with the end of hostilities between Israel and its most formidable military foe, Egypt. Egypt and Syria stunned Israel with a massive offensive on the holiest day in the Jewish calendar, Yom Kippur, in 1973, only to be defeated after Israel put up a desperate struggle for survival. The outcome of the Yom Kippur War convinced the Egyptian president to turn to the United States to negotiate the return of Egyptian territory lost in the Six Day War six years earlier. It also convinced Yasser Arafat, the PLO chairman, that U.S. mediation held the only hope for the creation of a Palestinian state. Arafat's tactical turn toward moderation angered those in the Palestinian national movement who clung to the credo that the birth of Palestine demanded the death of Israel. The inexorable result of such logic was the rejection of the peace process and a new wave of terror. So, a month before the American-mediated peace negotiations between Egypt and Israel were to begin, terrorists blew a U.S. airliner out of the sky over the Aegean Sea in the fall of 1974. "We do not want peace," the slogan went, "peace will be the end of all our hopes."

Terrorism lost its strategic coherence after the Americans began to broker what would become a separate peace between Egypt and Israel. The era of Palestinian nationalist terror began to fade in this political and geopolitical environment. In 1975 the factions that made up the Palestinian national movement found themselves drawn into a bloody civil war in Lebanon, much of it fratricidal violence between Palestinian factions backed by Iraq. But then there were the final episodes of the campaign the PFLP had begun in 1968. In the mid-1970s, terrorists tried to shoot down Israeli passenger jets, took delegates of OPEC countries hostage, and hijacked French and German jets carrying Israeli citizens. But the hijackings in particular became famous not for the audacity of the operations but for the lethal operations of elite Israeli and West German counterterrorism units. None of the violence impeded U.S. efforts to secure a separate peace between Egypt and Israel. In the fall of 1977, the Egyptian president addressed the Israeli parliament in words that would later cost him his life: "We accept to live with you in permanent peace."

President Jimmy Carter, who inherited the peace process from Ford and Nixon, managed to achieve a historic peace agreement between Egypt and Israel in 1979. An era of terror seemed to have come to an end. But another soon began with a revolution and an invasion. The Islamic Revolution in Iran at the beginning of 1979 and the Soviet invasion of Afghanistan at the end of that year marked the transmutation of terror. Although secular Palestinian organizations continued to commit random acts of terror, militant Islam replaced Palestinian nationalism as the most dangerous inspiration for terror. Jihad overtook national liberation as terrorism's rallying call. The Reagan administration poured money and materiel into jihad against the Soviets. Thousands of Arab men rushed to Afghanistan to fight as mujahideen alongside their Afghan brethren—this was the genesis of Al Qaeda. Then, in 1982, Israel invaded Lebanon to destroy the PLO and laid siege to Beirut. American intervention was inevitable but disastrous. The first U.S. encounter with militant Islam—and with mass casualty suicide attacks—came in Lebanon. Hizb'allah, the Party of God, destroyed the U.S. embassy in 1982 and the barracks housing Marine peacekeepers at the Beirut airport in 1983, killing 268 U.S. diplomats, spies, and Marines. The commander of the Marine contingent of the multilateral peacekeeping force had predicted that Reagan's decision to intervene in Lebanon's sectarian civil war would be catastrophic: "Don't you realize that if you do that, we will get slaughtered down there?"

This was the beginning of America's travails in Lebanon and its confrontation with militant Islam. Hizb'allah began seizing U.S. hostages in 1984 and conducted one of the longest hijackings of a U.S. passenger jet the following year. The hostage crises lasted through to the end of the decade and confounded the Reagan administration, which began selling U.S. arms to the Islamic Republic of Iran in the dim hope of gaining the release of Americans held hostage in Lebanon. The clandestine arms-for-hostage deals ended in a fiasco. During this period, remnants of Palestinian terror organizations mounted a series of lethal attacks, including massacres in Rome and Vienna airports. Libya lurked behind most of these attacks, and a military confrontation with the United States became inevitable. Reagan ordered an air strike in 1986; Libya retaliated by destroying a U.S. airliner over Scotland just before Christmas 1988. Ronald Reagan had been compelled to confront a hydra-headed threat of terror. But he could not entirely make good on his pledge that "America will never make concessions to terrorists."

There were no major acts of terror against Americans or U.S. interests during the administration of George Herbert Walker Bush. The last embers of Palestinian nationalist terror had burned out. Bill Clinton may have thought he had inherited a new world order that would permit him to focus on domestic issues when he entered office in 1993. But there would be consequences from Operation Desert Storm, the Bush administration's short war to expel Iraqi forces from Kuwait, and the withdrawal of the Soviet Union from Afghanistan. In Afghanistan, the Arab mujahideen formed the "Base" of a global terror network around Osama bin Laden. This base—Al Qaeda—would wage jihad against apostate governments in the Arab world and, eventually, the United States. The presence of U.S. forces in Saudi Arabia, the most holy land of Islam, convinced bin Laden, a Saudi, that the United States was Islam's mortal enemy. Others thought like him. Militant Muslims attacked the United States at regular intervals during Clinton's first term in office, in 1993, 1995, and 1996. The first of these attacks came on U.S. soil when a cell of Islamist terrorists attempted but failed to destroy the World Trade Center. Muslims had come to believe, as bin Laden exhorted them, that "the real enemy is America."

There was a deceptive two-year lull after bin Laden's "Declaration of War Against the Americans who Occupy the Land of the Two Holy Mosques" in 1996. But then, in February 1998, bin Laden and others issued a ruling of Islamic law that purported to impose a religious obligation on all Muslims to kill Americans. Al Qaeda destroyed two U.S. embassies in East Africa months later. Clinton retaliated with cruise missile strikes on Al Qaeda facilities in Afghanistan and gave instructions to the CIA to capture or kill bin Laden. America was now engaged in a covert, low-intensity war against militant Islam. Al Qaeda attempted unsuccessfully to conduct mass casualty attacks against Americans on the eve of the new millennium of the Christian era. At the end of 2000, Al Qaeda terrorists attacked and severely damaged the USS *Cole*. There could be no doubt that militant Muslims had taken it upon themselves as a religious obligation to attack Americans and "kill them on the land, on the sea, and in the air."

Americans went to the polls to elect a new president twenty-five days after the *Cole* attack. Al Qaeda had killed Americans on land and sea. By the time George W. Bush took the oath of office, the Al Qaeda terrorists who would kill Americans in the air on 9/11 had already entered the United States. The CIA knew this but never alerted the FBI. Vague warnings about a catastrophic Al Qaeda attack surged in the first months of the Bush administration. By the summer of 2001, counterterrorism officials were warning the national security advisor and the president about an imminent, mass casualty attack that would come without warning. The president was slow to appreciate the urgency of the situation and never took charge of the nation's security crisis. In the first week of August, the CIA briefed the president on bin Laden's determination to strike in the United States. Al Qaeda struck thirty-seven days later. On the night of 11 September, the president addressed the nation: "Today our nation saw evil."

The face of terrorism changed over the three decades between the spectacle of the PFLP's Skyjack Sunday operation in Black September 1970 and the atrocity of Al Qaeda's attack on 11 September 2001. Militant Islam replaced secular Palestinian nationalists as the ideology of terror. Jihad against apostates and infidels replaced the liberation of Palestine as the cause. Militant Islam was sworn to the destruction of the State of Israel, but now destruction of apostate Arab regimes and expulsion of Americans from Muslim lands became new strategic objectives of terror. Militant Islam proclaimed the murder of Americans, who had rarely been targeted by Palestinian terrorists, to be a religious duty. Terror became far more lethal with the advent of mass casualty suicide attacks. The face of terrorism has changed, but not its nature.

Acts of terror are war crimes. Terrorism is a crime against humanity. Terrorism is a form of irregular warfare that violates the laws and customs of war, as terrorists deliberately target noncombatants for the purpose of instilling fear and ultimately compelling governments to capitulate to their demands. Whatever the validity of the terrorists' political, social, or religious grievances, acts of terror negate the legitimacy of the cause. One of the air pirates who participated in Skyjack Sunday attempted to justify hostage-taking by saying "no one heard our screams or our suffering." The man behind the Black September terror operations attempted to distinguish "revolutionary violence, which is a political act" from "terrorism, which is not." But whether the ideological motivation for terror was secular Palestinian nationalism or militant Islam, terrorists justified murder. "The idea," said a leader of a secular Palestinian terror organization was "to take passengers hostage, kill them in the terminals, blow them out of the skies." This differs not at all from the Muslim imam's exhortation to all Muslims to kill Americans "on the land, on the sea, and in the air."

The crimes narrated in this book involve, fundamentally, acts that are "part of a widespread or systematic attack directed against any civilian population": murder and willful killing, the taking of hostages, torture, and destruction not justified by military necessity.[1] It is immaterial to me that terrorists reject these standards of lawful warfare; the standards have broad international acceptance in principle, albeit not always in practice, and I apply them to the conduct of my own government in the War on Terror.

The attacks on 9/11 clearly constituted a war crime. Al Qaeda intentionally launched an attack that was certain to cause loss of life or injury to civilians or damage to civilian objects—to paraphrase the language of the statute that established the International Criminal Court. But there is a deeper stratum to this criminality. Bin Laden's 1998 fatwa, discussed in Chapter 9, constituted direct and public incitement to commit acts intended to destroy a national group, to paraphrase the Genocide Convention.[2] Bin Laden's fatwa was incitement to genocide: "In compliance with God's order, the ruling to kill the Americans and their allies— civilians and military—is an individual duty for every Muslim who can do it in any country in which it is possible to do it."

In the three decades from the first PFLP hijacking to the Al Qaeda attack on 11 September, terrorists have sacrificed innocent human lives in the name of abstractions. Then it was a war for the liberation of Palestine, now it is jihad against apostates and infidels. Terrorism in the Middle East, from Black September to 11 September, began as a U.S. president struggled to avert a conventional war between Israel and the Arab states committed to Israel's destruction; it ended with an atrocity, unimaginable thirty years earlier, that led another president to declare a global war on terrorism.

Chapter 1
No One Heard Our Screams or Our Suffering

In the spring of 1967, Lyndon Johnson was agonizing over the escalating war in South East Asia. It had been nearly two years since he announced the fateful decision to commit U.S. combat forces in South Vietnam in order to defeat the Viet Cong guerrillas fighting to liberate South Vietnam and unify it with the Communist North. Johnson, who had assumed office after the assassination of John F. Kennedy in 1963, and went on to a landslide victory in the 1964 presidential election, saw his presidency destroyed by an intractable guerrilla war in the jungles of Vietnam. But by the spring of 1967 he was becoming concerned about a guerrilla war in the deserts of the Middle East and the possibility of a conventional war between Israel and the Arab states encircling it. Palestinian guerrillas were regularly conducting guerrilla raids against Israel from Jordan, Syria, and Lebanon. In May, the Egyptian president mobilized Egyptian forces, expelled the United Nations peacekeeping force deployed in the Sinai Peninsula, and closed the Gulf of Aqaba to Israeli shipping. "The danger implicit in every border incident in the Middle East," Johnson wrote after leaving office, "was not merely war between Israelis and Arabs but an ultimate confrontation between the Soviet Union and the United States." Johnson urged restraint on Israeli Prime Minister Levi Eshkol, but the president understood that the Egyptian provocations constituted a cause for war: "I used all the energy and experience I could muster to prevent war. But I was not too hopeful."[1] Under the exigent circumstances, to ask for Israel's forbearance was to ask for too much. On the morning of 5 June, Israel launched a massive preemptive strike against the Egyptian air force, destroying virtually all its Soviet-made combat aircraft on the ground. Over the next six days Israeli troops engaged Arab armies on three fronts. By the time the Israelis complied with UN Security Council Resolution 242 demanding an end to the fighting on 10 June, Israeli forces had occupied Egyptian territory in the Sinai Peninsula and the Gaza strip, Syrian territory in the Golan Heights, and Jordanian territory on the West Bank and Jerusalem, giving

Israel sovereignty over the site of its ancient Temple and one of Islam's holiest places, the Al-Aksa Mosque.[2] The Israeli victory in the Six Day War demoralized the Arab states, but it radicalized the Palestinian national movement and marked the onset of an era of terrorism directed against Israel, moderate Arab states and, inevitably, Europe and the Unites States. By the time Johnson left office in January 1969, Palestinian terrorists had launched a full-scale assault on civilian aviation intended to compel the world to consider the plight of the Palestinian people.

Origins

Palestinians refer to the creation of the state of Israel in 1948 as al-nakba, the catastrophe. Hundreds of thousands of Palestinians were displaced as result of the creation of the Jewish state, the ensuing war between the Arabs and Israelis, and an Israeli policy of expulsion.[3] As Jews—many of them Holocaust survivors—toiled to build a viable democratic state, the Palestinians chafed under Israeli occupation or languished in sprawling refugee camps in Jordan, Syria, and Lebanon or in the émigré communities throughout the Middle East. In the decades after the founding of Israel, and especially after the Arab's ignominious defeat in the Six Day War, thousands of Palestinians rushed to become fedayeen—"men of sacrifice" in Arabic—in the ranks of several guerrilla organizations later affiliated with the Palestine Liberation Organization. Founded in 1964, the PLO came to be identified with Yasser Arafat, its perennial chairman, and associated with the international terrorism committed under the banner of Palestinian nationalism after the Six Day War. The reality is more complex. Arafat actually resisted leading his guerrilla movement fully into the PLO until 1969, five years after its creation, when he was in a position to dominate it. By then another Palestinian organization had already committed the first acts of international terrorism.

Born in Cairo in August 1929 to Palestinian parents as Mohammed Abdel Rahman Raouf Arafat, Yasser Arafat would emerge as the acclaimed leader of the Palestinians before his fortieth birthday. Yet he lived only briefly in Palestine in the mid-1930s, as a young child when his father sent him to live with relatives in Jerusalem after the death of his mother.[4] Arafat returned to the Egyptian capital in 1937 and spent his formative years there. Soon after he entered the university to study engineering in 1947, he became engaged in the politics of the Palestinian émigré community, participating in Palestinian student organizations and smuggling weapons into a Palestine still under the British mandate. When Israel declared independence and war erupted between the Arabs and Jews in 1948, Arafat set off to fight with the irregular forces of the Muslim Brotherhood in Gaza, where he distinguished himself by his valor. The Arab defeat left Arafat with some inveterate judgments about the inclination of Arab states to betray their Palestinian brothers. The coup that brought Gamal Abdel Nasser to power in Egypt in 1952 did not substantially alter his thinking. In 1956, when Egypt went to war against combined forces of Israel, Great Britain, and France, Arafat was called up with other Egyptian reserve officers and sent to Port Said to clear mines. But a year after the Suez Crisis he left—or was compelled to leave—Egypt for Kuwait.

It was in Kuwait where Arafat and other Palestinian exiles incrementally formed the Palestine Liberation Movement, or Fatah, a process complete by 1959.[5] With Arafat was a tight group of close collaborators that included Khalil al-Wazir, who went by the name Abu Jihad, and Salah Khalaf, who took Abu Iyad as his nom de guerre. (Both men would be killed for their politics, al-Wazir in 1988 by Israeli commandos led by a future Israeli prime minister, Khalaf in 1991 by a rival Palestinian terrorist group.) Arafat called his movement Fatah, the Qur'an's word for "conquest," by inverting the Arabic acronym for the Palestine Liberation Movement, Harakat al-Tahrir al-Watani al-Filastini. But despite the allusion to Islam and his earlier connection with the Muslim Brotherhood, Arafat was a secular Palestinian nationalist who eschewed ideology in order to broaden Fatah's appeal. For Arafat and the men around him the armed struggle to liberate Palestine took priority over all else. Fatah's guiding principle approached heresy in 1959 when pan-Arab nationalism was at its zenith. Embodied by Egyptian president Gamal Abdel Nasser, the pan-Arab dream envisioned the liberation of Palestine, but only after the unification of the Arab nations made the military defeat of Israel practicable. Arafat inverted the logic of pan-Arabism. Whereas Nasser insisted that Arab unity was necessary for the liberation of Palestine, Arafat countered that the war to liberate Palestine would produce Arab unity: "an armed Palestinian revolution is the only way to liberate our homeland. . . . Only the idea of the armed struggle can bridge ideological differences and accelerate the process of unification."[6] The triumphs of revolutionary movements in China in 1949, Cuba in 1959, and Algeria in 1962 gave the Palestinian fedayeen reasons to believe in the efficacy of guerrilla warfare. (Each of these revolutionary states would provide Fatah substantial material support for the coming struggle.) Fatah was to become the preeminent guerrilla movement, Arafat the acclaimed leader of the Palestinians and eventually president of the Palestine National Authority, a title he held until his mysterious death in November 2004.

Nasser was aware of the Palestinian discontent with the hesitancy of the Arab states to confront Israel. Nasser, who came to power in the 1952 military coup that ousted King Farouk, emerged as the icon of secular Arab nationalism after he seized control of the Suez Canal and survived an assault by British, French, and Israeli forces in 1956 to retake it. Nasser could not forsake the Palestinian cause, but he was careful to subordinate it to his own grandiose vision of pan-Arab unity. Subordination of the Palestinian cause was critical because, unless controlled, the Palestinians would prematurely provoke war between Egypt and the militarily superior Israel. A master strategist who was ever mindful of other Arab leaders' ambitions to replace him as the symbol of the Arab nation, Nasser responded by attempting to coopt the Palestinian cause. This was the origin of the Palestine Liberation Organization, the PLO.

In January 1964 Nasser convened the first Arab Summit to plan for an eventual war with Israel. Although Nasser avoided the Palestinian question during the summit, he invited Ahmed Shuqayri, a Palestinian diplomat, to attend. At the conclusion of the summit, Shuqayri took the urging to continue consultations with Arab leaders as a mandate to create a separate Palestinian entity.[7] At the end of May, Shuqayri summoned Palestinian leaders to a conference in East Jerusalem to proclaim the creation of the Palestine Liberation Organization. The PLO was thus the creation of the old guard. The PLO charter provided for a Palestinian National Council (PNC), its supreme legislative body, and an executive committee to be elected annually. Shuqayri was the obvious choice for chairman. But although the Palestinians now had a distinct Palestinian entity, two issues were left unsettled—the PLO's relations with the Arab states and with Fatah and other guerrilla organizations committed to the liberation of Palestine by force of arms.

For Nasser and the other heads of state there could be no doubt about the imperative to subordinate the nascent PLO to the Arab states and to deny the Palestinian guerrillas freedom of action to confront Israel. That war with Israel was inevitable was never in doubt. But Nasser and the other heads of state demanded patience from the Palestinians while the Arab armies amassed weapons and forces for a conventional war. Palestinian impatience posed as great a challenge as the Palestinian demand for autonomy, because guerrilla raids into Israel from Syria and Jordan created the risk of Israeli retaliation and therefore the risk of war. In order to gain some measure of control of the Palestinian fedayeen, the Arab states pledged funds, weapons, and training to field the Palestine Liberation Army (PLA), but its under-strength units were deliberately scattered among the Arab states and integrated into the command structure of the Arab armies. The PLA was as much Arab as Palestinian. When the Israelis launched the preemptive war in June 1967, the PLA saw almost no action. Arafat understood that the Arab states created the

PLO not to advance the Palestinian struggle but to restrain it. But the mere existence of the PLO posed a formidable challenge to Fatah and Arafat's personal ambitions to dominate the Palestinian cause, because Arab recognition of the PLO bestowed legitimacy upon it. It became imperative for Fatah to take action to wrest the initiative from the nascent PLO and its liberation army. So, on New Year's Day 1965, Fatah's guerrilla forces—which Arafat called al-Asifa, the Storm—mounted their first attack against Israel. The war to liberate Palestine from Israeli occupation—and to provoke a war between the Arab and Jewish states— was reality.

Over the next two and a half years Fatah conducted hundreds of ineffectual guerrilla raids. The Israeli Defense Forces (IDF) repelled Fatah's incursions. But Fatah's strategy was not so much to inflict casualties on the Israelis or cripple the Israeli economy as to forge a Palestinian identity guided by the spirit of resistance and provoke Israeli retaliation that could precipitate the war that would reverse the catastrophe of 1948. Palestinian attacks, in fact, contributed to the May crisis and the June War. But the defeat of the Arab armies in the Six Day War actually strengthened Arafat, who intensified his appeal to Palestinians to liberate the new territories lost to Israeli conquest. Fatah was not alone. By the mid-1960s there were several guerrilla organizations pleading for arms and funds from Arab states. Most of them were small and ineffective. But the Six Day War was a catalyst for the Palestinian fedayeen. The conversion of the Arab Nationalist Movement into the PFLP in late 1967 was one of its most important consequences.

George Habash and Wadi Haddad created the Arab Nationalist Movement (ANM) in Beirut in 1951, almost a decade before Arafat, al-Wazir, and Khalaf founded Fatah. Born into a relatively wealthy Greek Orthodox family in 1925, Habash witnessed his family's expulsion from Lydda, known as Lod in present-day Israel, in 1948. Three years later Habash graduated from medical school at the prestigious American University in Beirut with a specialty in pediatrics.[8] Habash's determination to destroy the Jewish state motivated him to found the ANM. But as its name implied, Habash's ANM shared Nasser's views about Arab, and not merely Palestinian, national unity. The ANM did not form a separate Palestinian branch until 1961. Like Fatah, ANM mounted raids against Israel before the Six Day War and, like Fatah's operations, its attacks were inconsequential. Then came the Six Day War. Within months of Israel's victory, Habash converted the ANM into the PFLP. The PFLP was the fusion of the ANM and several small guerrilla organizations, the most notable the Palestine Liberation Front, formed in 1961 by Ahmed Jabril, a Palestinian who served as a captain in the Syrian army. With the transformation of the ANM into the PFLP came a radicalization in ideology. The PFLP adopted Marxism-Leninism and organized itself along classic Leninist lines. Habash became secretary general, but his Marxism did not run deep. The most important feature about the Marxist rhetoric was the call to establish alliances with revolutionary forces worldwide. In the coming years, this would translate into operational alliances with European and Japanese terrorist organizations.

The formation of the PFLP marked the beginning of a struggle for control of the PLO and the onset of a campaign of international terrorism in the cause of Palestinian liberation. The defeat in the Six Day War discredited the PLO almost as much as it discredited the Arab states. PLO chairman Ahmed Shuqayri was the first victim. Six months after the Israeli victory, the PLO executive committee replaced him with Yahya Hammouda, who proved to be as ineffective as Shuqayri. Arafat's hour was coming. Fatah's reputation was not damaged by the dismal performance of the Arab armies against the Israelis. On the contrary, because the defeat weakened the disciples of Nasser, it strengthened Arafat. Arafat was careful to cultivate a mystique about himself. The Palestinian leader managed to evade capture by Israeli intelligence during his forays into the occupied territories of Gaza and the West Bank, and Arafat's Fatah guerrillas crossed into Israel from Jordan to mount attacks. Fatah propaganda exaggerated the impact of the guerrilla raids, forcing other guerrilla organizations to press the attack and distort the truth about advances in the armed struggle. Arafat sought deliberately to embody the Palestinian nation in the popular perception, even though the effort to create a cult of personality conflicted with Fatah's principle of collective leadership. All this worked to his advantage. But Arafat benefited most from an Israeli operation to destroy the guerrillas in their enclave in Jordan.

In March 1968—the same month Lyndon Johnson astonished Americans with his decision to not seek reelection—some 15,000 Israeli troops supported by aircraft, artillery, and tanks assaulted Palestinian guerrilla bases near the Jordanian town of Karameh. The Israeli force was some fifteen times larger than the combined number of Fatah, PFLP, and PLA fedayeen amassed in Jordan. Rather than retreating in the face of superior enemy forces, Arafat ordered his men to stand their ground. Although the Israeli forces inflicted heavy casualties—killing more than one hundred Palestinians—Arafat's fedayeen managed to kill 29 Israelis and wound many more before the Israelis withdrew when the Jordanian army came to the defense of Fatah. In the popular perception, Fatah had forced an Israeli retreat, a feat of arms the combined armies of Egypt, Syria, and Jordan had never accomplished. The battle of Karameh transformed Arafat into the most credible leader of the Palestinians. In February 1969, Arafat was elevated to the chairmanship of the PLO.

The battle of Karameh forced the PFLP, as the principal opposition to Fatah, to take the offensive to restore its diminished image. The PFLP did not distinguish itself in the confrontation with the IDF, although PFLP secretary-general Habash bore no direct responsibility for his men's performance; he was in custody in Damascus when the Israelis moved against the guerrilla bases in Jordan. Nonetheless, while Fatah stood and fought, the PFLP fled to the mountains with the PLA. Withdrawal in the face of a superior enemy was sound guerrilla tactics, but it was politically damaging. All Palestinian guerrilla organizations were captive to the logic of armed struggle, which dictated that victory in battle is the measure of political legitimacy. To prove its militancy the PFLP made the ominous decision to attack Israel on its vulnerable "external front." Fatah had launched the guerrilla war of national liberation in 1965; the PFLP now launched an international terror campaign.

The Popular Front's Campaign of Air Piracy

On 23 July 1968, three PFLP terrorists hijacked an Israeli El Al flight en route from Rome to the Ben Gurion International Airport in Lod and directed it to Algeria.[9] The El Al hijacking was the first by a Palestinian terrorist organization and one of the longest in the history of air piracy—negotiations for the release of the hostages and the jet dragged on for 39 days. The PFLP action produced something no isolated guerrilla raid in Israel could produce, an international incident.

Terrorism is violence, but the violence is invariably symbolic. The symbolism was obvious. El Al is the national airline of the Jewish state, and attacking it was tantamount to attacking Israel. For Palestinians eager to see harm inflicted on Israel in retaliation for their sufferings, the PFLP's audacious action was cause for rejoicing. The decision to redirect the jet to Algeria had symbolic importance as well. The PFLP consciously entangled the Algerian government in the Palestinian struggle. The Algerian war of independence was the source of inspiration to the Palestinian fedayeen, and Algeria, which remained in a formal state of war with Israel, actively supported the guerrillas, principally Arafat's Fatah. Although a PFLP spokesman in Beirut insisted that the PFLP did not forewarn the Algerian government of the operation and would later demand that Algeria explain its reasons for resolving the crisis without consulting with the PFLP, it obviously was counting on the Algerian regime to abet an act of terrorism. Algeria's foreign minister, Abdelaziz Bouteflika, rebuked the PFLP for the action, but Algerian authorities took custody of the hostages and moved them a hotel.[10]

The day after the hijacking, Algerian authorities released nineteen passengers. Two days later they released ten more, all women and children. After their release, the passengers came close to praising their treatment. "The food was almost too good," said an Israeli flight attendant after her release.[11] But Algerian authorities refused to release the remaining seven passengers and five crew members on the pretext of conducting an investigation into the hijacking. The explanation was disingenuous in the extreme. By refusing to release the last hostages while the PFLP issued demands for the release of more than one thousand fedayeen imprisoned by the Israelis, Algeria implicated itself in the crime of air piracy. Israel demanded action from the United Nations and threatened to take action itself. Some Israeli politicians demanded retaliation by attacking Algerian civilian airliners on the ground.

In the end, it was not the threat of military action but the threat of an international boycott of Algeria, and Israeli concessions, that resolved the crisis. On 12 August, the International Association of Airline Pilots announced its members would refuse to fly to Algeria. The PFLP strategy to isolate Israel by making airline travel dangerous backfired. Although the Algerian government denounced these pressures, its position was untenable. While the Algerians held out, the Italians attempted to mediate. Unless Algeria was prepared to incur the wrath of the Palestinians by simply releasing the passengers, the only apparent hope for a resolution of the crisis was some movement by the Israelis. The PFLP demand for the exchange of more than one thousand fedayeen for the hostages was unconscionable. But as the crisis neared a second month, the Israelis modified their position. It was not an exchange of prisoners for hostages that was unacceptable, only the number of prisoners and the appearance of a quid pro quo. At the end of August the press leaked word that Israel was prepared to make a "humanitarian gesture" after the hostages and the aircraft were repatriated. Then, on 29 August, Palestinian guerrillas ambushed an Israeli patrol on the confrontation line on the Suez Canal, killing two Israelis and capturing a third. If the Israeli government needed another incentive to resolve the Algerian crisis, this was it. On 1 September, Algeria allowed the remaining hostages to fly to Israel via Rome. Israel made good on its pledge of a humanitarian gesture by quietly releasing 16 fedayeen held prisoner in Israel.

The hijacking initiated a terror campaign against civilian aviation that became more and more lethal over the next several years. Just after the hijacking, the PFLP called a press conference in the Beirut office of the al-Anwar newspaper. Ghassan Kanafani, the PFLP spokesperson, whom the Israelis would assassinate in July 1972, did all the speaking, but he repeatedly deferred to the man seated beside him. That man was Wadi Haddad, head of the PFLP Special Apparatus.[12] Known as the Master,

Haddad was among the founders of the ANM and later the PFLP. Like Habash, the PFLP secretary-general, Haddad was the son of Greek Orthodox parents and graduated from the American University with a degree in medicine. These two men were close. In 1956 both went to the Jordan Valley to lend their medical services to the United Nations Relief and Works Administration, an agency set up to attend to the flood of Palestinian refugees. There Jordanian officials became aware of Haddad and arrested him. It was a premonition: Haddad would make it his mission to overthrow the Jordanian monarchy as a prerequisite to the destruction of Israel. By the early 1960s Haddad was conspiring in Damascus. But while Habash was busying himself with political matters, Haddad worked to create a military strike force. He was among the first to advocate military operations against Israel. The ANM guerrilla operations were Haddad's. When those proved ineffective, and when Fatah gained ascendancy after the battle of Karameh, Haddad turned to air piracy—and to terror.

It is not known whether Habash knew of the El Al operation in advance, since he had been in custody in Damascus since March. Haddad's special apparatus organized his escape to Jordan two months after the last hostages left Algeria. What is certain is that as Haddad intensified the campaign against civilian aviation culminating in a spectacular operation in the fall of 1970, Habash endorsed Haddad's operations. The idea, said Habash, was "to turn passengers into hostages, blow them out of the sky, attack them in the terminals." Habash would not reverse his position until 1974, well after the Soviet Union, which had adopted the Palestinian cause, publicly condemned hijacking.[13] But Haddad never abandoned the strategy and continued to organize hijacking operations until failed operations in Entebbe in 1976 and Mogadishu in 1977 forced Habash to expel him from the PFLP. Haddad died the following year, but the disciples of the Master would sustain his campaign of aviation terror well into the 1980s, when Islamic fundamentalism was already replacing Palestinian nationalism as the ideological inspiration for violence.

The El Al operation was, in fact, the beginning of a lethal campaign to take hostages, blow passengers out of the sky, and attack them in the terminals. Two days after Christmas 1968, PFLP terrorists killed one passenger and wounded several others in attack on an El Al jet on the tarmac at the airport in Athens. Two days later, Israelis retaliated with a devastating air strike on Beirut International Airport, destroying thirteen passenger aircraft on the ground. On 18 February 1969 the PFLP attacked again, strafing an El Al aircraft in Zurich, killing a passenger and wounding four others. Six months passed without another major incident; then, at the end of August, PFLP terrorists led by Leila Khaled, a twenty-four-year-old woman who would soon become famous, hijacked a TWA flight after takeoff from Rome, diverted the plane to Damascus, and destroyed the jet on the ground after forcing the passengers off. The PFLP—with the connivance of the Syrian government—held two Israelis hostage for six weeks until Israel, in another humanitarian gesture, released two captured Syrian pilots.[14] The PFLP followed this with a September grenade attack on an El Al office in Munich that left two dead and an identical attack in Athens in November that killed a four-year-old boy. In December, airport security in Athens thwarted a PFLP attempt to seize another flight in Athens, but in February 1970 the PFLP raked the transit lounge at the Munich airport with gunfire, killing one El Al passenger and wounding many others.

The operations demonstrated a great deal about the PFLP's operational capabilities and commercial aviation's security vulnerabilities. Haddad proved that his special operations apparatus could strike in major European cities: Athens (where aviation officials routinely decried as unconscionably lax security), Zurich, Munich, and Rome. No airline was safe from attack. Although the Israelis would prevent Palestinians from hijacking El Al flights after the 1968 Algiers incident, they could not protect passengers and planes from ground attack in foreign cities, and soon the PFLP would demonstrate its capability to strike passengers in an Israeli airport. The August 1969 TWA hijacking proved the PFLP would not refrain from assaulting American commercial airlines. It was attacking on the external front, and it was beginning to attack Israel's U.S. and European allies. The PFLP operational capability was obvious, but the purpose behind the strategy was perplexing, even to some of its own fedayeen. If attacking El Al was tantamount to attacking Israel, then the operations were a continuation of the guerrilla war against Israel by other means. The attacks proved that the fedayeen were not impotent despite Israel's supremacy in conventional arms and dramatized the Palestinian problem even if they inevitably damaged the Palestinian cause. And inflicting casualties on Israeli passengers produced the psychological effect of exacting revenge for slain fedayeen and Palestinian civilians. But Haddad's strategy was more ambitious. The assault on civilian aviation was intended to isolate Israel, to strangle its economy by terrorizing pilgrims to the Holy Land, and to coerce commercial airlines to abandon their lucrative routes between the United States and Europe—and Israel.

The Destruction of Swiss Air 330

Haddad's assaults on aircraft raised the profile of the PFLP, but they also deepened the ideological rifts within it. Naif Hawatmeh, a young and charismatic member of the PFLP, broke ranks with Habash and Haddad over the strategy of air piracy. Hawatmeh's Marxism ran deeper than Habash's, and his orthodoxy led him to repudiate the hijacking operations as the desperate acts of elite commandos insulated from the masses. In February 1969, the same month of the attack in Zurich, Hawatmeh formed the Democratic Front for the Liberation of Palestine (DFLP) and set up operations in Jordan. Hawatmeh was a revolutionary who never wavered in his conviction that the destruction of Israel demanded the overthrow of reactionary Arab regimes. Hawatmeh's strident calls for the overthrow of King Hussein's monarchy in Jordan would have terrible consequences by the end of 1970.

The defection of Ahmed Jabril was more consequential for international terror. Jabril, who had merged his Palestine Liberation Front with the PFLP, drew the opposite conclusion about terrorism. In 1969, Jabril also broke away from the PFLP to form the Popular Front for the Liberation of Palestine-General Command in order to be free to act independently. On 22 February 1970, Jabril's PFLP-General Command went into action. On that day, bombs exploded aboard an Austrian Airlines jet en route to Israel from Frankfurt and a Swiss Air flight to Israel from Zurich. Although the Austrian Airlines jet was damaged, the pilot managed to land it. The pilot of Swiss Air 330 was less fortunate.

Fifteen minutes after takeoff from Zurich en route to Israel, the copilot of Swiss Air 330 calmly radioed the control tower with a report of an in-flight emergency: "I suspect there's been an explosion in the aft compartment."[15] The pilot struggled to put the Coronado jet back on the ground safely and swung out over Lake Lucerne. By then the cockpit was filling with dense, acrid smoke. The pilot nearly delivered his passengers to safety. Ground controllers watched the jet approach the airport, but then turn north instead of east. The crew was flying blind. It was the copilot's voice on flight 330's final transmission: "We are crashing. Good-bye everybody, good-bye everybody."[16] Swiss Air flight 330 crashed in a Zurich suburb, killing all 47 passengers and crew aboard. Eight Americans died in the worst act of terror up to that time. It did not take investigators long to determine that a bomb had brought down Swiss Air 330. The forensic science of proving airplane sabotage—and fixing responsibility—was still new in 1970; it would be well advanced by 1988 when a bomb destroyed Pan Am 103 over Lockerbie, Scotland. The evidence suggested the bomb, which exploded at 14,000 feet, was detonated by a barometric pressure devise, and that the bomb—disguised as a small radio manufactured in East Germany—was placed on board the jet along with mail bound for Israel. Compounding the tragedy was the fact that the crime was so simple—terrorists simply mailed in a bomb.

The PFLP-General Command claimed responsibility for the destruction of Swiss Air 330, but almost immediately disavowed it. The atrocity was such an unconscionable escalation of the war against civilian aviation that even other Palestinian organizations repudiated it. The PLO officially gave solemn assurances that it "strongly condemns such barbaric actions" and "no commando contingent would have carried out such an action." Arafat's Fatah went so far as to send its condolences to the families of the victims.[17] The condemnation may have been disingenuous or it may have evinced serious disagreements within and between the fedayeen organizations about terror. But the reality was that George Habash's threat—"to turn passengers into hostages, blow them out of the sky, attack them in the terminals"—was now real in each of its dimensions. Terrorists had taken the first passengers hostage when the PFLP hijacked jets to Algiers and Damascus in 1968 and 1969; they would seize jets and hostages thirteen more times before Haddad's death in 1978. Terrorists had attacked passengers in European terminals five times since Christmas 1968; they would strike airports in Athens and Rome in 1973, in Paris in 1975, in Istanbul in 1976, and in Rome and Vienna in 1985. Now Jabril's PFLP-General Command had blown the passengers of Swiss Air flight 330 out of the sky. A year later, in January 1971, authorities in London averted the mid-air bombing of an El Al flight when they discovered a young Latin American woman with explosives in her carry-on luggage. In August 1972, the PFLP-General Command managed to put a bomb aboard an El Al flight out of Rome. The bomb exploded but did not destroy the jet.[18] Terrorists would blow jets out of the sky again in 1974 and 1988. Regardless of the doctrinal disputes among the Palestinian factions over the strategy of terror, the Palestinian national movement was becoming equated with international terrorism.

Skyjack Sunday

The PFLP assault on civilian aviation began in the waning months of the Johnson administration in July 1968, but by the time Jabril's PFLP-General Command destroyed Swiss Air 330, Richard Nixon was president. Nixon had won the November 1968 election after a tumultuous year in the United States. In January the war in Vietnam took a dramatic turn after the Vietnamese mounted the famed Tet Offensive and opened a terrible political rift in American society. In March Johnson announced his decision to return to his ranch in Texas rather than stand for election to another term; in April an assassin cut down Dr. Martin Luther King, Jr., the influential civil rights leader; in June an angry young Syrian, Sirhan Sirhan, murdered Robert Kennedy in Los Angeles, only moments after voting returns in the California primary made him the presumptive Democratic nominee for president. Although the Middle East conflict was not the most urgent issue on the Republican administration's ambitious foreign policy agenda, Nixon could not ignore the escalating tensions on the ceasefire line between Egypt and Israel. The wave of terrorism further complicated an already complex region.

Nixon adopted a more active Middle East policy than Johnson's, and viewed movement on the complex array of issues as part of a global Cold War strategy.[19] As the Nixon administration approached the end of its first year, secretary of state William Rogers announced a peace plan based on Security Council Resolution 242, passed in November 1967 as the United Nations reaction to the Six Day War. The Rogers plan was doomed from the outset. The Arab League, meeting in Khartoum in August 1967, when the sting of the defeat was still acute, swore itself to three "No's": No negotiations with Israel, No recognition of Israel, No peace with Israel. Even Nixon admitted he believed the Rogers plan, because it envisioned Israel's return of the occupied territories, "had absolutely no chance of being accepted by Israel." Henry Kissinger, Nixon's ambitious national security advisor, was skeptical of what he derided as the "sacramental language" and "mystical ambiguities of Resolution 242."[20] But by the early fall of 1970, the administration was confronted with crises along the confrontation line between Egypt and Israel and in Jordan that compelled the administration to attempt to broker a ceasefire.

Clashes between Israel and Egypt along the Suez in the so-called War of Attrition were intensifying and, worse, the Soviet Union had begun arming Egypt with advanced surface-to-air-missiles to counteract Israel's air superiority. The White House soon suspected the Soviets were deploying advisors to operate them. The crisis threatened a repetition of Israel's preemptive strike in 1967. The administration succeeded in convincing Egypt, Jordan, and Israel to agree to a tenuous ceasefire on 7 August, but the chances the ceasefire would hold were nil. By early September both the Egyptians and the Israelis were accusing each other of breaches of the truce. But even though Egypt and Israel continued to exchange fire in violation of the August agreement, the Palestinians viewed even the dimmest prospect of meaningful negotiations between the Arab confrontation states and Israel as a betrayal of the Khartoum's "Three No's." Habash was explicit about it: "We do not want peace! Peace would be the end of all our hopes."[21] Those hopes now turned on the overthrow of the Jordanian monarchy in the belief captured in an incendiary slogan—the road to Tel Aviv leads through Amman.

By the fall of 1970, Palestinian militancy was beginning to shake the foundations of the Jordanian monarchy. The presence of the armed

PLO factions on Jordanian soil posed a danger for the very existence of Hussein's kingdom. Fedayeen incursions into Israel from Jordan put Jordan in Israel's line of fire. Moreover, the PLO was a force unto itself, a state within the Jordanian state. There were hundreds of violent confrontations between the Palestinians and the Jordanian population and army by 1970. Worse still, the PFLP and the DFLP openly militated for the overthrow of the Jordanian monarchy. Arafat, acting as both chairman of the PLO and chief of Fatah, was nearly as provocative. The hostility was more than verbal: in June 1970 the PFLP ambushed the Jordanian monarch's motorcade in Amman. By early September, with the Jordanian army and Palestinian guerrillas virtually at war, the king, whose grandfather was assassinated by a Palestinian in 1951 for his supposed collusion with Israel and the West, began to contemplate action to rid himself of the PLO. Meanwhile, the Mossad made an attempt on Haddad's life to rid Israel of the escalating threat of terror. In July 1970, Mossad agents fired rocket-propelled grenades into Haddad's Beirut apartment. Although the Mossad could not have known it at the time, the attack came as the Master was meeting with one his most experienced air pirates, Leila Khaled, to plan the PFLP's most audacious hijacking. Haddad and Khaled were not seriously wounded; Haddad's wife and eight-year-old son suffered minor cuts and burns. Undaunted, Haddad moved ahead with the planning of the most infamous simultaneous skyjacking in history until 9/11.

On 6 September 1970, Skyjack Sunday, squads of PFLP terrorists managed to board four New York bound flights and hijack three of them.[22] Two Palestinians took control of Pan Am flight 93 only minutes after the Boeing 747 left the ground in Amsterdam. Instead of crossing the Atlantic, the jet crossed Europe and landed in Beirut, where seven more terrorists boarded it and Lebanese airport personnel refueled it. Then the hijackers ordered it on to Cairo. The terrorists threatened no harm to the 152 passengers and 17 crew members. It was more like theater than terror. Passengers described the terrorists as "perfect gentlemen," who politely explained their intention to destroy the plane once it was on the ground. One crew member wondered whether the men were serious. But when the plane touched down the Palestinians ordered an evacuation of the plane and passengers scrabbled for escape chutes. The men who had rigged the explosives were barely off the jet when it exploded in flames. For the passengers aboard Pan Am 93 this was the end of the ordeal. The next morning all flew on to New York.

For the passengers aboard TWA flight 741 and Swissair 100 the hijacking was just the beginning of what proved to be a violent month in Jordan. The Boeing 707 left Frankfurt with 141 passengers and 10 crew members en route to New York. Fifteen minutes after takeoff, as the jet crossed West Germany's frontier with Luxembourg, two Palestinians seized it and ordered it to Dawson Field, a remote airstrip on a desert plateau 30 miles from Amman, the Jordanian capital. Swiss Air flight 100 out of Zurich was over France when two more Palestinians commandeered the DC-8 at almost the same moment.. Like those aboard the American jet, the 143 passengers and 12 crew members were suddenly en route to Dawson Field. As the pilot put his jet down he had to avoid the TWA jet already on the ground.

The two terrorists on El Al flight 219 failed in their mission to divert the jet to the Jordanian desert. Thirty minutes after the Boeing 707 left Amsterdam en route to New York with 148 passengers and 10 crew members, Leila Khaled and Patrick Arguello jumped into the aisle of the first class compartment and rushed the cockpit. Israeli intelligence knew Khaled's identity from the August 1969 TWA hijacking. That this young Palestinian woman managed to board an El Al flight demonstrated her resolve. She had undergone plastic surgery to alter her appearance and was traveling on a false Honduran passport posing as Arguello's Latin wife. Arguello was a U.S. citizen educated in Chile and living in Nicaragua. Not only had these two managed to board the jet, accomplices managed to place weapons aboard it. But the security failures prior to the departure of El Al 219 ended the moment Khaled and Arguello tried to commandeer the flight.

Arguello, armed with a pistol, rushed the cockpit door and shot an air steward who threw himself against it. An Israeli sky marshal shot him where he stood. Arguello, convulsing outside the cockpit, died before the plane made an emergency landing. (In a communiqué released the same day, the PFLP cynically charged Israel with a serious violation of international law by allowing El Al personnel to carry firearms aboard a civilian aircraft.) Khaled, who had leaped into the aisle holding two hand grenades, was supposed to hold the passengers and crew at bay while Arguello broke into the cockpit, but another marshal rapidly disarmed her and wrestled her to the cabin floor. The crew diverted the plane to London's Heathrow Airport, where British authorities took Khaled into custody, angering the Israelis, who claimed jurisdiction over air pirates for crimes aboard Israeli aircraft. In another seventy-two hours the British would come to regret their entanglement in the affair.

Haddad's operation on Skyjack Sunday was a triumph. Although the Israelis thwarted the seizure of El Al flight 219, the PFLP commandeered three jets, destroyed one, and held two others in Jordan with nearly three hundred hostages. Flush with bravado, the PFLP explained that it had hijacked the jets to manifest its abhorrence of the August cease-fire agreement Egypt and Jordan conceded to Israel and the United States. The PFLP seized the Pan Am and TWA flights—symbols of American global presence—to punish the United States for its support of Israel; it went after the El Al flight simply because the Palestinians were at war with Israel. Haddad's commandos had more pragmatic reasons for hijacking Swiss Air 100: the release of the three fedayeen serving twelve-year prison sentences for the February 1969 attack on an El Al jet in Zurich. Because Germans were aboard the flight, the PFLP demanded the release of three more Palestinians imprisoned for the September 1969 attack on an El Al office in Munich. And it reiterated its demand for the release of Sirhan Sirhan, the assassin of Robert Kennedy. Once Leila Khaled fell into British hands, the PFLP also demanded her release and the body of her fallen comrade. This was just the opening round of demands. The PFLP would reveal its specific demands for the release of fedayeen imprisoned in Israel only after the terrorists in England, Switzerland, and West Germany went free.

The PFLP's position was formidable. It held two multimillion-dollar aircraft and more than three hundred hostages of many nationalities. PFLP spokesmen threatened to destroy the jets—although not to kill the hostages—in seventy-two hours, at 10 p.m. New York time, on Wednesday, 9 September. The hostages sat confined to their seats in the sweltering desert heat. PFLP guerrillas encircled Dawson Field; the Jordanian army encircled the PFLP. It was a dangerous confrontation, but the Jordanian army was powerless to rescue the hostages without endangering their lives. On Monday, the PFLP released more than half the hostages, mostly women and children who could not tolerate the conditions. They were free but not safe. They made the overland journey to the capital in a country descending into civil war; in Amman, fierce fighting in the streets forced them to take shelter in the basement of the hotel where the Jordanians had put them up. But the terrorists still held more than 150 Israeli, American, British, West German, and Swiss nationals. The crisis was just beginning.

President Nixon was relaxing at his house in San Clemente for Labor Day weekend when the PFLP seized the airliners. Terrorists were holding an unknown number of Americans hostage and threatening the destruction of the aircraft within seventy-two hours, yet the president's thinking ran to geostrategic considerations. Nixon recorded in his memoir that after the hijackings "it seemed likely that a serious showdown was going to be unavoidable." Kissinger, the national security advisor, was of a like mind. As Kissinger saw things, the United States "faced two problems, the safety of the hostages and the future of Jordan." But the future of Jordan mattered most to him: the survival of the man Kissinger patronizingly called the "tough little king" was a strategic imperative. Here the United States had options.[23] Nixon ordered U.S. naval forces in the Mediterranean to move into striking distance of Jordan to deter

Syrian and Iraqi intervention in defense of the Palestinian fedayeen, and he discreetly indicated that the United States would favor an Israeli attack to save Jordan and crush the Palestinians. The threat of a U.S. and Israeli attack could at least buttress King Hussein. But the United States could not guarantee the safety of the hostages—the Pentagon advised that it could not organize a rescue operation—and the president and his national security advisor refused to bargain for their lives. "Israel had a policy of never yielding to blackmail," Kissinger wrote later; "our own view was roughly the same." The reality was that Israel's policy was not that rigid; Israel made "humanitarian gestures" after the release of Israeli hostages in 1968 and again in 1969. The Nixon administration's fidelity to a doctrine would be challenged again—with dire consequences—before Nixon left office. The Swiss and the West Germans, however, saw no wisdom in risking innocent lives in defense of an abstract principle. The Swiss immediately announced their intention to comply with the demand for the release of the three fedayeen held in Swiss custody, and the West Germans gave assurances they would trade Palestinian terrorists for West German tourists a few days after the Swiss announcement. But both governments refused to release the Palestinians until all the hostages were released, regardless of nationality. No one was certain about the position of British prime minister Edward Heath. Haddad knew how to influence his thinking.

British Overseas Airways Corporation (BOAC) flight 755 departed Bombay en route to London on 9 September with 117 passengers and crew. The flight was scheduled to make stopovers in Bahrain and Beirut before proceeding to London. The BOAC jet never arrived in London. PFLP terrorists boarded it in Bahrain and commandeered it during its final approach to Beirut. It was the second time in three days that a hijacked jetliner approached the airport in the Lebanese capital. To heighten the drama, the terrorists ordered the pilot to circle the city for a full hour before putting down to refuel. By the time the plane landed, both the British ambassador and the Lebanese transportation minister were on the radio urging the terrorists to release the women and children aboard the jet. This the terrorists were not willing to consider: "We are leaving with everybody" they warned "or we are blowing up the airplane with everybody." It was the first—and last—explicit threat to the passengers. After refueling in Beirut, the plane made the short journey to Dawson Field outside Amman. The pilot, a twenty-two-year veteran, remembers one of the terrorists pondering aloud as he took off for Jordan: "Let's see what Heath does now."[24]

The United States, Switzerland, West Germany, and Britain were already negotiating through the International Committee of the Red Cross when the third jet arrived in Jordan with 117 more hostages. The passengers aboard BOAC flight 755 brought the number of hostages back up to nearly 300. A Red Cross mediator convinced the PFLP to push back its original deadline by another seventy-two hours, but even the Red Cross was confused about the exact time those hours expired. The guerrillas surrounding the jets began to ease the restrictions on the hostages. The flight crews spoke at news conferences, small groups of hostages walked around the jets, photographers photographed them, and journalists spoke with them. It was an international media spectacle Haddad would never again achieve. But conditions on the jets were horrendous. Food was scanty, the heat was intolerable, toilets overflowed. On Thursday, the fifth day of the ordeal for the TWA and Swiss Air passengers, an American passenger gave birth to another hostage. The terrorists did not overtly threaten the hostages—a PFLP spokesman threatened to destroy the planes, but did not repeat the threat uttered in Beirut to blow up the planes with the hostages aboard them—but the tension was palpable.

Israel's position was critical, because even after the Swiss, West Germans, and British announced the fedayeen would go free, the fate of the remaining hostages depended on Golda Meir, who had become prime minister when Levi Eshkol was struck down by a heart attack in 1969. Meier would confront the taking and killing of hostages throughout her term in office. On 11 September, the PFLP released 88 hostages, moved another 23 to hotels in Amman, and offered to free all women and children for the release of the seven fedayeen in Switzerland, West Germany, and England. The same day, Israel made vague statements about an agreement "in principle" to make an exchange. The hostage crisis outside of Amman appeared to be moving toward resolution, but appearances were deceiving. The Palestinians, alarmed by the menacing deployments of Israeli and U.S. forces, and engaged in intensifying combat with Jordanian troops, decided to act. On 12 September, the PFLP released all but 54 of the hostages. But then, thirteen hours before the deadline, the guerrillas destroyed the empty jets one by one as news photographers captured some of the most dramatic images in the history of terrorism in the media age. The world would not see anything like this until 9/11.

The destruction of the jets stunned Arafat, who was by then struggling to maintain the unity of the fedayeen militias and to deny the United States and Israel justification for an attack. Arafat, as PLO chairman, suspended the PFLP from the PLO executive committee, but he would have to relent because he could not afford to lose the PFLP with the Palestinian guerrillas virtually at war with the Jordanian army. The reaction in London was different. The day after the jets exploded into flames, and after intense discussions within the cabinet and between the

United States and Great Britain, Her Majesty's Government announced it would free Leila Khaled when all the remaining hostages came home. That was still weeks off.

For the 54 hostages left behind, the squalor of the jets was replaced by the squalor of the Wahdat refugee camp. The U.S. State Department could not be certain, but reports indicated that 37 or 38 of the hostages were American. Their captors still did not threaten them with death; a PFLP communiqué stated only that it would hold them indefinitely as prisoners of war. This was a different kind of threat—interminable captivity—Americans would face in the 1980s in Lebanon. A Palestinian refugee camp was not a safe haven. On 17 September, what had been armed clashes between the Palestinians and Jordanians erupted into full-scale civil war. The same Jordanian army that had come to the defense of the Palestinians at Karameh two years before launched a full-scale assault on PLO positions. The ensuing combat was terrible. Over the next ten days, International Committee of the Red Cross (ICRC) mediators attempted to sustain negotiations over the fate of the hostages but, by the third week of September, ICRC officials acknowledged there had been no direct contact for days with the guerrillas holding the hostages. The guerrillas were on the defensive.

On 26 September, the Jordanians proudly announced troops loyal to the king had rescued 15 hostages from the Wahdat refugee camp; the PFLP predictably announced it had freed them. The next day, the PFLP released 33 more hostages. Now the PFLP held only six hostages, one fewer than the seven fedayeen whose release they demanded. On 28 September, as the violence spiraled out of control, Egyptian president Nasser convened an emergency meeting of the Arab League to end the internecine violence in Jordan. When envoys were unable to broker a settlement, Nasser summoned the king and the chairman of the PLO to Cairo to work out the details of a fragile truce. But neither the truce nor Nasser survived what the Palestinians regard as "Black September." Already frail, Nasser collapsed and died of a heart attack on 28 September. The internecine violence of Black September killed Nasser, and his dream of pan-Arabism died with him.

The next day the PFLP released the remaining six hostages. Leila Khaled and her comrades imprisoned in Switzerland and West Germany went free soon after. Years later, the BBC tracked down Khaled and asked her about Skyjack Sunday and the decision to free her. "No one heard our screams and our suffering," she said; "all we got from the world was more tents and old clothes. After 1967, we were obliged to explain to the world that the Palestinians had a cause." Asked about the negotiations, Khaled remembered that the terrorists had an advantage. "They could not do anything but accept the demands. We just wanted these governments to recognize that these people had a legitimate strug-gle. I think the European governments recognized us in a situation when we had power. It was a good step for us because [it showed] that governments could be negotiated with and that we could impose our demands."[25]

For Khaled and the leadership of the PFLP the obligation to explain to the world that the Palestinians had a legitimate struggle justified mass hostage-taking. The tactic was reprehensible, but it was effective because hostage-taking propelled Western governments into an insuperable moral dilemma. The British prime minister and his counterparts in Israel, Europe, and the United States understood that appeasement of the terrorists would embolden them. But despite the declared policy to reject negotiations at all costs, the potential costs in human lives because of inflexible adherence to the policy were too great. Confronted with an onslaught against civilian aviation, governments would have to tighten airport security to prevent terrorists from boarding aircraft, or they would have to form elite counterterrorist units to assault hijacked planes and kill hijackers. This was not a dilemma for governments alone. Even in the days before instantaneous broadcast of news via satellite, the inevi-table news coverage of the crisis in Jordan intensified the pressure on the governments to capitulate to terrorist demands. Governments were in a moral dilemma, so too were the sentinels of a free society—the new organizations. The ethical debate about media coverage of terrorist operations is a direct consequence of terrorists' determination to manipulate the news. Because terrorism is inherently newsworthy, the reality is that media organizations cannot simply decline to cover terror-ism. The terrorists understand all of this perfectly well. The hijackings were a means to broadcast a set of demands and advance a set of politi-cal objectives. In the media age, terrorism is politics by other means.

Arafat's Terror Option

September 1970, Black September, was a terrible ordeal for Arab unity: the Palestinians were killed not by Israelis but by their Jordanian broth-ers. The truce between the Palestinians and Jordanians, called out of respect for Nasser, did not hold. Fighting inevitably resumed. Before the last Palestinian enclaves were eliminated in July 1971, PLO fighters suf-fered appalling casualties; estimates fall in the range of five to fifteen thousand killed.[26] King Hussein's Bedouin army had driven Arafat and the PLO from Jordan, but the PLO was vengeful, not vanquished.

In August and again in September 1971, senior PLO leaders met in Damascus, Syria, and endorsed the strategy of international terrorism George Habash and Wadi Haddad had initiated in 1968. Guerrilla attacks against Israeli border positions had accomplished nothing. And now the PLO was consumed with avenging the betrayal of Jordan and the moderate Arab states. Wadi Haddad's assault on civilian aviation at least forced Western governments to negotiate with the Palestinians over the lives of passengers and crews, if not yet to resolve the broader political question of the political status of the Palestinian people. International terrorism became an option in the absence of real military capabilities or a commitment to political settlement. Except for Arafat, whose attitude mattered most, the PLO leaders did not pause to consider the possibility that the strategy would actually damage Palestinian aspirations by creating the perception that the Palestinians were criminals undeserving of a state of their own. But PLO chairman Arafat faced a dilemma. If he opposed the terrorist option, the PFLP and smaller groups could act autonomously, but that entailed the risk of fracturing the unity of the PLO and losing power. And Fatah itself was divided over terror. Abu Iyad, head of Fatah intelligence, raised his voice in defense of terror, although he was careful to characterize his actions as revolutionary violence. When the moment came to decide, Arafat absented himself from the meeting. It was act of moral ambiguity that did not absolve the future president of the Palestinian National Authority of complicity in terrorism.[27] Arafat merely adapted the adage of Mao—a revolutionary he admired—to the circumstances of the Palestinian revolution: if power proceeds from the barrel of a gun, Chairman Arafat was intent on controlling the gun. At the conclusion of the Damascus conference, the chieftains of the PLO militias decided to intensify the campaign of terror. For the next few years, until the Yom Kippur War in October 1973, terror would have a new name.

On 28 November 1971, a Palestinian assassination squad murdered Wasfi Tel, the Jordanian prime minister, in the ornate lobby of the Sheraton Hotel in Cairo where Tel was attending a meeting of the Arab League. It was a gruesome spectacle. No one, not even Tel's bodyguards, noticed the two Palestinians who followed Tel into the Sheraton, and no one sensed the danger until one of them, Essat Rabah, fired five gunshots into the Jordanian politician at point blank range. As Tel lay bleeding to death, a second Palestinian, Mozar Khalifa, stooped down and licked the blood flowing out over the marble as the crowd watched on aghast, and he claimed the act in the name of Black September. "One of the Butchers of the Palestinian people was thus executed," is how Abu Iyad expressed it, "Black September, the underground organization set up early that autumn, had just carried out its first operation."[28] It was the first anyone had heard of Black September; it would not be the last.

Chapter 2

Revolutionary Violence Is a Political Act, Terrorism Is Not

The year 1972 was an election year in the United States. Richard Nixon, who had come into office in 1969 amid mounting protests against the interminable war in Vietnam, already the longest in U.S. history, was seeking a second term. Nixon's foreign policy agenda was ambitious. Henry Kissinger, who would become both national security advisor and secretary of state in the second Nixon administration, was simultaneously pursuing détente with the Soviet Union, making overtures to the People's Republic of China, and negotiating the extrication from Vietnam. But by the time Nixon and Kissinger negotiated "peace with honor" in the Paris peace talks with the Vietnamese delegation in 1972, which led to a complete U.S. withdrawal the following year, the crisis in the Middle East had worsened. Egypt and Syria acted to reverse the humiliation of 1967.

This was also the year of Black September. Black September struck out with a vengeance to compel the world to understand the Palestinian conflict would not be confined to the Middle East. Terror seeped into Europe, and Americans fell victim to terror. The organization that congealed in the bloodshed in Jordan nearly assassinated King Hussein's envoy in London only a week after it murdered his prime minister in Cairo. In February it sabotaged a West German electrical installation and a Dutch natural gas plant. In March it attempted its first hijacking, and at the end of May it attacked a petroleum refinery in Trieste. Black September would attack four more times at different points of the compass before its final operation in March 1973: Europe in September, Asia in December, the Middle East in February, and North Africa in March.

Black September

The principal figures in Black September—Abu Iyad, Mohammed Najjar, Abu Daoud, and Ali Hassan Salameh—were all were powerful actors in Fatah.[1] Abu Iyad, a founder of Fatah, was chief of Fatah's intelligence, Jihaz al-Razd. Mohammed Najjar was Abu Iyad's chief of operations until the Israelis killed him in April 1973. Abu Daoud commanded Fatah guerrilla forces in Jordan before the Jordanians expelled them. Ali Hassan Salameh was Abu Iyad's deputy and would eventually become chief of Arafat's security detail, Force 17, until the Israelis killed him in January 1979. Abu Iyad never acknowledged his connection to Black September, and his public statements about the terror organization are almost undecipherable. "Black September was never a terrorist organization," he wrote in his memoir, "it acted as an auxiliary to the Resistance, when the resistance was no longer in a position to fully assume its military and political tasks. . . . Its members always insisted that they had no organic tie with Fatah or the PLO. But I knew a number of them, and I can assure you that most of them belonged to various fedayeen organizations." The fact is that Abu Iyad not only knew many of the members of Black September, he recruited them—Abu Iyad *was* the organic link to Fatah. That Black September did not commit acts of terrorism was a question of semantics because, said Iyad, "I do not confuse revolutionary violence, which is a political act, with terrorism, which is not."[2]

Abu Daoud's public statements about Black September were made in February 1972 while he was under a sentence of death for conspiracy to seize the U.S. embassy in Amman. "There is no such organization called Black September," Daoud confessed in a televised spectacle, "Black September is only the intelligence apparatus [of Fatah] Jihaz el-Razd."[3] Daoud named Iyad, Najjar, and Salameh in his public confession, but uttered not a word about Yasser Arafat. Because these men formed the circle around Arafat, Arafat himself was at the epicenter of Black September, even if he was not specifically aware of the details of Black September's operations. This was Arafat's cynicism at its worst. Black September was the concession Arafat made to Fatah's radicals to the dismay of the movement's moderates. One of those moderates, Khalad Hassan, swears he was secretly negotiating a rapprochement between the PLO and Jordan with Wasfi Tel in Egypt when Black September murdered the Jordanian prime minister.[4]

One of the more intriguing figures in Black September was Ali Hassan Salameh. Palestinian militancy was in his lineage. He was only seven when his father, Sheikh Hassan Salameh, died fighting to prevent the Catastrophe in 1948 and became legendary for his sacrifice. The sheikh's son would live up to the family's reputation and eventually share his father's fate. Ali Hassan Salameh took the nom de guerre Abu Hassan, following the practice of affixing Abu, "father," to his family name, but Israeli intelligence called him the Red Prince. Prince because of his opulent lifestyle, red because of the blood on his hands. Salameh was flamboyant—he had a flare for the good life and a passion for beautiful women. (His second wife, Georgina Rizk, a Lebanese Christian, won the Miss Universe pageant in 1971.) After joining Fatah, he became Abu Iyad's deputy in Fatah intelligence and, eventually, Commander of European Operations in Black September. After Black September ceased terror operations, Arafat made Ali Hassan Salameh chief of Force 17.

The Central Intelligence Agency knew of Ali Hassan Salameh's connection to Fatah intelligence well before Black September's appearance, and the agency worked with him after Black September murdered Americans.[5] Some time in 1969, Robert Ames, a CIA case officer in Beirut, made contact with Salameh in an effort to establish an informal—and deniable—back channel between U.S. intelligence and the PLO. It was a prudent move, although this sort of back channel violated assurances the Nixon administration later offered the Israelis that the United States would not recognize the PLO. Ames and Salameh met face-to-face in Kuwait in early 1970, months before the Jordanian crisis and more than a year before Fatah set up Black September. Ames, fluent in Arabic, apparently established a rapport with the Palestinian. The men had mutual interests in establishing contact, but their interests were not identical, and they did not have the final authority to reach an accommodation. Salameh, whose contacts must have been sanctioned by Arafat, was interested in a political opening to the United States. Ames was acting in the much more limited interest of the United States in gathering intelligence about threats to Americans and American interests. Arafat could offer intelligence through Salameh in the hope of making a diplomatic breakthrough.

The contact between Ames and Salameh—and between U.S. and Fatah intelligence—would result in a back channel security arrangement, but not until 1974 after Black September actually murdered U.S. diplomats. At the end of 1970, Salameh broke off contact with the CIA, after a senior CIA officer attempted to recruit him in Rome with an offer of a $1 million. The CIA's clumsy effort to buy an asset would have its consequences. Over the next three years, Salameh was directly involved in some, although not all, of Black September's terror operations. It was Salameh who organized the assassination of Wasfi Tel in November 1971 and the attacks in West Germany, Holland, and Italy in early 1972. He then became involved in the planning of a late summer operation in the heart of Europe, an operation that more than any other, including even Haddad's Skyjack Sunday hijackings, defined the threat of terror in the 1970s in the mind of most Americans.

The appearance of Black September was ominous because it meant another killer was roaming in search of victims. But the appearance of

Black September did not mean the disappearance of the PFLP. Actually, the PFLP struck first in 1972.

The Lod Massacre

Wadi Haddad never sought the approval of the PLO to conduct terror operations, just as he never heeded the organization's chastisements. George Habash, the nominal secretary general of the PFLP, was in prison in Damascus when Haddad organized the first hijacking, and in Communist China on Skyjack Sunday. Haddad was his own man. George Habash alternated between deep-throated threats against passengers and cautiously phrased denials of responsibility, but by 1971 Haddad commanded the loyalty of his own faction within the PFLP. At the end of February, Haddad's men resumed the offensive.

On 22 February, five PFLP terrorists broke into the cockpit of a Lufthansa Boeing 747 soon after departure from New Delhi en route to Athens.[6] It was only weeks after the Black September attack on the West German electrical plant. The year 1972 was to be a year of reckoning for West Germany. The terrorists ordered the crew to continue across the Arabian Sea and put down in Aden, in what was then South Yemen, where they could count on the tacit collaboration of the radical government. There the terrorists rigged the plane with explosives and began to issue demands laced with threats against the 175 passengers and 15 crew members. First, the terrorists demanded release of the Black September assassins who murdered Wasfi Tel in Cairo in November 1971. Then they demanded the release of Sirhan Sirhan, the man who assassinated Robert F. Kennedy in June 1968. The PFLP later denied ever having demanded the freedom of Kennedy's assassin, but it issued the denial after it learned that Joseph Kennedy, III, son of the slain presidential candidate, was among the hostages the terrorists had already released.[7] The prominent American escaped harm with the other passengers, but the terrorists still held the crew. Thousands of miles away, in Beirut, the PFLP discreetly presented its ransom demand to the Lufthansa office. Twenty-four hours later, the terrorists released the last hostages and surrendered to the Yemeni officials.

The resolution of the Lufthansa incident came at a price. The West German transport minister acknowledged Lufthansa's payment of $5 million for the lives of the crew and the return of the plane intact.[8] In previous hijackings to Damascus, Amman, and Cairo, airline executives and stockholders watched in horror as the Palestinians destroyed the multimillion-dollar jets. The West Germans avoided the monetary losses and averted the loss of life. The West German government managed the September 1970 hostage crisis in Jordan this same way. With the lives of hostages at risk, Bonn offered assurances of the release of imprisoned fedayeen, but only after British and Israeli hostages went free. When the chance of a peaceful resolution presented itself, and the decision was the West Germans' to make, the government acted to save lives. But in a few months time, the West Germans would find themselves entangled in another incident, this time on their own soil, without the option to make concessions.

The terrorists went free soon after the passengers were released. The Yemenis, like the Algerians and the Syrians before them, saw no reason to incarcerate the Palestinian terrorists. The Egyptians, too, would eventually see the prudence of quietly freeing Wasfi Tel's assassins. West German authorities later complained about the terrorists' brief detention, despite the fact that West German intelligence already knew the identities "of at least several of them."[9] Several of the terrorists were, in fact, already known to Western intelligence. When the hijacked Lufthansa flight arrived in Aden, Ali Taha was there waiting for it. Taha, who went by the name of Kamal Rafat, personally took charge of the negotiations that produced the release of the hostages and the extortion of Lufthansa. Taha was known to intelligence services because he commanded all the previous PFLP air piracy operations going back to the Algiers incident in 1968.[10] By now, Taha was so well known that he could not board a flight without the risk of compromising an operation. The temptation to commandeer another planeload of hostages must have been tremendous. Eight weeks later Taha succumbed to the temptation, and this desire to see action one more time cost him his life.

In May, Black September, impressed by the spectacular PFLP operations, decided to mount its own hijacking operation. Mohammad Najjar conceived the operation, Salameh, Black September's operational commander in Europe, organized it, and Ali Taha conducted it.[11] In May 1972, Najjar was acting as chief of Fatah intelligence, replacing Salah Khalaf, who was quarreling with Arafat. Under the circumstances, Najjar was concerned with his standing among the more militant fedayeen. To compensate for Fatah's lack of experience with air piracy, Najjar enlisted Taha to command a combined Fatah-PFLP operation under the banner of Black September. On 8 May, Taha led three Fatah terrorists in an operation to seize a Belgian Sabena flight en route from Vienna to Tel Aviv. Taha was living dangerously. Even before the flight left Vienna, officials in Brussels warned security in Vienna of a plot to commandeer the flight. Security searched three Arabs for weapons, but inexplicably the search turned up nothing.[12] En route to Tel Aviv, Taha and three confederates, a man and two women, took control of the plane and its 101 passengers and crew in the name of Black September.[13] Taha had defied the risks of direct participation in the operation and had narrowly escaped capture. Now, instead of directing the flight to a secure location in a friendly country like Algeria, Syria, or South Yemen, he ordered the pilot to continue Ben Gurion International Airport, the original destination. It was an act of utter contempt for the Israeli security forces. But because the risk was great the propaganda value of putting the plane down in Israel was even greater. It was a fatal miscalculation.

Taha's audacity may have astonished the IDF, but it also gave them a tactical advantage. When the plane put down, ground controllers directed the Boeing 707 to a remote area of the airport, and Taha began direct radio communications with senior IDF officers in the control tower. Moshe Dyan, the defense minister and hero of the Six Day War, was present, but Shimon Peres, the transportation minister and future prime minister, handled the negotiations. Taha demanded a straight exchange: 101 passengers and crew for 300 fedayeen held in Israel. The Israelis should deliver the Palestinians directly to the jet; Taha would deliver them to freedom. But Peres refused to make the concession. The most the government could contemplate was the release of perhaps twenty Palestinians as a "gesture of good will," the innocuous phrase used during the 1968 Algiers incident. In fact, the Israelis were preparing for a demonstration of force rather than a gesture of good will. As night fell on the first day of the hijacking, Israeli commandos disabled the aircraft's landing gear to prevent the hijackers' departure to a more secure location. For the pilot, Captain Reginald Levy, the Israeli action heightened the danger. After Taha threatened murder-suicide unless the Israelis repaired and refueled the jet, Levy appealed over the cockpit radio, "I think they will blow it up, they are serious."[14] In fact, the Palestinians let 10 P.M. and 5 A.M. deadlines pass without acting on their threat. The delays, and the apparent loss of will, gave the Israelis the time to organize a rescue.

Twenty-three hours after the hostage crisis began, the Israelis communicated their intention to repair the jet in the interest of saving lives. In fact, Israel was mounting its first takedown of a hijacked airliner. The El Al mechanics who assembled beneath the fuselage were really Lieutenant Colonel Ehud Barak's elite Sayaret Matkal commandos.[15] Before the Palestinians could react, the commandos rushed up ladders onto the wings and forced open the emergency doors. The assault was over in moments. The Israelis killed Taha and another hijacker and captured the two women. The bullets that ripped through the cabin wounded five passengers, killing one. That same evening the Israeli chief of staff, Lt. General David Elazar, issued a challenge: "If all the countries would do as we did, there wouldn't be the disgrace of hijacking in the world."[16]

The Sabena incident marked a turning point in assault on civilian aviation. It did not end "the disgrace of hijacking in the world," but it raised the risks to the hijackers. The hazards to the hijackers had been negligible thus far. Israeli sky marshals had captured Leila Khaled and killed her accomplice in the El Al incident in September 1970. But the terrorists involved in other operations were not even imprisoned—or not for very long—much less killed. The British, after all, set Khaled free. After the commandos burst into the Sabena jet and killed Taha, terrorists understood that governments had options other than capitulation. Khaled's statement, made after her release in September 1970, that the hijackings proved "we could impose our demands" was no longer valid. Israeli commandos would mount a more spectacular rescue operation at Entebbe, Uganda, in 1976; West German commandos would do so in Mogadishu, Somalia, in 1977. In both operations the commandos killed hijackers and rescued hostages. The glory days of the air pirates came to an end in Lod. But the risks increased on all sides. Palestinian hijackers did not execute a single passenger or crew member until December 1973. In future hijackings, terrorists would realize that the credibility of their threats depended on their willingness to kill.

Wadi Haddad grasped the new dynamic. Black September claimed the Sabena operation, but when it failed Haddad lost his most experienced air pirate. Three weeks after Israeli commandos cut down Ali Taha, Haddad turned the Ben Gurion International Airport at Lod into the scene of an atrocity. The Israelis were learning to combat air piracy, and El Al had begun to throw up extraordinary security around airliners after the ground attacks against airliners in Athens, Zurich, and Munich between December 1968 and February 1970. The Israelis were on high alert for Palestinian terrorists, and they had reason to be alert to threats posed by Europeans. The spectacular terror operations of previous years succeeded in attracting mercenaries to the Palestinian cause. Because of its Marxist rhetoric, the PFLP held special appeal. The German Revolutionary Cells provided recruits in search of battlefronts in the world revolution. In April 1971, Israeli security personnel seized four French terrorists with explosives inside the terminal at Lod.[17] But the Japanese were the first to join forces with the Palestinians. The Japanese Red Army, or JRA, was the radicalized Japanese students' answer to the call for revolutionary violence. The JRA, although small, already had carried out its first hijacking in March 1970, months before Skyjack Sunday in September. In February 1971, the JRA's leader, Fusako Shigenobu, traveled to Lebanon to establish relations with Habash and the PFLP. By 1972, JRA militants were training there. Haddad sent them into action at the end of May.

On 31 May, three members of the JRA boarded Air France flight 132 from Paris to Tel Aviv during a stopover in Rome. The three men had no intention of commandeering the plane, because theirs was a suicide mission to massacre passengers in the arrival terminal at Ben Gurion International Airport. Shortly after arriving at 10:30 P.M., the three retrieved their baggage inside the terminal, drew automatic weapons and grenades from their bags, and opened fire indiscriminately. The Japanese killed 24 in the massacre, including 19 Puerto Rican Catholics on a pilgrimage to the Holy Land, and wounded more than seventy others in the rampage. Two of the attackers were killed, one when he crossed in front of his comrades' line of fire, a second when a grenade exploded in his hands. The third, Kozo Okamoto, was captured and imprisoned in Israel.[18] Witnesses described the rampage: "all of a sudden I saw a tall man in a brown shirt pulling a machine gun and cocking it. . . . I heard bursts of fire that lasted a few minutes. . . . I saw people rolling, scattering away. . . . I saw two people limping through the exit doors." Emergency personnel arrived to find a scene of carnage, shards of glass, and pools of blood. Shimon Peres, minister of transportation, arrived at Ben Gurion and gave the first briefing to the media: "I am sorry to say that the bloodbath was extremely terrible." He vowed that Israel would "take every step to fight this new madness." The PFLP viewed things differently. The PFLP immediately announced "its complete responsibility for the brave operation" and identified the fallen heroes as members of the Squad of the Martyr Patrick Arguello, a reference to the air pirate killed by Israeli security on the El Al flight during the Skyjack Sunday operation. The PFLP believed it had ample justification to describe the operation as brave and the fallen terrorists as martyrs. It timed the operation to coincide with the fifth anniversary of Israel's aggression in the June 1967 Six Day War, and claimed it was a reprisal for the Sayaret Matkal killing of Ali Taha during the takedown of the hijacked Sabena flight earlier in the month. The attack was "the revolutionary answer to the Israeli massacre performed in cold blood . . . a tribute to the blood of two heroes who fell as a result of a cheap trick."[19]

Israeli authorities interrogated Kozo Okamoto the terrorist who survived the attack. The twenty-four-year-old gave critical details of the planning of the attack and the operational alliance between the JRA and the PFLP. The Lod massacre was to have been a suicide operation, and Okamoto pleaded with the Israelis to permit him to take his own life. But Okamoto would live a long life. He languished in an Israeli prison for twelve years, but he was not forsaken. He went free in 1985 as a result of a prisoner exchange between Israel and the PFLP and disappeared into Lebanon. Japanese authorities never abandoned efforts to bring him to justice and in 2000 persuaded their Lebanese counterparts to arrest him and three other JRA militants. The Lebanese extradited three, but Okamoto escaped prosecution. News of his arrest sparked protests by Lebanese Muslims, who regarded him as a hero for his actions at Lod, and the Lebanese government granted him asylum.[20]

The Lod massacre revealed the power of ideology to incite to murder. The Japanese militants killed without regard to the innocence of their victims in the name of a struggle that was not their own. Israelis understood that hatred of the Jewish state could justify indiscriminate murder of Jews in the minds of Palestinian terrorists. But the Japanese had no personal connection to Palestine. Their motivation for undertaking a suicide operation for the PFLP was a vague ideological notion that the liberation of Palestine would somehow promote a global revolution. European terrorists who would soon enlist in the PFLP as mercenaries shared this view without ever articulating how indiscriminate slaughter could lead to a more just revolutionary world order.

The Israelis were swift to exact vengeance. On 8 July, the Mossad assassinated Ghassan Kanafani, the PFLP spokesperson in Beirut, with a car bomb. It was Kanafani who, beginning with the July 1968 press conference during the El Al hijacking in Algiers, justified the most unjustifiable acts of violence as the voice of the PFLP. The Mossad must have taken great satisfaction at his death, even though in killing him the Mossad also killed his seventeen-year-old niece. Over the next few weeks, Mossad letter bombs maimed the director of a PLO research center and editor of a PFLP newspaper.[21] Kanafani's assassination was a prelude to a Mossad assassination campaign sanctioned by the Israeli cabinet at the end of the year in reaction to Black September's next operation—in Munich.

The Games of Peace and Joy

After Lod, Black September became the most clear and present danger. The Sabena hijacking in March went badly, but by the summer of 1972 Black September was preparing for its most infamous operation "to affirm the existence of the Palestinian people," as Abu Iyad explained it, "by taking advantage of the extraordinary concentration of mass media."[22] In 1972 there was only one event that could demand extraordinary media coverage: the Games of the XX Olympiad in Munich.

The West German government welcomed the summer Olympics as an historic opportunity to erase the ignominious memories of Hitler's 1936 Berlin games. Chancellor Willy Brandt hoped to prove that West Germany was a different state. The venue for the games held great significance for the twenty-one-member Israeli delegation as well. Because Germany under Nazi rule was the epicenter of the Holocaust, by participating in the games the Israeli Olympians would prove the Jewish nation would forever survive. But for the Palestinians the games were something else entirely. If the West believed the creation of a Jewish state somehow assuaged European guilt, the Palestinians demanded the world know that the birth of Israel was their collective Catastrophe by mounting an attack during a sporting festival that in ancient times prompted warring city-states to observe a temporary truce.

In mid-July 1972 Abu Iyad and Abu Daoud—the core leadership of Black September—rendezvoused at a café in Rome. The International Olympics Committee had just announced its rejection of a Palestinian petition to send a Palestinian team to compete in the Games. Abu Iyad was incensed because, he wrote later, it seemed to confirm the international community's belief that Palestinians "didn't deserve to exist."[23] Two days after their meeting in the Italian capital, Abu Daoud flew to Munich to see the Olympic Village for himself.[24] Operation Iqrit and Biri'm—an allusion to Palestinian villages outside Jerusalem cleansed by the Israelis in 1948—was in motion.[25]

The Games of the XX Olympiad—the Games of Peace and Joy—were set to begin on 26 August. As the world's finest athletes were preparing for competition around the globe, a contingent of Palestinians was training for hand-to-hand combat in a Libyan camp for a mission to infiltrate the Olympic Village and take Israeli Olympians hostage. Yasser Arafat certainly knew of the operation, but he prudently left the operational details to Abu Iyad and Abu Daoud, who selected two men—known to the world only as Issa and Tony—to lead the assault. On 7 August, Abu Daoud returned to Munich with Tony to reconnoiter the Olympic Village for a second time. On 24 August Abu Iyad and Abu Daoud rendezvoused again in Frankfurt. Iyad and a female companion flew in from Paris carrying weapons for the assault—Kalashnikovs and grenades—in their luggage. A West German customs official inspected one bag but found only women's lingerie and waved the couple through. Over the next few days, Abu Daoud transported the weapons from Frankfurt to Munich by train and concealed them in lockers in the terminal building.

The failure of West German—and U.S. and European—intelligence agencies was catastrophic. Abu Iyad and Abu Daoud, senior members of Fatah and Black September, managed to move around European capitals without detection. Now they were in West Germany, a country that had already had brushes with Palestinian terror. PFLP terrorists attacked Israelis on West German soil in Munich in February 1970, hurling grenades at the El Al ticket counter. Black September sabotaged a West German electrical plant in February 1971, and later that month the PFLP hijacked a Lufthansa flight to Yemen. After the Lufthansa incident, West German authorities complained about the Yemeni leniency because some of the terrorists were known to the West Germans. Yet inexplicably, West German authorities, who should also have known about Abu

Iyad, failed to detect him at the airport with weapons of war. And the West Germans had their own indigenous terrorism. The German Red Army Faction and the Revolutionary Cells, which were already planting bombs in West German cities by the time RAF leader Andreas Baader made contact with the PFLP in February 1972, only seven months before the West Germans would welcome the world to a restored West Germany. In fact, the West Germans had Baader in custody when the games began and after the Palestinians seized the Israeli athletes they included the release of Baader among their demands. Despite all this, the authorities were unaware of the presence of armed guerrillas in Munich until Black September violently seized the Israeli Olympians and captured the world's attention. West German and Olympic officials may have believed that the sanctity of the Olympic spirit would ward off evil, but that very attitude gave the Palestinians an advantage.

Abu Daoud visited the Olympic Village with a young woman on the day of the opening ceremonies. Posing as Brazilians, the Palestinians talked their way past security and entered the village. As Abu Daoud tells the story, a female member of the Israeli delegation unwittingly invited them into the foyer of the Israeli athletes' apartment complex at 31 Connollystrasse. "She had no way of knowing she had considerably facilitated our task," Abu Daoud wrote almost three decades later.[26] The operational commander of Operation Iqrit and Biri'm now had detailed knowledge of the layout of the apartments he would order his men to storm.

Eleven days later, Black September transformed the Games of Peace and Joy into a spectacle of terror and death. Just after 4 A.M. on 5 September, the eve of the second anniversary of Skyjack Sunday, eight Palestinians converged outside the Olympic Village near the Israelis' apartments on 31 Connollystrasse. Their running suits and athletic bags completed the disguise of athletes returning from local pubs after curfew. Other athletes saw them but suspected nothing. No security guards patrolled the parameter. Only a low wall stood between the Palestinian terrorists and the Jewish athletes asleep in separate apartments. Thirty minutes later, after a swift assault on two apartments, two Israelis were dead and nine others taken hostage. It was their last day of life.

The Palestinians encountered resistance trying to enter one apartment, but forced their way in past an Israeli who threw himself against the door. They shot and wounded another Israeli, Moshe Weinberg, who struggled for a terrorist's weapon. The bullet tore through his jaw, causing a horrible wound, but did not knock him unconscious. One Israeli escaped through a window when he was awakened by the sounds of struggle outside his bedroom. Within minutes the Palestinians held six Israelis and moved on to a second apartment, forcing Weinberg, who was bleeding profusely, to come with them. The Palestinians seized the six Israelis sleeping in the second apartment without resistance. But as they forced the athletes at gunpoint back to the first apartment, one Israeli broke free and ran down a flight of stairs, into a parking garage beneath the apartments and to safety. In the same instant, Moshe Weinberg lunged at the Palestinians again. The act probably saved his compatriot's life, but it cost him his own, as a terrorist shot him to death in the act. When the Palestinians gathered the second group of hostages together with the first in an upper bedroom, another Israeli, Yossef Romano, made a desperate grab for one of the terrorist's weapons. The Palestinian killed him instantly with a burst from his Kalashnikov. The assault ended with Romano's death. There, in a bedroom before dawn, nine Israelis were bound and forced to sit in a circle around Romano's corpse on the floor in a pool of blood as a warning to the Israelis about the punishment for resistance.

By 5 A.M. the Israelis who escaped alerted officials in the Olympic Village to the assault. Word spread throughout West German officialdom and the media. As police arrived at the scene, Issa, the commander of the operation, appeared outside the apartment to communicate demands for the release of hundreds of fedayeen from Israeli prisons and Andreas Baader and Ulrike Meinhoff, the leaders of the Red Army Faction, whom West German authorities had finally arrested in June. Issa set a 9 A.M. deadline for compliance with the demands; after that Palestinians would begin executing the Israelis one by one. To prove their seriousness, the Palestinians threw Weinberg's body into the street in front of the apartment where they held the other Olympians.

The West German government conveyed Black September's demands to Golda Meir, the indomitable Israeli prime minister, who immediately rejected them in principle. Meir refused even to contemplate negotiations. Instead, Meir immediately dispatched the head of the Mossad, Zvi Zamir, to Munich as she pleaded with the West German authorities to permit an elite Sayaret Matkal counterterrorist unit to assist in a rescue. The Israeli special forces had proven their abilities just last May, when they took down the Sabena hijackers. Meir put them on alert to leave for West Germany at a moment's notice. The call to action never came.

West Germany's highest officials rushed to Munich before day's end. Chancellor Willy Brandt arrived in the afternoon. Hans-Dietrich Genscher, the interior minister and future foreign minister, arrived at the same time and met face-to-face with Issa. Genscher even offered himself as a hostage in exchange for the release of the Israelis. Then the West Germans offered an undisclosed sum of money and safe passage for the Palestinians in exchange for the lives of the Jewish athletes and the swift termination of an embarrassing incident. A cash offer worked in February when the PFLP seized a Lufthansa flight and diverted it to Aden. It was the PFLP that seized the Lufthansa flight, but Black September was not content with a massive infusion of cash into its war chest. Israel's adamant refusal to capitulate to the terrorists' demands—or to make a good will gesture like those offered during the El Al crisis in Algeria in 1968—left the West Germans with few options. The most promising possibility was to persuade the Egyptian government to mediate. In fact, the terrorists' contingency plan involved departure to an Arab state with the hostages. But Egyptian president Anwar Sadat would not assume responsibility for their lives. With Israel refusing to negotiate and Egypt refusing to mediate, the West Germans could only attempt to delay and deceive the eight terrorists barricaded inside 31 Connollystrasse with the nine Olympians.

The West Germans managed to push back the 9 A.M. deadline for the beginning of the executions until noon, then one o'clock, then three, then five, then seven. By early afternoon they were reluctantly planning a rescue operation. The first attempt at an armed rescue came after the deadline was pushed back to seven. By then officials, including Genscher, had entered the Israeli apartment and seen the terror in the eyes of the Jewish athletes for themselves. "I will never forget those faces," Genscher would say later.[27] Rescue must have seemed the last best option. But there was no elite counterterrorism unit up to the task. The best the Munich police could muster were a dozen or so police for an assault, police whose courage surpassed their training. Fortunately for them, their superiors never gave the order to attack. Issa, who saw live television images of the police assembling on the roof above them, forced the West Germans to pull back with the threat of the immediate execution of hostages. The journalistic impulse to broadcast breaking news compromised the mission and, although the indiscretion could have cost lives, it probably saved them for the time being. Even some of the police selected to break into the apartments through the air vents admitted the operation was suicide. But the disaster that was adverted in the Olympic Village was awaiting the Israeli athletes, and the terrorists who abducted them, on the outskirts of Munich.

The West Germans seized on another stratagem: they would lure the Palestinians to Fürstenfeldbruck, an airport outside Munich, with the false promise that a Lufthansa 737 would fly them and the hostages to Cairo. Genscher informed Issa that a peaceful resolution of the crisis was near. Issa had only to allow the West Germans time to arrange the complicated logistics: helicopters to transport the Palestinians and the Israeli Olympians to Fürstenfeldbruck, a jet to fly them to Egypt, pilots who would risk becoming hostages or casualties. It would take another three hours for the West Germans to put everything in place. The reality was that the West Germans wanted to lure the Palestinians into a field of fire. Snipers took positions in the parking garage beneath the apartment complex. It was nearly two hundred yards from the Israeli apartment to the field where the helicopters were waiting. But Issa, who took the precaution of walking the distance with officials to observe the route for himself, demanded a bus. The West Germans were forced to move the ambush to Fürstenfeldbruck. It was after 10:00 P.M. before Issa, the seven other fedayeen, and the nine Israelis made their way from 31 Connollystrasse to the bus and through the parking garage to the helicopters for the thirty-minute flight to Fürstenfeldbruck. Twenty minutes later, the two helicopters were airborne. The Israelis were bound inside, five in one helicopter, four in the other.

The fatal tactical errors at Fürstenfeldbruck were those of a police force that had not contemplated a terror attack in the Bavarian capital. The snipers deployed at the darkened airport were poorly armed and inadequately trained for a firefight with hardened commandos. They had only hours to organize an ambush. Those on the ground were not even in direct radio contact with each other. The police might have stood some chance of success against fatigued Palestinians if the crisis had dragged on for days, but the Palestinians, aware of the fate of the Black September hijackers of the Sabena flight in May, did not commit the failure of permitting the West Germans or the Israelis to wear them down. The West German refusal to permit Israel's Sayaret Matkal to take charge of the rescue, or even to give tactical advice, was about to have terrible consequences. And in an incredible intelligence failure, the West Germans deployed only five snipers. Authorities in the Olympic Village never conveyed an accurate count of the Palestinians to the police who were assembling to ambush them.

The helicopters arrived just after 10:30 P.M. Most of the terrorists stepped off, exposing themselves to snipers concealed on the roof of the small control tower building directly in front of them. Issa and another terrorist walked across the tarmac to inspect the jet awaiting them with engines revving. But when they boarded it they found no crew and sensed a trap. West German police, who were to have overpowered the men, abandoned their positions only minutes before the helicopters put down. The rescue failed then and there. As the Palestinians ran back to the helicopters shouting over the roar of the engines, the West Germans opened fire. But the snipers' aim was not true. One terrorist was killed in the first volley of shots, another wounded. But the others took cover beneath the helicopters and returned fire. The nine Israelis bound together inside the helicopters were defenseless as bullets ricocheted off the tarmac. The firefight at Fürstenfeldbruck lasted more than an hour. It ended in a massacre. As the West Germans brought up armored vehicles in support of the snipers, the Palestinians acted on their orders to defend themselves. One Palestinian fired at point-blank range into one helicopter, killing four of the Jewish athletes, another threw a grenade into the second helicopter killing the other five. When it was over, nine Israelis, five Palestinians, and a West German policeman were dead.

The carnage on the tarmac at Fürstenfeldbruck was not the end of the incident for either the Palestinians or the Israelis. Black September felt duty-bound to liberate the three imprisoned survivors of Operation Iqrit and Biri'm. It took them less than two months to force the West Germans to free them. On 29 October, Black September terrorists seized control of a Lufthansa flight out of Beirut for Munich and diverted it to Damascus. On the ground in the Syrian capital the hijackers threatened to blow up the plane and the passengers unless the German chancellor released fedayeen incarcerated in West Germany. Willy Brandt complied, and the survivors of the firefight in Munich went free.[28] It was the end of a bad run for West German counterterrorism. The authorities failed to intercept the terrorists who attacked the Olympics, killed the Israeli hostages trying to save them, and now submitted to demands for the release of terrorists from their jurisdiction.

Committee X

Judaism teaches that anyone who saves a life saves the world; it also teaches an eye for an eye. Golda Meir resolved to be true to the ancient tradition. In the aftermath of the atrocity in West Germany, Golda Meir convened a meeting of her senior national security and counterterrorism advisors. At their urging, Meir resolved to hunt down the leadership of Black September. This was the origin of the Mossad Operation Wrath of God. Even for a state at war with implacable adversaries, the decision to sanction assassination crossed an invisible line into morally ambiguous territory. Plausible deniability became critical for political as well as the obvious operational reasons. Operation Wrath of God became a closely guarded secret of an ad hoc Committee X composed of the highest authorities of the Jewish state.[29] Committee X sent covert teams of assassins across the Middle East and Europe to hunt down Black September terrorists. Without making the error of moral equivalence, the assassination teams were not unlike Black September. If the Palestinians adopted the name Black September to obscure the connections between its actions and the PLO leadership, the assassination teams attempted to distance themselves from the Mossad. The assassination teams led by the shadowy "Mike"—Mike Harari, who decades later became involved with Panamanian dictator Manual Noriega—and "Avner" went so far as to resign their commissions in the Mossad to create the conditions for plausible deniability in the argot of the intelligence community.

In fact, Committee X only decided to intensify and broaden a campaign of selective assassinations the Israeli government had begun years earlier. In July, before Munich, the Mossad assassinated Ghassan Kanafani and maimed lesser-known PLO figures with letter bombs; two years before that, in July 1970, the Mossad nearly assassinated Wadi Haddad in his Beirut apartment. Assassination was nothing new. The national clamor to avenge the Israeli Olympians only provided Israel more justification for reprisal killings or preemptive strikes to smite its terrorist enemies. Not all those marked for death belonged to Black September; PFLP cadres were hunted down and killed as well. And, the assassinations Committee X sanctioned served a broader strategic purpose. Not all those killed were terrorists; some were PLO moderates, who were killed at a moment when Israel had reasons to fear Arafat's tilt toward moderation.

The three survivors of Black September's Munich operation figured prominently on the Mossad hit list, but the chieftains of Black September—Abu Iyad, Mohammed Najjar, Abu Daoud, and Ali Hassan Salameh—were the' principal targets. The Israelis never managed to kill Abu Iyad; he would be killed by a dissident Palestinian he had recruited into Fatah; Sayaret Matkal, Israeli special forces, killed Najjar in Beirut in 1973; the Mossad seriously wounded Abu Daoud in 1981, but he survived and, a decade after the assassination attempt, voted as a member of the Palestinian National Council to rescind the clause in the PLO charter calling for the destruction of Israel.[30] Ali Hassan Salameh, whom the Israelis called the Red Prince, frustrated the Israeli assassination squads until 1979; in fact, Israeli intelligence committed one of its most damaging blunders in 1974 when it killed a man it mistook for the Red Prince in Norway. Committee X also marked Wadi Haddad, the "Master" of PFLP operations, for death. The Israelis, who attempted to assassinate him as early as 1970, never managed to kill him; he died of cancer in 1978. Mohammed Boudia was the chief of PFLP operations in Europe and superior to the infamous Carlos the Jackal; the Israelis planted the bomb that killed him in his car in Paris in June 1973. Basil al-Kubaisi managed logistics for the PFLP; the Israelis killed him in Paris in April 1973.

Committee X's assassination squads struck within weeks of Munich, killing men who did not suspect the Mossad was hunting them. On 16 October 1972, the Israelis tracked Wael Zwaiter to Rome and shot him to death in the lobby of his apartment building. On 8 December, a Mossad assassination squad killed Mahmoud Hamshari in Paris. This time the assassination was more imaginative. Hamshari's killers placed a bomb under his telephone table and detonated it when he identified himself to a caller posing as a journalist interested in interviewing him. In January 1973, the Mossad killed Hussein Abad al-Chir in Cyprus by detonating a bomb placed under his bed. None of these men were directly involved in the Munich atrocity; indeed, there are doubts about their involvement in Black September. The Israelis had reason to believe that Zwaiter, PLO representative in Rome, had been involved in the El Al hijacking in July 1968. Hamshari was an intellectual, not a terrorist operative, but the Mossad believed he had had a hand in the Munich operation; the Israelis were certain al-Chir was the PLO contact with the Soviet KGB.[31] These were only the first in a series of assassinations—and counter-assassinations—in a dirty war that would continue through 1973 and into 1974.

At the end of the year, Black September mounted its second major operation, on the other side of the world from the first. On 28 December, four Palestinian terrorists raided the Israeli Embassy in Bangkok.[32] They seized six Israeli diplomats, among them the ambassador to neighboring Cambodia, who happened to be visiting. They issued the usual demands: the release of 36 imprisoned comrades. The terrorists' sense of solidarity was inclusive: the name of Kozo Okamoto, the Japanese Red Army survivor of the Lod massacre, figured on the list. The Munich incident was still vivid in the memories of the Israeli and Thai governments. Golda Meir, whose intelligence agency was just beginning to hunt down those responsible for Munich, reasserted the Israeli government's policy of non-negotiation. The government of Thailand, embarrassed by the breach of security, made a daunting show of force by encircling the embassy with security forces. As important as the Israeli and Thai reaction was that of Egypt. President Sadat had refused to become embroiled in the Munich incident. His refusal to grant the Black September commandos safe passage to Cairo not only contributed to the tragedy at Fürstenfeldbruck, but damaged his diplomacy. By the end of 1972, Sadat was interested in gaining support for a negotiated return of the Sinai, lost to the Israelis in the Six Day War.

The intervention of the Egyptian ambassador proved critical. Whatever encouragement the terrorists may have taken from the release of the three survivors of the Munich, the deaths of the other five must have weighed heavily on their minds. With no other viable options, the four Palestinians accepted the Egyptian offer of safe passage and surrendered without harming their captives. Everyone took away different lessons from the Bangkok incident. For governments confronted with the threat to their diplomats—this included the Nixon administration—Bangkok taught the efficacy of absolute refusal to strike deals with terrorists. For the terrorists, Bangkok taught the futility of threats and the imperative to kill.

Abu Iyad and Ali Hassan Salameh had shifted tactics from hijacking airliners to seizing embassies. The change was first evident in Munich. Instead of seizing random passengers, Black September would pursue high officials and dignitaries. There was another critical change in strategy. Black September's major operations after Bangkok—an embassy takeover in Amman in February that failed and one in Khartoum in March that succeeded—revealed its perception of its real enemy, the United States.

Chapter 3

Much Blood Will Flow, Not All of It Ours

The year 1972 was a year of terrible violence; 1973 would be worse. The year began triumphantly for Richard Nixon, who took the oath of office for a second time in January. The electoral returns the previous November seemed to vindicate the career of one of the more controversial politicians in recent decades. Within days of his second inauguration, Nixon addressed the nation to announce that Henry Kissinger and Le Duc Tho, the North Vietnamese envoy, had initialed the Paris Peace Accords, which ended the Vietnam War and earned the two men the Nobel Prize for Peace. But 1973 would be a year marked by scandal in Washington and violence in the Middle East. Within weeks of his second inauguration, the president would confront the same wrenching moral dilemma the Israeli prime minister faced the previous September. The Israeli Mossad was engaged in an escalating dirty war of counterterrorism against the PFLP and Black September, and renegade organizations backed by Iraq and Libya launched a wave of terror operations in Europe to destroy any appearance of Palestinian moderation. Not a month passed without terrorist or counterterrorist violence. Moreover, it was almost inevitable that Egypt, Syria, and Jordan would seek to reconquer the territory they lost to Israel in the Six Day War. By the end of the year, while Nixon's presidency crashed down around him as a consequence of the Watergate scandal, the fourth Arab-Israeli war would bring the United States and the Soviet Union into a confrontation and would reshape the political terrain in the Middle East.

Black September's Final Operations

The campaign of Palestinian terrorism and Israeli counterterrorism had by now escalated into low-intensity warfare. The resolution of the hostage incident in Bangkok in December 1973 seemed proof that governments could compel terrorists to back down simply by refusing to capitulate to their demands. The Israelis were actively engaged in a covert counterterrorism of reprisal killings and preemptive assassinations. Operation Wrath of God, the Mossad's covert campaign of assassinations of the PLO middle echelon, had claimed its first two victims in October in Rome and December in Paris. In January, the Mossad struck again, killing Hussein Abad al-Chir in Cyprus. The operation was almost identical to the one that eliminated Mahmoud Hamshari in Paris the previous month; the Mossad's avengers placed a bomb under al-Chir's bed. The next day, Black September struck back in Madrid, assassinating Baruch Cohen, a Mossad agent who recruited Palestinian university students in Spain as Mossad informants.[1] Abu Iyad, whose life depended on counterintelligence, discovered Cohen's operations and ordered his assassination.

The violence was only beginning. On 20 February, the Israeli armed forces assaulted two Palestinian refugee camps near Tripoli, Lebanon—Badawi and Nahr al-Bard—where PFLP trained fedayeen. The Israeli commandos killed 40 in the raid. The following day, as the Israeli forces were completing the operation in Lebanon, Israel's acute security concerns caused a catastrophe. The waste of innocent life marked the Arab-Israeli conflict from the beginning. Palestinian terrorists found justification for killing innocent Israelis, Israeli soldiers rationalized the deaths of innocent Palestinians as collateral damage. But what happened in the skies over the Israeli-occupied Sinai Peninsula claimed more lives than any terrorist act up to that time. On 21 February, the pilot of a Libyan airliner en route to Cairo became disoriented in one of North Africa's blinding sandstorms. Before the pilot realized the error in navigation, the plane had strayed into Israel's security zone over the occupied Sinai where Israeli fighter jets intercepted it. Israeli efforts to hail the pilot were to no avail. The Israelis later insisted that the pilot ignored orders to land, but there is another explanation. The French-speaking pilot apparently did not understand the commands coming over the civilian radio channel. The Israelis feared the worst. No terrorist had deliberately crashed a civilian airliner in a population center or military installation—none did until 9/11. But the Israeli authorities acted to preempt the possibility of a suicide attack on Israel's nuclear weapons installation at Dimona. It was a tragic miscalculation. The pilot of the doomed Libyan airliner had already reversed course when the Israelis fighters opened fire; 106 passengers and crew died when the plane crashed in the desert.[2]

That same month, Black September set in motion its third major operation after Munich and Bangkok. Like Bangkok, the mission was an embassy seizure. As Abu Iyad tells it, it was an "ambitious plan." Coming only two months after the demoralizing failure in Bangkok, Black September needed a bold strike.[3] If the plan was ambitious, it was also dangerous. The embassy was in Amman. Jordan remained hostile territory for the Palestinians, especially for Black September. whose name is an allusion to the fratricide of 1970. Jordanian intelligence was alert to the threat of Black September, whose first operation was the assassination of the Jordanian prime minister in Cairo. Jordanian intelligence was collaborating with the Israeli Mossad and the CIA. The collaboration of the intelligence agencies was important, but the brutality of Jordanian intelligence toward suspected enemies of the kingdom gave it a critical advantage. There was something else about the ambitious operation that Iyad later reported was months in planning. Black September planned to take down the U.S. embassy in the Jordanian capital and hold American diplomats hostage until the Jordanians freed imprisoned fedayeen and the Americans freed Sirhan Sirhan, Robert Kennedy's assassin. It was the first time the Palestinians deliberately targeted Americans. The Amman operation marked a critical turning point in Middle Eastern terrorism.

Because of the importance of the mission—and the urgency of success—Iyad selected Abu Daoud to take charge of the mission. Daoud commanded Fatah forces in Jordan during the confrontation with Hussein's troops in September 1970 and planned the Munich Olympics operation with Abu Iyad. Iyad considered him courageous, capable, and a close friend. That Daoud managed to enter Jordan through Iraq and set himself up in a safe house was a remarkable achievement. Actually, fifteen fedayeen operating in two squads infiltrated Amman, one to storm the U.S. embassy, the second to seize the adjacent offices of the Jordanian prime minister if the assault on the Americans failed. In fact, the entire operation failed. Daoud planned the preparation for 14 February. After putting all the elements in place, Daoud left Jordan en route to Syria. He never reached the border. Jordanian intelligence arrested Daoud and a woman posing as his wife as they drove from Amman to Damascus. It was not a chance encounter. At the same time Jordanian intelligence raided the safe houses where the fedayeen were mustering for the operation. Daoud had been betrayed by an agent within the conspiracy. The arrest of a senior figure in Black September—and Fatah—was an intelligence coup. Under interrogation Daoud made damaging statements about Black September, Fatah, and Abu Iyad.[4] That the Jordanians tortured him is a reasonable certainty; Black September did not condemn him to death for his moral weakness under interrogation. But a Jordanian court did sentence him to death. King Hussein prudently commuted the sentence to life, fearing for his own life if the monarchy killed a Palestinian of Daoud's stature. But that was not the end of the Daoud affair. Inevitably, Black September would act to liberate him. Less than a month after Daoud's capture, Black September set in motion its fourth major operation. It had struck in Europe, Asia, the Middle East, now it would strike North Africa, demonstrating its reach to all points on the compass.

The planning for what Black September would call Operation Nahr al-Bard began in Beirut in mid-February, even before Daoud's capture in Jordan and the Israeli assault on the Badawi and Nahr al-Bard refugee camps in Lebanon. Abu Iyad was behind it, but another Fatah operative, known only as Abu Jamal—his true identity was never established—coordinated it with the most senior PLO representatives in the Sudan, Fawaz Yassin and his deputy, Rizig Abu Ghassan.[5] Yassin, who traveled between the Sudan and Libya in the days before and after the operation, was in charge of logistics; Ghassan actually commanded the armed fedayeen who carried it out. Operation Nahr al-Bard was to be a raid on a diplomatic reception at the Saudi Arabian embassy in Khartoum, where Black September would seize the CIA's principal operative in the Middle East. The Palestinians, aware of the CIA's collaboration with Jordanian intelligence, accused the agency of complicity in the slaughter in Jordan in September 1970. Whatever the truth about CIA involvement in Jordan, the information about the man identified as the CIA's chief in the Middle East, George Curtis Moore, was false. Moore was a career diplomat, not a professional intelligence officer. He was just completing a tour as the chargé d'affaires of the U.S. mission in the Sudanese capital, and the gathering in Khartoum was a farewell reception hosted by the Saudis.

On the evening of 1 March, just as the diplomatic reception was breaking up, Abu Ghassan and seven other Palestinians, armed with Kalashnikov assault rifles and grenades, rushed the front gate and shot their way into the Saudi Arabian embassy. They killed a Sudanese policeman and wounded the U.S. ambassador Cleo Noel, Jr. and Belgian chargé d'affaires Guy Eid. In the panic of the first moments of the assault a number of diplomats managed to escape over the garden wall in the rear of the Saudi compound. The Palestinians seized many others. But their mission was not to take as many dignitaries hostage as possible, but to capture and kill Americans. Moore, Noel, and Eid were bound and beaten. Within hours, word reached Washington that terrorists again held Americans hostage.

The crisis in Khartoum compelled President Nixon to confront the same moral dilemma that the Munich attack forced on Golda Meir. It was not the first time a U.S. diplomat had been taken hostage and threatened with death. In September 1969, Brazilian terrorists abducted the U.S. ambassador to the country, Charles Elbrick. Nixon, still in his first year in office, encouraged the Brazilians to comply with the terrorists' demands for the release of imprisoned Brazilian terrorists. The Brazilian military government, known for its hard line, accommodated the White

House. The Brazilians were more concerned about the prospect of the death of a U.S. diplomat on Brazilian soil than about freeing political prisoners. The U.S. ambassador went free after a few days of captivity; the terrorists and their freed comrades flew to Algeria aboard a military transport. But in 1973 Nixon was adamant in the refusal to make concessions to terrorists. The president drew the lessons from Bangkok, while ignoring those of Munich.

Golda Meir made the policy of no negotiations an article of faith: if Israelis died in Munich, their death was due to the malevolence of the Palestinians and the incompetence of the West Germans, not the intransigence of the Israelis. In Bangkok, Thai authorities reacted to Black September's seizure of the Israeli embassy with a formidable display of force. Golda Meir's intransigence and Thai armed posturing appeared to break the four terrorists holding the Israeli diplomats. The crisis unfolding in Khartoum resembled the crisis in Bangkok in that respect: the Sudanese also rushed forces to the Saudi embassy. In Bangkok unlike Munich, however, the Egyptian government saw an interest in mediating the crisis. But that apparently made less impression on the White House situation room than did Golda Meir's resolute adherence to the doctrine of no negotiation or the psychological effects of military threats.

Nixon apparently did not consider all the psychological dynamics of the hostage situation. The Sudanese made a show of force but also intervened to resolve the crisis. Sudanese vice president Mohammed al-Baghir Ahmad personally took charge of negotiations. A general, al-Baghir understood the language of force, but with the Palestinians he preferred the language of mediation. Even after he was certain Nixon would offer him nothing he could offer to Black September, al-Baghir understood the need to convince the Palestinians to keep lines of communication open. In reality he understood the need to wear the Palestinians down and erode their resolve. Then, in an unguarded remark, Nixon destroyed that possibility. Asked by a reporter to comment on the crisis as it was entering its second day, Nixon said: "As far as the United States as a government giving into blackmail demands, we cannot do so and we will not do so. . . . We will do everything we can to get them released, but we will not pay blackmail."[6] Three hours later, the eight Palestinians murdered Moore, Noel, and Eid with bursts of Kalashnikov fire in the basement of the Saudi embassy. The order to kill the diplomats came via a coded radio message instructing the Black September commando to "remember the martyrs of Nahr al-Bard," a reference to the Palestinians killed in the Israeli operation in Tripoli in February. The Israelis who intercepted the transmission have always alleged, but never proven, that the voice was Arafat's. But the order to kill came from the highest echelon of Black September, meaning the militant core of Arafat's Fatah, and almost certainly from Abu Iyad.[7]

After executing George Curtis Moore, Cleo Noel, Jr., and Guy Eid, the eight fedayeen surrendered to Sudanese authorities. U.S. officials put considerable pressure on Sudan's president, Gaafur Nimeiry, to prosecute the killers. The affair says a great deal about the politics of the Arab-Israeli conflict, and about justice. Nimeiry was deeply embarrassed by the operation and correctly suspected that Muammar Qaddafi, the Libyan dictator, was behind the murder of the diplomats. Qaddafi, who was already emerging as a principal figure in the intricate web of state sponsorship of Palestinian terror, would become even more involved as a sponsor of the Rejection Front, which emerged after the official PLO opted to participate in the nascent peace process in 1974. Nimeiry had reason to expose Qaddafi. Moreover, Nimeiry felt betrayed by Fatah. He had become personally involved in the September 1970 crisis in Jordan, flying to Amman to help mediate between the Jordanians and the Palestinians. From his perspective, Arafat owed his life to the Sudanese president's intervention.

This same ideological commitment to the Palestinian cause prevented Nimeiry from punishing the Black September terrorists who embarrassed him in his own capital. The same perverse logic applied to the Egyptians who released Wasfi Tel's assassins on narrow legal grounds. Nimeiry would have preferred not to alienate the United States. The two countries had only recently renewed diplomatic relations which were suspended after the Six Day War. The most important task of the two slain U.S. diplomats had been to achieve a full rapprochement. But passion prevailed over reason. Nimeiry, after considerable delay, forced a Sudanese court to try the diplomats' killers, although the Palestinians transformed the trial into a forum to voice Black September's grievances. On 24 June 1973, a Sudanese court found six of the eight guilty of murder. But twenty-four hours later Nimeiry released the men into PLO custody with the understanding that Arafat's security would imprison them in Beirut for the duration of their sentences. This was not the end of the incident: in one of those small ironies of the history of Palestinian terrorism, in November 1974 dissident Palestinians would hijack a British airliner to demand that the PLO free brother Palestinians.

The Khartoum incident alerted the Nixon administration to the dangers the escalating terror campaign posed for U.S. emissaries. These were dangers Americans traveling to Israel confronted once the PFLP turned to air piracy. But apart from applying diplomatic pressures on the Sudan, the Nixon administration had few options. Its myopic efforts to frame a negotiated solution were focused on ending hostilities between Egypt and Israel. The idea of a comprehensive peace that accommodated the Palestinians fell outside the administration's strategic vision. Not until months later, after the October War, did Nixon and Kissinger even contemplate discreet communications with the PLO, though the CIA had once established contact with Arafat via Ali Hassan Salameh, the Red Prince. When Kissinger finally dispatched an envoy to speak with PLO representatives in November, he gave instructions to warn of dire consequences for future acts of violence rather than to explore prospects for meaningful dialogue.

Operation Youth of Spring

Even before Munich the Mossad was gathering intelligence on the senior PLO cadre and terrorists. By April Mossad agents identified the residences of three of them in an apartment building on Rue Verdun in Beirut's Fakhani district, which by 1973 the Palestinians had converted into a principality. Mohammed Najjar was the most dangerous of the three. A senior member of Fatah intelligence and an operational commander of Black September, Najjar was behind the May 1972 Sabena hijacking. And although Munich was principally the work of Abu Iyad and Abu Daoud, the Israelis were certain of Najjar's involvement. Kamal Adwan also belonged to Black September. He was a staunch supporter of terror, even after Arafat began to have second thoughts about hijackings and hostage-taking for strategic, though certainly not moral, reasons. In the wake of the PFLP-JRA massacre at Lod, Adwan had quipped "this was an ordinary attack similar to any other attack conducted by a combat unit on a settlement or military camp."[8] Committee X did not specifically mark Kamal Nasser for a Wrath of God assassination. But as a principal apologist for the PLO, the Israelis reviled him—as they reviled the PFLP's Ghassan Kanafani, whom they killed on a Beirut street the previous year—for his words as much as his deeds. The Israelis killed Najjar, Adwan, and Nasser on an April night in an operation with a disconcertingly idyllic code word, Youth of Spring.

Operation Youth of Spring was a coordinated Mossad-Sayaret Matkal operation. On the night of 10 April, Lieutenant Colonel Ehud Barak's commandos came ashore on a Beirut beach in Zodiac boats and rendezvoused with Mossad agents, who rushed them to Rue Verdun in rented cars.[9] Some of the commandos were disguised as women to deceive Lebanese police and Palestinian militants patrolling the Fakhani district; Barak, the future prime minister, disguised as a brunette woman, began the killing, shooting a guard posted outside the apartment building. A silencer muffled the shots. Then Barak's men rushed up flights of stairs to the apartments where the men slept and blew open the doors to

Kamal Adwan's apartment. Barak is not reticent about telling the details in his imperfect English: "It was only the split-second hesitation of the terrorist when he sees it's (sic) civilian people, that ended up our officer shot the terrorist and not the other way around." Adwan was racked with as many as 55 bullets. His daughter witnessed the attack "glass was being shattered on our heads and he just fell."[10] It was the same in Najjar's apartment, except that there the Israelis killed Najjar's wife, who threw herself in the line of fire to save her husband. Her son, who heard the burst of fire from the adjoining room, remembers his father cursing the Israelis—"You killed her you dogs"—an instant before they killed him. Within minutes a battle erupted in the Fahkani. As Barak's men were killing Najjar, Adwan, and Nasser, another Sayaret Matkal team was attacking the nearby headquarters of the Democratic Front for the Liberation of Palestine. Abu Iyad, who improbably claims he was in a nearby apartment debriefing the survivors of the Munich operation the West Germans released the previous October, heard gunfire and deafening explosions.[11] Out on the street the Israeli commandos came under fire from Lebanese and Palestinians.

Operation Youth of Spring inflicted heavy damage on Black September. The Israelis killed three of the senior cadre; and almost a fourth. Abu Iyad had dined with the slain men earlier in the evening, attended a PLO central committee meeting with them, and was briefly at Nasser's apartment that night.[12] Yasser Arafat and the DFLP's Naif Hawatmeh lived within blocks of the epicenter of the Israeli assault. But the damage went beyond the body count. The deepest wounds were psychological. Iyad was convinced that the "commandos would never have been able to operate with such impunity for three hours in the heart of Beirut if they hadn't benefited from important local complicity." In fact, the raid lasted thirty minutes, not three hours, but the nighttime assault not only shook what the PLO's sense of invulnerability, it deepened their suspicions of the Lebanese, especially the minority Maronite Christians.[13] This was not coincidental because the Israelis came to inflame tensions between Lebanese and Palestinians as much as they came to kill Palestinians terrorists. Over the next three weeks, Palestinian fedayeen and Lebanese security forces clashed, and in May President Frenjieh ordered the Lebanese air force to bomb and strafe the Sabra and Shatila refugee camps. The possibility of a wider conflict was averted only through the mediation of Arab states. It was a prelude of bad times to come. In less than two years Lebanese and Palestinians would be killing each other with the same ferocity that the Jordanians and Palestinians had killed each other in September 1970.

Israel was not winning the war on terrorism, but it was inflicting great harm on its terrorist enemies. Two days after Operation Youth of Spring, a Mossad Wrath of God assassination squad struck again in Athens, killing Zaid Muchassi with a bomb in his room in the Hotel Aristides. Muchassi was filling in for Abad al-Chir, the PLO liaison with the Soviet KGB, whom the Israelis had killed in Rome in October. Making their escape, the Israelis ran into Muchassi's KGB contact in a car outside the hotel and shot and killed him.[14] In the months since the Munich massacre, the Mossad had struck five times: against Black September with the Wrath of God assassinations in Rome, Paris, and Cyprus between October and January; against the PFLP with the devastating attack on the PFLP camps in Tripoli, Lebanon, in February, and again against Black September with the audacious April assault in Beirut. The Palestinians were finding it harder and harder to mount operations in the spring of 1973.

On 15 March, French and Italian authorities arrested two Palestinians who planned to attack the Israeli and Jordanian embassies in Paris. On 4 April, Italian police arrested two more Palestinians, forestalling an attack on El Al passengers at the Leonardo Da Vinci Airport in Rome. Five days later, authorities in Cyprus arrested four Palestinians before they could mount simultaneous attacks on an Israeli Arika passenger jet and the Israeli ambassador's residence in Nicosia. The Mossad and Sayaret Matkal executed Operation Youth of Spring in the heart of Beirut the next night. Seventeen days later the Palestinians tried to retaliate. On 27 April, security officials at Beirut's international airport apprehended three more Palestinians who tried to board a plane for France with explosives. That same day a Palestinian opened fire at the El Al office in Rome, this time managing to kill an Italian clerk who had crossed the path of Palestinian terror. It was a succession of Palestinian failures punctuated by Israeli successes. In June, the Mossad struck in Paris again. This time it was a preemptive strike rather than a reprisal killing.

A Dirty War

The PFLP had not conducted a major international terror operation since May 1972, when Wadi Haddad sent the Japanese Red Army mercenaries on a suicide mission to slaughter disembarking passengers at the Ben Gurion International Airport in Lod. By 1973, tensions between George Habash, the PFLP's nominal secretary general, and Haddad, the master of PFLP terror, had begun to divide the PFLP into factions. The devastating attack on the PFLP training camps in Tripoli in February disrupted Haddad's operations. But the master had not laid down the gun. In mid-1973, Haddad was carefully expanding the PFLP terror network in Europe from safe houses in Paris and London. The man at the center of the network was Mohammed Boudia. As chief of PFLP operations in Europe, Boudia had a range of responsibilities that included the recruitment of foreign nationals to the Palestinian cause in the name of world revolution. Among his recruits was Illich Ramírez Sánchez, a megalomaniac young Venezuelan known as Carlos the Jackal, who throughout much of 1974 and 1975 would be one of the world's most hunted terrorists. The Israelis discovered Boudia's activities in Paris. Late in the morning of 28 June, Mossad planted a bomb beneath the seat of Boudia's car; the pressure of his weight detonated it, killing him.[15] The assassination of Mohammed Boudia was the ninth assassination sanctioned by Committee X and the last successful killing in a series of Wrath of God killings. But it was not the last attempt on the life of a Palestinian terrorist. A month later, the Mossad struck again, this time with disastrous consequences. But first Wadi Haddad's faction of the PFLP suddenly went back into action.

On 20 July, five terrorists hijacked a Japanese Airways flight out of Amsterdam en route to Tokyo with 145 passengers and crew. The hijacking was a combined PFLP and JRA operation. JRA terrorists proved useful to Wadi Haddad at Lod in 1972, but this time the master ordered PFLP members to accompany the Japanese. The operation was a fiasco. One of the hijackers, a Palestinian woman, inadvertently exploded a grenade, killing herself and severely wounding a member of the crew.[16] Miraculously, the Boeing 747 remained airworthy and the terrorists ordered the plane to fly to the Persian Gulf in search of a country that would permit the plane to land. Iraqi authorities denied permission to land at Basra, and Bahraini authorities refused to allow the plane to touch down in Manama before the United Arab Emirates decided to try to resolve the crisis in Dubai. The UAE defense minister took personal charge of the negotiations and boarded the plane after the wounded crew member and the body of the dead terrorist came off it. But the incident did not end in Dubai. The terrorists ordered the plane on to Benghazi, Libya, without issuing a single demand in Dubai. Safe in Muammar Qaddafi's territory, the terrorists released the hostages without gaining anything in return, and then destroyed the huge jet on the ground before surrendering to Libyan authorities. It was an absolutely futile operation that only succeeded in widening the rift between George Habash, the PFLP general-secretary, who denied PFLP involvement in the operation, and Wadi Haddad, the master terrorist, who ordered it.

A month later, the Mossad carried out another Wrath of God killing, this time in Lillehammer, Norway. Mossad had managed to kill nine Palestinians belonging to the PFLP or Black September. None were of the highest echelon of the terror hierarchy. Black September's Mohammad

Najjar and the PFLP's Mohammed Boudia were operational command-ers, but not masterminds like Abu Iyad or Wadi Haddad. There was one man among the many marked for assassination whose death the Mos-sad's assassination squads coveted most, the elusive Ali Hassan Salameh. The Mossad attributed Munich to the Red Prince, although Abu Iyad and Abu Daoud planned the operation, selected the men who carried it out, and transported the weapons that killed the Israelis. But Salameh, who ran operations in Europe and organized Black September's early sabotage operations there, provided logistical support. The intensity of the Mossad's passion to kill him burned for years—even after Golda Meier called off Operation Wrath of God because of the operational errors the Mossad was about to commit in Lillehammer—and may have been due to Salameh's personal relationship to Yasser Arafat.[17] The leg-end of the Red Prince may be larger than the life.

In July, the Mossad tracked a man it was certain was the Red Prince to Lillehammer. But the intelligence that led Mossad to the small Norwe-gian city was false; in fact, Salameh, whose survival depended on coun-terintelligence, may have provided the Israelis the false intelligence to expose Operation Wrath of God. But in July 1973, Mossad chieftain Zvi Zamir, who personally observed the slaughter of the Israeli Olympians at Fürstenfeldbruck, was so certain of the information that he sanc-tioned the action in Lillehammer.[18] Mike Harari commanded the seven Mossad agents in the operation. The assassination squad acquired cars and lodging and tracked the movements of a man resembling Salameh for a full day before killing him. In what turned out to be a calamitous error, Harari dismissed one agent's doubts about the identity of the man living modestly in Lillehammer. On the night of 21 August, Ahmed Bou-chiki and his wife stepped off a bus and were walking down a darkened Lillehammer street when the madness of the Israeli-Palestinian conflict violently collided with their lives. Bouchiki was not a clandestine Pales-tinian agent, he was a Moroccan waiter whose great misfortune was to bear a striking resemblance to the darkly handsome Salameh. Two Mos-sad agents fired fourteen shots into Bouchiki and left him to die in front of his wife, Torill Larsen, who was pregnant with their child.

The Mossad had murdered an innocent man. Zvi Zamir, the Mossad chief, rationalized the mistake, "this may happen in this sort of activ-ity."[19] But this was only one of many of the assassination squad's opera-tional errors. The day after the murder, Lillehammer police arrested two members of the squad at the airport as they attempted to flee the coun-try. On the night of the murder an alert policeman had taken down the license number of the assassins' car as it sped from the scene; the Mos-sad agents had failed to exchange cars before fleeing Lillehammer. Dur-ing the interrogations the Israelis gave up critical information about the

operation that led to the arrest of four more members of the assassination squad and compromised Mossad operations in Europe. The
damage to Israeli intelligence operations was tremendous. In secret
proceedings, a Norwegian court convicted six Israeli intelligence agents
for the murder of Ahmed Bouchiki and sentenced them to various
prison terms, none longer than twenty-one months.

The murder of Ahmed Bouchiki remained shrouded in official
secrecy for more than a quarter of a century. The principal facts were
known, but the sealed court records and the lenient sentences of the
six Mossad agents raised suspicions about the involvement of Norwegian
security officials. Then came another clandestine encounter between
Palestinians and Israelis in Norway. In 1993, twenty years after Bouchiki's murder, PLO and Israeli representatives met secretly in Oslo to
work out the details of an agreement that would lead to mutual recognition between Arafat's liberation organization and the Jewish state. Three
years later, the Israeli government secretly paid compensation to Torill
Larsen, Bouchiki's widow. Israel did not publicly acknowledge complicity in the crime, but Bouchiki's widow knew better: "No one pays out
compensation unless they are guilty."[20]

The violence of summer 1973 ended with an atrocity in one European
airport and a near catastrophe in another. The atrocity occurred in Athens, where on 5 August two Palestinian terrorists opened fire in a passenger lounge on passengers awaiting a TWA flight to New York. In a
shocking repetition of the Lod massacre fifteen months earlier, the terrorists wounded fifty-five and killed three before capture. Two of the
dead were Americans, one a sixteen-year-old girl. Greek authorities sentenced the men to death for the atrocity, but released them in early 1974
after Palestinians seized a Greek freighter. A month after the atrocity in
Athens, authorities in Rome narrowly averted a catastrophe by arresting
five men who somehow had smuggled Soviet-made shoulder-launched
(SAM-5) surface-to-air missiles into the Italian capital. It was a truly international conspiracy: Libya supplied the weapons, the terrorists came
from Lebanon, Iraq, Syria, Algeria and Libya, and their mission was to
shoot down an Israeli passenger jet after takeoff from the airport.[21]

The Appearance of Abu Nidal

It had been a violent spring and summer. The Palestinians managed to
mount terror operations despite the Israeli campaign to terrorize the
terrorists. But the failure rate was high, attesting to heightened security
and better intelligence in a now fully involved European theater of terror and counterterror operations. There was something else. Palestinian
terrorism underwent a metamorphosis in the first six months of 1973.

The two principal nuclei—Wadi Haddad's faction of the PFLP and Abu Iyad's Black September faction of Fatah—were fragmenting into dissident organizations. The failed PFLP-JRA hijacking in July was the first PFLP operation in more than a year. Black September quietly disappeared after the Khartoum operation in March and death of Najjar, Adwan, and Nasser in April. Neither the PFLP nor Black September was responsible for the operations in Paris, Nicosia, Beirut, Rome, and Athens between March and September. These were acts of Palestinian dissidents who rejected the PLO's discernible tilt toward moderation, men like Abd al-Ghafur, who was behind the Rome and Athens attacks in the spring, and Sabri al-Banna.[22] Both would strike again before the end of the year—al-Banna in Paris in September, al-Ghafur in November and December, after the October War.

Sabri Khalil al-Banna adopted Abu Nidal as his nom de guerre when he joined the Palestinian nationalist movement. Abu Nidal's trajectory was similar to that of many prominent figures in Fatah or the PFLP. Exiled in Saudi Arabia, Abu Nidal moved in conspiratorial circles of young Palestinians who dreamed of liberating Palestine; he even formed a small liberation organization, but it did not survive. After the Six Day War, Abu Iyad, Arafat's intelligence chieftain, recruited Abu Nidal into Fatah. He was posted to the Sudan as Fatah's representative in Khartoum in 1969. It was a brief assignment. He was back in Jordan in 1970, but was sent to Iraq as Fatah's representative to Baghdad before the Palestinian-Jordanian confrontation. In Baghdad, the Baath regime, which seized power in a 1968 bloodletting, encouraged him to organize a radical Fatah faction to challenge Arafat. Abu Nidal was thus originally a creature of Iraqi intelligence, although in later years he transferred his loyalties to Syria and eventually Libya. In September 1973, while he was still nominally under the discipline of Fatah, Abu Nidal carried out his first terror operation.

On the morning of 5 September, the same day the Italian authorities discovered the conspiracy to shoot down an El Al jet in Rome, five terrorists claiming membership in a new organization, al-Icab ("punishment" in Arabic), seized the Saudi Arabian embassy in Paris. They took fifteen hostages, whom they threatened to kill unless Jordan complied with their sole demand: the release of Abu Daoud, who was serving a life sentence for his involvement in the February plot to take U.S. diplomats hostage in Amman. The terrorists were Abu Nidal's men. In fact, the operation's commander, Samir Muhammad al-Abbasi, was the husband of one Abu Nidal's nieces.[23]

Al-Icab was the first in a series of fictitious names Abu Nidal would use in the operations of what he eventually called Fatah-Revolutionary Council. The name was meant to ridicule Arafat, the chief of Fatah and the chairman of the PLO executive committee. Abu Nidal no longer considered Fatah, or the PLO, revolutionary. Abu Nidal admired the imprisoned Abu Daoud and expected that once freed Daoud would join his dissident Fatah faction. Rumors flew that a senior member of Fatah, perhaps even Abu Iyad himself, had betrayed Abu Daoud in Amman at the behest of Arafat, who opposed the embassy operation. But there was another motive. The Paris operation was organized to embarrass Arafat, who was in Morocco attending a meeting of the Non-Aligned Movement. By fall 1973, Arafat was already trying to remake himself in the image of a statesman. Abu Nidal was determined to strew wreckage in his path in the interest of the new Baath regime in Iraq. The terrorists made this clear in a statement that denounced "Arab regimes that disguised themselves behind progressive slogans but move in the line of surrender."[24]

The hostage crisis in Paris lasted forty-eight hours. As evening fell on 5 September, the terrorists apologized to the French for conducting the operation on French soil, and then demanded a jet to fly them and their hostages to an Arab country, any Arab country. As dawn broke on 6 September, they threatened to begin killing the hostages at intervals, but either their resolve was weak or their orders were firm—deadlines for the beginning of executions came and went without a killing. At one point the terrorists speaking through journalists acting as intermediaries told French authorities they wanted to avoid "another Munich." The incident was becoming more and more bizarre. The Iraqi ambassador entered the Saudi embassy on the morning of 6 September to offer himself as a hostage. That same evening, Syrian president Hafez al-Asad offered the terrorists a Syrian jet to fly them out of France. A compromise was in place. The terrorists released ten hostages but took Saudi nationals with them to the plane that would take them first to Cairo for refueling and then to Damascus. The plane never arrived in Syria, but diverted to Kuwait. That was not the end of it. The terrorists forced the pilots back into the air and into Saudi airspace. Over the Saudi capital, they threatened to throw the Saudi hostages from the plane unless the Saudi monarch pressured Jordanian monarch to release Abu Daoud. The threats changed nothing. After a short flight the terrorists returned to Kuwait City, where they released the hostages and surrendered on 7 September.

Abu Iyad, in his memoir five years after the Paris incident, denounced the operation as "a completely senseless exploit."[25] In fact, it infuriated Arafat, who issued a statement from Rabat denouncing the operation and promising to bring those responsible to account. After the closure of the Non-Aligned Summit, Arafat dispatched Abu Iyad and a trusted moderate, Mahmoud Abbas, known as Abu Mazen, to Baghdad to confront the renegade Abu Nidal. Abu Iyad might have believed it feasible to subject Abu Nidal to Fatah discipline, but what he learned in Baghdad should have been a warning. Iraqi intelligence officials present at the meeting revealed that Iraq set the Paris operation in motion, and Abu Nidal merely carried it out.[26] The alliance between Iraq's Baath regime and Abu Nidal's Fatah-Revolutionary Council would prove fatal for PLO moderates. Over the next few years, Abu Nidal acted more as a contract killer than as an international terrorist, systematically assassinating PLO and Arab moderates and Syrian rivals in pursuit of Iraq's national aspiration to become the center of the Arab political universe. In June 1974, Fatah intelligence discovered Abu Nidal's plot to assassinate Abu Mazen and sentenced Nidal to death for treason in absentia. In 1991, Abu Nidal ordered the assassination of Abu Iyad in Tunis as punishment for his drift to moderation.

Less than three weeks after the Saudi embassy operation, Abu Daoud walked free with hundreds of other Palestinian fedayeen. But neither Abu Nidal nor Iraq could claim credit when Jordan's prison gates swung open. King Hussein granted general amnesty to Palestinians at the behest of Egypt and Syria, who needed the Palestinian guerrillas for operations in an imminent war with Israel.

The Yom Kippur War

Israel's victory in the June 1967 Six Day War was deeply humiliating to Egypt, which lost the oil fields of the Sinai Peninsula to Israeli occupation. Anwar Sadat, the Egyptian president who had come to power after Nasser's death during the 1970 Jordanian crisis, could not accept the status quo. By late 1971, Sadat was signaling his preference was for a negotiated return of the occupied Egyptian territory, and he beckoned the United States to frame an agreement with Israel. In April 1972, Egypt began to communicate to Washington through a secret back channel, and in July Sadat announced Egypt's expulsion of 15,000 Soviet military advisors.[27] But the Nixon administration, then heavily engaged in the Paris Peace Talks aimed at ending the Vietnam War, and bent on prying Egypt out of the Soviet sphere of influence, did not vigorously pursue Sadat's overtures. In April 1973, three months after Kissinger and Le Duc Tho initialed the Paris Peace Agreement, Sadat gave a speech warning of war. By September, the Egyptian and Syrian high commands had finalized plans to a two-front war on Israel. The events of October 1973 would alter the entire Middle Eastern political terrain.

Yom Kippur, the Day of Atonement, the holiest day in Judaism, fell on 6 October in 1972. That day, Egyptian and Syrian forces launched Operation Spark. Eighty thousand Egyptian troops crossed the Suez Canal, overwhelming the 500 Israeli troops dug in on the canal's western bank. To the north, 1,400 Syrian tanks engaged the 180 Israeli tanks positioned in the Golan Heights. It was a spectacular intelligence failure for both the Mossad and the CIA that nearly translated into a military catastrophe for Israel. Despite signs that the Egyptians and Syrians were massed for an attack, U.S. intelligence concluded that the Arab states would not risk another defeat by the superior Israeli forces. Nixon, who was in the throes of the Watergate crisis, admitted surprise: "I was disappointed by our own intelligence shortcomings, and I was stunned by the failure of Israeli intelligence." Israel was thrown back on the defensive. The IDF suffered substantial losses of men and materiel during the first three days of the fighting, and on 9 October appealed to Washington for a massive shipment of weapons to mount a counteroffensive. Nixon did not hesitate to come to Israel's defense. For the Republican president the "disturbing question mark . . . [was] the role of the Soviet Union."

But Nixon had other worries. An appeals court had ruled in favor of the Watergate special prosecutor's subpoena for secret Oval Office tapes that would reveal the president's culpability in the cover-up of the Watergate break-in; the vice president was forced to resign on the same day the Israelis appealed for arms and, as the war entered a dangerous phase on Saturday 20 October, Nixon ordered the "Saturday night massacre" firing of the Watergate special prosecutor. The next day, the United States and the Soviet Union agreed to the text of UN Security Council Resolution 338, calling on the belligerents to "terminate all military activity immediately," and to begin negotiations "aimed at establishing a just and durable peace in the Middle East." As important, the Super Powers agreed to host a peace conference, which would eventually be scheduled to begin on 17 December in Geneva. The Security Council passed Resolution 338 on 22 October and set a 12-hour deadline for termination of hostilities. From the onset of the crisis Nixon adhered to the simple principle that the United States should not impose a diplomatic cease-fire: "it would be better to wait until the war had reached a point at which neither side had a decisive military advantage." The reasoning was straightforward: "only a battlefield stalemate would provide the foundation on which fruitful negotiations begin."[28]

Israel and Egypt accepted the terms of Resolution 338, but that did not end the fighting. Israel alleged Egyptian violations of the cease-fire and pressed ahead with an attack on the Egyptian Third Army Corps, which it had already driven back across the Suez, encircling the Egyptian elite troops. The United States and the Soviet Union quickly brokered another cease-fire agreement on 24 October. To monitor it, Anwar Sadat requested deployment of an international peacekeeping force. The Soviets responded by proposing that the United States and the Soviet

Union deploy armed peacekeepers in the Sinai, and threatened a unilateral deployment of Soviet forces when Nixon rejected the proposal. Nixon's response to Soviet premier Leonid Brezhnev was stark: "we must view your suggestion of unilateral action as a matter of the gravest concern involving incalculable actions."[29] To help the Soviet leader calculate the incalculable, Nixon ordered U.S. conventional and nuclear forces on alert. Hostilities concluded the next day.

The CIA and the PLO

Anwar Sadat waged war to compel the United States to broker a peace that would restore the Sinai to Egypt. In fact, the October War was the catalyst for Kissinger's famous shuttle diplomacy that produced a series of agreements between Israel and Egypt, culminating in Sadat's historic—and heroic—visit to Jerusalem in November 1978 and the Camp David Accords in 1979. The Palestinians felt betrayed. Abu Iyad, who was euphoric when the Egyptian president announced Operation Spark, was caustic now: "The October War in Sadat's eyes must indeed have been a 'spark' . . . not the raging fire that the entire Arab world was hoping for."[30] But Iyad was among the first to realize the war had transformed the strategic equation. The Palestinians were compelled to reconsider the policy of no negotiation with Israel, no recognition of Israel, no peace with Israel. The mere possibility of Palestinian participation in the Geneva negotiations provoked a violent schism within the Palestinian national movement. Abu Nidal's seizure of the Saudi Embassy in September was an early sign of the Rejectionist terror and internecine warfare to come. Other signs would come at the end of November and again in December.

The PLO disunity over the question of negotiations was matched by the U.S. and Israeli unity: there was no room at the peace table for Arafat's PLO. Golda Meir, whose Committee X had been systematically hunting down PLO figures in the months leading up to the October War, rejected the very notion of a Palestinian national identity. Kissinger, who assumed near total authority to conduct U.S. foreign policy while Nixon sank deeper into the mire of the Watergate scandal, was more concerned with dividing Egypt from the Arab world than with finding a just and durable peace. The Arab League, meeting in Algiers in November, tried to force the issue by declaring the PLO the "sole legitimate representative of the Palestinian people." Arafat, who had long coveted this recognition of his legitimacy, took it as a mandate to move the PLO in the direction of calculated moderation. A discreet dialogue with the United States became his best option.

At the beginning of November 1973, Henry Kissinger dispatched Vernon Walters to make contact with the PLO. Walters, a career army officer, had become a lieutenant general in March 1972 after a distinguished career as a soldier, military liaison, and covert operator. That same month, Nixon appointed him deputy director of the CIA, and the Senate confirmed him in May. When the intelligence community's involvement in the Watergate affair forced Richard Helms to resign as director of the CIA in July 1973, Walters served as acting director until September, a month before the eruption of the Yom Kippur War. In November, immediately after the war, Kissinger sent Walters to deliver a stern warning to the PLO. Walters arrived in Rabat, Morocco, in the first week of November. King Hassan arranged for his clandestine meeting with PLO moderates, Khaled Hassan, who chaired the Palestinian National Council's foreign relations committee, and Maje Abu Sharer, who directed Fatah's information department.[31]

Walters delivered a forceful message, but in his memoir he was secretive about the mission: "On one occasion the U.S. government sent me to talk to a most hostile group of terrorists. . . . We were able to communicate and there were no further acts of blood between us."[32] Somehow U.S. diplomats learned Walter's verbatim remarks: "The violence against us has got to stop, or much blood will flow, and you may be sure that not all of it will be ours."[33] But for the Palestinians, who were suffering the blows of Israel's Wrath of God operation, the threat of American retaliation was less important than the prospect of a diplomatic dialogue. Kissinger had foreclosed that possibility: "at this stage, involving the PLO [in negotiations] was incompatible with the interests of any of the parties to the Middle East conflict."[34] But the PLO representatives, who viewed the PLO as a legitimate party to the conflict, came away with the impression that dialogue was possible. As they tell it, Walters had some probing questions for the Palestinians about Soviet support for the Palestinian struggle, about the PLO moderates' ideas about a future democratic Palestinian state, and about the PLO's relations with Jordan.[35] The Palestinians left the secret meeting with expectations for future encounters endorsed by Nixon. But Kissinger had dispatched Walters to deliver a stern message, not to initiate a dialogue. The meeting did not produce a secret back channel between PLO moderates and the Department of State or the White House. Kissinger may have disdained contacts with the PLO, but the CIA saw the wisdom of an accommodation. In fact, the CIA had already renewed its overtures to PLO moderates the previous year. In September 1972, immediately after Black September's horrific failure in Munich, Robert Ames, the CIA's operative in the Middle East, sent a cryptic message to Ali Hassan Salameh, the Red Prince: "My company [CIA] is still interested in getting together with Ali's company [the PLO]. The Southern company [Israel]

. . . knew about our contacts."[36] The CIA would have its opportunity to reestablish communications with Salameh in less than a year, when Arafat addressed the UN General Assembly in New York.

At the end of the month Walters met with PLO moderates in Rabat, Palestinian dissidents took the first of two actions to poison the atmosphere for the coming negotiations in Geneva. On 25 November, three Palestinians hijacked a Dutch KLM Boeing 747 bound for New Delhi from Beirut with 288 passengers and crew. Although it made political sense for Israel and the United States simply to blame the PLO for all terror, the PLO denounced the hijacking. The new reality of renegade terror further complicated already complicated matters. The men who hijacked the KLM flight claimed to belong to the Nationalist Arab Youth for the Liberation of Palestine, a new organization whose command structure Western intelligence was just beginning to piece together. But the hijackers revealed their connection to earlier terror operations when they issued their sole demand: release of the terrorists captured during the failed operation to attack the residence of the Israeli ambassador and hijack an Israeli passenger jet in Cyprus in April. To make the demand more forcefully, the hijackers ordered the crew to fly to Nicosia after a stopover in Damascus to take on fuel. But the Cypriot president refused to be intimidated, and the terrorists ordered the plane to Abu Dhabi and released the hostages without winning the release of their comrades. In a familiar pattern, the terrorists opted for surrender in an Arab state they knew would not dare punish them for air piracy, much less terrorism.

The KLM hijacking was an act of solidarity between fedayeen. Captured terrorists knew their comrades would never forsake them —freedom was a hijacking away, experience taught them. Few governments obstinately refused to surrender to terrorist blackmail, and most saw humanitarian and political reasons for exchanging the guilty for the innocent. The September operation in Paris was different. Abu Nidal's men demanded the release of Abu Daoud from a Jordanian prison, but the deeper motive for the operation was to embarrass Arafat. After the October War, sabotaging PLO diplomacy became even more urgent. Nixon and Kissinger understood the October War as creating conditions for negotiations that would ultimately lure Egypt away from the Palestinian cause. With the Geneva talks set to begin at the end of December, Arafat prudently decided adapt to the radically changed geopolitical circumstances. The official PLO began convoluted internal debates about the necessity of endorsing the Geneva talks, if for no other reason than to prevent the devolution of the occupied West Bank to Jordan on the basis of Security Council Resolution 242. The renegades viewed things differently and vowed to keep the fires of Palestinian revolution burning. In December Abd al-Ghafur, the dissident who had organized a series of Libyan-backed operations beginning in the spring, put his own torch to the plans for the Geneva peace conference. He struck in Rome.

The Pan Am Massacre

Italian authorities knew the Eternal City was the crossroads for Palestinian terrorists. The JRA terrorists who attacked the Ben Gurion International Airport in Lod in May 1972 acquired their weapons in Rome. Abu Iyad and Abu Daoud rendezvoused in the city six weeks before the Munich Olympics operation. In April, Italian authorities arrested two Palestinians planning an attack in the Leonardo Da Vinci airport. In September, they arrested five terrorists who planned to shoot down an Israeli passenger jet there; their trial was actually set to begin in mid-December, around the time the United States and the Soviet Union originally planned to convene the Geneva peace conference. In mid-December Rome was on alert for a terror attack. It was then and there that Abd al-Ghafur sent his men into action.

On 17 December, five terrorists arrived at the Leonardo Da Vinci Airport aboard a flight from Madrid. The men acquired weapons outside the terminal from accomplices and then approached a security check point where passengers were filing through newly installed metal detectors on the way to connecting flights. The attack began there just before 1 P.M. Drawing their weapons, the terrorists broke into two assault squads, one to kill at random, the second to secure an avenue for escape. Two Palestinians opened fire through the thin fuselage of a Pan Am Boeing 707 standing at the gate, then charged the plane, hurling phosphorus grenades into the cabin. Passengers scrambled for emergency exists as the jet exploded into flames. Twenty-nine passengers, ten of them American, were burned to death in the conflagration. The second squad rushed onto the tarmac to commandeer a Lufthansa jet, shooting two Italian security guards dead and taking seventeen passengers and crew hostage. The ground attack was over in only twenty-two terrifying minutes. Then began the terror of the Lufthansa hostages.[37]

The terrorists forced the pilots into the air and on to Athens, where the plane landed that evening. While Italian authorities were left to put out the fires, tend the wounded, and identify the dead, Greek authorities were thrust into tense negotiations. The Palestinians never identified their organization, but told Greek authorities "we love liberty, especially Palestinian liberty." Their only demand was like the one made in the name of the National Arab Youth for the Liberation of Palestinian a month earlier: the liberation of the men captured in the Athens airport attack in August. The demand came with a threat. "We are going to conduct a slaughter at the Athens airport," one of the terrorists told the tower. If the carnage in Rome was not enough to convince Greek authorities the seriousness of the threats, the Dutch pilot, Captain Joe Kroese, dispelled any doubts. "They're serious . . . they've already killed four"—and they were threatening the life of a fifth hostage—"They're going to shoot him." But before authorities could arrange for an Arab speaker to calm the terrorists, the sound of gunfire came over the cockpit radio. "It's too late" was all the pilot could say.

In fact, the pilot was hearing simulated executions. The terrorists had not killed four or five but only one hostage, an Italian airport employee they selected at random. "He was sitting there all alone," another passenger later told authorities. The hijackers "asked him, even very politely, to come to the galley" from his seat in the rear of the plane. "He walked up calmly. Nobody had any idea of what was about to happen." Nobody except the terrorists. Another passenger could see through an opening in the curtain that he was pleading for his life. One of the terrorists shot him twice at point blank range. This was the first hostage murdered aboard a hijacked jet since the PFLP initiated the campaign of hijackings in 1968. That same night, the Palestinians ordered the crew to fly them to Kuwait. They left the body of the murdered Italian hostage on the tarmac in Athens as proof of their love of liberty. The incident ended in Kuwait City thirty hours after it began in Rome with the explosion of automatic weapon fire and grenades. After arrival, the terrorists simply surrendered.

The year 1973 ended as violently as it began with terror claiming victims along a wide arc from the Holy Land to the Old World. But the illogic of terror was shifting. The conflagration in Rome served a very different purpose than previous operations. The purpose of the hijacking of the El Al flight in July 1968 was to raise Palestinian morale by demonstrating the fighting spirit of fedayeen at a moment when the Arab armies and Palestinian guerrillas felt dispirited. The Skyjack Sunday operations two years later were intended, in Leila Khaled's words, to demonstrate to the world that the Palestinians had a legitimate cause at a moment when the world would offer no more than tents and old clothes. The purpose of Black September's Munich Olympic operation was to force the world to be alarmed by the consequences of neglect of the Palestinian national aspirations. But the purpose of this latest outrage was not to embolden Palestinians by harming Israelis or to force indifferent or hostile Western powers to alter their foreign policies, its purpose was to damage Arafat and to destroy an incipient peace process that would promise less than the destruction of the Jewish state and a complete reversal of the Catastrophe of 1948. And to succeed in this, Palestinian extremists would strive to prove to the world that Palestinians were incapable of moderation.

Chapter 4

Peace Would Be the End of All Our Hopes

The year 1974 began with the Nixon administration in the throes of the Watergate scandal. Nixon's abuse of power, coming when American society was already torn by the Vietnam conflict, shook American confidence in the integrity of government. Nixon resigned office on 9 August 1974, leaving Gerald Ford the daunting challenge of restoring the presidency and healing a nation. To ensure continuity, Ford asked Henry Kissinger to stay on as secretary of state and encouraged him to continue his efforts to forge a peace in the Middle East compatible with United States geopolitical interests. Kissinger brokered disengagement agreements between Israel and Egypt in January and between Israel and Syria in May, but a comprehensive peace settlement involving the Palestinians lay beyond the horizon of Kissinger's strategic thinking. The Palestinian national movement entered 1974 in disarray. Arafat signaled his interest in dialogue and scored a series of diplomatic successes that could have opened a pathway to a two-state solution, but the emergence of the Rejection Front, led by the PFLP, proved Arafat could not keep the more radical PLO factions in line. Predictably, new terrorist threats emerged. In 1975, civil war erupted in Lebanon, and for the better part of a year, until the Syrian military intervened to safeguard Syria's interests in Lebanon, the Palestinians were thrown into a struggle for survival.

The Rejection Front

While Nixon struggled to save his political life, Kissinger assiduously pursued peace in the Middle East. Although the Yom Kippur War the previous October had altered the strategic equation in the volatile region, the Geneva conference in December accomplished nothing. The White House had serious misgivings about Soviet participation in peace talks. In an unguarded remark, Kissinger admitted to reporters that the administration sought "to expel the Soviet Union from the Middle East." The administration had even more serious misgivings about the participation of the PLO. "The best way to deal with the Palestinian issue," Kissinger told the Senate Foreign Relations Committee in May, was to "draw the Jordanians into the West Bank and thereby turn the debate . . . into one between the Jordanians and the Palestinians." The strategy served Israel's interests well. In June, Yitzak Rabin, a former general who had served as Israel's ambassador to the United States, replaced Golda Meir as prime minister. In September, Kissinger told Rabin during a visit to Washington "a Palestinian state is likely to have as its objective the destruction of both Jordan and Israel."[1] The diplomatic strategy precluded anything approaching a comprehensive settlement. But it did yield incremental successes. Kissinger's famed shuttle diplomacy produced disengagement agreements between Israel and Egypt in January and between Israel and Syria in May.

The Palestinians did everything in their power to compel Kissinger to take their interests seriously. Between April and June, as Kissinger was trading time between Cairo, Damascus, and Jerusalem trying to stabilize the lines redrawn in the October war, Palestinian guerrillas mounted a series of operations in Israel. All the major PLO factions attacked. The bloodshed was awful. On 5 March, eight Fatah guerrillas seized a hotel in Tel Aviv. Kissinger was in Amman for talks with King Hussein and preparing to travel to Israel the following day. He returned to Washington instead. The Israelis launched a rescue operation, but it proved deadly. Seven guerrillas were killed in the fighting; twenty Israelis were killed, including the general commanding the operation. On 11 April, three guerrillas from Jabril's PFLP-General Command seized a group of Israelis in Qirayt Shemona. The IDF attempted a rescue, but it ended in bloodshed. The IDF killed three guerrillas, but nineteen hostages and soldiers were killed. Hawatmeh's DFLP mounted its own operation a month later. Three DFLP guerrillas took 100 Israeli high school students hostage in Ma'alot in northern Israel. The incident ended violently on 15 May, the twenty-sixth anniversary of the declaration of the State of Israel. All three guerrillas and 23 children were killed. On 13 June, the PFLP struck a kibbutz. This time four guerrillas and a number of Israelis died in the ensuing firefight. On 26 June, Fatah guerrillas came ashore by boat near Nahariya, Israel, on a mission to take hostages. Three Israelis and all the terrorists were killed in a firefight.[2]

The renewal of attacks in Israel proved the Palestinians could inflict harm even if they could not influence events. The factitious PLO was obsessed with its doctrine of no recognition of Israel, no negotiations with Israel, no peace with Israel. Egypt's acceptance of U.S. mediation to regain Egyptian territory was an ominous sign that direct negotiations, recognition, and peace were in the offing. Yasser Arafat understood the new dynamic; in fact, he had already tried to establish a secret back channel to the United States. Just as Sadat understood that U.S. mediation, not Egyptian arms, could restore the Sinai to Egypt, Arafat understood that only U.S. mediation, not Palestinian terrorism, could secure a Palestinian state. This was not the vision of the destruction of Israel and the total liberation of Palestine that Palestinians had been conditioned to embrace, but it was a realistic glimpse at the only possible future—a Palestinian ministate on the West Bank and Gaza coexisting with Israel.

In June, the same month the PFLP and Fatah mounted their deadly attacks, Arafat convened a meeting of the Palestinian National Council (PNC) in Cairo. The PNC was supposedly the supreme legislative body of the PLO, but in practice Arafat dominated the PLO by controlling the executive committee as its chairman. The PNC was useful to him only to authenticate his decisions. Now Arafat convinced the PNC to accept the principle of PLO authority over any piece of Palestinian territory liberated from Israeli occupation. It was shrewd maneuver. Foremost in Arafat's mind was the possibility that Kissinger might actually succeed in convincing Israel to restore the occupied West Bank to Jordan, foreclosing the possibility of a sovereign Palestinian state governed by the PLO. Kissinger was already making headway. Egypt was already showing signs of its willingness to back away from the principle that the PLO was the sole legitimate representative of the Palestinian people endorsed by the Arab League the previous November in Algiers. In July, Sadat recognized King Hussein's right to speak for the one million Palestinians living in the West Bank and Jordan. Arafat's proposal was controversial, but it gained the support of Fatah's major leaders. Abu Iyad, for one, realized that the changed dynamics forced the PLO to end its "all or nothing" policy.[3] Arafat struggled to convince Palestinians that the new policy was not capitulation. Instead he proclaimed the declaration to be the centerpiece of a new policy to liberate Palestine in stages, implying any territory liberated, or ceded in negotiations, would become the staging ground for the guerrilla war of total liberation.

Arafat's enemies within the PLO, led as always by George Habash, the PFLP secretary-general, were not deceived by the rhetoric of liberation in stages. Habash grasped that Arafat was staking his hopes on the negotiations despite the efforts of Israel and the United States to exclude the PLO from the talks. Worse still, the negotiations were based on Security Council Resolution 242, which called for Israeli withdrawal from the territories occupied in the 1967 Six Day War and the right of Israel "to live in peace within secure and recognized boundaries free from threats or acts of force." Habash's thinking conformed to the PLO's official line—"We can by no means accept that the end of the aggression of 1967 should come at the price of confirming the aggression of 1948"—until Arafat succeeded in changing that line.[4] The PNC vote caused a schism. Immediately following the PNC meeting in Cairo, George Habash broke ranks with the Fatah-dominated PLO and, in October, convened the first meeting of the Front for the Rejection of Capitulationist Solutions, or the Rejection Front, in Baghdad. Ahmed Jabril brought his PFLP-General Command into the new Rejection Front as did the leaders of smaller fedayeen organizations. Abd al-Ghafur and Abu Nidal, who had been working to sabotage the peace process for more than a year already, aligned themselves with the Rejection Front without formally joining it. It was no coincidence that Habash called the meeting in Baghdad. Iraq would become a principal backer of the Rejection Front, together with Libya and Yemen. The schism in the PLO would have deadly consequences. Over the next few years, the Rejectionists would assassinate PLO moderates and their Arab allies and would mount a series of international terror operations. In fact, the first deadly attack came even before the Rejectionists met in the Iraqi capital. There had not been a major international terrorist operation since Abd al-Ghafur organized the December 1973 atrocity at the Leonardo Da Vinci airport in Rome. The eight-month lull ended in a few moments of sheer terror over the Ionian Sea on a clear evening of 8 September 1974.

The Destruction of TWA 841

TWA flight 841 arrived in Athens after strict passenger screening in Israel had put it forty-five minutes behind schedule. Security in Israel was tight; it should have been rigorous in Athens. The previous August, terrorists had killed three in the passenger terminal there. But Athens was notorious for its security breaches. For the fedayeen, Greece was the transit point for weapons transfers to Europe. Athens was the first of three stops before TWA flight 841 was to reach its final destination in New York. Thirty minutes after leaving the Greek capital, the captain reported the flight reached its cruising level. It was his final transmission. The crew of Pan Am flight 110 en route to Beirut from Rome witnessed the final moments of TWA flight 841.

The captain of Pan Am 110 was the first to catch a glimpse of TWA 841 seven miles away approaching from the east some 3,000 feet below Pan Am 110. It was a beautiful evening over the Ionian Sea. The visibility was unlimited, and the scattered clouds below did not obscure the sea. All was routine. He looked away for a moment and in that instant the bomb that destroyed TWA 841 exploded. When he saw TWA 841 again the plane was climbing steeply, one of its engines was falling away, fuel leaking from the wing was leaving a whitish vapor trail, and luggage blown out of the rear baggage compartment was forming a cloud of debris in the wake of plane's and fluttering back to earth. The climb was so steep that in those moments it took the two planes to close from seven miles to a mile and a half, TWA 841 was nearly level with Pan Am 110.

Then TWA 841 rolled over to the left, plunged into a steep descent, and began to spiral slowly toward the sea. It passed behind Pan Am 110 and from its passengers' and crew's field of vision. No one saw the impact with the water.

The crash of TWA 841 killed all 79 passengers and 9 crew members aboard the plane, 17 of them American. The next day, a U.S. warship recovered 24 bodies and enough wreckage for the FBI and the National Transportation Safety Board to determine the cause of the disaster. That same day, Abd al-Ghafur's Nationalist Arab Youth Organization for the Liberation of Palestine claimed responsibility for the destruction of the jet. The organization's communiqué reported a Chilean national of Palestinian descent detonated the bomb killing him and a number of Mossad agents who were aboard the plane. If the claim was true, this was the first time Palestinian terrorists had resorted to a suicide bombing. No one has ever confirmed that Israeli agents died aboard TWA 841; it is certain that seven children and two infants were killed when the plane plunged into the sea.[5]

TWA 841 was Abd al-Ghafur's attempt to embarrass Arafat on the eve of the Arab League summit in Morocco in October. It was also al-Ghafur's final act of terror in a campaign that began the previous spring. Four days after the TWA disaster, Fatah assassins killed al-Ghafur in Beirut on Arafat's orders.[6] Arafat denounced the terror operation in Paris and Rome in September and December and vowed to punish the men responsible. But Arafat ordered al-Ghafur's death not for terrorism but for breach of discipline. Arafat did not denounce Black September's terror when it served his aims. His calculations were different now. Abu Iyad, who as intelligence chief kept in contact with the more radical PLO factions, later lamented al-Ghafur's assassination because, he said, it turned internal disputes about strategy into a violent struggle for power.[7] Iyad was especially worried that al-Ghafur's assassination would prompt his confederate, Abu Nidal, to seek revenge. In fact, Abu Nidal had already resolved to assassinate PLO moderates. In June, Fatah intelligence had thwarted the assassination of Mahmoud Abbas, also known as Abu Mazen, the man who accompanied Abu Iyad to Baghdad to confront Abu Nidal after the seizure of the Saudi embassy in Paris. For whatever reason, Abu Nidal believed Mahmoud Abbas's death was imperative. No one doubted that Abu Nidal's ultimate aim was the assassination of Arafat himself. In October, a month after the TWA atrocity, a Fatah tribunal tried Abu Nidal in absentia and sentenced him to death. Fatah never carried out the death sentence. Instead, Abu Nidal did most of the killing.

That same month, October, the Arab League reconvened in Rabat, Morocco, to consider the state of the Arab world. Eleven months earlier, during the Algiers summit, the League recognized the PLO as the sole legitimate representative of the Palestinian people. Arafat could count the declaration as a diplomatic triumph. But the Algiers declaration was under attack. King Hussein, with Kissinger's firm support, held out for recognition of his kingdom's right to represent the interests of the nearly one million Palestinians living in Jordan. Anwar Sadat, who was by then committed to U.S. mediation, had endorsed this reinterpretation of the Algiers declaration in July. Arafat was determined that Arab League reaffirm the PLO's—and Arafat's—exclusive right to speak for all Palestinians. The Arab heads of state who traveled to Rabat in October were keenly aware of the risks of angering the PLO. In the weeks before the Arab League summit, Moroccan intelligence arrested a number of Palestinians who entered the country under aliases. Abu Iyad had sent them to assassinate King Hussein, but wild rumors about a conspiracy to assassinate any representative who did not reaffirm PLO's representation of the Palestinians swirled around the Moroccan capital. Abu Iyad later boasted of his involvement in the Palestinians plot to assassinate King Hussein—"I assume full responsibility for it and the honor of supporting their action"—but indignantly denied the rumors about a conspiracy to kill other Arab heads of state.[8] In the end, the Arab League reaffirmed the PLO's unique status and proclaimed the right of the Palestinians to return to their homeland. Even King Hussein, who had risen to the floor to deliver an impassioned but ultimately futile defense of Jordan's territorial rights over the West Bank, voted in favor of the resolution. Henry Kissinger was crestfallen: "the collapse of the Jordanian option," he lamented, "was a major lost opportunity." Because the PLO rejected Israel's right to existence, and because the PLO remained committed to terror, the Rabat decision "guaranteed nineteen years of impasse on West Bank negotiations."[9]

Arafat at the United Nations

Arafat was riding a rising tide of diplomatic success. He had convinced the PNC to endorse his desideratum of a Palestinian authority in the West Bank in June, and he had won the Arab League's reaffirmation of the PLO's right to speak for all Palestinians in October. In November, he triumphed again, this time in New York. On 13 November, Arafat addressed the UN General Assembly. In a lengthy speech that aired Palestinian grievances, Arafat promised the Jews living in Palestine the opportunity to live in Palestine in "peace and without discrimination," but without a state of their own. Speaking as chairman of the PLO and "leader of the Palestinian revolution" Arafat offered Jews "the most generous solution, that we might live together in a framework of just peace in our democratic Palestine." Although the maneuvering in Cairo demonstrated his still secret inclination to achieve a Palestinian state through negotiations, Arafat could not explicitly recognize Israel's right to exist within secure borders per Resolution 242. The most generous solution he could offer was not the most reasonable solution that could be envisioned: separate Jewish and Palestinian states. The most Arafat could offer Jews was the opportunity to live in a democratic Palestine under PLO rule. Because Arafat's speech had to resonate with the PLO rank and file, the leader of the Palestinian Revolution could not abandon the rhetoric of violence, so he concluded with a threat: "Today I have come bearing an olive branch and a freedom fighter's gun. Do not let the olive branch fall from my hand." It was not an empty threat. Arafat would not explicitly renounce violence for another thirteen years when the political terrain shifted still again, and even then violence forever remained an option for him. Still, Arafat understood the path to the creation of a Palestinian state wound through the labyrinth of American-brokered negotiations. The address before the General Assembly was a triumph. After the speech the General Assembly bestowed observer status on the PLO, placing it on the same plane as the Vatican.

Arafat's triumph was an affront to Israel. The General Assembly had rewarded terror by recognizing an organization whose members practiced it. After the General Assembly granted the PLO observer status, a PLO spokesman conceded "now that we are observers at the United Nations, we will think more deeply and thoroughly regarding armed operations."[10] Arafat had tried to distance himself from the terror of Black September, and in recent months had missed no opportunity to disavow the terror operations of PLO organizations hostile to him. But his personal connections with Black September's commanders were undeniable. Abu Iyad, a founding member of Fatah, was the force behind Black September and the person most responsible for the murder of the Israeli Olympians in Munich. Iyad feuded with Arafat, but he still served him. Ali Hassan Salameh, who once commanded Black September's European operations, was even closer to Arafat. Arafat's trust in him was an endorsement of Black September.

In the fall of 1974, Salameh was acting as chief of Arafat's security detail, Force 17. When Arafat addressed the General Assembly, Salameh was by his side. U.S. officials knew of Salameh's terrorist past with Black September; they knew too that Black September had murdered George Curtis Moore and Cleo Noel in Khartoum the previous March. But the State Department approved visas for Salameh and other members of Arafat's New York delegation with connections to Black September and the Khartoum operation because the CIA had a professional interest in reaching an accommodation with the Red Prince. The agency had squandered one opportunity before the emergence of Black September and it would not waste another.

It had been a year since Vernon Walters met secretly with Fatah moderates in Rabat, seventeen months since Black September murdered U.S. diplomats in Khartoum. With the United States deeply immersed in Middle East diplomacy, the threat to Americans was greater than ever. Salameh was the one man who could warn the CIA of gathering dangers. This was the pragmatism that led the CIA to meet with Salameh in his suite at New York's Waldorf Astoria. No one has come forward with a verbatim account of the meeting, but it is certain that the CIA made a pact with the Red Prince. The pact served its purpose. In the darkest hours of the Lebanese Civil War in 1975 and 1976, Salameh alerted Americans to threats against them. Salameh was alert, but he was not omniscient. He did not learn of the plot against Francis Meloy, Jr., U.S. ambassador to Lebanon, until militants of the Lebanese off-shoot of the PFLP abducted Meloy and an advisor at a check point in Beirut and executed them in June 1976.[11] The murder of two more U.S. diplomats aside, American intelligence was well pleased with Salameh. In 1976, the CIA brought Salameh to the United States, where he met with Robert Ames, his principal CIA contact, and other intelligence officers, before Salameh embarked on a leisurely tour of New Orleans, Los Angeles, and Honolulu.[12] Salameh did his part for his own pragmatic reasons. But the CIA refused to place Salameh under its own protection. The Americans knew the Israelis were determined to kill the Red Prince, and Salameh knew the Americans knew. One of Salameh's CIA contacts in Beirut, Sam Wyman, has been candid about it in a series of interviews: "Certain things go unsaid. I mean, he knew that I knew who he was, what he had done, so on and so forth. So why bring it up. . . . Had you asked me at the time I would have said it's only a matter of time before they try to get him."[13]

In fact, Salameh might never have made it to New York for the meeting with the CIA in November 1974. In January, a Wrath of God assassination squad tracked him to a small Swiss village, only four months after Mossad agents mistakenly killed Ahmed Bouchiki, thinking the Moroccan was Salameh. This time the Mossad had found the real Red Prince, in Switzerland to where he was to rendezvous with a contact. Golda Meir had not abandoned operation Wrath of God after the fiasco in Lillehammer; and killing the Red Prince now would rectify a tragic case of mistaken identity. Salameh chose a church for the rendezvous; the Mossad was not concerned about the sanctity of the site. Three Israelis followed Salameh into the church but never had the chance to kill him. Inside the church three of Salameh's bodyguards confronted the Israelis. Shots were fired. The Israelis who had come to kill Salameh killed his bodyguards instead and then broke off the pursuit of the Red Prince to avoid another fiasco. This was the closest Mossad would come to Salameh for another five years.

Things went badly for Mossad after that. In May, an alluring young woman seduced an assassination squad member in a London hotel bar and killed him during a tryst in his room. In September, an assassin in the pay of the Palestinians, posing as an informant, killed another Israeli. In October, the Mossad located Salameh in a house overlooking the Atlantic on the cliffs of Gibraltar. The operation was a repetition of the one in Switzerland five months earlier; the Israelis came near the house but never made contact with Salameh. In an exchange of fire, the Israelis killed another bodyguard and then withdrew for their own safety.[14] Exactly a month later, the Israelis saw Salameh again, this time in New York, guarding Arafat.

Arafat's triumph was scandalous to Israel, but it was treasonous to Palestinian militants dead set against the course the PLO chairman was charting. Terror again became a means of subverting Arafat. On 22 November, three Palestinians hijacked a British Airways flight from London to Brunei during a stopover in Dubai. Forty-seven passengers and crew members became the latest hostages to an internal Palestinian feud. The terrorists claimed the operation in the name of the Martyr Abu Mahmoud Squad, a reference to the nom de guerre of Abd al-Ghafur, the man Arafat ordered killed in September. Al-Ghafur was dead, but his disciples lived on, and one of them, Abu Mustafa Qaddura, was behind the hijacking.[15] Air pirates had learned the importance of keeping on the move and searching out the best location for negotiations. The day after the hijacking, the terrorists ordered the pilots into the air. It landed in Tunis, where authorities summoned Abu Iyad to conduct the negotiations and to sort out the intricacies of the internal Palestinian feud.

Abu Iyad later boasted of his mediation of the crisis. But in fact, the terrorists seized their hostages to challenge Arafat and Fatah. Their demand was the release of fifteen Palestinians—the eight terrorists responsible for the murder of the U.S. and Belgian diplomats in Khartoum in March 1972, whom Fatah held in custody; the five responsible for the massacre in Rome the previous December, whom Egyptians authorities held, and two captured in the Netherlands before they could mount an operation there. As Iyad tells it, the hijackers were basically patriotic youths who had wandered into the apostasy of the Rejection Front with men like Abd al-Ghafur, who Iyad wrote was "killed under mysterious circumstances," and Abu Nidal, the two responsible for the upsurge in terror over the past year.

So, while Abu Iyad understood he was "dealing with resolute adversaries," he was confident he could convert them to Fatah orthodoxy. He began the negotiations by assuring the men of the Martyr Abu Mahmoud Squad that he had been on good terms with al-Ghafur before he broke with Fatah. This was the time and place to end the violent feud between Palestinian factions. Iyad's only concern now was "to save the lives of the hostages while safeguarding the reputation of the Resistance." Iyad would use his considerable influence to gain the release of the men imprisoned for the Rome atrocity, but Fatah would never yield to the demand for the release of the eight men who murdered Noel, Moore, and Eid in Khartoum, because, he said, they fell under Fatah's inviolable jurisdiction.[16]

In the early morning of the third day of the hostage crisis in Tunis the Palestinians dispassionately selected a forty-three-year-old West German businessman from among the hostages, walked him to the open door of the jet, and shot him in the back of the head at point blank range.[17] Gustav Kehl's body fell to the tarmac. Kehl became the second hostage whom terrorists executed during a hijacking. Abu Iyad never mentions the murder in his memoir, but the murder ended the impasse. The Martyr Abu Mahmoud Squad gained the freedom of seven Palestinians, not fifteen. The Egyptian government freed the five men in its custody; the Dutch government released the two it held. In a supreme irony, only Arafat refused to yield to the terrorists' demands—the eight Black September murderers of the diplomats in Khartoum remained in the protective custody of Fatah.

The terror that began aboard the British Airways flight in Dubai ended three days after it began in Tripoli, Libya. With assurances of safe conduct and the release of seven Palestinians, the Martyr Abu Mahmoud Squad ordered the pilots to make a short flight to the Libyan capital where they surrendered to authorities. Libya's Muammar Qaddafi, who had backed Abdel Ghafur, welcomed the Martyr Abu Mahmoud Squad as a gesture to end the crisis. This was more than a humanitarian gesture; it was complicity in air piracy.

In his account, Abu Iyad claimed to have recruited the three members of the Martyr Abu Mahmoud Squad into the ranks of Fatah after the incident. During the hostage negotiations in Tunis, the men secretly conveyed their real demand: the withdrawal of the PLO's observer mission to the United Nations. Sometime after the end of the hostage incident, Iyad met with the three Palestinians and convinced them of the error at the core of the Rejection's Front strategy of diplomatic sabotage by posing two questions about Arafat's triumph at the United Nations. "Have you read Arafat's speech at the UN General Assembly?" Should the PLO "scorn a moral and political victory?"[18] Iyad's account sounds apocryphal, but the claim about recruiting the murderers of a passenger to the ranks of Fatah reveals something about his attitude about terror—saving the lives of hostages was to him less important than safeguarding the reputation of the Resistance and depleting the ranks of the Rejection Front.

Carlos and Commando Boudia

Palestinian terror was beginning to lose its strategic coherence even before the October 1973 War. Abd al-Ghafur's operations in the spring and summer of that year, and Abu Nidal's seizure of the Saudi Embassy in Paris in September, were early signs that terror was beginning to be driven by the dynamics of Palestinian factionalism. After the October War and the beginning of the peace process, the operations of al-Ghafur and his disciples in December 1973 and September and November 1974, proved that factional terror was a wildfire. The new terrorism destroyed of any hope the Palestinians could air their legitimate grievances in a diplomatic forum. That was its purpose. The Rejection Front formed around the hostility to the idea of a negotiated compromise to the Israelis' and Palestinians' territorial claims. That hostility became manifest in this new terror.

Wadi Haddad, the Master of the PFLP's terror, thrived in this environment. The emergence of the Rejection Front in 1974 marked the beginning of the final phase of a decade-long campaign of terror that began with the El Al hijacking in 1968 and ended with the Master's death of natural causes in 1978. Haddad's final operations—attacks on El Al jets in Paris in January, and a raid on the OPEC meeting in Vienna in December, 1975; a hijacking of an Air France jet to Entebbe, Uganda, in June, and an airport attack in Istanbul in August, 1976; and a hijacking of a Lufthansa flight to Mogadishu, Somalia, in October 1977—were all dismal failures. In fact, the Entebbe and Mogadishu hijackings became legendary not for the PFLP's audacity, but because of Israeli and West German special forces' spectacular rescue operations.

The PFLP did not organize a successful major international terror operation in 1973 or 1974. There was no mystery to the hiatus. In June 1973, the Mossad assassinated Mohammed Boudia, the PFLP's operational commander in Europe. After Boudia's death, Haddad selected a Lebanese militant, Michel Moukharbal, to assume command of the European operations. But Moukharbal commandos, who claimed operations under the banner of Commando Boudia, were not hardened Palestinians who survived the deprivations of the refugee camps and who fought to liberate their homeland from Israeli occupation, they were Japanese, German, and Latin American mercenaries seeking thrills in the cause of world revolution. Haddad began calling upon mercenaries in 1972, when a JRA suicide squad massacred passengers at Lod. Haddad called on the JRA again in July 1973 for a hijacking that ended in failure in Libya. (By 1974, the JRA was mainly operating in Europe under Haddad's instructions.) In August 1976, after suffering a series of arrests, the JRA carried out another airport massacre, this time in Istanbul, on Haddad's orders. By then Germans, who began their revolutionary careers in the Revolutionary Cells and the Red Army Faction, had joined the ranks of the PFLP in Europe. At the center of this network of international mercenaries was one man, Carlos, who became the face of this new international terror.

Illich Ramírez Sánchez was the son of a wealthy Venezuelan attorney whose devotion to Marxism inspired him to name his son after Vladimir Ilich Ulyanov, Lenin. Ramirez traveled widely, with extended stays in London, Paris, and finally Moscow. It was there in 1970 that PFLP spokesman Abu Bassam al-Sharif recruited Ramírez while the Venezuelan was studying at the Patrice Lumumba University.[19] By July 1970, Ramírez was training in PFLP camps in Jordan, where he took the name Carlos. Carlos was in Jordan in September when Haddad's Special Apparatus shocked the world with Skyjack Sunday, and when King Hussein retaliated by forcibly expelling the Palestinians. The following year, Carlos was traveling between Paris and London, setting up safe houses and integrating himself into Mohammed Boudia's PFLP cells in Europe. After the Mossad struck down Boudia, and Michel Moukharbal assumed command of European operations, Carlos effectively became second-in-command of Commando Boudia.

Carlos's first task was simple, to draw up a list of Jews and moderate Arabs the PFLP could take hostage or murder. At the end of 1973 Carlos, acting on orders, selected a name on the list. On 30 December he forced his way into the London home of Joseph Sieff, vice president of the British Zionist Federation. Carlos shot Sieff in the face, seriously wounding but not killing him. In August 1974, Carlos bombed the offices of French newspapers the PFLP deemed sympathetic to Israel. The bombs killed no one. In September, Carlos and Moukharbal organized another operation, this time in support of the JRA.

In July 1974, French authorities had arrested Yamada Yoskiaki, a JRA member connected to the Commando Boudia, at Orly airport in Paris.[20] It was an intelligence coup. Yamada kept silent during interrogations, but documents in his possession led French authorities to break a JRA cell in the French capital. Yamada's freedom became an imperative for the mercenaries of Commando Boudia. In September, three Japanese terrorists seized thirteen hostages in the French Embassy in The Hague and demanded Yamada's release. Carlos, who organized the operation, was in The Hague when the Japanese stormed the embassy, but fled to

Paris to monitor negotiations. The French complied immediately and flew Yamada to an airport outside The Hague. Over the next two days, the Dutch negotiated with the Japanese over the details of the hostage release and the terrorists' departure. To intensify the pressure, Carlos decided to make a bold strike back in the French capital. On a quiet Sunday afternoon, two days after the Japanese seized French diplomats in The Hague, Carlos hurled grenades into a fashionable Paris café, killing two and seriously wounding others. It was Carlos's first blood.

Neither the embassy seizure nor the café attack figured in Wadi Haddad's operational plans for Europe. They were improvised actions of a mercenary cell trying to free a comrade whose own breach of security procedures led to his capture. Haddad might have begun to lose confidence in Moukharbal's and Carlos's Commando Boudia, but he sent them back into action. In fact, Haddad was planning something spectacular. In January 1975, Wadi Haddad instructed Michel Moukharbal to take the fight where the master's operations had always been most deadly—airports.

On Monday, 13 January, Carlos and a mercenary from Germany's Revolutionary Cells, Johannes Weinrich, drove to Orly Airport in Paris armed with an RPG-7, a Soviet-made rocket-propelled grenade launcher. From the very onset of his campaign against civilian aviation, the master had alternated between hijacking jets and attacking them on the ground with grenades and Kalashnikovs. Now there was a new weapon in the arsenal of terror. The rocket-propelled grenades (RPG) were potentially lethal weapons because of their capabilities as shoulder-held, surface-to-air missiles. The Soviet bloc made RPG antitank weapons as well as surface-to-air missiles (SAMs),widely available to the Palestinians for defense against the Israelis. Terrorists had already tried to use SAMs against civilian aircraft. In September 1973, Italian authorities seized SAM-5s near the Leonardo Da Vinci airport. The operation at Orly was identical to the failed operation at Leonardo Da Vinci—Carlos and Weinrich had come to destroy an Israeli El Al airliner on takeoff.

This time the terrorists managed to bring the weapons into striking distance. Weinrich shouldered the weapon and took aim at an Israeli Boeing 707 taxiing toward the main runway with 143 passengers and crew aboard. The men were less than 150 meters away, standing beside a fence on an airport access road, when Weinrich fired the weapon. The missile streaked across the airport but veered off its mark, tore through a parked car beyond the jet, and exploded in a service building, injuring no one. Weinrich fired a second missile, but this also missed its mark and struck an empty Yugoslav jet. Carlos and Weinrich escaped. French authorities later discovered the abandoned car, the RPG-7 launcher, and two rockets.

Whether it was Weinrich's training or nerves that failed him, his poor marksmanship averted a disaster. Moukarbal was not deterred and ordered a second attack at Orly. Within days, Carlos returned with three Palestinians to reconnoiter the airport again.[21] They found a massive security presence. Even so, Carlos and his men managed to enter the terminal in search of a new firing position and a location to conceal weapons. Commando Boudia decided to mount the new attack from the observation balcony inside the terminal. Over the next few days, the terrorists smuggled weapons into Orly and concealed them in the public restrooms near the observation balcony. Moukharbal set the attack for Sunday, 19 January. But Commando Boudia had lost the element of surprise as well as its most lethal weapon, the Soviet RPG-7, which Carlos and Weinrich abandoned after the first attack. Now it would mount an attack from within the terminal with a less advanced RPG-2.

Carlos later admitted to a journalist that he had apprehensions. Attacking from within the terminal meant having to take hostages to escape, making the operation a repeat of Abd al-Ghafur's horrific operation at the Leonardo Da Vinci Airport in December 1973. "There was the very real possibility," Carlos admitted, "that many people would be killed and we wished to avoid that." The statement is revealing. The entire purpose of the mission was to kill the passengers aboard a departing El Al jet, but Carlos had managed to mark the coordinates of an inverted moral world by separating those aboard a doomed Israeli jet from those inside the terminal. Air passage on an Israeli air carrier was all the difference. The message of the attack was unambiguous, "never fly El Al."[22]

The Sunday attack failed like the previous one, but the aftermath was very different. For all their audacity, Commando Boudia had planned the operation poorly. The terrorists were late in arriving at their rendezvous point, and by the time they assembled the RPG and rushed out onto the observation balcony to take aim, the Israeli jet had taxied out of range. The terrorists were in plain sight of passengers and French security personnel. An alert guard opened fire on the terrorists before they could launch a rocket. The terrorists returned fire, hurled grenades, and began seizing hostages. They seized ten in all, including a ten-year-old girl, and barricaded themselves in the restrooms. Carlos himself escaped in the chaos of the first moments of the shooting, but his comrades were trapped with their human shields. For the next seventeen hours the French authorities were confronted with a hostage crisis in the capital's international airport. The government sought to avert a slaughter. In the two most recent hijackings—in Rome in December 1973 in ominously similar circumstances, and Dubai in November 1974—the terrorists murdered hostages. The morning after this attack, after tense negotiations, the French government permitted the terrorists to fly out of Orly. They took refuge in Baghdad, capital of the Rejection Front's principal state sponsor.

Michel Moukharbal's Commando Boudia lurched from failure to failure. In fact, the Orly airport attacks were Moukharbal's final operations. In June he traveled to Beirut to confer with Wadi Haddad about future operations. It was there that Moukharbal made a fatal error. On 7 June, Lebanese authorities detained him as he attempted to board a direct flight from Beirut to Paris. It was a serious breach of security procedures. By now the Lebanese were scrutinizing passengers traveling to France. Haddad had given instructions to his men to fly circuitous routes to avoid raising suspicions. Worse still, Moukarbal was in possession of forged passports, the stock in trade of international terrorists. Lebanese officials interrogated Moukharbal for two full days without discovering he was Haddad's man in Europe.

With no formal charges to bring, the Lebanese released Moukharbal, who flew on to Paris on 13 June. Alerted, the French placed him under surveillance and managed to photograph him standing beside another man, Carlos. This was another breach of security. Instead of avoiding direct contact, the two most important figures of Commando Boudia allowed themselves to be seen together near a safe house. The surveillance photograph became a critical piece of evidence in the French police's dossier on Commando Boudia. Soon the pursuit of the man in the photograph would come at the cost of three lives, including Moukharbal's. A week later, Moukharbal evaded French surveillance and boarded a flight to London where the British detained him. The United Kingdom expelled Moukharbal to France the following day, 21 June. The French police arrested him upon his arrival.

Moukharbal spent the final week of his life under interrogation by the French Direction de la Surveillance du Territoire, the DST. On 27 June, the DST implicitly threatened his life by threatening to expel him to Beirut to face Haddad's wrath as a French informant—to turn Moukharbal the French authorities merely had to make him understand that they intended to inform Haddad they had already turned him. The implied threat broke Moukharbal, who agreed to lead police to the man in the surveillance photograph. Late in the night of 27 June, Moukharbal led three detectives to an apartment in Paris's famed Latin Quarter—and to Carlos. Detective Jean Herranz and a subordinate were the first to enter the apartment, where Carlos was entertaining friends. They left Moukharbal behind in the police car under guard by a third detective. It was only moments before Herranz began questioning Carlos because of his resemblance to the man in the surveillance photograph. Carlos, who claimed to be a Peruvian businessman, kept his composure. For the better part of an hour he answered questions. He denied knowing Mouk-harbal. Herranz confronted Carlos with the photograph, and still Carlos denied knowing him. Then Herranz summoned Moukharbal himself. It seems never to have occurred to Herranz that the detectives' lives were in danger. The police were not armed, and they did not search Carlos for a weapon. It was a fatal error. In the short minutes it took the detectives to bring Haddad's commander of European operations to the apartment, Carlos had made up his mind to kill. Moukharbal came into the apartment and pointed directly at Carlos, "this is the man." In that same instant Carlos drew a concealed weapon from his jacket and opened fire, killing two detectives and grievously wounding Herranz. Then he executed Moukharbal, who was cowering in a corner, with a single shot to the head. Moukharbal, Carlos remembered, looked like "a broken shadow."[23]

Carlos fled the apartment and soon escaped France. Authorities in France and the United Kingdom—Carlos also kept a safe house and a lover in London—began a thorough investigation of the mysterious man who had been moving between their two countries. In Carlos's London safe house, police found documents, weapons, and a copy of Frederick Forsyth's novel, *The Day of the Jackal.* From that moment on, Ilich Ramirez Sanchez, Carlos, became Carlos the Jackal. Carlos eventually made his way to Beirut to confer with Haddad, who accepted Carlos's explanation that by killing Moukharbal he had executed a traitor. The Master did not lose confidence in the Venezuelan mercenary just yet; in fact, he entrusted him with another mission. Six months after the massacre in the Latin Quarter, Carlos would reappear in another European capital, Vienna.

The PLO in Lebanon's Civil War

Wadi Haddad's terror campaign against civilian aviation was criminal from inception, and now it was drifting into strategic incoherence. At this juncture of the Palestinians' struggle for a state, the only purpose of a random act of terror—like the attempts, which failed, to destroy an El Al jet in Paris—was to kill for the sake of killing. Terror demonstrated the Rejection Front's implacable hostility to Middle East negotiations. But no act of terror could alter the direction or the pace of the peace process. The Rejection Front's violence did not compel Kissinger to reconsider the Palestinian problem; it only reinforced the U.S. and Israeli determination to exclude the Palestinians from the negotiations. Rejection of negotiations did not prevent Sadat from falling further under the influence of the United States; it only drove him to separate

Egypt's strategic interests from the national aspirations of the Palestinians.

The peace process the Rejection Front vowed to destroy began to gather momentum in the spring and summer of 1975. In December 1973, the United States and the Soviet Union convened the Geneva Talks. In January 1974, Kissinger had managed to convince the Israelis and Egyptians to conclude a disengagement agreement. He convinced the Israelis and the Syrians to disengage in May. But the interim agreements did nothing to restore the Sinai Peninsula to Egypt or the Golan Heights to Syria. They did nothing at all to end the formal state of belligerency between the countries or to address the Palestinian question. After that, negotiations stalled. President Nixon visited the Middle East in June, only two months before his resignation, but by then the Watergate scandal took the oxygen out his presidency. In the spring of 1975, Gerald Ford, concerned about the possibility of another war unless Egypt and Israel reached an agreement, sent Kissinger back to the region. Ford found the Israelis inflexible. "The Israelis were stronger militarily than all their Arab neighbors combined, yet peace was no closer than it had ever been," Ford wrote later. "If we were going to build up their military capabilities, we in turn had to see some flexibility to achieve a fair, secure and permanent peace."[24] By early summer there were signs of progress. In the first week of June, President Sadat visited Washington to meet with President Ford, and Prime Minister Rabin visited two weeks later. In August, Kissinger traveled to the Middle East to finalize a second disengagement agreement. The Israelis and Egyptians signed Sinai II, as the agreement is known, on 4 September. Although the agreement concerned the redeployment of Egyptian and Israeli forces in the Sinai, it affected the Palestinians. In secret protocol, the Ford Administration made official an informal pledge to Israel that the United States would not recognize the PLO until the PLO accepted Security Council Resolutions 242 and 338 and, implicitly, the right of the Jewish state to live at peace on land the Palestinians claimed as their own.[25] Revelation of the secret agreement infuriated Arafat, although not to the point that he abandoned hope in the eventual conversion of the United States to the Palestinian point of view. The secret agreement also endangered Arafat's chief of security, Ali Hassan Salameh, who secretly had been sharing intelligence with the CIA ever since the Red Prince met with CIA officers in the Waldorf-Astoria the previous November. The U.S. pledge to Israel about contacts with the PLO meant Ali Hassan Salameh could not count on U.S. protection from Israel's wrath.

The pledge to Israel to exclude Arafat's PLO from negotiations bolstered the Rejection Front, which believed no good could come from dialogue premised on the Jewish state's right to exist. But during the spring and summer of 1975, sectarian violence in Lebanon posed a more serious threat to the Palestinians than any agreement between Egypt and Israel or any secret protocol between the United States and the Jewish state. By the end of the year, Lebanon was descending into civil war. Lebanon threatened to become another Jordan.

The Palestinian presence in Lebanon put enormous stress on the foundations of Lebanon's archaic political order. The threat to Lebanon's Maronite Christian minority was greatest. The National Covenant, crafted by Lebanon's Maronite Christian, Muslim, and Druze communities in 1943, bestowed inordinate power on the Maronites, who dominated the presidency. The Covenant's provision for a Muslim prime minister created the facade of power-sharing, but as Lebanon's demographics changed, segments of the country's Muslim and Druze populations, backed by the Lebanese left, began to militate for the abrogation of the National Covenant under the banner of the Lebanese National Movement (LNM), formed in 1975. The Palestinians, comprising 10 percent of the population by 1975, complicated matters. The PLO had transformed Beirut's Fakhani district into a principality; thousands of Palestinian refugees in the sprawling refugee camps threatened to become permanent residents; and Palestinian guerrillas, operating in the south, mounted armed attacks on Israel, provoking retaliatory strikes. The deteriorating situation on the ground made irrelevant an official agreement, worked out in Cairo in 1969, concerning the status of the Palestinians in Lebanon. Worse still, the Palestinian Rejection Front, Hawatmeh's DFLP, and even elements of Arafat's Fatah, openly aligned themselves with the LNM.

The Lebanese president, Sulayman Franjieh, a Maronite, sensed the danger of an implosion. Arafat, who could foresee a repetition of the disaster in Jordan, gave Franjieh assurances about the PLO's respect for Lebanese sovereignty. But the PLO chairman did not speak for the Palestinian factions aligned with the LNM. Nor did Franjieh speak for the Maronite Christian Phalange or its leader, Pierre Gemayel. Born of the fascist movements in Spain and Italy in the 1930s, the Phalange viewed the alignment between the Palestinians and LNM as a mortal threat to the Maronites' sectarian interests. Gemayel, son of the movement's founder, warned a party congress that "the Palestinian Revolution is a revolution against us."[26] Lebanon fractured into armed camps. Between April and December the situation went from bad to worse to calamitous.

On 13 April 1975, Gemayel's entourage came under fire outside a Beirut church. Gemayel escaped assassination, but three members of the Phalange were killed. The Phalange blamed the Palestinians. In retaliation Phalange militiamen ambushed a bus carrying Palestinians, massacring twenty-six.[27] Within days the LNM and Palestinian guerrillas

engaged the Phalange militia in Beirut. These were the first shots in Lebanon's civil war. Over the next weeks Arafat struggled to keep Fatah
guerrillas out of combat and to find a way out of the crisis. In May, he
sent Ali Hassan Salameh to meet with senior Maronite representatives
to assure them the PLO would limit itself to defensive operations. In
June, Arafat met with Franjieh, but the Lebanese president berated the
Palestinians for violating the terms of the 1969 Cairo agreement that
specified the limits of Palestinian actions in Lebanon. On 25 June, two
days after the meeting with Franjieh, Arafat issued another public statement pledging Palestinian neutrality and urging all parties "despite
everything that has happened" to look beyond the "mad violence."[28]
Then, in September, came the announcement of the Sinai II agreement
and the revelation of America's secret agreement with Israel. Although
one thing had nothing to do with the other, Palestinians saw a vast U.S.-
Israeli conspiracy to isolate and destroy the Palestinian resistance. Kissinger's maneuvering with Egypt was one part of the conspiracy, the
other was the U.S. and Israeli covert support for the Christians in Lebanon. This was fiction inspired by the coincidence of facts. Back in June,
around the time of Sadat's and Rabin's visits to Washington, a cache of
Israeli weapons bound for the Phalange turned up on a beach in southern Lebanon. Further escalation seemed inevitable. In October, the
Phalange began rocket attacks on the Palestinian Tal al-Zataar refugee
camp. On the twenty-fourth, the LNM, reinforced by Palestinian guerrillas, launched major operations against the Christian district in the capital. The final opportunity to reach a cease-fire before the eruption of
full-scale civil war was lost in the first week of December. On 6 December, Hafez al-Asad, the Syrian president, invited Pierre Gemayel to
Damascus for talks. That day—Black Saturday—Christian militiamen
began seizing hundreds of hostages in Muslim West Beirut. They murdered more than seventy.[29] Palestinians in Beirut would begin 1976
besieged in their camps under bombardment by Christian militias. Four
years after Black September, Lebanon was becoming Jordan.

Carlos Seizes the OPEC Ministers

In September 1970, after the Palestinian fedayeen and Jordanian forces
exchanged the first shots in their internecine war, Wadi Haddad
ordered his air pirates to seize jets and hostages in Europe and bring
them to Jordan. It was an act intended to dramatize the Palestinian
plight and to inflict the final destabilizing blow on King Hussein's pro-
U.S. regime. The operation was successful by half. Skyjack Sunday dramatized the Palestinians cause, but it fortified King Hussein's resolve to
rid himself of the Palestinian fedayeen. Now, four years after the Pales-

tinian's expulsion from Jordan, with Palestinians battling for their survival in Lebanon, Wadi Haddad decided to punish moderate Arab states for their betrayal of the Palestinians by striking at the symbol of Arab economic power, OPEC.

By 1975, OPEC was a force. Two years earlier, Nixon had ordered the airlift of U.S. weapons and ammunition to the beleaguered Israelis during the Yom Kippur War. OPEC retaliated by imposing an oil embargo that drove up the price of oil. Revenues soared and petrodollars became the currency that capitalized development schemes throughout the developing world. Kissinger threw himself into a diplomatic effort to lift the embargo with the same intensity that he worked for an Egyptian-Israeli disengagement. In March 1974, OPEC, dominated by moderate states like Saudi Arabia and Iran, saw the wisdom of putting profits before principles and lifted the embargo. Haddad was determined to punish them for that, so was Muammar Qaddafi, the Libyan dictator behind the Rejection Front, because the lifting of the embargo meant a fall in Libya's oil revenues. So, Qaddafi called on Haddad to deliver a message to OPEC's moderates. Haddad called on Carlos to make that happen.

So it was that, four days before Christmas, Carlos reappeared in Vienna. He had six terrorists with him, three Palestinians, including his second-in-command, and three Germans, Wilfred Böse, Hans-Joachim Klein, and Gabriele Kröcher-Tiedemann, all recruited from the German Revolutionary Cells. Carlos, who had worked with Böse before in Paris, entrusted Böse with surveillance and logistics for this new operation, but he did not include him in the operational plans. Carlos was flush with bravado and basked in self-importance. No longer second in command to Moukharbal, whom he had murdered in Paris, Carlos issued orders as though he were commanding a great army. The killings in Paris in June had given Carlos notoriety, but instead of concealing his identify to safeguard future operations, Carlos proclaimed it as if he, Carlos, and the Arab Revolution were now one and the same.

Just before noon on Sunday, 21 December, Carlos and the six members of his renamed Arm of the Arab Revolution walked into the Texaco Building housing the European offices of the Texas Oil Company, the Canadian embassy, and OPEC headquarters. They carried Adidas bags filled with automatic pistols, grenades, and explosives. There were no metal detectors, no identity checks—there was no security at all, except for two Austrian policemen posted outside the second floor conference room where the OPEC ministers were discussing oil production and pricing. As they ascended the stairway to the second floor past journalists covering the OPEC meeting, one journalist mistook them for a small African delegation, another joked, "wait till they pull their machine guns out of their bags."[30] Coming into the reception area on the second floor the terrorists drew their weapons. Within minutes the terrorists had killed three. Gabriele Kröcher-Tiedemann killed a policeman and an Iraqi bodyguard. Carlos shot and killed a Libyan bodyguard in the conference room where the delegates suddenly found themselves hostages. The seizure was swift, but in the confusion one policeman managed to alert the Special Command unit of the Austrian police. Within minutes officers armed with machine guns rushed into the building, up to the second floor, and into a firefight with Hans-Joachim Klein, who was assigned to cover access to the second floor. In a brief exchange of fire, a ricocheting bullet struck Klein. Bullet fragments tore though his colon and pancreas and nicked an artery. But fearing a massacre, the police withdrew. Carlos controlled the building. Within the hour, Bruno Kriesky, the vacationing Austrian chancellor, learned of the OPEC raid: there were three dead, more than sixty hostages. Carlos released some hostages, and sent Klein, who was hemorrhaging internally, to receive medical attention.

Inside the OPEC conference room Carlos began dividing the hostages into groupings that reflected the Rejection Front's geopolitical map of the world. Carlos separated the ministers from neutral Arab, African, and Latin American states, then he separated the ministers from the progressive Arab states, Algeria, Iraq, Libya, and Kuwait from the ministers of states the Rejection Front considered reactionary, Saudi Arabia, Iran, and Qatar. Carlos had no quarrel with the progressives, all of whom actively supported the Rejection Front's strategy to prevent Arafat's capitulation to the United States and Israel. In fact, Iraq was behind the operation at Orly airport, Libya was behind this operation.[31] So, it was a terrible irony in the fog of battle an Iraqi and a Libyan were struck down by friendly fire. Carlos had come to make a statement—and to kill the two most hated moderates, Sheik Yamani, the Saudi minister, and his Iranian counterpart, Jamshid Amuzegar.

Carlos did not intend to remain in Vienna for very long. As night fell over Vienna, Carlos began issuing demands through the Iraqi ambassador to Austria. It was he who gave the first indications that the Spanish speaking man inside OPEC headquarters might be Carlos. Both the Austrians and the French denied the reports, neither wanted to face recriminations for failing to prevent the man responsible for killing three men in Paris six months earlier from escaping capture or detection. But all doubts about Carlos's identity vanished when he gave the Venezuelan oil minister, whom he later released, a handwritten letter to his mother. Carlos's poor discipline would actually save lives before the ordeal was over.

Carlos's first demand was that the Austrian authorities provide a bus to take the terrorists and their hostages to the airport and a jet to fly them to an Arab state. Carlos intended to fly his hostages out of Austria within twenty-four hours. Klein would come with them despite physicians' warnings about the seriousness of his wounds. Carlos's—or Haddad's—plan was a clever piece of propaganda. Carlos would fly from country to country throughout the Middle East, releasing the OPEC ministers in their own capitals, after authorities there broadcasted a propaganda statement. Carlos would free them all, except the Saudi and Iranian ministers—Haddad's orders were to execute them. Austrian authorities, desperate to avoid more bloodshed, began airing the statement at two hour intervals that evening. It began by proclaiming the seizure of the OPEC ministers was "an act of political contestation" directed at "the alliance between American imperialism and the capitulating reactionary forces in the Arab homeland." The rest read like the Rejection Front's manifesto: the Arab states must reaffirm the policy of no recognition of Israel, no negotiation, no peace; they must maintain economic pressure on the United States through the oil embargo; they must come to the aid of the embattled Palestinians in Lebanon where Zionist and Imperialist forces were attempting to break the resistance; Egypt and Syria must shun the path of peace and mount another full-scale offensive against Israel.[32]

Chancellor Bruno Kriesky had learned the lessons of Munich; lives could be spared by meeting the terrorists' demands. Carlos was in a position to dictate policy. The Austrian government had agreed to all of Carlos's terms. Carlos would leave Vienna in an Austrian airline DC-9 with his weapons, half the hostages, and Hans-Joachim Klein, who lay critically wounded in a Vienna hospital. Kriesky told journalists later, "We were pressured into this decision by the fear that the hostage's lives would be taken."[33] Kriesky did not know Carlos's orders were to murder Yamani and Amuzegar, but Yamani knew, because Carlos personally told him to prepare to die. Yamani could expect a bullet in Riyadh, Amuzegar could expect one in Tehran. To Carlos, and Wadi Haddad, these men embodied the reprehensible allegiance of their governments to the United States. Saudi Arabia meekly capitulated to the Americans in the hope of selling oil. Iran, still under the Shah, was the pillar of the Nixon Doctrine that directed the United States support for regimes able to protect U.S. interests in strategic regions of the Cold War world. Their government's foreign policies were their death sentences.

Shortly after 7 A.M., Carlos appeared outside the Texaco building standing beside the bus that would take them to the airport. He was in his prime. He was photographed embracing or shaking the hands of released hostages. Carlos freed more than twenty hostages, but he kept forty others, including eleven OPEC ministers. Two hours later Carlos was airborne, en route to Algiers. Seven years after Wadi Haddad hijacked the El Al flight initiating the campaign against civilian aviation, Algiers again became the destination of choice for terrorists. But things were different now. When the plane touched down in Algiers, Carlos released a number of hostages, sent Hans-Joachim Klien off for medical attention, and then deplaned to confer with the Algerian foreign minister, Abdelaziz Bouteflika. This was the very same Algerian official who met the PFLP hijackers in July 1968. Carlos and Bouteflika conferred inside a passenger lounge. After seven hours Carlos left the terminal and reboarded the jet. Within minutes it was in the air again bound for Tripoli, the capital of Qaddafi's Libya. When Bouteflika emerged from the negotiations he assured journalists the jet would make a series of stops, the terrorists would release hostages in several capitals, and there was "no reason to fear that there will be other victims."[34] In fact, the stop in Algiers was the flight's penultimate stop. Carlos would be back in the Algerian capital that same day.

Carlos touched down in Libya in the afternoon of 22 December where he released some of his hostages, including the Libyan OPEC minister. He expected cooperation from the Libyans. But Qaddafi, who stood in the shadows of the operation, did not want to reveal his complicity in it. Qaddafi, through intermediaries, refused Carlos's request for a longer range Boeing 707 to replace the DC-9 to make the sojourn around Arab capitals possible. Qaddafi could not grant a demand Kriesky and Bouteflika had denied without appearing to aid and abet. Carlos, dismayed, ordered the exhausted Austrian pilots to depart that same afternoon. When Tunisian authorities closed the airport to Carlos, the only option left was to return to Algiers. The end of the crisis was near. In Algiers, Carlos met with Bouteflika in the airport lounge yet again. This time the Algerian foreign minister made Carlos an offer he could not refuse: amnesty and a cash payment of $20 million, put up by Saudi Arabia, for the lives Yamani and Amuzegar. Carlos, known for his extravagance, accepted the offer on the condition the money be paid to him rather than the PFLP. Carlos's comrades were furious. "My people are without their country," one of the Palestinians, Carlos's second-in-command during the operation, recalled later, "and all he could think about was the money." But Carlos, who was defying Haddad's orders, demanded that his comrades-in-arms obey his. In the early morning hours of 23 December, Carlos walked off the plane followed by the mercenaries of his Arm of the Arab Revolution. The hostages walked off minutes later.[35]

Carlos remained in Algiers for several weeks but eventually returned to Yemen to meet with Wadi Haddad. The Master, incensed by Carlos's insubordination, expelled him from the PFLP and turned to Wilfred Böse, the German terrorist Carlos recruited, for his next operation.

Expulsion from the PFLP actually freed Carlos to strike off on his own using the Saudi cash to finance his own operations. Carlos was quiet for nearly six years. In 1979, he took Magdelena Kopp, a German revolutionary, as his wife and had a daughter with her. But Carlos did not settle down. In the early 1980s, Carlos organized a series of terror attacks, including the bombing of a Paris-bound express train in March 1982 that killed five, the bombing of a French cultural center in West Berlin in August 1983 that killed one, and the bombing of a rail terminal in Marseilles on New Year's Eve in 1983 that killed two. Carlos faded into obscurity in the mid-1980s—when Abu Nidal had already replaced Carlos as the world's most feared terrorist—and eventually sought refuge in the Sudan. French authorities finally caught up with Carlos in Khartoum in August 1994, and convinced the Sudanese government to extradite the Jackal for the murder of Michel Moukharbal and two French detectives in June 1975. In December 1997, a French court convicted Carlos of the murders and sentenced him to life.[36] In one of history's small ironies, when Sudanese authorities captured Carlos and delivered him into French custody, Khartoum had already become the sanctuary of a tall, fanatical Saudi national who was organizing a global jihad against Crusaders and Jews—Osama bin Laden.

Haddad ordered the Vienna operation, Carlos carried it out, but Muammar Qaddafi was its real sponsor. Qaddafi denied the allegations and denied he subsequently gave Carlos sanctuary. If Carlos ever set foot in Libya, Qaddafi told a journalist, he would prosecute him for the murder of a Libyan national in Vienna.[37] But Qaddafi's fervent sponsorship of the Rejection Front and terrorists, like Carlos and later Abu Nidal, earned Libya a place high on Washington's list of rogue states. A decade after the incident in Vienna, an assertive Reagan administration would strike out at Qaddafi in 1986 only to have Qaddafi strike back in 1988 in one of the most horrendous acts of terror, the destruction of Pan Am 103.

Chapter 5

We Accept to Live with You in Permanent Peace

In the summer of 1976, Americans celebrated two hundred years of independence, and in the fall they went to the polls to elect the nation's thirty-ninth president. It was the final year of Gerald Ford's presidency and Henry Kissinger's dominance of U.S. foreign policy. The Ford administration could not claim any great foreign policy triumphs. The events that brought the former Representative from Michigan to Washington all but precluded that. Much of Ford's presidency was consumed by crises whose origins could be traced to the misadventures of his predecessors. So, when Saigon fell to the communists in 1975, after a decent interval the Paris Accords afforded United States pride, it fell to Ford to order the humiliating evacuation of the few remaining Americans and some of the remnant of the defeated South Vietnamese allies. Ford might have suspended U.S. Middle East diplomacy in order to concentrate on political survival, but to his great credit he pressed ahead with the process Kissinger had set in motion. The Egyptians and Israelis concluded the Sinai II agreement during Ford's watch. For that matter, Arafat addressed the United Nations General Assembly while Ford occupied the White House. There were opportunities in the Middle East— but also grave challenges. In 1976, after Lebanon descended into a full-scale civil war, Ford would be compelled to evacuate Americans from a foreign capital for the second time in his presidency. And like his predecessor, Ford would have to contend with the murder of U.S. diplomats by Palestinian radicals. In November of America's bicentennial year, Americans chose Jimmy Carter president in the hope that this virtually unknown governor from Georgia would return virtue to Washington. Carter's presidency appeared to mark the end of the Kissinger era of U.S. foreign policy. Carter's faith in solutions to intractable problems produced a peace agreement between Egypt and Israel that forever transformed the conflict in the Middle East, even if it did not end it. Palestinian groups opposed to the prospect of peace still resorted to terror to disrupt diplomacy. Wadi Haddad organized his final acts of piracy, and Abu Nidal initiated a campaign of assassinations. But as the first decade of Palestinian terror drew to a close, Palestinians turned on each other, or they turned to European mercenaries to commit their outrages. The most spectacular acts of terror, the hijackings in 1976 and 1977, ended with the death of the terrorists instead of their hostages. Wadi Haddad died the following year. One era of Middle Eastern terrorism ended with the Master's death. Another began with a revolution.

Lebanon's Black June

In January 1976, the sporadic violence in Lebanon exploded in a full-scale civil war when Maronite Christian militias, who a month earlier had wantonly murdered more than seventy Muslims in Beirut, laid siege to two Palestinian refugee camps, Tal al-Zaatar and Jisr al-Basha. The fighting would last until October, when Saudi Arabia, Egypt, and Kuwait imposed a cease fire on the warring factions. By then, Syria had mounted an invasion of Lebanon to secure its own interests. For a time, Palestinians were too involved in a fight for their survival in Lebanon to fight for the destruction of Israel.

Over the previous months, Arafat had tried to restrain PLO military action, but now he rushed frontline Palestinian units into the fight to relieve the Maronite siege of Tal al-Zaatar and Jisr al-Basha. Then, under pressure from the leftist PLO factions, Arafat led PLO formations into an open military alliance with Kamal Jumblatt's Lebanese National Movement. The decision effectively negated Arafat's diplomatic triumphs of 1974. By taking up arms in the sectarian conflict in Lebanon, the Palestinians deepened the suspicion that Palestinian militancy posed a mortal danger, not to Israel, but to any state that permitted the Palestinians to set up camp. In Lebanon, as in Jordan, the Palestinians' determination to establish a militant state within the state had caused war. Now called the Joint Forces, the Palestinians and Lebanese Muslim and Druze militias possessed both the firepower and troop strength to take the battle to the Pierre Gemayel's Phalange and other Christian militias. Both sides committed atrocities. On 14 January, Christian forces overwhelmed the defenders of the Dbayeh refugee camp and slaughtered its inhabitants. The Palestinians retaliated by laying waste to the Christian stronghold in the coastal town of Damour. As Lebanon split into sectarian factions, the Lebanese army crumbled. Muslim officers in the Bekaa Valley and in Beirut mutinied in March and formed the Lebanese Arab Army. By the spring of 1976, the PLO and LNM Joint Forces held the advantage: by one estimate, nearly 80 percent of Lebanese territory fell under Joint Forces control.[1]

The crisis in Lebanon reverberated throughout the region. Israel's strategic concerns were acute. In 1969, Lebanon became the first state to formally permit the PLO to operate from its territory, and in the ensuing years various PLO factions mounted guerrilla operations against northern Israel from southern Lebanon. These were deadly but manageable. A victory of the PLO and Lebanese National Movement over the Maronite Christians would transform Lebanon into a radical state and a mortal threat. The U.S. interests in the outcome of the Lebanese conflict were fundamentally the same as its interests during the Jordanian civil war six years earlier—Israel's security and the denial of geopolitical advantage to the Soviet Union. Israel and the United States provided covert support for the Maronite militias, but both Jerusalem and Washington had to contemplate direct intervention to thwart a PLO-LNM victory. So, Syria could not remain impassive.

In January, as the crisis deepened, the Syrian president Hafez al-Asad mobilized Syrian forces along the Lebanese border as a warning to Lebanese president Sulayman Franjieh and Phalangist chieftain Pierre Gemayel that Syria would intervene to prevent a Maronite victory. In February, Syria attempted to impose a political settlement, but it did not hold. In March, the Palestinian factions forming the Rejection Front, with the support of Fatah's militant left, publicly proclaimed their aim to achieve a military solution. The intensifying fighting prompted Asad to demand a PLO cease-fire and then deploy more troops in Lebanon's Bekaa Valley. Syria followed this with another peace proposal, which led to the resignation of President Franjieh and to new elections in May. But the new president, Ilayes Sarkis, was not the candidate of the PLO and LNM Joint Forces, which took steps to consolidate political control over conquered territory. The Christian militias, now operating under the Lebanese Front, struck back.

As the rhythm of battle shifted in favor of the radical Joint Forces, Asad realized a PLO-LNM victory posed threats to Syria's own strategic interests.[2] Except for the status quo ante bellum or something resembling it, Damascus viewed all the possible scenarios with alarm. An outright victory of the radical forces would diminish Syria's considerable influence over Lebanon. A partition of Lebanon into Muslim and Christian cantons would have the same effect. An Israeli invasion to secure its northern border would bring the militarily superior IDF to the western approaches of Syria. Given the alternatives, Asad felt compelled to act. On the final day of May, Asad ordered a full scale Syrian invasion of Lebanon with the intent of imposing order in the capital. By the end of the first week of June, Syrian forces were fully engaged in combat, not with the Maronite Lebanese Front, but with the PLO and LNM Joint Forces in the mountain passes leading to Beirut. The following week, the Arab League summoned its foreign ministers and approved deployment of a peacekeeping force, misleadingly called the Arab Security Force. The small ASF deployed on 13 June, but there was no peace to keep. For five more months, until the principals to the conflict accepted conditions for a cease fire put before them in the Saudi capital, the Joint Forces, the Lebanese Front, and the Syrian army clawed at each other.

The conflict in Lebanon predictably endangered Americans. Four days after the first Arab peacekeepers deployed in Beirut, radicals belonging to the minuscule Arab Socialist Action Party abducted and murdered Francis Meloy, Jr., the U.S. ambassador, Robert Waring, his economic advisor, and their Lebanese chauffeur, at a checkpoint dividing the Christian and Muslim sectors of Beirut.[3] Meloy was en route to meet with the Lebanese president-elect. This was the second time Palestinians had assassinated U.S. diplomats. Fatah's Black September faction murdered George Curtis Moore and Cleo Noel in Khartoum in 1973 under the false assumption that Moore was somehow involved in the bloodletting of Black September in Jordan in 1970. Now the ASAP, the Lebanese affiliate of the PFLP, murdered Meloy and Warring under the assumption that the United States had a hand in the Black June bloodletting in Lebanon. Two days after the murder, President Ford, in the midst of a fierce battle with Ronald Reagan for the Republican presidential nomination, ordered the evacuation of Americans from Beirut.[4]

The murders were a blow to the secret security arrangement Ali Hassan Salameh, now head of Arafat's Force 17 security detail, had worked out with the Americans during the meeting at the Waldorf Astoria in November 1974. Salameh, who discreetly provided security for the ambassador's entourage, was not aware of Meloy's movements that day and so could not prevent the assassination. But Fatah, under the personal direction of Abu Iyad, the very man who ordered the murder of the Americans in Khartoum four years earlier, conducted an investigation that convinced U.S. intelligence that Fatah was still a reliable security partner. In fact, Salameh provided the security to cover the evacuation of U.S. diplomatic personnel from Beirut.[5] The murder of the Meloy and Waring was an ominous reminder that the Middle East's violence would not be confined to the region's geographic boundaries or limited to the principal belligerents. At the end of June, there came another reminder.

Operation Thunderball

Eleven days after the murder of the U.S. diplomats, Wadi Haddad ordered yet another act of air piracy. It might have been predicted. As the fighting in Jordan climbed towards its zenith back in September 1970, Wadi Haddad mounted the Skyjack Sunday operation in the

expectation that it would inflict a fatal blow on King Hussein's monarchy. A month into the Syrian offensive in Lebanon, as Palestinian and
Lebanese militants fought pitched battles with Syrian troops, Haddad
attempted to conjure up his magic one more time. But Haddad's Special
Apparatus was not the formidable force it once was. When the operation
was over, it was weaker still.

In the early morning of Sunday, 27 June 1976, four terrorists, three
men and a woman, arrived in Athens aboard a Singapore Airlines flight
from Bahrain. They went to the passenger lounge to await a connecting
flight, Air France flight 139 from Tel Aviv to Paris during its stopover in
the Greek capital. The Athens airport was as insecure as ever, despite the
violence in previous years, and the terrorists easily acquired weapons. At
noon they boarded Air France flight 139, and thirty minutes later the
huge Airbus was airborne with 257 passengers and crew; 9 were American, 70 were Israeli. Minutes into the flight, the pilot, Michel Bacos,
heard screams from the cabin. "I thought there was a fire on board," he
said later. It did not occur to him that terrorists were commandeering
his airplane.[6] A moment later the flight engineer opened the cockpit
door to find himself face to face with Wilfred Böse, Carlos's accomplice
in Paris and Vienna. Böse, armed with a pistol and a grenade, identified
himself as Achmed el-Kibesi, and commandeered the jet in the name of
the Che Guevara Group of the Gaza Brigade of the PFLP. The Guevara
group, like the squad that seized the OPEC ministers in December, was
an amalgam of German mercenaries and Arab militants. Böse was in
command and with him was a German woman, Brigette Kuhlmann, his
lover.

Böse ordered the pilots to divert to Benghazi, Libya, where he demanded fuel, released a passenger who convinced him she was pregnant, then methodically collected passengers' passports to determine
their nationality. Böse was searching out Jews. After six hours on the
ground, he ordered the plane airborne on a course to the southwest,
across Libya and over the Sudan to Uganda. The flight pushed the Airbus, the most modern wide-body jet in the Air France fleet, to the outer
limits of its range. At three o'clock in the morning, fifteen hours after
departure from Athens, Captain Bacos put the plane down at the airport
in Entebbe on the western shore of Lake Victoria; he had just enough
fuel for twenty more minutes of flight.

In the PFLP's previous hijackings, the air pirates could count on the
tacit complicity of the authorities whose states proclaimed their belligerency with Israel. The regimes in Libya and Iraq were by now financing
and even directing Rejection Front operations, but Libya's Muammar
Qaddafi and Iraq's Ahmed Hassan al-Bakr—or behind him, Saddam
Hussein—were careful to conceal their involvement. Just the previous

December, Qaddafi had refused Carlos's demand for a longer-range Boeing 707 out of concern for Libya's image. But the regime in Uganda, despite later protests of its innocence, revealed its direct complicity through its actions from the moment the Airbus touched down. When the plane taxied to a spot near the Old Terminal building, Ugandan troops rushed to surround it. Within the hour Uganda's dictator, Idi Amin Dada, arrived, ostensibly to conduct negotiations with the hijackers. In fact, he had come to confer with them. Doctor Idi Amin Dada, who came to power in a coup in 1971 and then proclaimed himself president for life, had by 1976 become one of the most vicious despots on a continent rife with despotism. A hulking man, Amin actually prided himself on the paratrooper insignia he earned in an Israeli training course. But, after the Yom Kippur War, Amin began to denounce the Jewish state in order to demonstrate solidarity with the Palestinian liberation movement and bolster his revolutionary image. When Air France flight 139 arrived outside his capital, he had a chance to turn his hostile words into even more hostile actions. Amin, in fact, had turned his airport over to the PFLP.

When Air France flight 139 arrived with the 257 hostages and four hijackers, other members of the PFLP were already there. The Mossad managed to identify some of them. It took a day to identify Böse, dispelling initial speculation that the man who called himself Achmed el-Kibesi was really Ilich Ramirez Sanchez, Carlos. It took longer to discover that his female accomplice was not Gabrielle Kröcher-Tiedemann, Carlos's comrade during the OPEC operation the past December, but Brigette Kuhlmann. The Israelis did not identify the Palestinians until after they killed them a week later. And there was another man who arrived at Entebbe but who vanished before the hostage crisis ended in violence. The press, citing Israeli sources, identified him as Anton Degas Bouvier, an associate of Carlos. In fact, Bouvier was probably Fouad Awad, a former Lebanese army officer, who was now an operational commander for the PFLP.[7]

In a communiqué released later, the PFLP explained it had seized the Air France flight in reaction to France's sale of Mirage jet fighters to Israel and French companies' collaboration in an Israeli nuclear reactor project. France's commercial ties with the Jewish state made it "a tool of U.S. imperialism." The communiqué denounced Israel as genocidal, the regimes in Egypt and Syria as reactionary—Egypt for its conformity to Kissinger's diplomatic agenda, Syria for its intervention against the Palestinians. And the PFLP demanded the release 54 terrorists. The Israelis held forty of them, including Kozo Okamoto, the lone survivor of the Lod massacre. The others were Germans belonging to the German Red Army Faction serving sentences in Europe. Böse set a deadline, Thursday at noon, three days away.[8]

Now, eight years after the PFLP began the campaign against civilian aviation, everyone knew the rhythm of the hostage ritual. Monday afternoon, Böse, who was already showing signs of fatigue, allowed the hostages to leave the jet for the Old Terminal building. "I want to be human," he told the hostages, "but I am very tired and a little confused."[9] That evening Idi Amin, dressed in uniform replete with his Israeli paratrooper insignia, visited the hostages. Amin boasted that it was he who had persuaded the terrorists to move to passengers off the jet into the Old Terminal. Inside, Ugandan airport personnel served the hostages food and coffee as the terrorists stood guard over them. Outside, Ugandan troops took up positions around the building. But unlike Bangkok in 1972 or Khartoum in 1973, where the Thais and the Sudanese made displays of force, the Ugandan troops were not there to menace the terrorists but to defend them. As night fell, the Israeli government's announcement of its refusal to negotiate came over Ugandan radio. Then Böse, a German, began selecting out the Israeli and Jewish passengers from the others. The Holocaust survivors among the hostages knew from experience what this meant.

By Wednesday the hostages settled into a routine of tedium and fear, aware that the Thursday deadline was fast approaching. The terrorists had not threatened to begin killing hostages singly to intensify the pressure on Israel. But there was cruelty. Brigette Kuhlmann was especially cruel. The Palestinians singled out a young Israeli they thought to be a soldier, and interrogated him harshly to draw out sensitive military intelligence he could not possibly have known. But the hostages' spirit of resistance was strong. One Israeli, a Nazi death camp survivor, confronted Böse demanding to know how Germans who professed to be concerned with a more just world order, and who accused Israel of genocide against the Palestinians, could threaten mass murder: "Today when I see you and your girlfriend, it is difficult for us to believe the Nazi movement has died."[10] That afternoon the terrorists released 47 hostages, none of them Jews or Israelis. The next day the freed hostages flew on to Paris where Mossad agents met up with them to glean intelligence on the terrorists, the deployment of Ugandan troops, and the condition and location of the hostages. The terrorists' gesture would prove costly to them.

The hostages awoke on Thursday with the 1 P.M. deadline hanging over them. But at noon, Idi Amin arrived with his wife and son to announce he had convinced Böse to stay the killing for three more days, until Sunday. Amin was preparing to leave for Mauritius to attend the Organization of African Unity summit; the prospect of a slaughter in his

Uganda during a diplomatic conference was reason enough to allow the Israeli cabinet more time to yield to the terrorists' demands. The delay doomed the Che Guevara group of the Gaza Brigade of the PFLP. That same day, the terrorists released another 100 hostages, again none of them Jews or Israelis. Courageously, Captain Bacos and his flight crew refused to abandon the passengers. That same evening, the Israeli cabinet voted unanimously to authorize Prime Minister Yitzak Rabin to open negotiations on the fate of the hostages and the release of imprisoned terrorists.[11] It was an announcement that would have required no explanation had it come from France or West Germany or Austria, but Israel had declared a policy of non-negotiation after the first hijackings to Algeria and Syria in 1968 and 1969. Fidelity to the policy had cost lives in Munich in 1972. The United States adopted the policy, and it had cost lives in Khartoum in 1973. Those facts must have weighed heavily on the Israeli government. Rabin's cabinet took the decision after concluding that Idi Amin was not acting in good faith. Instead of offering his good offices, he was offering aid and comfort to terrorists, who were separating Jews from gentiles with the intent to kill. The cabinet explained its decision to open negotiations as a necessary evil in the absence of alternatives. In fact, Rabin was already contemplating an alternative.

On the second day of the crisis, Prime Minister Rabin ordered the IDF to begin to draw up contingency plans for an armed rescue operation. Uganda is 2,500 miles from Israel, a fact that must have convinced the Che Guevara group and the Ugandan army that they were safe from the Israelis. But until Idi Amin had severed diplomatic relations with Israel after the Yom Kippur War, Israeli Hercules transports regularly had flown aid into Entebbe. An Israeli company had constructed the Old Terminal where the terrorists were standing guard over the hostages, and the blueprints were on file in Israel. Mossad agents gathered and analyzed information on the situation on the ground from released hostages. The IDF had commandos with the training for the mission. The prime minister, Yitzak Rabin, a former general known for his valor, had the political will to take risks. And Israel, a nation still stunned by the loss of 11 Olympians in Munich, was desperate to avert a tenfold loss of life. All this fortified Israel's resolve to act.

By Thursday evening, Brigadier General Dan Shomron, commander of Israel's elite paratroop forces, had developed an operational plan and assembled a strike force. Over the next three days the lives of the hostages and the commandos moved in different rhythms on parallel planes. The hostages sat confined to a dilapidated terminal building in Uganda under the threat of death. The commandos were confined to a base in Israel where they prepared frantically for an assault with the risk of failure on their minds. Early Friday morning, Idi Amin paid the hostages another visit, his third, to instruct them to draft a letter to Rabin urging Israel's acceptance of the terrorists' demands. The hostages could not refuse under the circumstances, but the letter was not the emotional appeal for Israeli capitulation Amin and Böse had hoped would break Rabin's spirit. The letter flattered Amin for his efforts and asked only that the Israeli government "react positively." None of the hostages signed it. Later that afternoon one of the hostages, Dora Bloch, fell ill and was transported to a hospital; a dual British and Israeli national, Mrs. Bloch would be murdered in Idi Amin's Uganda.[12] That evening, Amin was back at the Old Terminal building to inform the hostages that the Israeli government was not reacting positively, and that he, Idi Amin, had done everything that could be done to resolve the crisis. It was a warning, and an effort at self-absolution. That night the Israeli strike force began rehearsing Operation Thunderball with an assault on a full-scale mockup of the Old Terminal building.

On Saturday morning the hostages awoke thinking for a second time this could be the last day of their lives. The psychological torment was great, and now most of them became physically ill with vomiting and diarrhea from badly cooked food or filthy water. Yitzak Rabin could not have known this, nor could the hostages have known that Rabin was about to ask his cabinet for authorization to liberate them. At 11:00 A.M., Rabin convened a meeting of his cabinet. The simulated assault on the mockup of the Old Terminal building in the predawn hours bolstered his confidence that the IDF could cover the distance, take the terrorists by surprise, and deliver the Jews to safety. By the time the cabinet convened, the strike force had loaded equipment aboard aircraft. The planes were already airborne at 1:00 P.M., when Rabin revealed the plan to his cabinet. The deadline for the murder of the hostages was just over twenty-four hours away.

The strike force left the Israeli base at Ophir aboard three C-130 Hercules transports and two Boeing 707s, one equipped for airborne command and control, the other as a mobile field hospital. The planes flew separate courses over Israeli territory to avoid detection and then rendezvoused over the Red Sea. They flew south along the African coast before turning east over Kenya where the airmobile hospital put down to await casualties. At 11:00 P.M., the first of three C-130 transports carrying lead elements of the strike force landed at Entebbe and taxied within yards of the Old Terminal. Seven minutes later the other two Hercules landed. The main assault group, commanded by Yonathan Netanyahu, brother of the future prime minister, Binyamin, stormed off the Hercules near the Old Terminal. To ensure surprise as they closed the distance to the Old Terminal, the Israelis brought a black Mercedes made to look like Idi Amin's limousine. The deception paralyzed the Ugandan troops standing guard, who for an instant thought Amin was making a surprise late night visit to the hostages. The Israelis opened fire on them.

The hostages' lives depended on the speed of the Israelis' actions and the terrorists' reactions. General Shomron's plan for the assault on Entebbe was superlative. But when the shooting was over, Böse's inaction had spared almost as many lives as the Israelis' actions. When the paratroopers assaulted the Old Terminal, Böse ran into the building where the hostages lay on the floor. He could have killed scores with a burst from his Kalashnikov; instead, he shouted to them to stay down.[13] An Israeli paratrooper shot him to death as he turned his weapon on the attackers.

The Israelis killed seven terrorists—the four original hijackers and three Palestinians from the PFLP who joined them at the airport—and twenty Ugandan soldiers at Entebbe. To cover their withdrawal, they destroyed Uganda's air force, a squadron of Soviet MiG-21 fighters, on the tarmac. They inadvertently killed three hostages and wounded seven, and lost Yonathan Netanyahu, the assault team commander, who was struck by a bullet in the back and died aboard the C-130 en route to Nairobi. Fifty-two minutes after the paratroopers arrived, a Hercules carried the hostages out of Uganda. At 2:00 a.m., after refueling in Kenya, the planes departed for Israel. They crossed the Israeli frontier at Eilat in the Gulf of Aqaba at dawn.

That afternoon, Rabin addressed the Knesset and called Operation Thunderball "one [the IDF's] most exemplary victories," and offered it as "Israel's contribution to humanity's struggle against terrorism." Rabin did not utter a word about Munich, but the memory of the eleven Olympians infused his reference to the "manifestation of Jewish fraternity and Israeli valor" in Uganda. But the joy at the rescue of the hostages was tempered by the loss of four Israelis. The next day, Israel would be shocked by news that a fifth Israeli had disappeared. Dora Bloch was not in the Old Terminal when the paratroops liberated the hostages; she had been in a hospital in Kampala under the care of physicians and presumably under the protection of the Ugandan government since Thursday. On Sunday morning, after the airport assault, the British consul visited Bloch in the hospital in Kampala. Thirty minutes later witnesses saw Ugandan secret police drag her from her bed. The murder of Dora Bloch was a final outrage of Idi Amin's complicity in the hijacking. In his speech to the Knesset, Rabin publicly charged Amin with complicity, "all indications showed that the Uganda leader was collaborating with the terrorists, while using deceit and false pretenses."[14] That fact compelled Rabin to order Operation Thunderball, and it should have prompted the international community to condemn Amin.

In the days following the raid, international condemnation flowed from official spokesmen—but it was condemnation of the Israelis' actions, not those of the PFLP or Amin. The PLO, while condemning the hijacking, characterized the Israel action as an act of terrorism. The Egyptian foreign minister was even more scathing. "The Israel military aggression against Uganda," he said, revealed "the real terrorist face of the Zionist state." Even the UN secretary general, Kurt Waldheim, in an extemporaneous remark, after participating in the meeting of the OAU in Mauritius—the same OAU meeting Amin attended during the hostage crisis—referred to the raid as "a serious violation" of Uganda's sovereignty.[15]

Five days after Entebbe, Idi Amin's ambassador to the UN demanded that the Security Council condemn Israel and that Israel pay monetary compensation for the deaths of Ugandan soldiers and the destruction of the MiGs. He had the unconditional support of the entire 47 members of the Organization of African Unity, which characterized the raid as "a wanton act of aggression." But Ugandan officials could not provide plausible answers to questions about Dora Bloch's fate and whereabouts. Uganda's claim that she had returned to Entebbe before the assault where blatantly false, because the British consul had seen her in a Kampala hospital on Sunday after the raid. Israel's ambassador, Chaim Herzog, laid out the circumstantial evidence of Uganda's direct complicity, then turned allegations of Israel's aggression back on Uganda: "Before us stands accused this rotten, corrupt, brutal, cynical, bloodthirsty monster of international terrorism and all of those who support it."[16]

Five weeks after Entebbe the bloodthirsty monster struck again. On 12 August, four terrorists attacked an Israeli jet at the airport in Istanbul, Turkey. This was another PFLP-JRA operation. The terrorists killed four passengers and wounded twenty others.[17] Whether it was retaliation for Entebbe or for Israel's shipment of arms to the Maronites, who had just overrun the Tal al-Zaatar camp in Beirut, or both, the atrocity proved the truth of Rabin's remarks before the Knesset five weeks earlier—humanity's struggle against terrorism was not over. But there was a reprieve. Wadi Haddad would not strike again for more than a year, when the PFLP mounted yet another hijacking, its last, in an operation that would end just as the operation in Uganda ended.

Saddam's Assassin

The Syrian intervention in Lebanon in June forestalled an Israel invasion, but it effectively served Israel's strategic interests. For that reason,

Hafez al-Asad's decision earned him the enmity of the Arab confrontation states, and Iraq's enmity most of all. Iraq's Arab Baath Socialist Party had conspired to seize power in Baghdad since the overthrow of the monarchy. Inspired by Nasser's pan-Arabism, the Baath movement was dedicated to the renewal of a united Arab nation—Baath means renewal in Arabic. Iraq's tepid post-coup government, headed by General Abdel Karim Kassem, so disillusioned the Baathists that they attempted to assassinate him in 1958. A young Saddam Hussein was a member of the assassination squad. Five years later the Baathists staged a coup with CIA backing, but the 1963 revolution was aborted in a counter coup within months. Five years after that, in 1968, Baath saw another chance to make revolution in Iraq. Israel's decisive victory in the Six Day War and President Abdel Rahman Aref's refusal to send troops into battle against the Jews gave Baath the impetus it needed to sweep Aref from power. This time, Baath took precautions to defend its revolution against its enemies. The new president, Ahmed Hassan al-Bakr, empowered his protégé, Saddam Hussein, to construct a police state. Within two years, Saddam Hussein was effectively ruling Iraq behind the facade of al-Bakr's presidency.[18]

Instead of negating national rivalries, the supposedly unifying vision of Arab renewal actually deepened personal rivalries. The tensions with Nasser in the 1960s were part of this reality. In the mid-1970s, the friction was between Iraq's Baath party and its sister, Syria's Baath party. Now Iraq, determined to weaken its rivals to its claim to be the standard bearer of Arab renewal, acted to punish Syria for its betrayal. Because open warfare was impossible, Iraq turned to assassination. And for this, Iraq had an assassin.

Sabri Khalil al-Banna, Abu Nidal, had the temperament and the ambition to become Iraq's avenger. Al-Banna had once belonged to the most radical fringe of Fatah's left wing. Abu Iyad recruited him and then protected him when Abu Nidal's personal enmity to Arafat began to become manifest even prior to the October 1973 War. In September of that year, Abu Nidal's men, calling themselves al-Icab—punishment—stormed the Saudi embassy in Paris. When Abu Iyad and Abu Mazen confronted Abu Nidal in Baghdad after the incident, they came away with their first impressions about the threat al-Banna posed. The following year, after Fatah intelligence thwarted Abu Nidal's conspiracy to assassinate Abu Mazen, Fatah tried Abu Nidal in absentia and sentenced him to death. Fatah succeeded in eliminating Abu Nidal's confederate, Abd al-Ghafur, after the mid-air destruction of TWA 841 in September 1974, but the Iraqi state protected Abu Nidal.[19]

Saddam Hussein and Abu Nidal did not strike up a personal relationship, but they shared personality traits. Both men were ambitious, paranoid, and psychopathic. Saddam coveted President Al-Bakr's office, even though by 1970 he was Iraq's de facto tyrant. Saddam never wavered in his pursuit of the Iraqi presidency until he managed to wrest it from al-Bakr in a palace coup in July 1979. And he coveted acclaim as the symbol of the Arab nation in the tradition of Nasser. In 1972, even before becoming president, Saddam nationalized the petroleum industry in a move that was reminiscent of Nasser's nationalization of the Suez Canal in 1956. And like Nasser, Saddam adopted the Palestinian cause. This was the meaning of Iraq's backing of the Rejection Front and Abu Nidal's Fatah-Revolutionary Council. For Saddam, it was not enough to demand the international community's respect for the Palestinian right to self-determination, because the creation of a Palestinian state was less important to Saddam than the Arab world's adulation of him as the true defender of the Palestinians' absolutist demands. This was an ambition that demanded violence. And Saddam Hussein was a violent man. Saddam began his rise up through the ranks of Iraq's Baath party as a gunman, then consolidated his hold on power behind al-Bakr as the architect of the state's security apparatus. Violence was inculcated in Saddam as a child, but as a man Saddam grasped that Baath ideology, because it was totalitarian, was violent at its core. Once in control of the coercive institutions of the Iraqi state, Saddam persecuted the revolution's enemies, and his own, with equal cruelty. And Saddam saw an infinite universe of enemies. This explains the episodic purges of the Baath party, the relentless state terrorism, the war against Iran, the seizure of Kuwait, the fetish for weapons of mass destruction, and the genocidal campaign against Iraq's Kurds.

Abu Nidal's ambitions were not as grandiose as Saddam's. Abu Nidal coveted Arafat's position as PLO chieftain and the symbol of Palestinian revolution. This was the meaning of Abu Nidal's attempt to usurp the name of Arafat's Fatah. But his Fatah-Revolutionary Council never became the movement Arafat succeeded in creating and legitimizing as the dominant force within the PLO. Abu Nidal's organization never became a political movement; it was never more than a terror organization. Like Saddam, Abu Nidal invoked ideology to vindicate a personal affinity for violence. His radicalism in the cause of Palestinian liberation was meant to establish his legitimacy, but most of his early victims were not Zionists or Imperialists, they were Palestinians and Arabs.[20] It is for this reason that his first intended victim, in 1974, was Mahmoud Abbas, know as Abu Mazen, the PLO moderate destined to become, three decades later, the U.S.-endorsed prime minister of the Palestinian National Authority. But after 1976, Abu Nidal turned his guns on Iraq's rival, Syria.

The Syrian intervention in Lebanon in June 1976 provided the justification for Abu Nidal's first sustained wave of attacks. The Fatah-Revolutionary Council mounted its first terror operation in Paris in September 1973 under the name al-Icab. Now Abu Nidal chose a new name, Black June, an allusion to Syrian's invasion of Lebanon. In July, Abu Nidal sent Black June terror squads to bomb the offices of the Syrian national airline in Rome and Kuwait City. In late September, he sent another squad on what was tantamount to a suicide operation in Damascus. On 26 September, four terrorists seized more than ninety hostages in the Semiramis Hotel in the Syrian capital. Syrian commandos raided the hotel, killing one of the terrorists and capturing the others. Hafez al-Asad reacted harshly, ordering them hanged in public a day later. In October, Abu Nidal struck again with attacks on the Syrian embassies in Islamabad and Rome. That same month, Saudi Arabia, Egypt, and Kuwait brokered the end of the Lebanese civil war, but that did not mean the end of Abu Nidal's violence. In December, Black June attacked the Syrian consulates in Ankara and Istanbul and attempted to assassinate Syria's foreign minister, Abd al-Halim Khaddam. In January 1977, Black June attempted, and failed, to kill the Syrian defense minister, Mustafa Tlas, who directed Syrian military operations in Lebanon. Al-Banna ordered another attempt on the life of the Syrian foreign minister a year later, in October 1977, at the airport in Abu Dhabi, where Khaddam was on a state visit. Khaddam survived this attempt, but the shots that missed Khaddam killed his counterpart, the United Arab Emirates minister of state for foreign affairs, who was standing beside him.[21] All these attacks only served Saddam Hussein's interests vis-à-vis his nemesis, Hafez al-Asad. They did nothing to bring Palestinians any closer to a homeland. And, the moment Saddam decided to suspend the internecine warfare, Black June suspended operations. The lull would last for nearly a year until Abu Nidal struck at the Syria foreign minister a second time. In 1978, Abu Nidal would mount another wave of attacks, this time against Palestinian moderates.

Abu Nidal changed allegiances over the years. Saddam Hussein expelled him from Iraq in 1983 to appease the Reagan administration, which was then surreptitiously aiding Iraq in its futile war with Iran. Abu Nidal found refuge in the Syria that was once his enemy. Abu Nidal would launch another wave of terror from Syria, this time against Europeans and Americans, making him for a time the world's most wanted terrorist. In 1987, he moved to Libya, where he organized his final terror and assassination operations. But after Libya's Muammar Qaddafi expelled him, and his rage burned out, Abu Nidal returned to Baghdad. He commited suicide there—or Saddam's agents killed him—in August 2002, when Saddam sent his security forces to arrest him.

Sadat at the Knesset

A month after the end of the Lebanese civil war, Americans went to the polls and elected Jimmy Carter president of the United States. Carter, a Georgia peanut farmer turned naval officer turned governor, was swept into Washington on a tide of popular discontent with politics in the nation's capital. Carter, upon taking the oath of office in January 1977, proclaimed human rights the cornerstone of U.S. foreign policy and set out to right some of the wrongs U.S. power had wrought from Latin American to the Middle East. The thrust of Carter's foreign policy was a repudiation of the previous Republican administration's realpolitik. It was the dawn of a very short lived era of American good will.

The Arab-Israeli conflict figured high on the administration's agenda. This Carter inherited from the Nixon and Ford administrations, which recognized the conflict's implications for U.S. geopolitical interests. But Carter and his secretary of state, Cyrus Vance, eschewed Kissinger's incremental approach, which focused on interim settlements between Egypt and Israel but ignored the Palestinian question. "Most previous peace efforts," Carter wrote after leaving office, "had been designed to end one of the frequent military engagements or merely to devise some means by which negotiations could begin." But Carter, viewing the world through the prism of his concern for human rights, saw a fundamentally moral problem: "Since I had made our nation's commitment to human rights a central tenet of our foreign policy, it was impossible for me to ignore the very serious problems on the West Bank. . . . The continued deprivation of Palestinian rights . . . was contrary to the basic moral and ethical principles of both our countries [Israel and the U.S.]." And, while Carter "recognized the legitimate needs of the Israelis to protect themselves against terrorism," he believed the United States and Israel "needed to resolve the underlying problems."[22] So, Carter boldly decided to frame the principles of a comprehensive peace, although the great irony of the administration's major achievement, the Camp David Accords, was that those accords would in fact produce only a separate peace between Egypt and Israel.

In February, a month into his term in office, Carter sent Cyrus Vance to the Middle East where he found substantial support for another Geneva conference under U.S. and Soviet auspices. Anwar Sadat, who had proven his determination to find a way to peace when he put his name to the Sinai II agreement, was the driving force in the push for a negotiated settlement. Sadat's motivations were principally domestic. The Egyptian economy cried out for attention, and perennial belligerency with Israel bled Egyptian treasure. But Sadat insisted that the United States and Israel address the Palestinian question. In practical terms this meant finding a formula for Palestinian participation that would circumnavigate Israel's adamant opposition to negotiations with the PLO and the United States pledge, made by Kissinger, to shun Arafat's organization. The pressure was great. The previous September, the Arab League had voted to admit the PLO as a formal member. In March, at the thirteenth session of the Palestinian National Council in Cairo, the PNC approved the contentious idea of an independent Palestinian state in any part of Palestine. The vote extended the idea of the establishment of Palestinian authority on any parcel of liberated territory that Arafat forced through the PNC in June 1974—the vote that had been the catalyst for the creation of the Rejection Front.

There was the appearance of movement, and the United States had expressed a commitment to a comprehensive peace; Egypt, an eagerness to end the state of belligerency with Israel; moderate Arab states, an endorsement of the Geneva conference; and, Arafat had long ago concluded that U.S.-brokered negotiations that triangulated Egyptian, Palestinian, and Israeli interests offered the only realistic hope for the realization of his dream to preside over a Palestinian state. Arafat's hopes were bolstered in March when President Carter worked a cautious a reference to a "Palestinian homeland" into a speech. The effect of the word *homeland* was thunderous—it would not be for another quarter of a century, until 2003, that a U.S. president actually called for a Palestinian *state*—and Carter paid a political price for it. But he pressed ahead. At the end of June, Secretary of State Vance released a statement reiterating the administration's position.[23] But the positions of the Israelis and the Palestinians mattered most. Yitzak Rabin, the Israeli prime minister, might have been able to make progress toward a final settlement; he would eventually shake hands with Arafat in the Rose Garden, but not until his second term in office, which began in 1992 and ended three years later when a Jewish zealot murdered him after a peace rally. But, by the time the State Department repeated President Carter's words about a Palestinian homeland, Rabin was out of power. On 21 June 1977, Menachem Begin's Likud party gained enough seats in the Knesset to force a change of government—and a drastic change in direction.

Begin, born in Russia before the era of the Soviet Union, was a Zionist militant from his teenage years. His commitment to a Jewish state, and his determination to use violence to achieve one, resembled Arafat's unyielding resolve to create a Palestinian state. Begin immigrated to Palestine during the Second World War, and during the years of the British mandate took up arms as a commander of the Zionist Irgun Zevai Leumi, a clandestine organization the British had reason to consider a terrorist organization. In 1946, Begin participated in the bombing of the King David Hotel, the headquarters of the British military command, which killed 91 and wounded half as many. During the war that followed Israel's declaration of statehood, the Irgun massacred Palestinians in Dier Yassin; a massacre that Palestinians would forever cite as justification for their own atrocities. After independence, Begin rose to political prominence in opposition to Israel's Labor Party. He became a member of the Knesset during Israel's government of national unity, formed on the eve of the 1967 war, and was instrumental in the creation of the Likud. Likud's victory in the 1977 elections was the culmination of a long trajectory, and a hardening of Israeli politics.[24]

A month after Begin took office, Cyrus Vance presented the Israeli prime minister with a draft peace plan during his state visit to the United States. The plan, intended as a working document for the Geneva conference, was framed around five principles. Begin could not countenance the fifth, which concerned "self-determination by the Palestinians in deciding on their future status."[25] Begin's agenda was not the exchange of land for peace, it was the settlement of land conquered in war. In September, Begin gave his blessing to the establishment of Jewish settlements on Palestinian land. Nonetheless, even after Begin's election, Arafat continued to send signals of moderation to Washington. In August, after Secretary of State Vance visited the region, Abu Iyad, once the chieftain of Black September, hinted that the PLO could accept Security Council Resolution 242 now that Washington understood the Palestinian problem in terms of self-determination rather than merely the repatriation of refugees.[26] In September, Egypt and Israel began exchanging peace plans through the State Department. A month later, on 1 October, in the lead up to the Geneva conference, the United States and the Soviet Union issued a joint communiqué that contained language about the "legitimate rights of the Palestinian people"—but nothing explicit about their right to self-determination—and the participation of all parties, including the Palestinians, in the talks.

Then, on 9 November, Anwar Sadat summoned Yasser Arafat to Cairo to hear his address before a special session of the Egyptian People's Assembly. Arafat, whose political clairvoyance is one of his most intriguing qualities, sensed something momentous. But he could not have predicted what happened next. Sadat, in a memorable phrase, told the Peoples Assembly: "I state in all seriousness that I am prepared to go to the end of the world—and Israel will be surprised to hear me tell you that I am ready to go to their home, to the Knesset itself, to argue with them."[27] Sadat's statement may have surprised Israel, but it stunned the Arab world. Arafat's presence in the audience created the false impression of prior consultation. After the speech, Arafat left Cairo in a rage. The same day Sadat announced his intention to travel to Israel, Israeli forces attacked Palestinian positions in southern Lebanon, killing 78.

Civilian casualties were high.[28] The killing did not dissuade Sadat from traveling to Israel.

Eleven days later, on 20 November, Sadat stood before the Israeli Knesset to explain that he had come "to avert from all the Arab people the horrors of shocking and destructive wars" and "to declare it to the whole world, that we accept to live with you in permanent peace based on justice." He offered Egypt's acceptance of Security Council resolutions and "all the international guarantees you envisage and accept." Resolution 242, adopted after the Six Day War, was especially significant and controversial. Kissinger had once disparaged Resolution 242's "sacramental language" and "mystical ambiguities." Menachem Begin had already reinterpreted it to permit Israeli annexation of occupied territories he forever called by their biblical names, Samaria and Galilee. The Palestinians were nowhere near accepting it, despite Arafat's inclinations. Then Sadat uttered a series of phrases that would have raised the Palestinians' spirits, if they had not already understood the words to be empty: "I have not come here for a separate agreement between Egypt and Israel. . . . An interim peace between Egypt and Israel, or between any Arab confrontation state and Israel, will not bring permanent peace based on justice in the entire region. . . . In the absence of a just solution of the Palestinian problem, never will there be that durable and just peace upon which the entire world insists." Sadat made no reference to the PLO. Arafat was certain that either Menachem Begin or Moshe Dyan prevailed on the Egyptian president to excise all references to the sole legitimate representative of the Palestinian people from his speech.[29] Sadat's gesture effectively canceled the Geneva conference planned for December and rendered moot any discussion about Palestinian representation. Despite his insistence that he had not come to negotiate a separate peace, that would be Sadat's legacy. The Knesset speech was the prelude to the Camp David Accords in September 1978 and Egypt's separate peace with Israel in March 1979.

The Master's Final Operation

For the better part of a decade, since William Rogers announced his doomed plan in 1970, diplomatic moves in the Middle East had provoked acts of terror. Wadi Haddad had an instinct for using violence to throw those searching for peace off balance. The fast- moving diplomatic efforts throughout 1977 to end the state of belligerency between Egypt and Israel gave those who rejected compromise, or capitulation, motive to attack. No one could have been surprised that some act of terror was in the planning. It came in October, only weeks before Sadat's historic visit to Jerusalem. The surprise was that the act would be so tangential to the Palestinian-Israeli conflict.

On 13 October, four Palestinian members of the PFLP, two men and two women, boarded Lufthansa flight 181 from Palma de Mallorca in the Mediterranean to Frankfurt, West Germany. They were armed with pistols and grenades. Shortly after takeoff they commandeered the flight and ordered the pilot, Captain Jurgen Schumann, to fly to Rome. A PFLP terror squad now had 91 hostages, 86 passengers and 5 crew members. This was the beginning of a four-day terror odyssey that covered 6,000 miles and took the hostages to six countries in the Mediterranean, the Persian Gulf, and East Africa.[30]

The hijacking had no direct connection to events in the Middle East. Rather, it it was connected to a German Red Army Faction operation in West Germany. Six weeks earlier, on 5 September, six members of the German Red Army Faction ambushed Hans-Martin Schleyer's limousine on a narrow street near his home in Cologne, shot his chauffeur, raked the follow-up car carrying his bodyguards with automatic weapons and shotguns, and pulled Schleyer from the car. They whisked him away in a Volkswagen bus, leaving behind four dead. This was a relatively new terror tactic. Brazilian terrorists used it in 1969 when they kidnapped U.S. ambassador Charles Elbrick; Italian terrorists would use it in 1978 when they kidnapped former Italian prime minister Aldo Moro, the former Italian prime minister. Within hours the RAF issued a communiqué demanding a fifteen million dollar ransom for Schleyer's life and the release of eleven RAF members imprisoned in Germany, including Andreas Baader of the Baader-Meinhoff gang. Schleyer, a wealthy industrialist, was symbolic of everything the RAF detested about West German capitalism. As a young man Schleyer had joined the Nazi party and served in the SS and the Nazi administration in occupied Czechoslovakia. His awesome financial power in the Federal Republic of Germany must have been proof to the RAF that West Germany's democracy was a façade for fascism.

The only connections between Schleyer's kidnapping and events in the Middle East were the date—5 September was the anniversary of both Skyjack Sunday and the Munich Olympic operations—and the RAF's collaboration with Wadi Haddad's PFLP special operations apparatus, because the terrorists had trained for the operation in a PFLP camp in Yemen. The connections between the PFLP and German terrorists were by now solid. For years, German terrorists had served in the PFLP's European cells as mercenaries. Former members of the German Revolutionary Cells, like Hans Joachim Klein and Wilfred Böse, had participated in the Orly airport, Vienna OPEC, and Entebbe operations, acting on behalf of the Palestinians. The Lufthansa hijacking was different—the Arabs who seized the flight were returning a favor.

The Lufthansa operation was classic PFLP. Two of the four hijackers were women. From the beginning of Wadi Haddad's assault on civilian aviation in 1968 women were integrated into the PFLP's special operations. Leila Khaled led the 1969 hijacking that ended in Damascus and was captured on board the El Al flight during the Skyjack Sunday operation. Two Palestinian women were aboard the Sabena flight hijacked to Lod in 1972; both survived the Israeli assault on the jet. Gabrielle Kröcher-Tiedemann and Brigette Kuhlmann, both Germans, participated in the OPEC headquarters seizure in Vienna in December 1975 and the Air France hijacking that ended with the Israeli assault in Entebbe in 1976.

Lufthansa flight 181 arrived in Rome at 3:00 P.M. Italian authorities immediately ordered counterterrorism units to surround the jet and waited for the operational commander of the hijacking operation to make his demands from the cockpit. The man identified himself over the radio as Mohammed Walter and claimed the operation in the name of the Organization for World Struggle against Imperialism. Both names were fictitious. Mohammed was a pseudonym for Zuhair Akkash; the Organization, like the Che Guevara group that perished at Entebbe, was a cover for the PFLP. The four hijackers were all PFLP militants who had trained for this operation at a terrorist training camp outside Baghdad.[31] Akkash issued a simple set of demands: $15 million in ransom and the release of eleven members of the RAF imprisoned in West Germany and two Palestinians imprisoned in Turkey for the murder of four passengers in the August 1976 Istanbul airport attack in the aftermath of the Entebbe raid. The RAF had demanded the release of these same eleven prisoners six weeks earlier when it took Hans Martin Schleyer hostage in Cologne. At the same time Akkash made his demand, Gundrun Ensslen, one of the eleven, communicated the identical demand to prison officials from her cell in West Germany. The demands came with a threat: the destruction of the jet and the murder of all aboard it.

Suddenly Italian and West German authorities were in the same predicament as in December 1973, when Abd al-Ghafur's National Arab Youth for the Liberation of Palestine killed 29 passengers aboard a Pan Am jet and then seized a Lufthansa jet at Leonardo Da Vinci airport. Before that incident ended thirty hours later in Kuwait, the terrorists had executed an Italian airport employee in Athens. Terror had returned to the Eternal City. This time Italian authorities were resolute. Their inclination was to storm the jet, and West German authorities concurred. But neither the Italians nor the West Germans would have the chance to attempt a rescue in Rome; the chance would come days later.

At 5:40 that afternoon, Akkash ordered the jet back into the skies for Larnaca, Cyprus, where it arrived three hours later. Two hours after that, the jet was airborne again. Akkash directed it to Beirut, but when Lebanese authorities refused to be drawn into a hostage crisis, he had no alternative but to continue across the Middle East. Then authorities in Syria, Iraq—where Akkash had trained for the operation,—and Kuwait closed their airports. In the early morning hours of Friday, the jet appeared in the skies over Bahrain. The plane orbited Bahrain for nearly two hours before authorities allowed the plane to land for fueling at 2:30 A.M. on. There Akkash issued an ultimatum. The government in Bonn must comply with his demands or he would destroy the jet, with the hostages aboard, by 9 A.M. on Sunday the sixteenth. An hour later, Lufthansa flight 181 was on the move again. It arrived in Dubai just before 6 A.M. That is where West German authorities caught up with the Lufthansa hostages.

In Bonn, West German chancellor Helmut Schmidt was consumed by the crisis. The West Germans had learned terrible lessons in the Olympic Village and at Fürstenfeldbruck in September 1972, but The situation was different now. Willy Brandt could not offer concessions to terrorists in 1972 because the hostages were Israelis, not West Germans. Schmidt had the authority to exchange terrorists for innocents. He first would have to back off from earlier public statements opposing negotiations with terrorists as a matter of principle, but he could explain that earlier West German governments had seen the wisdom of avoiding the loss of life ever since the PFLP had seized a Lufthansa flight to Aden in 1971. There was something else. Brandt had no elite counterterrorist unit to take down the Black September terrorists on the tarmac at Fürstenfeldbruck in 1972. Now Helmut Schmidt had the Border Security Group Nine, or Grenzshustzgruppe 9, GSG-9. Formed in the aftermath of the calamity at Fürstenfeldbruck, the GSG-9 was an elite counterterrorist unit waiting for an opportunity to prove itself in action. In fact, within hours of the hijacking, members of the GSG-9 were in pursuit of the Lufthansa jet. Soon after Lufthansa 181 arrived in Larnaca, only seven hours after the hijacking, the unit was on the ground in Cyprus, fifty miles from the airport in Larnaca. When Akkash ordered the plane to fly toward the Middle East, the unit redeployed to Ankara, Turkey. Another GSG-9 unit flew to Tehran to await orders. So, the West Germans had options; they now confronted the same choices the Israelis confronted during the Entebbe crisis a year earlier.

Schmidt's inclination was to open a dialogue. On Friday, he sent a confidant, Hans-Jurgen Wischnewski, the minister of state, to Dubai.[32] Wischnewski arrived just before midnight and opened communications with Akkash via radio from the control tower. All day Saturday, the fifteenth, Wischnewski tried to reason with Akkash. Conditions on the jet were atrocious, the heat and fear overcame passengers, especially the young and the elderly. In Rome, Larnaca, and Bahrain, authorities had asked Akkash to release some hostages as a gesture. The PLO representative personally appealed to Akkash in Bahrain. Akkash refused. And he refused to push back the Sunday morning deadline for the destruction of the jet.

Akkash knew counterterrorism tactics, and he knew the scenarios. He knew Israeli commandos had assaulted the Sabena jet in Lod in 1972 and the Old Terminal building in Entebbe in 1976, so he knew the danger of delay and darkness. And he had specific intelligence about the movement of West German commando units. Wadi Haddad's PFLP intelligence network became aware of the GSG-9 unit's arrival in Ankara, where it redeployed from Larnaca. Akkash demanded that the West German authorities recall the commandos, and they complied. PFLP intelligence let Akkash know when the plane carrying the commandos reached West German soil. But neither Akkash nor the PFLP knew that other GSG-9 units were in Crete and Iran. As darkness fell in Dubai, Akkash's apprehensions grew. When airport personnel approached the jet to attach a mobile generator, the terrorists opened fire on them. Dubai's defense minister, Sheik Mohammed bin Rashid al-Maktum, who negotiated with Akkash beside Wischnewski, almost ordered an assault on the jet during those tense moments. But he doubted Akkash's determination to destroy the plane and held off. "I think perhaps [he] will kill some of the hostages," he chillingly told journalists. He admitted he had considered an armed rescue, "everything was considered," but he chose to avoid "anything that would have exposed lives to danger."[33]

Sunday dawned with the 9 A.M. deadline hanging in the air. Akkash let it pass without explanation. At noon Akkash, convinced the West Germans were preparing an assault, ordered the pilots on to another capital. Nearly four hours later Lufthansa arrived over Aden in South Yemen, the fifth city in four days. At 3:40 P.M., Captain Schumann appealed to airport authorities in Aden for permission to land his jet before it ran out of fuel. Yemeni authorities who had abetted the PFLP hijacking of a Lufthansa flight in 1971 refused to become entangled now and blocked the runways. Without the fuel to fly on to another capital, Captain Schumann put the jet down on the hard sand beside the runway. Lufthansa flight 181 would remain on Yemeni soil for twenty-one hours. Now there was a problem of a different order. Schumann, concerned that the hard landing had damaged the Boeing 737's landing gear, now feared it could collapse on takeoff. He convinced Akkash to allow him to leave the plane and inspect it for damage. Outside the jet

Schumann reacted like a man under crushing pressure—he fled. Schumann may have been trying to strand the jet in Aden without a pilot: he may have put the plane down in the sand to damage its landing gear for that same reason. Whatever his motive, the decision to flee was his last.

Akkash demanded Yemeni authorities return Schumann to the plane. Schumann's act shifted the moral burden onto the Yemenis. Whether to avoid bloodshed or to rid themselves of the problem of hostages on their soil, the Yemenis complied. A witness, Christiane Maria Santiago, one of two Americans aboard Lufthansa flight 181—the other was her child—later described Schumann's final moments. The Yemenis brought Captain Schumann to the exit ramp at the rear of the Boeing 737, a stewardess helped him aboard, and then Schumann "ran forward through the aisle, then got on his knees and begged."[34] Akkash stood over Captain Schumann with a pistol pointed at his head and delivered a speech—about what no one remembered—then murdered him with a single shot to the back of the head. Jurgen Schumann, like the Italian airport employee killed aboard a Lufthansa flight in Athens in December 1973 or the West German businessman executed aboard a British Airways flight in Tunis in November 1974, became another random victim of a terrorist who took innocent life as proof of the justice of his cause. Twenty hours after Captain Schumann landed the jet in Aden, his copilot flew the jet out with Schumann's body lying in the aisle. Akkash left the body there—just as Black September's Issa left Yossef Romano's body lying in the Israeli Olympians' apartment in 1972—as a warning to the others about the futility of escape. Lufthansa flight 181 flew south over the Red Sea into Africa. The copilot put the plane down in Mogadishu, Somalia, just before 4:30 A.M. on Monday the seventeenth. Lufthansa flight 181 had arrived at its final destination.

With the jet's arrival in Mogadishu the hijacking of Lufthansa flight 181 moved toward its climax. When Akkash threw Schumann's body from the jet to the tarmac the anguish in Bonn deepened and the West German government's resolve hardened. Somali troops surrounded the jet just as Ugandan troops had surrounded the Air France jet at Entebbe a year earlier. But the Somali dictator, Mohammed Siad Barre, was not Idi Amin. Helmut Schmidt placed an urgent call to Barre after the crisis moved to Somalia, and found Barre sympathetic to the hostages rather than the hostage-takers. Events began to move quickly. Hans-Jurgen Wischnewski, the West German negotiator, arrived from Dubai soon after the Lufthansa jet put down in Mogadishu. With him was the West German chargé d'affaires in Somalia, Michael Libal. They had no illusions. The terrorists had already identified Jewish passengers by their passports, selected three young Jewish girls for execution, bound the passengers in their seats, and doused the aisles with flammable liquor.

Wischnewski did not know this, but he suspected it. The West German minister of state called Schmidt to urge him to order the GSG-9 to assault the plane.

Now, because time meant life, Wischnewski lied to Akkash.[35] Speaking to Akkash over the radio, Michael Libal assured Akkash that the West German government had decided to free the eleven RAF prisoners in West Germany and was preparing to fly them to Mogadishu. But he said that they needed time, until 9 A.M. Tuesday. Akkash faced a life and death decision. He knew the probabilities. The Israeli government had freed fedayeen in humanitarian gestures after PFLP hijackings in 1968 and 1969; European governments had exchanged imprisoned terrorists for hostages in during the Skyjack Sunday crisis in 1970; the West Germans had freed prisoners in exchange for Lufthansa hostages in Aden 1972, and had freed the survivors of the Munich Olympic operation when another Lufthansa jet was commandeered in 1972; the Egyptians and Dutch governments freed terrorists after Salah Khalaf, the PLO intelligence chieftain, intervened to end a hijacking of a British Airways jet in Tunis in 1974. But after 1974, the attitude of Western governments hardened. So, many of the PFLP's hijackings ended in failure—at Lod in 1972 and at Entebbe 1976—and failure meant death. Akkash knew that death came with failure; he also knew glory came with triumph. He decided to move the deadline. But because he knew time could mean death, he told the West Germans 9 A.M. was too long to wait. "It is seven hours flying time from Germany," he told the hostages, "I give them seven hours," or until 3:30 A.M. Tuesday. Akkash understood perfectly well what he was risking. Over the radio he warned, "this will not be another Entebbe."[36]

The 3:30 A.M. deadline gave the GSG-9 just enough time to turn Mogadishu into another Entebbe. Sometime after midnight, more than sixty GSG-9 commandos landed in Mogadishu aboard a specially equipped Boeing 707. The commandos had been stalking the hijackers for days. One squad had deployed in Cyprus on Thursday, only seven hours after Akkash seized Lufthansa flight 181. They redeployed to Ankara after Akkash ordered the plane to cross the Middle East in search of a capital that would allow the hijacked jet to land, then returned to base outside Bonn when Akkash learned of their presence in Turkey. This was an elaborate deception. When the West German media reported the commandos' return, Akkash believed the threat had departed. He did not know that another GSG-9 unit was in Tehran and still another was in Crete. The lives of the hostages, and the commandos, depended on speed and stealth. Here the news media's obligations to report the news conflicted with the GSG-9's mission to save hostages' lives. Newswires carried Reuters, Associated Press, and Agence France-

Presse reports of a mysterious Boeing 707 landing in Mogadishu with only its navigation lights. Reuters was specific, reporting that the plane carried an elite West German police unit. The information could have proved lethal. Within minutes of the first wire reports, the West German government appealed to news services to withhold information. By then it might have been too late, except Akkash never heard the reports that the West Germans were organizing what he had warned them against—another Entebbe.

When Akkash realized he was under attack, it was already too late. At 2 A.M., Somali commandos who had surrounded the plane lit a fire 200 feet in front of the jet. It was a diversion. Akkash and two of the three other hijackers rushed to the cockpit to view the fire, isolating themselves from the cabin. Within seconds West German commandos were scaling ladders on the aircraft's wings. With them were two members of the elite British Special Air Services who detonated flash-bang grenades to stun the terrorists. The operation was over in seven minutes. Once the commandos breached the emergency doors, Akkash's ability to repel the attackers, or to kill the hostages who were asleep in their seats, was gone. In a matter of moments, the West Germans shot and killed two terrorists and wounded Akkash and one of the two women, Suhaila al-Sayeh. Akkash died of his wounds hours later in a Mogadishu hospital. The GSG-9 operation was even more effective than the Israeli Sayaret Matkal's operation in Lod five years earlier—no passengers died, and only one passenger and two commandos were wounded.[37]

The Lufthansa hostages survived their ordeal, but Hans-Martin Schleyer did not survive his. When news of the Mogadishu operation reached West Germany, Schleyer's abductors slashed his throat. French authorities found his body in the trunk of a car in a village near the German border. The near certainty that the RAF would execute Schleyer must have figured in Helmut Schmidt's moral calculus when he ordered the takedown of Lufthansa flight 181. The reprisal killing of Schleyer came as a surprise to no one, but what occurred in Stammheim prison surprised everyone. The day of the Mogadishu rescue, Andreas Baader, Jan-Carl Raspe and Gundrun Ensslen, three of the eleven imprisoned RAF terrorists whose release Akkash demanded, killed themselves in their cells. Baader and Raspe shot themselves with pistols secreted in their cells, Ensslen hanged herself with a bed sheet. A fourth, Irmgard Moller, attempted suicide with a knife, but prison guards prevented her. West German authorities, who were never able to explain how terrorists managed to come into possession of guns in a maximum security prison, found themselves belying allegations that prison guards murdered them.[38] As inexplicable is why Baader and Raspe chose to kill themselves rather than fight their way out of Stammheim.

The Lufthansa hijacking was the Master's final terror operation. Wadi Haddad's life was something of a parable of the Palestinian-Israeli conflict. A man who began a career as a physician devoted to saving lives ended life as an archterrorist dedicated to sacrificing them. Haddad's assault on civil aviation gave the PFLP a mystique that saved it from obscurity after Fatah's victory at Karameh in 1968 propelled Arafat into the leadership of the Palestinian national movement. The master's terror campaign made the world aware of the Palestinian struggle, even though it made the Palestinian cause synonymous with hostage taking, random murder, and terrorism. The first hijackings—in Algiers in 1968, Damascus in 1969, Amman and Cairo in 1970, and Aden in 1972—were spectacles of Palestinian militancy. The Skyjack Sunday operation in September 1970 was the most spectacular of all. It would not be for another three decades—until 9/11—that terrorists managed to synchronize the hijacking of four jets and hold the world in thrall to the power of terror. Haddad's air pirates did not kill a single passenger in any of those early hijacking operations. But then there were the airport assaults. The taking of hostages for the purpose of making a statement, exacting ransom, and freeing comrades-in-arms was reprehensible. But the random murder of air travelers in airports in Israel and Europe was criminal in the extreme.

The terror campaign did nothing to create a Palestinian state; it was calculated only to destroy—to destroy the Jewish state, the Jordanian monarchy, and the peace process. Haddad's campaign failed even in that. The terror campaign ultimately failed, and even the final terror operations ended in failure. By the end of his campaign Haddad was calling on foreign mercenaries like Carlos and Wilfred Böse, but they were incompetent. Carlos' megalomania eclipsed the Palestinian revolution, Böse was a lost soul. The final operations at Entebbe and Mogadishu were spectacular failures that obviated the mystique of Skyjack Sunday. Even the PFLP repudiated them. After Mogadishu, the PFLP issued a communiqué announcing it had actually expelled Haddad from the movement in 1976, after the Entebbe debacle.[39] It did not matter. Mogadishu was Haddad's final act of terror, although his disciples would attempt to resurrect his Special Apparatus in the 1980s when they carried out sporadic terrorist acts. Wadi Haddad, the Master whom the Israelis attempted to kill with rockets in Beirut in 1970, died of cancer in March 1978.

Camp David

Sadat's appearance before the Israeli Knesset was to be the most important diplomatic breakthroughs in the Middle East peace process until

December 1988, when Washington agreed to initiate a dialogue with the PLO after the Palestine National Congress finally accepted Resolutions 242 and 338 and Arafat publicly condemned terrorism. That was more than a decade off. The breakthrough of November 1977 created a dilemma for Arafat. The Arab states, led by the Rejection Front's staunchest supporters, Iraq, Libya, Algeria, and Yemen, condemned Sadat for treason, isolated Egypt, and vowed to establish a "Steadfastness and Confrontation Front." In December, Libya's Muammar Qaddafi invited the leaders of the Palestinian factions to Tripoli, not as representatives of the PLO, but as chieftains of their separate movements. It was a rebuke to Arafat. Arafat had been outraged by Sadat's move, although he later lamented only that Sadat had not coordinated his strategy with the Arab states and the PLO and thereby squandered an opportunity to challenge Israel to make concessions.[40] Nonetheless, Arafat did not want to break completely with Sadat. Arafat had not yet despaired of the notion that Egypt's rapprochement with the United States was critical for the creation of a Palestinian state. Arafat's refusal to throw himself behind the Steadfastness and Confrontation Front only deepened the hostility of the most radical confrontation states, most especially Iraq. The consequences were predictable.

In January 1978, Abu Nidal renewed his assassination campaign at the behest of Iraq's Saddam Hussein. On 4 January, Abu Nidal's assassins murdered Said Hammami, the PLO representative in London. Hammami paid with his life for Arafat's peace overtures. Hammami, at Arafat's instigation, repeatedly made public statements concerning the possibility the peaceful coexistence of Palestinian and Jewish states. This was Arafat's way of preparing the Palestinians for something less than complete liberation, something he had been attempting since 1974. Worse still, Hammami was known to be in discreet contact with an Israeli peace advocate, Uri Avnery. Hammami's assassination was only the beginning. On 18 February, Abu Nidal ordered the murder in Cyprus of Yusif al-Sibai, an Egyptian writer who was close to Sadat. Two months later, on 15 May, the anniversary of the creation of the State of Israel, assassins killed Ali Yassin, the PLO's envoy in Kuwait. A month later, Fatah publicly accused Iraq of complicity in the assassination campaign and mounted attacks on the Iraqi embassy in Beirut and on Iraqi diplomats in England, France, Pakistan, Lebanon, and Libya. Then on 3 August, Abu Nidal killed Izz al-Din Qalaq, another PLO envoy, his assistant, and four others in a bloody attack in Islamabad. Just when the dirty war within the Palestinian camp was beginning to resemble the Mossad's campaign of assassinations in Europe five years earlier, Abu Nidal suspended the assassination campaign for two years, until 1980, when he reemerged.[41]

Not all the killing was Palestinian on Palestinian. On 11 March, Fatah infiltrated eleven guerrillas into Israel by sea on the coast near Tel Aviv. As Abu Iyad tells it, the operation was intended to be a guerrilla raid on an Israeli military base, not a terrorist attack on civilians. Like the raids in early 1974, which came in the wake of diplomatic developments after the Yom Kippur War, the purpose of the operation was to preempt any further progress in the U.S.-brokered negotiations between Egypt and Israel that ignored the Palestinians' interests. As Abu Iyad explains it, "We weren't going to let Carter, Begin, and Sadat get away with a so-called peace which would deprive the Palestinian people of their future."[42] And, like the raids in early 1974, the law of unintended consequences dictated high civilian casualties. The operation went awry from the beginning. The guerrillas were supposed to come ashore separately, but one unit never made it to shore. Instead of aborting the mission, the commander, a young woman who had been tested under fire during the Lebanese conflict, ordered the fedayeen to commandeer a passenger bus. It is impossible to know her intentions—she ordered the bus on to Tel Aviv, perhaps to transform an armed raid into a hostage incident in a major Israeli city—but her actions were deadly. The inevitable happened. The Palestinians and the IDF exchanged fire at a roadblock. The firefight killed nine Palestinian guerrillas, two Israeli soldiers, and thirty-four Israeli civilians. Abu Iyad characteristically blamed the Israelis who, just has they had done at Munich, "chose to sacrifice their own civilians rather than allow us to score a political success."

Two days later, Menachem Begin ordered the IDF to retaliate. Begin was not a man for half measures. On 14 March, the IDF mounted a massive invasion of southern Lebanon. Some 25,000 troops supported by tanks crossed Israel's northern and northwestern borders with Lebanon. The operation lasted a week. When the fighting stopped on the twenty-first, the day after the UN Security Council adopted Resolution 425 calling on Israel "immediately to cease its military action against Lebanese territorial integrity," Israeli forces had swept over virtually all Lebanese territory south of the Litani River, creating a buffer zone between PLO forces and Israel. The IDF lost 21 soldiers, but killed three times as many Palestinian guerrillas. Israeli troops did not withdraw until mid-June, when a UN peacekeeping force, UNFIL, was deployed in southern Lebanon. Operation Litani was more massive than the Israeli incursion into Jordan in March 1968. And it was a prelude of worse things to come. Four years later, in 1982, Begin would launch Operation Peace for Galilee, a full-scale invasion of Lebanon that brought Israeli troops into Beirut, with deadly consequences for Americans.

Operation Litani and the acceleration of the construction of Jewish settlements in the occupied West Bank forced Sadat into a precarious position. By January, Carter was concerned that Begin was damaging the prospects for peace: "Whenever we seemed to be having some success with the Arabs, Begin would proclaim the establishment of another group of settlements . . . the repeated Israeli invasions or bombings of Lebanon also precipitated crises."[43] Then Carter seized on the idea of a summit at the presidential retreat at Camp David. Carter remained convinced of the need for a comprehensive framework that addressed the Palestinian question, and Sadat had made the same point in his speech to the Israeli Knesset in November. But meaningful movement on the Palestinian question was not possible. The Palestinian leadership was violently divided, neither the United States nor Israel recognized the PLO as a legitimate interlocutor, and the Likud government was not prepared to offer the Palestinians anything more than limited autonomy on the West Bank and Gaza where Israel insisted on the right to establish Jewish settlements. Indeed, Begin did not even believe Security Council Resolution 242 demanded Israeli withdrawal from the occupied West Bank.

Anwar Sadat and Menachem Begin arrived at Camp David on 5 September 1978, the anniversary of the Munich Olympic massacre. Jimmy Carter knew that Israeli withdrawal from the Sinai Peninsula, occupied since the Six Day War, was within his reach. He knew also that even an interim agreement on the West Bank and Gaza was most likely beyond it. Fifteen days after they confined themselves to Camp David, Carter, Sadat, and Begin emerged from isolation to announce that the Egyptian president and the Israeli prime minister had agreed to the texts of two "frameworks" for the negotiation of peace: Peace Between Israel and Egypt, and, ambitiously, Peace in the Middle East. Over the next six months, Carter labored to transform the hopes of Camp David into a durable peace. In March 1979, Israel and Egypt concluded the separate peace agreement Sadat had once warned could not hold unless the parties eventually resolved the Palestinian problem. In fact, the peace between Israel and Egypt held. The Palestinian problem, although transformed, remained open. Begin, to the consternation of Jimmy Carter, almost immediately disavowed Israel's commitment to withdraw from the West Bank and to grant autonomy to the Palestinians under Israeli occupation.[44]

The Camp David Accords framed the separate peace between Egypt and Israel concluded in March 1979 and earned Menachem Begin and Anwar Sadat the Nobel Prize for Peace. The Nobel Prize committee did not so honor Jimmy Carter for his tenacity and vision. The committee would wait almost a quarter century, until 2002, to award Carter the prestigious award for his indefatigable pursuit of peace in war ravaged countries around the world. By then, both Begin and Sadat were dead.

Begin died of natural causes in 1992. Sadat's fate was very different, and almost inexorable. Islamic militants, who by the beginning of the 1980s represented the new threat of terror, assassinated Sadat in 1981.

Final Reckoning

Even as the Americans labored to finalize the terms of the peace treaty between Israel and Egypt, the Israelis took action to avenge the deaths of Israeli Olympians in Munich in 1972. In January 1979, Ali Hassan Salameh, the Red Prince, was thrity-eight years old, the father of two sons, and living with his second wife, the former Miss Universe. Salameh was also commander of Arafat's security detachment, Force 17, and a valued security contact for the CIA. Israel considered Salameh, a principal figure of Black September, an archterrorist. It did not matter that Salameh was working with the United States. Even the Americans understood Salameh was a marked man. Sam Wyman, his CIA contact in Lebanon, knew this. Salameh knew this too, but Salameh, Wyman later said, "relaxed and he shouldn't have."[45] The Mossad thought it had killed Salameh in Lillehammer in 1973 but murdered an innocent man instead. A year later, the Mossad watched as the Red Prince appeared beside Arafat at the United Nations. In January 1979, the Mossad acted on the imperatives to exact vengeance for the crime at Munich and to rectify the error of mistaken identity in Lillehammer.

In late 1978, the Mossad found Salameh in Beirut and positioned Monika Chambers, an English-born Mossad agent, in an apartment with a panoramic view of the streets Salameh regularly traveled in his Chevrolet station wagon. Chambers kept Salameh under surveillance for weeks until she knew his movements and the Mossad could devise an assassination plan. By the third week of January, the Mossad was prepared to act. On 21 January, Mossad agents smuggled plastic explosives into Beirut, packed them into a Volkswagen Beetle, and then parked the car on the street. On the afternoon of 22 January, as Salameh passed by in his Chevrolet, Monika Chambers detonated the explosives in the Volkswagen by remote control from her balcony. The blast killed Salameh and ended an era. Another was about to begin in the city where Salameh died, Beirut.

Chapter 6

We Will Get Slaughtered Down There

In January 1980, Jimmy Carter entered an electoral year and the final
year of his presidency. The historic triumph at Camp David in September 1978 and the conclusion of a formal peace treaty between Israel and
Egypt in March 1979 seemed to validate Carter's foreign policy idealism
after so many years of Nixon's and Kissinger's Cold War realpolitik. But
a series of geopolitical defeats throughout 1979—the Islamic Revolution
in Iran in February, the Sandinista Revolution in Nicaragua in July, the
seizure of U.S. hostages in Tehran in November, and the Soviet invasion
of Afghanistan in December—strangled Carter's presidency. Then in
September 1980, Iraq attacked Iran, initiating a war that would last
nearly as long as the Soviet's doomed war in Afghanistan. The Republican presidential candidate, Ronald Reagan, seized on all these foreign
policy disasters in chiding the Democratic incumbent for making
human rights the cornerstone of U.S. foreign policy to the detriment
of its Cold War allies. Reagan won the presidency in November 1980 and
took office the following January zealous to restore the United States as
a superpower. Reagan was not eager to engage in the Middle East. In
fact, the Reagan administration came to office concerned more about
the situation in Central America than the intersecting Middle East conflicts. But Reagan could not avoid the Middle East. Israel's invasion of
Lebanon in June 1982 pulled the United States back into the geopolitics
of the region. The consequences of Israel's Lebanon war would be
dreadful. By the time Reagan stood for reelection in 1984, Islamic terrorists had killed hundreds of U.S. diplomats, intelligence agents, and
Marines in a series of destructive suicide truck bombings in Lebanon.
Terror entered a new era, and the sequence of events that culminated
in 9/11 was in motion.

The Islamic Revolution in Iran

In January 1979, Muhammad Reza Pahlavi, the Shah of Iran, abdicated
the Peacock throne to which the CIA had restored the Pahlavi dynasty in
1954. Two weeks later the spiritual leader of Iran's Shi'a, the Ayatollah

Ruhollah Khomeini, returned to Iran after sixteen years in exile, in Iraq and then in France. At the end of March, Iranians went to the polls to vote in a national referendum and overwhelmingly approved the declaration of an Islamic republic. In December, Khomeini, who had published a seminal tract on the principles of an Islamic government while in exile, established a theocracy with himself as the supreme jurisprudent of Islamic law.[1]

The Iranian revolution resonated throughout the Muslim world, Arab and non-Arab. The Palestinian struggle for national liberation had served the cause of a mythical Arab unity, even though support for the Palestinian fedayeen was more often rhetorical than real. But the Iranian revolution gave the struggle against oppression a religious intensity that surpassed anything secular Palestinian or pan-Arab nationalism could ever generate. Although Iranians are Persian not Arab, and Shi'a not Sunni, the potency of the Ayatollah's message was tremendous: Because Muslims had strayed from the one truth path, Muslims chaffed under the yoke of Western imperialism. Muslim holy places in Jerusalem were desecrated by Zionism; Muslim states were mired in political corruption; only the revival of Islam could lead to the restoration of Muslim land, including Palestine, to the Dar al-Islam, the abode of Islam. Islam demanded more than the liberation of Palestine, it demanded the establishment of Islamic governments faithful to the Qur'an and the Sharia, or Islamic law, throughout the Muslim world. And for this Muslims must be prepared to sacrifice themselves in jihad, holy war. Islamist thought was far more radical than the pan-Arab nationalism that competed with it for decades. So revolutionary was the message that the nationalist and Arab socialist regimes in Egypt, Syria, and Iraq struggled to silence it. The year before Israel dealt a death blow to Nasser's pan-Arab nationalism by defeating Egypt and its allies in the Six Day War, Nasser had Sayyid Qutb, Egypt's most prolific and influential Islamic scholar, publicly executed.[2] The reverberations of Iran's Islamic revolution were felt everywhere. In November 1979, some 1,500 Islamic radicals seized the holiest of Muslim shrines, the Grand Mosque in Mecca, and held it for nearly two weeks. The siege ended in violence when Saudi National Guards, aided by French special forces, stormed the mosque. In coming years, Islamic violence would spread to Egypt (where Islamist officers would assassinate Sadat), Kuwait, Algeria, and other states where fundamentalists heeded the call to overthrow apostate regimes.

Iran's Islamic revolution was intrinsically hostile to the United States because of its embrace of the Shah (even Carter, the human rights advocate, called Iran under the Shah an island of stability), its unfaltering defense of Israel, and its global hegemony. That hostility became manifest first in an overt act, then in sustained covert support for terrorism.

On Sunday, 4 November 1979, Iranian students stormed the U.S. embassy compound in Tehran and seized diplomats and members of the embassy staff. Jimmy Carter understandably called it a date he would never forget.[3] The Islamic militants released nineteen hostages, all African Americans or women, within a few weeks, but held the remaining 52 Americans for 444 days, until Ronald Reagan's inauguration day in January 1981. The hostage crisis paralyzed the Carter White House. Carter attempted everything within the considerable U.S. capacity except military action, until military action appeared to the former naval officer as the last best hope. When it failed, Carter's presidency failed.

On 24 April 1980, only a month after the conclusion of the separate peace between Egypt and Israel, Carter ordered Colonel Charles Beckwith to lead America's elite Delta Force commandos in an operation to rescue the U.S. diplomats. Had it succeeded, Operation Eagle Claw would have surpassed the Israeli operation at Entebbe in 1976 as the most spectacular rescue operation. Beckwith commanded 139 Special Operation Forces troops and the crews of eight helicopters and six transport and tanker aircraft. The mission, planned to unfold over two days, appeared impossible. The commandos would fly to a remote location in the desert—Desert One—and rendezvous with helicopters. The helicopters would have to fly 600 miles from the USS *Nimitz* in the Gulf of Oman. From Desert One the commandos would move to a second location outside Tehran where they would pass the night. The next day, the commandos would penetrate the center of Tehran aboard trucks, free the hostages, fly out on the helicopters, board transport aircraft in the desert landing zone, and fly out of Iran. But Operation Eagle Claw failed. Two of the helicopters developed mechanical trouble and never arrived at the Desert One landing zone, and a third developed mechanical problems there. With too few helicopters for the mission, Beckwith chose to abort it. Then disaster struck: a helicopter flying blind in the desert dust collided with a C-130 Hercules transport and exploded into flames. Eight U.S. commandos died in the flames: Carter's hopes for reelection died with them.[4]

The Soviet Invasion of Afghanistan

On 26 December 1979, Leonid Brezhnev ordered the fearsome Red Army to invade Afghanistan, fearing that chaos in the Muslim country could reverberate among the Muslim population of the Soviet republics bordering Afghanistan. A year earlier the Marxist People's Democratic Party of Afghanistan had seized power, but the revolutionary government was beset by internal power struggles that blunted its efforts to transform tribal Afghanistan into a socialist state. In September 1979,

Afghan premier Hafizullah Amin staged a palace coup and made himself president. By then, Afghan tribesmen, whose Islamic fundamentalism was indomitable, were already taking up arms against the Marxist regime. Amin's coup only heightened the Soviet Union's anxiety about the deteriorating situation in its newest client state. Breshnev moved against him the day after Christmas and installed his own man, Babrak Karmal, as president. But the Soviet invasion did not pacify Afghanistan—it ignited a jihad.

The Carter administration, still reeling from the Soviet willingness to jeopardize superpower relations after more than a decade of détente, began aiding Afghan fighters. It was the beginning of a decade of war and the demise of the Soviet Union. When Reagan took office, U.S. support for the Afghan mujahideen soared to hundreds of millions of dollars annually. The CIA's covert operation became the largest undertaken by the agency and the first that actually killed Russians instead of Russian proxies.[5] Najibullah, head of Afghanistan's secret police, replaced Babrak Karmal in 1986. But by then the Afghan mujahideen, armed by the CIA with advanced weapons, were inflicting heavy casualties on the once invincible Red Army. But there was a dark side to the CIA's Afghan war. The CIA rarely made direct contact with the Afghan mujahideen because the Pakistani intelligence agency, the Inter-Services Intelligence, or ISI, ran the Afghanis. And the ISI favored the most radical fundamentalists, with consequences yet unseen. As ominously, the war to drive the Soviet invaders from Afghanistan became a jihad for Muslims throughout the Arab world. Saudi Arabia poured billions of dollars into the jihad, matching the funds Congress had authorized for the CIA crusade with barely a debate.

More ominous than the money were the mujahideen. Many thousands of Muslims trekked to Afghanistan to wage jihad. The influx of Arab-Afghans, as they came to be known, multiplied the guerrilla forces but created a logistical burden. The Pakistani ISI, the CIA, and even the Agency for International Development hurled themselves at the problem of moving men, weapons, and supplies. But the Arab-Afghans took up the task of operating a guerrilla jihad as well. By the early 1980s, two men, a Palestinian and a Saudi, created the Maktab al-Khidamat—Mujahideen Services Bureau—to recruit holy warriors and to manage the logistics of their martyrdom. It was a global enterprise. One affiliate, the al-Kifah Refugee Services Center, operated in Brooklyn and in time would recruit mujahideen for the jihad against the United States. The Palestinian, Abdallah Youssef Azzam, an esteemed Muslim cleric, did not survive the Afghan war; a car bomb killed him in November 1989 after the war in Afghanistan entered a new phase. The Saudi would

become the one man whose name became synonymous with mega-ter-
rorism—Osama bin Laden.[6]

President Mikhail Gorbachev withdrew the battered Red Army from
Afghanistan in February 1989, but by then his efforts to reform the
Soviet Union had created the dynamic that ultimately led to its demise.
The Berlin Wall fell in November that year, and the Soviet Union disintegrated three years later. But the Soviet withdrawal did not end the conflict in Afghanistan as mujahideen commanders hastened to destroy
Najibullah's regime. They drove Najibullah from power in 1992 and
imprisoned him until 1996 when they publicly hanged him. By then a
new force had emerged in Afghanistan, who, calling themselves religious students—Taliban—would impose a brutally fundamentalist
Islamic state and permit Osama bin Laden to set up terrorist encamp-
ments in Afghanistan. The antecedents of 9/11 and America's war in
Afghanistan were in place.

Iraq's Invasion of Kuwait

In July 1979, eleven years after the Baath party seized power in Iraq, Saddam Hussein, nominal vice president of Iraq, overthrew President
Ahmed Hassan al-Bakr in a palace coup. In fact, Saddam Hussein had
ruled Iraq for years, making the critical decisions and constructing a
regime of terror that was obedient to his will. Thirteen months after he
seized power, the new Iraqi president launched an invasion of Iran for
reasons that are idiosyncratic to Saddam's way of thinking. The provocations were there. The Ayatollah Khomeini had denounced the secular
Baath regime in Iraq and made territorial claims on the Shi'a holy places
in the Iraqi cities of Karbala and Najjaf that Saddam Hussein correctly
interpreted as a threat to Iraq's territorial integrity as well as his narcissis-
tic rule. Sensing both danger and an opportunity to settle a perennial
territorial dispute over the Shat al-Arab waterway, Saddam Hussein
ordered the invasion of Iran in September. The war dragged on for
eight years until August 1988, and saw all the depredations of warfare:
human wave assaults, aerial bombardment of cities, attacks on shipping
in the Persian Gulf, and poison gas attacks.[7] The numbers of killed and
maimed ran into the millions.

The Reagan administration reacted to the war between the two most
powerful states in the strategically vital and oil-rich Persian Gulf with the
cynicism inherent to realist calculations about geopolitics. A prolonged
war served U.S. interests, because as long as Iran and Iraq mauled each
other, neither could achieve regional supremacy or threaten America's
geostrategic position. So, Reagan found it in the U.S. interest to assist
both Iran and Iraq. The administration began providing weapons to

Iran via Israel in 1985 in exchange for American hostages held by the Iranian-backed Hizb'allah in Lebanon. The covert arms-for-hostages deals violated the declared U.S. policy to embargo both sides in the war and reject negotiations with terrorist states. Inevitably, Hizb'allah seized more hostages to exchange for still more arms. The arms deals with Iran later intersected with another covert operation in Nicaragua. This was the genesis of the Iran-Contra scandal that would cause the Reagan administration so much grief when the press and the Congress learned of the administration's duplicity.

The Reagan administration was just as duplicitous with Saddam Hussein's Iraq. The United States began providing the Iraqi military with limited intelligence about Iranian movements on the battlefield early in the war. The covert intelligence was not intended to make an Iraqi victory possible, but only to make an Iranian victory impossible. There were overt dealings as well. In early 1981, the Reagan administration began to make overtures to Saddam Hussein. Alexander Haig, the secretary of state, issued carefully calibrated statements about Saddam that cast his regime in a positive light. The CIA station chief in Amman, Tom Twitten, began visiting Baghdad regularly in 1982. Saddam was discovering the most unlikely of allies, although the alliance was driven by the administration's anxieties about Iran. In July 1983, Saddam banished Abu Nidal, the Palestinian dissident turned Iraqi agent provocateur, who by then had already committed his most provocative act of terror and sparked a war in Lebanon, to placate the Reagan administration.[8] Then in December, Reagan dispatched Donald Rumsfeld, the past and future secretary of defense, to establish "direct contact between an envoy of the president of the United States and President Saddam Hussein."[9]

Rumsfeld was already a powerful figure in Washington when Reagan entrusted him with this mission. A former navy pilot, Rumsfeld served in Congress for seven years before serving in the Nixon White House as an advisor on economic matters. President Ford appointed him ambassador to NATO, then White House chief of staff, then secretary of defense at the age of thirty. In a supreme irony, Rumsfeld would return to the Pentagon as secretary of defense in 2001 in George W. Bush's administration to supervise America's war against Saddam Hussein in 2003.[10] Rumsfeld visited Baghdad in December 1983 when he met with Saddam Hussein in a now famous photo opportunity. A month earlier, American intelligence officers on the ground in Iraq had reported to Washington that Iraqi forces were using chemical weapons almost daily.[11] Rumsfeld traveled to Baghdad again in March 1984, when he met with Tariq Aziz, a Saddam loyalist who served the Iraqi dictator in several capacities over the years. Just before this second visit, the United

States openly condemned Iraq's poison gas attacks. But Reagan officials assured the Iraqis that the Reagan administration found it in U.S. interests to continue "to improve bilateral relations with Iraq, at a pace of Iraq's choosing." To emphasize the point, the American officials conveyed then vice president George Bush's invitation to Tariq Aziz to visit the White House.[12] Tariq Aziz, who became the Eight of Spades on the Defense Department's famous deck of cards during Operation Iraqi Freedom two decades later, met with Ronald Reagan in the Oval Office on 26 November 1984 to celebrate the restoration of diplomatic relations, severed since the Six Day War, between the United States and Saddam Hussein's Iraq.

The Reagan administration's reactions to the events in Iran, Afghanistan, and Iraq bore consequences for the United States that became fully manifest decades later—wars in Iraq in 1991 and 2003 and Afghanistan in 2001, as well as the atrocity of 11 September. But as the brief Carter era drew to a close and the Reagan years opened, none of that could be foreseen.

The conflict between the Israelis and Palestinians was virtually lost in this geopolitical maze. The peace treaty Carter achieved in March 1979 marked the outer limit of diplomatic possibility, and Washington lapsed into inertia after Reagan took office. Palestinian terrorism appeared to be on the decline after the triumphs of Israeli and West German counterterrorism operations in Entebbe and Mogadishu in 1976 and 1977 and the death of Wadi Haddad the following year. Then Abu Nidal suddenly reappeared.

Over a period of months in 1976 and 1977, Abu Nidal's Fatah-Revolutionary Council, calling itself Black June in remembrance of Syria's intervention in Lebanon, preyed on Syrians at the behest of Iraq. Then Abu Nidal turned on Palestinian and Egyptian moderates, killing four between January and August 1978. A sixteen-month hiatus ended suddenly in 1980, when Abu Nidal turned on Palestinian and Arab moderates and began attacking Jews in Europe. In July 1980, Abu Nidal's assassins murdered Na'im Khudr, the PLO envoy in Brussels. In April 1983, his killers assassinated Issam Sartawi, another PLO moderate who was in contact with Israeli peace activists in Lisbon.[13] But these were not major figures. The men Abu Nidal most wanted to kill, Abu Iyad and Abu Daoud, eluded him. Abu Nidal tried and failed to murder them both between 1980 and 1981.

In the summer of 1980, even as he pursued this vendetta against his Palestinian brothers, Abu Nidal suddenly began attacking Jews. Still operating under the protection of Saddam Hussein's regime in Baghdad, Abu Nidal sent terror squads to roam Europe looking for targets of opportunity. The killing and the maiming came at regular intervals: a grenade attack on a Jewish school in Antwerp on 27 July 1980 killed one student and wounded nineteen others; an automatic weapons and grenade attack on a synagogue in Vienna on 29 August 1981 killed two and wounded nineteen; an attack on a Jewish restaurant in Paris on 9 August 1982 wounded several patrons but killed no one; an attack on a synagogue in Rome in October 1982 killed one child and wounded ten.[14] This was the beginning of a wave of European terror that would continue even after Saddam Hussein expelled Abu Nidal from Baghdad to placate the Reagan administration. But it was a botched assassination in London in June 1982 that was to have the gravest consequences: a war in Lebanon that would burn for nearly a decade. Abu Nidal waged terror well into the 1980s. And new Palestinian terror organizations, constructed from the remnants of Wadi Haddad's faction of the PFLP, began hurling bombs and attacking airliners. But by mid-decade a new terror materialized with consequences, which in terms of loss of life and geopolitics, was infinitely greater than the terror of the consequences of secular Palestinian national movement. The first sign came in Cairo, although few grasped the meaning of the attack or appreciated that the men behind it would one day become the most dangerous of all terrorists.

The Assassination of Sadat

On 6 October 1981, Anwar Sadat left the Egyptian capital to review a display of Egypt's renewed military might. It was the anniversary of the Egyptian army's assault across the Suez Canal eight years earlier. For the Egyptian army the assault against the IDF dug in on the eastern bank of the canal was a rare triumph of arms. It did not matter that Israel eventually defeated Egypt and Syria in the Yom Kippur War or that only a year earlier Sadat had signed a separate peace agreement with the Jewish state. Sadat's presidency depended on his army's loyalty, and this was his officers' moment to celebrate a fleeting victory in battle that was not tarnished by the defeat in the war. Sadat, looking relaxed and jovial, arrived dressed in full military regalia and took the seat of honor between his vice president, Hosni Mubarak, and his defense minister. Americans were there. The parade was a celebration of the assault across the Suez, but it was equally a demonstration of the American weapons that began to stock Egypt's arsenals after Sadat's shift in allegiance from the Soviet Union to the United States. Sadat made U.S. military officers and defense contractors honored guests.

But in October 1981 Sadat was under challenge, and not just because of his peace treaty with Israel. Throughout the previous month, Sadat's security forces had methodically arrested hundreds of opponents, including Islamic militants, who were agitating against his government. Sadat lived under threat of assassination, but the possibility that assassins would come from the ranks of the army did not occur to him until a group of parading soldiers turned their guns on him. The parade was nearly over when four soldiers leaped from a truck passing in front of the reviewing stand, brandishing rifles and grenades and charged toward Sadat. The attack lasted only minutes. The assassins killed eight and wounded nearly 200, including three Americans. Anwar Sadat was struck in the head, neck, chest, arm, and legs. He died en route to a hospital aboard an Egyptian army helicopter. Somehow Vice President Mubarak emerged unscathed to find himself president.

That night, ABC's *Nightline* program—created originally as America's nightly line to news about the American hostages in Iran—devoted a special to the Sadat assassination. Former U.S. officials were invited to speculate about the identity of the assassins and the implications for the Middle East. Jimmy Carter, Henry Kissinger, and former CIA director Richard Helms appeared. All suspected the complicity of Libya's Muammar Qaddafi, whose rivalry with Sadat was dangerous. But even a year and a half after the Islamic Revolution in Iran, and a year after the seizure of the Grand Mosque in Saudi Arabia, these former officials did not so much as mention the possibility that militant Islam had struck down the most visible symbol of Arab collusion with the United States.

In fact, the assassins were all militant Muslims belonging to Jama'at al-Jihad, the Jihad Group. Khalid al-Islambuli, a lieutenant colonel, led the assassins. Grainy images of the massacre at the parade ground show him blasting his assault rifle at Sadat. Islambuli reveled in his act. When captured he exclaimed "I have killed Pharaoh!"[15] For him to be this close to Sadat was incredible; Islambuli's own brother was then under suspicion for subversion. The Egyptian state executed al-Islambuli and the three other soldiers who killed Sadat. It also executed Muhammad Abd al-Salam Faraj, the electrical engineer who authored the incendiary tract, *The Neglected Duty*, which explained the duty to murder the Egyptian head of state.[16] Then the Egyptian state struck out against al-Jihad and militant groups like it.

Two decades after Nasser executed Qutb, the threat of Islamic radicalism again became a matter of secular Egypt's survival. Al-Jihad was one of several radical Islamist organizations that turned to terror in Egypt in the 1980s. Although the Egyptian security services would prevent them from ever mounting a serious challenge to the survival of Egypt's secular state or Mubarak's presidency, the Islamists would prove their ability to kill government officials, whom they considered apostates, Coptic Christians, whom they considered infidels, and foreign tourists, who they believed defiled Muslim lands.[17] Some of the future's most dangerous terrorists came from the ranks of Egyptian Islamic Jihad or gave religious sanction to its actions.

One such man was Sheikh Omar Abdel Rahman, a blind cleric, whom an Egyptian court tried for subversion along with more than 300 Islamic militants detained by Egyptian security forces in the aftermath of the Sadat assassination.[18] The state charged Rahman with issuing a fatwa justifying violence against Christians in the defense of Islam and the assassination of politicians who had drifted into apostasy. Convictions on the charges could have led to a death sentence, but Sheikh Rahman did not cower before the court during his 1982 trial. He defended jihad and "the legal punishments of Allah and his law" as doctrines of faith established by fourteen centuries of Islamic jurisprudence.[19] The court actually acquitted Rahman, reasoning that although the blind cleric had justified murder he had not specifically sanctioned the murder of Sadat or anyone else. The court gave those it did convict lenient sentences on the grounds that the security forces extracted confessions under duress. In early 1985, Rahman traveled to Afghanistan where he met Abdullah Azzam and Osama bin Laden, who had already organized the Mujahideen Services Bureau, the forerunner of Al Qaeda. By now Sheikh Rahman was a renowned theologian of jihad. It was a meeting of like minds. Eventually Rahman returned to Egypt, where security forces placed him under house arrest cognizant that his advocacy of militant Islam made him an enduring threat. Disciples subsequently freed Rahman by force and organized his escape to the Sudan, a state that would soon suffer its own Islamization and where Osama bin Laden would eventually find safe haven. In 1990, the U.S. consulate in the Sudan granted Sheikh Rahman a U.S. visa under mysterious circumstances—a CIA officer at the embassy signed the visa. That proved to be a fatal error. Rahman moved to the United States and established himself as the imam of a New Jersey mosque.[20] There Rahman made converts to his call for jihad against the United States. Among those who heeded his call were the terrorists who bombed the World Trade Center in February 1993. Sheikh Rahman continued to inspire Islamists to violence after the first World Trade Center attack. The Justice Department would eventually convict Sheikh Omar Abdel Rahman on charges of conspiracy to bomb New York-area landmarks. He is imprisoned in the United States. Two of Rahman's sons, proving themselves worthy of their father's militancy, joined Osama bin Laden in Afghanistan.[21]

More fascinating is Ayman al-Zawahiri. Al-Zawahiri is the child of prominent families. His father was a professor of pharmacology.[22] Al-Zawahiri himself would eventually become a surgeon. His father's uncle became the Grand Imam of the Al-Azhar University in Cairo, the most prestigious center of Islamic theology. His maternal grandfather was president of Cairo University and founded the Kind Saud University in Riyadh, Saudi Arabia. Al-Zawahiri chose his father's profession by becoming a surgeon, but became involved with clandestine Islamist organizations before the age of fifteen. Al- Zawahiri was among al-Jihad's founders and, like Sheikh Omar Abdel Rahman, stood trial for acts of Islamist violence. Al-Zawahiri was not implicated directly in the conspiracy to kill Sadat; he only learned about the conspiracy on the morning of the massacre. His crime was inciting armed uprisings in Upper Egypt in the aftermath of the assassination. And like Sheikh Rahman, al-Zawahiri turned his prosecution into propaganda. Confined to a huge cage in the courtroom with other defendants, al-Zawahiri, fluent in English, gave an impassioned impromptu speech proclaiming the faith: "Now we want to speak to the whole world. Who are we? We are Muslims. We are Muslims who believe in our religion. . . . We are not sorry for what we have done for our religion, and we have sacrificed, and we stand ready to make more sacrifices."[23] An Egyptian court convicted al-Zawahiri and sentenced him to three years' imprisonment. Al-Zawahiri went free in 1984, and in 1985 he fled Egypt for Afghanistan as leader of Egyptian Islamic Jihad. It was there he met Osama bin Laden, before bin Laden became a major figure among the Arab-Afghans and before he established the Base, Al Qaeda. In time al-Zawahiri effectively merged Egyptian Islamic Jihad with Al Qaeda, but terror operations against Egypt did not cease. In 1999, another Egyptian court sentenced al-Zawahiri, and his brother Mohammed, to death in absentia for conspiracy to assassinate Egyptian leaders, including an attempt on the life Hosni Mubarak in Ethiopia in 1995.[24]

Sadat's assassination shocked U.S. policy-makers, but it did not awaken them to the threat that the United States was actually feeding and arming in Afghanistan. In 1981, the Reagan administration made allies with the same mujahideen who killed Egypt's pharaoh because they also killed Russians. The United States could not see beyond the immediate challenges cluttering the path of U.S. foreign policy. And, after Sadat's murder, those challenges surged in Lebanon.

Operation Peace for Galilee

Sadat's assassination gave the world its first glimpse at the Islamist terror that would kill in the name of piety with utter ruthlessness for the remainder of the twentieth century and ignite a global war on terror in the twenty-first. The world would see it next in Lebanon, although, ironically, the catalyst for the surge of Islamist violence was an act of terror by a secular terror organization, Abu Nidal's Fatah-Revolutionary Council. Abu Nidal committed his most consequential act of terror on

3 June 1982, when his assassins shot Shlomo Argov, the Israeli envoy in London, leaving him paralyzed. The attack provided the Israelis with the justification Menachem Begin's Likud government had been seeking to set into motion the invasion of Lebanon that the IDF had been meticulously planning for months. The provocation damaged the PLO's careful effort to recast itself as a responsible party deserving U.S. recognition, a fact that has always aroused suspicion that Abu Nidal's organization was manipulated by Israeli intelligence.

In an exchange with a journalist three years after the Argov incident three years later and on the eve of airport attacks in Rome and Vienna, Abu Nidal casually acknowledged that "the Israelis looked for an excuse to invade and the assassination of the ambassador was the spark they needed."

"Arafat said that you were an agent for the Israelis and you caused them to invade Lebanon; that you were, in a way, working for them."

"You know what Arafat says sometimes makes me laugh."

But Abu Nidal, the supreme rejectionist, had his own rationale. He told his interviewer the Israeli embassy in London was the center of the Mossad's European operations and that Argov was a Mossad agent. Nidal, who took pleasure in being "the ghost which walks through the night," vowed to strike at the British, the Americans, anyone who supported Zionism, and "every Arab or Palestinian who had contact with the Mossad."[25] There is another possibility. Abu Nidal was operating from Baghdad when his assassins shot Argov. Iraq was mired in its war with Iran, and Saddam Hussein was desperate to find an exit strategy. In the contorted logic of the Middle East conflict, provoking Israel to attack the PLO in Lebanon could have forced the Arab states to settle the Iran-Iraq War in order to unite the faithful against the Zionist aggressor. If that was the stratagem, it failed.

The day after the assassination attempt on Shlomo Argov in London, Israeli warplanes streaked into action over Lebanon and began pounding PLO positions in preparation for an invasion. The Israeli ground offensive began on 6 June 1982, the fifteenth anniversary of Israel's pre-emptive strike that gave Israel victory in six days of fighting in 1967. But Operation Peace for Galilee would be different from the Six Day War. Israel's first all-out war against the Palestinians would take ten weeks, not six days, and would cost Israel 368 killed in action and more than 2,300 wounded. More Israelis would die before Israeli troops finally withdrew from Lebanon in June 2000, eighteen years after Begin launched Operation Peace for Galilee. The Israeli invasion would also compel the United States to deploy troops in Lebanon. And Americans would die there. Almost as many Americans as Israelis would die in Lebanon—291 Americans, Marines, and sailors, embassy officials, CIA agents, and ordinary citizens—as a consequence of the Israeli war for peace in Galilee. The PLO would lose nearly twice as many. But Lebanese and Palestinian civilians bore the brunt of the offensive, with nearly 18,000 dead, among them the victims of a horrific massacre in the Sabra and Shatila refugee camps.[26]

The code name for the invasion was a misnomer. The real purpose of Operation Peace for Galilee was not to drive PLO artillery batteries from the border where they were shelling Israel's northern settlements but to annihilate the PLO. And to accomplish that the Israelis would have to march on Beirut. But the Begin government, which had been planning the operation for months, needed a provocation. Ronald Reagan saw this clearly: "Begin, who believed in the biblical maxim of 'an eye for an eye,' and his defense minister, Ariel Sharon, a bellicose man who seemed to be chomping at the bit to start a war, were preparing for a full-scale invasion of Lebanon, waiting for the slightest provocation to launch it."[27] If at first Arafat and senior PLO military and political leaders did not grasp Israel's real war aims, the scale of the operation and the IDF willingness to incur heavy casualties soon convinced them that Israel intended to lay siege to the Lebanese capital. Before Operation Peace for Galilee, Israel's triumphs came in days rather than weeks, and the United Nations, the United States, and the international community invariably intervened to halt the fighting. But this time things would be different.

The Israelis met tenacious resistance in southern Lebanon from the PLO factions and the Lebanese National Movement, a loose coalition of leftist, nationalist, Muslim, and Druze parties originally formed prior to the first Lebanese civil war in 1975–1976.[28] PLO and LNM formations engaged the IDF in fierce combat around Sidon and Khaldeh, south of the Beirut international airport where U.S. Marines would later deploy, but they could do no more than slow the Israeli's advance on Beirut because of Israel's overwhelming military superiority. On 9 June, the Israeli air force dealt a devastating blow to Syrian air defenses in the Bekaa Valley, simultaneously bringing Syria into the war and ensuring its eventual defeat. That same day Reagan wrote Begin to express his concern about the escalation in fighting: "I am extremely concerned by the latest reports of additional advances of Israel into Lebanon and the escalation of violence between Israel and Syria." But foremost in Reagan's mind was the possibility of Soviet intervention. Reagan had just received a note from Brezhnev expressing the Soviet leader's concerns for Syria, the Soviet Union's ally. Reagan urged the Israelis to accept a cease-fire effective on the morning of 10 June, then ended with a warning: "Menachem, a refusal by Israel to accept a ceasefire will aggravate further the serious threat to world peace and will create extreme tension in our relations."[29] Begin did not heed Reagan's appeal. In coming weeks and months Israel's disregard for its staunchest ally's concerns would cost American lives.

The Israelis pressed ahead with their advance and took Khaldeh on 12 June. The following day Israeli forces arrived at the gates of Beirut. For the next two months, the IDF and their ally, the Maronite Christian Lebanese Forces, laid siege to the Lebanese capital. The Israelis never mounted a full-scale assault on the city. Beirut's defenders repulsed forays by IDF armored and infantry units around the siege parameter. Rather than incurring the costs of urban combat, Israeli defense minister Ariel Sharon ordered an artillery and air bombardment. With Beirut isolated, the Israelis began a fierce battle to wrest control of the Shouf mountains above Beirut in the east from Syrian forces and Druze militias. By 26 June, the IDF had defeated Syrian forces in the Shouf, and Syria agreed to a ceasefire, leaving Israel free to prosecute its war on the PLO. On 6 August, the Israelis began a continuous six-day bombardment of Beirut. President Reagan later wrote that this "new and even more brutal attack on civilian neighborhoods sickened me."[30] The Israeli bombardment ended on 12 August when Arafat agreed to evacuate the PLO from Beirut under the protection of a multinational force.

Arafat's decision was forced on him. The Israelis had driven the Palestinian leadership from Lebanon. These were the circumstances that in the past produced acts of terror. And they came. The day before Arafat announced his decision to evacuate Beirut, a small Palestinian faction, the 15 May Organization, struck out thousands of miles from the fighting in Lebanon. The 15 May Organization was a small terrorist cell with origins in Wadi Haddad's PFLP Special Apparatus. Wadi Haddad died in 1978, but some of his disciples carried on his work. One man to claim Haddad's mantle was Muhammad al-Umari. Al-Umari, who took Abu Ibrahim as his nom de guerre, formed the 15 May Organization in 1979. The name commemorates the date of the founding of Israel. Over the next two years, the 15 May Organization carried out a series of bombings in London, Rome, Athens, West Berlin, and Vienna. Abu Ibrahim's chief accomplice was a skilled bomb maker, Mohammed Rashid. Now Rashid turned on civilian aviation. On 11 August, Mohammed Rashid boarded Pan Am flight 830 from Tokyo to Honolulu with his wife and child—and a bomb—then deplaned during a stopover.[31] Rashid concealed the bomb under his seat. The jet was on its final approach into Honolulu when the bomb exploded, blasting a hole in the plane's fuselage. The explosion killed one passenger, a fifteen-year-old Japanese boy, and wounded fourteen others, but the jet remained airworthy. It was an act devoid of any purpose. The death of a boy or even the death of all the passengers aboard the jet several miles above the earth and thousands of miles from the frontline in Beirut could accomplish nothing to relieve the military pressure on the PLO.

Palestinian militants had attacked airplanes before, after the Israelis inflicted military defeats on them or diplomats sat down to discuss peace. Wadi Haddad began the assault on civilian aviation after the Six Day War; Ahmed Jabril's PFLP-General Command destroyed Swissair flight 330 in flight in February 1970; Abd al-Ghafur's National Arab Youth for the Liberation of Palestine destroyed TWA 841 over the Ionian Sea in September 1974. There had been other attempts to destroy airliners with bombs and even surface-to-air missiles. Now the 15 May Organization, with Mohammed Rashid acting as its chief terrorist, adopted the tactic. The bombing of Pan Am 830 was the first of a series of attempts at sabotage. The others failed. On 25 August, two weeks after the bombing of Pan Am 830 and the day after U.S. peacekeepers went ashore in Beirut to supervise the evacuation of the PLO, security personnel discovered a bomb concealed below a seat on another Pan Am flight from Miami soon after its arrival in Rio de Janeiro, Brazil. Then, in December 1983, Rashid managed to get a bomb aboard an El Al flight from London to Tel Aviv. Fuad Shara, an accomplice who later testified against Rashid, had convinced a British woman to carry a bag containing a bomb aboard the plane. But, the bomb failed to explode. Security personnel later discovered and diffused it.[32] Rashid disappeared for some time after that, until April 1986 when he bombed again.

The day after the Pan Am 830 bombing, Arafat and the senior PLO leaders accepted the U.S. envoy's plan for the evacuation of the Palestinian fedayeen under the protection of a Multinational Force (MNF) composed of French, Italian, and U.S, forces. Thirteen days later, the French contingent of the multinational force arrived to oversee the evacuation of the PLO. A battalion of Marines went ashore four days after that and, except for a few critical days, would remain in Lebanon for eighteen turbulent months. When the Marines finally withdrew from Lebanon on 26 February 1984, the Corps had suffered its worst day of casualties since the Second World War and Americans living and working in Lebanon would be swept up in the maelstrom of violence Operation Peace for Galilee had stirred up.

Ronald Reagan must have believed that U.S. intervention created an opportunity for peace. On 1 September, nine days before the PLO completed its evacuation, Reagan announced a peace plan that would bear his name. The Reagan plan called for a "fresh start," but in substance the Reagan plan offered the Palestinians only limited autonomy on the West Bank and Gaza after a five-year transition period, despite Reagan's acknowledgement that the Camp David Accords had "recognized the legitimate rights of the Palestinian people." Like the Rogers Plan enunciated by the Nixon administration or Kissinger's Jordanian Option, which it resembled, the Reagan plan was bound to go nowhere. To the president's dismay, the Israeli cabinet unanimously rejected it even before it was made public.[33] Then, America's presence in Lebanon took a dangerous turn.

Sabra and Shatila

Ronald Reagan was eager to withdraw the Marines from Beirut. As soon as the PLO evacuated the Lebanese capital, Reagan ordered the Marines back to the safety of the ships anchored in the Mediterranean. That was not the end of American involvement. U.S. and Israeli interests in a stable Lebanon depended on the establishment of a government favorable to those interests. The Americans and the Israelis believed they found the man to lead just such a government. On 23 August, the Lebanese parliament elected Bashir Gemayel president in a preordained act that did nothing to pacify the country. Gemayel, the leader of the Christian Phalange and son of the movement's founder, was Israel's and the United States' choice as the man to guide a renewed Lebanon towards the West. But Reagan withdrew the Marine peacekeeping contingent on 10 September, before Gemayel took office, without consultation with the Italians or the French, who contributed troops to the MNF. Four days after the Americans returned to their ships, the remainder of the MNF abandoned Beirut to its fate. The consequences were immediate. On 14 September, a Syrian agent planted a bomb in the apartment building directly above the room where president-elect Gemayel was holding a meeting of his closest associates. The blast brought the building down, killing Gemayel and killing or wounding more than eighty others.[34] Syria sent an unambiguous message that its interests in Lebanon were to be taken seriously. (The Lebanese parliament reacted by selecting Amin Gemayel, the assassinated president-elect's brother, president.) The next evening, vengeful Phalangists went on the killing rampage that everyone anticipated—and that the multinational force had presumably been deployed to avert.

In reaction to the Gemayel assassination, IDF entered Beirut on 15 September in violation of the cease-fire agreement and Israel's pledge to the United States. The next evening the Israelis sent the Phalange into two sprawling refugee camps in search of the PLO fedayeen Israeli intelligence claimed remained behind. Over the next forty-eight hours, Sabra and Shatila became killing grounds. Journalists, some of whom had been covering the Lebanese tragedy since the 1975–76 civil war, entered the camps on the morning of the eighteenth and gave the world the first descriptions of the carnage. There were hundreds of dead:

"they were everywhere . . . there were women lying in houses, with their skirts torn up to their waists and their legs wide apart, children with their throats cut, rows of young men shot in the back after being lined up at an execution wall. There were babies."[35] No one knows with certainty the number of Palestinians slaughtered in Sabra and Shatila, but it was no fewer than 700 and perhaps three times that many.

Israel's complicity in the massacres is beyond reasonable doubt. Israeli soldiers transported the Phalangist militiamen to Sabra and Shatila, and they were present just outside the camps throughout the massacre. U.S. diplomats informed the Israelis about the massacre while the Phalangists were in the act of committing it. Morris Draper, an U.S. diplomat, confronted an Israeli attached to the foreign ministry with the truth at ten o'clock Saturday morning: "You must stop the massacres. They are obscene. I have an officer in there counting bodies . . . they are killing children. You are in absolute control of the area and you are therefore responsible for that area."[36] What resistance was offered belied Israeli claims that as many as 2,000 PLO fighters hid in Sabra and Shatila. The same men who engaged the Israelis in fierce fighting in the first week of Operation Peace for Galilee then halted the IDF at the gates of Beirut would certainly have inflicted heavy losses on the relatively small number of Phalangists who moved around the camps for more than two days.

An Israeli commission inquiry chaired by the president of the Israeli Supreme Court later concluded that senior officials in the Israeli government bore "indirect" responsibility for Sabra and Shatila, because the Israeli leadership was "obligated to foresee . . . that the phalangists would commit massacres and pogroms against the inhabitants of the camps." The commission reproached Prime Minister Menachem Begin and Ariel Sharon, his defense minister: Begin because his lack of involvement in the decision-making process "cast on him a certain degree of responsibility," Sharon because the possibility of a massacre "did not concern him in the least."[37] Ronald Reagan said publicly that he was "horrified" by the killings of the Palestinians, and he summoned the Israeli ambassador to "demand that the Israeli government immediately withdraw its forces from West Beirut." Reagan did not mention that his envoy, Philip Habib, had given the PLO verbal assurances about the safety of the Palestinians left behind in the camps, but Habib has acknowledged that Americans gave those assurances.[38] The president would say only that "during the negotiations leading to the PLO withdrawal from Beirut, we were assured that Israeli forces would not enter West Beirut." But Reagan did blame the Israelis: "Israel, by yesterday in military control of Beirut, claimed that its moves would prevent the kind of tragedy that has now occurred." Coming only weeks after Reagan unveiled his peace plan for the Middle East, the atrocity threatened to undermine U.S. diplomacy as much as any act of Palestinian terror. The atrocity at Sabra and Shatila compelled Ronald Reagan to order the Marines to return to Beirut—and into harm's way. Sending the Marines back into Beirut, Reagan wrote later, was the source of his "greatest regret and greatest sorrow."[39]

America's Presence

The Marines deployed at the Beirut International Airport on 29 September and hunkered down for a mission encrypted in a single word—"presence"—not found in the Corps lexicon.[40] Ronald Reagan told the nation he had sent the Marines back to Beirut to enable "the Lebanese government to restore full sovereignty over its capital, the essential precondition for extending its control over the entire country." He came closer to the truth in his memoir writing that the purpose of the mission was "to help keep the peace and to free the Lebanese army to go after the various militias and warlords who were terrorizing the country." Then he acknowledged that it was "a moral commitment to Israel that originally sent our marines to Lebanon." The president expected that the Marines' mere presence would keep the peace and, without sensing the contradiction, allowed the Lebanese army to go after the various militias. But Reagan remained convinced of U.S. neutrality: "We never had the intention of getting involved in Lebanon's civil war." The Israelis, unlike the Americans, whom they would draw into the conflict, did not equivocate. The Israeli high command informed the Israeli troops that "the main goal of the Israelis in Lebanon is to secure the existence of the Christians and to make possible a political arrangement that will enable Lebanon to recover its sovereignty."[41] The Israelis at least acknowledged the mission was defense of the Christians in Lebanon's civil war; the Americans remained oblivious to that reality. So, the Marines were left to interpret the mission, then suffer the consequences when the White House changed the mission on them.

"Presence as a mission is not in any military dictionary," the Marine Corps commandant told a congressional committee investigating the disaster that later befell the Marines. "I guess the best description is that we are a visible manifestation of U.S. strength and resolve to Lebanon and the free world."[42] Thus the Americans were drawn into a labyrinth of sectarian violence that erupted into open warfare after the Israeli invasion and the evacuation of the PLO. It was inevitable that the Americans would lose their way. In fact, the Marines entered an environment that was rapidly turning hostile, because America's new archenemy—the Islamic Republic of Iran—chose to punish the United States in Beirut. As 1982 drew to a close, a new, even more militant force began to take shape among Lebanon's long-suffering Shi'a. Within months the Marines found themselves confronted with adherents of a militant Islam who lived just beyond their gate.

The Marines' mission was not a classic military mission, and the location of their deployment was a military nightmare. The Beirut International Airport sits beside the Mediterranean Sea south of Beirut in the shadow of the Shouf Mountains to the east. There was only one point on the compass, west, where a small U.S. armada stood off shore, where the Marines' flank was secure. The airport remained open, except when fighting erupted and incoming artillery, mortars, or rockets forced suspension of flights. The Lebanese armed forces were nominally responsible for airport security. Civilians came and went. The IDF controlled the area to the south of the airport and in the Shouf Mountains, and transported men and materiel to the Shouf along a road running adjacent to the airport. Confrontations between Americans and Israelis were inevitable. The Marines were determined to maintain their neutrality until the moment the White House destroyed it. The Israelis were determined to cross through U.S. lines to pursue the guerrillas that ambushed their convoys. Tensions between the Marines and the IDF culminated in February when a Marine captain drew his weapon on an Israeli tank commander who tried to lead an armored column past the Marines' position. The situation to the east in the Shouf Mountains was even more critical. As long as the Israelis commanded the heights overlooking Beirut and the airport, the Marines were relatively secure. That would change in September 1983, when the Israelis hastily withdrew from the Shouf, prompting warring factions to fight for control of the ridgeline and leaving the Americans dangerously exposed. To the north, just outside the airport parameter, sat Hay es Salaam, a Shi'a village that did not even appear on the Marine Corps maps. The Marines called it Hooterville. Hay es Salaam was terra incognita. A Marine lieutenant colonel, who commanded one of the Marines' Battalion Landing Teams that rotated in and out of Lebanon, expressed the frustration: "my [intelligence officer] can tell me what's going on in the Bekaa Valley and he can tell me what's going on in Tripoli [but] we have no foggy idea of what's going on right outside our gate . . . we have no capability [of] understanding how those people out there are feeling about us."[43] Within a year the Marines would come to understand the depth of the feelings about them, when one of those Shi'a crashed through the Marines' gate.

Hizb'allah

Shi'a militancy was born of a centuries-old sense of oppression and subjugation. Outcast as virtual heretics by the dominant Sunni sect of Islam, the Shi'a minority felt embattled even in Muslim countries with Shi'a enclaves, Iraq and, most of all, Lebanon. The Lebanese national accord divided power between the Maronite Christians and the Sunni Muslims but ignored the Shi'a. The Druze were nearly as marginalized, but they at least had an enclave in the Shouf Mountains. The Lebanese Shi'a were fatalistic about their status until 1974, when their spiritual leader called on them to awaken. Musa al-Sadr was born in Qom, Iran's holy city; he studied Islam in the Shi'a's holiest city, Najjaf, in Iraq. He became a spiritual leader—the imam—of the Lebanese Shi'a in 1959. Al-Sadr witnessed the disintegration of Lebanon's social compact and the subjugation of Lebanon's Shi'a. In 1974, Imam al-Sadr formed the Organization of the Disinherited and the following year, after the Lebanese civil war erupted, he formed the Lebanese Resistance Battalions, whose acronym, Amal, is Arabic for "hope."[44] The PLO trained Amal militiamen, but there was friction between Arafat's secular Palestinian national movement and al-Sadr's Lebanese Shi'a movement. The PLO's omnipresence in the heavily Shi'a south Lebanon was a cause for friction. Another was the PLO's operations against Israel—the civilian Shi'a population inevitably bore the brunt of Israeli military retaliation. The Shi'a suffered greatly when Menachem Begin launched Litani in 1978. That same year, al-Sadr toured Arab states in search of material and moral support. The tour ended in Muammar Qaddafi's Libya where the imam mysteriously disappeared. The speculation was that Qaddafi ordered his murder, possibly because Qaddafi viewed al-Sadr's Amal more as a rival than an ally of the Palestinian extremists Libya financed. After al-Sadr's disappearance, Nabih Berri assumed leadership of Amal, but Berri was an attorney, not a cleric. And, Nabih Berri was a moderate who ascended to the leadership of a Shi'a movement at a moment the Shi'a were about to turn militant.

The Israeli invasion ignited the Shi'a militancy that would pose the threat outside the Marines' gate at the Beirut International Airport. The Shi'a did not rise to the PLO's defense when the Israelis came to destroy Palestinian guerrillas because the Shi'a regarded the PLO as a menace. But the Shi'a would eventually rise up, after Israel's military operation became a military occupation and the Americans' presence became U.S. intervention—and after the Iranians arrived in Lebanon to organize a jihad. The Ayatollah Khomeini reacted immediately to Israel's invasion of Lebanon by sending a contingent of Revolutionary Guards, Pasadran, to train Lebanese Shi'a. Two senior Iranian clerics oversaw the clandestine operation: Ayatollah Ali Akbar Mohtashemi, Iran's ambassador to Syria, and Ayatollah Hussein Ali Montazeri, director of the Department of Islamic Liberation Movements.[45] Some 1,500 Pasadran—almost the same number as the Marines at the Beirut International Airport—

arrived in Baalbeck in the northern Bekaa Valley in June. This was Syrian controlled territory. Hafez al-Asad, the Syrian president, had his motives for permitting the Iranians to begin training mujahideen for terror operations. Violence against the Israelis and the multinational force served Syrian interests in Lebanon. And, Syria's cooperation with Iran was an extension of Syria's enmity toward Iraq, which was now in the second year of its catastrophic war with Iran. By the end of 1982, the Iranians succeeded in radicalizing the Lebanese Shi'a, first in the Bekaa, then in Beirut, and finally in southern Lebanon. The signs were almost immediate. In June, the month Israel invaded, Amal's spokesman, Hussein al-Musawi, publicly broke with the movement's moderate leader, Nabih Berri, and formed Islamic Amal. (Terry Anderson, the Associated Press Beirut bureau chief whom Shi'a radicals would hold hostage for seven full years, had deep impressions of al-Musawi: "this man," he wrote after his release from captivity, "is evil.")[46] This was the visible deepening radicalization. Less visible was the Iranian effort to form an entirely new clandestine organization whose allegiance to Ayatollah Khomeini was absolute and whose purpose was to mount a jihad against Israel and the United States—Hizb'allah, the Party of God.

Hizb'allah existed by the end of the 1982, and it launched a jihad early in 1983. But Hizb'allah was veiled in an impenetrable secrecy. It did not publicly proclaim its own existence until the anniversary of the Sabra and Shatila massacres in 1984. Instead, it claimed acts under a host of names: Islamic Jihad, the Revolutionary Justice Organization, the Organization of the Oppressed of the Earth, and others. Its original spiritual guide, Sheikh Mohammed Hussein Fadlallah, has always denied his direct membership in Hizb'allah. Hizb'allah's enmity toward Israel and the United States was theological, but the Reagan administration's strategy in Lebanon—"to free the Lebanese army to go after various militias," as Reagan put it in his memoir—deepened it. The Americans made no secret about their preference for a political order constructed around Maronite president Amin Gemayel. By December, the Marines were training predominantly Maronite Lebanese army units. In the early months of 1983, Reagan's special envoy to Lebanon, Philip Habib, worked to secure an agreement that would lead to the withdrawal of all forces in Lebanon—Israeli, Palestinian, and Syrian. The Israelis pushed for the agreement, because it would entail the withdrawal of Syrian forces and because it would consolidate Amin Gemayel's power. Israel was maneuvering for a peace agreement between Lebanon and Israel that would have the symbolic, although not the military, importance of the separate peace Sadat, the late Egyptian president, had concluded with Israel.[47] Only the Maronites and the Israelis had an interest in the agreement. The Shi'a decided to resort to terror to prevent it. On 15

March, an Italian peacekeeper was killed in an ambush, a day later five Marines were wounded in a grenade on their patrol. The attacks represented an escalation of the dangers, but not a serious military threat. Then, exactly one month and two days later, the United States had its first horrifying experience with the mass-casualty terror attacks Islamist militants would mount against Americans for the next twenty years.

A few minutes after 1 P.M. on 18 April 1983, a suicide attacker drove a van laden with 2,000 pounds of explosives past a Lebanese sentry into the lobby of the U.S. embassy in Beirut and detonated it. The concussion shook Beirut, threw a sheet of flame and cloud of dense smoke hundreds of feet into sky, and tore off a section of the façade of a seven-story building. It was devastation: 63 people were killed by the blast or crushed beneath the rubble, 46 Lebanese and 17 Americans.[48] The day of the attack someone called various news agencies and claimed the attack in the name of Islamic Jihad.

The suicide bombing of the U.S. embassy devastated the United States intelligence capabilities in Lebanon at the very moment the Marines at the airport desperately needed to understand what was going on outside their gate. Among the bodies pulled from the embassy wreckage were those of Robert Ames, the CIA's chief Middle East intelligence analyst, and eight of his colleagues. It was Ames who, a decade earlier, had initiated contact with Ali Hassan Salameh, the Red Prince, in an effort reach an accommodation between the Americans and Arafat's Fatah. Now both men were dead. The Israelis killed Salameh with a car bomb in January 1979, ending one era of Middle East terror. When Hizb'allah killed Ames with a car bomb it opened another.

The car bomb that destroyed the U.S. embassy was not the first to explode in Beirut. What set the embassy car bombing apart was not that it was mass murder, but that it was a lone suicide. From that moment on, Americans had to contend with the zealotry of men whose religious faith inspired them to martyrdom.[49] But even for Hizb'allah clerics who found justifications for jihad in Islamic jurisprudence, suicide attacks forced a reexamination of religious doctrine, because Islam prohibits suicide.[50] Islamist clerics evaded the prohibition by redefining the ignoble act of suicide as the noble acceptance of martyrdom: death in the act of killing the enemies of religion differs not at all from death in battle against a numerically superior force when joining the battle means certain death. The infusion of this belief into Hizb'allah operational doctrine was more portentous than the introduction of the vehicle bomb in the arsenal of terror. Now, religion imposed no moral constraints either on killing others or killing oneself; to the contrary, suicide terrorists could find inspiration in Islamist teachings beckoning martyrs to the pleasures of paradise.[51] The ideology of liberation became transformed into the theology of death.

These were the ideas behind the suicide bombing of the U.S. embassy and even more devastating suicide attacks to come. But there was a man behind the embassy attack—Imad Fayez Mugniyah.[52] Mugniyah personified the transfiguration of secular Palestinian terrorism into terror of militant Islam. Born in 1962 in southern Lebanon, Mugniyah was the son of a Shi'a cleric. In his late teens, Mugniyah enlisted in Arafat's Fatah and soon made his way into the elite security detachment, Force 17. Mugniyah was a subordinate to Ali Hassan Salameh. The personal connection is ironic: Mugniyah, the Red Prince's lieutenant, organized the operation that killed Robert Ames, the Red Prince's CIA contact. This was the shift in the winds of international terror that the United States was slow to discern. After the Israeli invasion of Lebanon, Mugniyah changed allegiances. Instead of evacuating Beirut with the PLO, Mugniyah stayed behind. When the Iranian Revolutionary Guards arrived to mobilize the mujahideen, Mugniyah gravitated toward the nascent Hizb'allah. His expertise in security made him invaluable. Mugniyah became head of the Hizb'allah security apparatus, responsible for Sheikh Fadlallah's safety and the Party of God's terror operations. And Mugniyah became one of America's most dangerous adversaries—and the world's most lethal terrorists—over the next decade. He killed Americans with massive vehicle bombs twice more in Lebanon, in October in the worst attack on Americans until 9/11, and again in September 1984. Then he turned to hostage-taking and airline hijacking.

Mugniyah lost two brothers to the violence in Lebanon. One, whose name, Jihad, captured the family's spirit of Shi'a militancy, was killed in a massive car bomb explosion in 1985 outside a Beirut mosque. The bomb was intended to kill Sheikh Fadlallah, Hizb'allah's spiritual guide. The CIA, the Mossad, and Saudi Arabian intelligence have always denied claims of their collective involvement of the bombing that killed eighty-five and precipitated a new wave of hostage-taking.[53] Nine years later, in 1994, another car bomb killed Mugniyah's brother Fuad. This was a Mossad operation intended to kill Imad, not his brother. When the Mossad killed the wrong man, operatives laid a trap for Mugniyah at his brother's funeral, but he knew better than to attend.

Few Americans knew Imad Mugniyah's name, because in the 1980s U.S. officials publicly declared Abu Nidal the world's most dangerous terrorist. But Imad Mugniyah killed more Americans in a single act of terror than Abu Nidal and all terrorists combined managed to kill during all the years of Middle East terrorism, until 9/11. After Hizb'allah freed the last U.S. hostage in 1991, Mugniyah became a critical actor in the World Islamic Front for Jihad against Jews and Crusaders, as the net-work of Islamist terror organizations called itself. Mugniyah was behind two murderous car bombings in Argentina, one in 1992 that killed 28 and another in 1994 that killed 85. Then, Mugniyah entered the orbit of two men who formed Al Qaeda's senior leadership, Osama bin Laden and Ayman al-Zawahiri. There has been speculation of his involvement in terror attacks linked to Al Qaeda, such as the 1996 attack on the Kho-bar Towers in Dahran, Saudi Arabia.[54] U.S. intelligence came close to capturing Mugniyah at least twice, once in 1986 when Mugniyah passed through Charles de Gaulle airport in Paris, and again in 1995 in Jeddah, Saudi Arabia. French authorities declined the CIA's appeals for permis-sion to apprehend Mugniyah while in Paris, concerned that Mugniyah's arrest on French soil would imperil the lives of French hostages in Leba-non. Nine years later, Saudi officials prevented Mugniyah's capture after the FBI had learned Mugniyah was aboard a flight from Khartoum to Beirut with a stopover in Jeddah. The Saudis saw the wisdom of avoiding trouble and refused the plane permission to put down in Saudi Arabia.[55] The April bombing of the U.S. embassy was Mugniyah's first major oper-ation, but it was neither his last nor his most deadly. By the time the Americans could bury their dead, Mugniyah was already planning his next operation.

The embassy bombing drove the Reagan administration to achieve a political settlement in Lebanon that conformed to United States and Israeli strategic interests. From the beginning, Washington was blind to the error of its assumptions about the ability of the Gemayel government to exercise authority over Lebanon or ever implement an agreement with Israel. Now the administration pressed ahead with its diplomatic efforts in the belief that a reassessment of its Lebanon policy would be to yield to terrorism and dishonor the slain Americans. Prime Minister Begin would realize the futility of his efforts before Reagan. In the first week of September, Begin ordered a hasty Israeli withdrawal from the Shouf to more secure positions in southern Lebanon. Two weeks later, a grieving and war-weary Begin resigned office. Reagan would eventually order the termination of the Marines' mission, but not until February 1984, after the Marines suffered the consequences of the Reagan admin-istration's fallacies. But initially, the American determination to succeed produced the appearance of success. On 17 May, near enough to the anniversary of the founding of Israel to make it an act of contempt for Muslims, President Gemayel signed his name to agreement that suppos-edly ended the state of war with Israel. But forces opposed to the agree-ment soon proved Gemayel's government did not rule Lebanon.

The Marine Barracks Bombing

In June, the Marines and the Lebanese Armed Forces, which the Marines had begun to train back in December, began to conduct joint patrols. The new Marine commander, Colonel Timothy Geraghty, the fourth man to assume command there, must have had a premonition of gathering dangers because that same month he ordered an exercise: the evacuation of mass casualties suffered in an attack on the Marines at the airport. In July, the Lebanese Armed Forces and Walid Jumblatt's Druze militia began exchanging fire near the airport. Americans came under fire as artillery and stray mortar rounds fell near their position, but these were not deliberate attacks on the Americans. That changed at the end of August when Marines began coming under heavy mortar attacks. Colonel Geraghty, concerned for the safety of his Marines, ordered another 150 of them to move into the five-story building housing the Battalion Landing Team headquarters, bringing the total of Marines and Navy personnel bunked there to more than 300, one quarter of the Marines at the airport. On the twenty-ninth, the Marines returned fire for the first time. Two Marines were killed in the firefight.[56] By September, the Marines' mission as well as their position at the airport became untenable.

The Israeli withdrawal from the Shouf came on 4 September. Then hell broke loose. Maronite and Druze forces rushed into the breach to gain tactical advantage in the mountains. On the sixth, intense fighting spilled over and Druze fire from the Shouf killed two more Americans at the airport. On the eighth, a U.S. warship, the USS *Bowen*, fired on the Druze artillery position in the Shouf that had fired down at the Marines at the airport. Eight days later, the USS *Bowen* and the USS *John Rodgers* opened fire to defend the Marines. Then on the nineteenth, the Americans crossed the line that separates defense of the Marines at the airport from support of the Maronite Christians in combat operations against the Druze and Muslims. On the morning of the nineteenth, the commander of the Lebanese Armed Forces alerted the military aide of Reagan's new special envoy to Lebanon, Robert "Bud" McFarlane, to a desperate battle for control of Shuq al-Gharb, a village in the Shouf Mountains. Unless the Americans intervened, he told him, the Shouf would fall to hostile forces and imperil the Gemayel's presidential palace and the Marines at the airport. McFarlane, a former Marine lieutenant colonel who had replaced a dispirited Philip Habib as special envoy to Lebanon, advised President Reagan to authorize U.S. intervention. When Reagan gave the order, Colonel Timothy Geraghty, the Marine commander on the ground, was stunned. He told McFarlane that an attack on the Druze in support of the Christians "will cost us our neutrality." The protest came with a warning, "Don't you realize that if you do that we'll get slaughtered down here?" Neither the president nor his special envoy paid Geraghty any heed.[57] That same day, the nineteenth, the USS *John Rodgers* and the USS *Virginia* fired 360 rounds of high explosives in a five-hour naval bombardment of the Shouf. The U.S. navy opened fire again on the twenty-first and the twenty-third. But by then the Americans had become combatants.[58]

The Marine Commandant, General P. X. Kelly, later told a congressional committee "our naval gunfire support for the LAF [Lebanese army] [could have] increased Moslem perception that our Marines were pro-Christian and no longer neutral." The president of the United States had ignored the consequences of that possibility. Reagan noted in his diary that the expansion "of our mission to aid the Lebanese army with artillery and air support . . . could be seen as putting us in the war." But a week later, on 19 September, Reagan dismissed the perception and ordered the five-hour bombardment of Shuq al-Gharb. "Our Navy guns turned loose in support of the Lebanese army fighting to hold a position on a hill overlooking our Marines at the Beirut airport," Reagan wrote. He then added: "This still comes under the head of defense."[59] But only Ronald Reagan saw it that way. Exactly thirty-seven days later, just as Colonel Geraghty had warned, wrathful mujahideen slaughtered Marines at the Beirut International Airport.

At 2:00 A.M. on Sunday, 23 October, Robert McFarlane woke Ronald Reagan, who was vacationing at the Augusta National Golf Club in Georgia, with news of the Marines' worst day of casualties since the Second World War.[60] Reagan had combat on his mind. That morning he had intended to review contingency plans for Operation Urgent Fury, an invasion of the tiny Caribbean island of Grenada, where dissident Marxists had overthrown the government and American medical students were in danger of being taken hostage or killed. (Two days later, on 25 October, Reagan ordered U.S. troops, including the 22nd Marine Amphibious Unit, which was en route to relieve Colonel Geraghty's Marines in Beirut, to invade Grenada.) But on that morning, news of conflict came from a different quarter.

On the other side of the world from the Augusta National Gulf Club, Lance Corporals Eddie Di Franco and Henry Linkkila were at their separate posts in front of the Marine Battalion Landing Team headquarters at Beirut International Airport when they saw a yellow Mercedes truck enter the airport parking lot in front of their position.[61] The truck circled the parking lot twice and disappeared. It was just after dawn. The truck reappeared an hour later. This time it circled the parking lot once, gathered speed, then tore through a wire fence and sped directly toward the Marine's BLT headquarters. The Mercedes was moving at more than fifty miles per hour when it passed between the two Marines' posts. Di Franco caught a glimpse of the suicide attacker as he sped by his position, "He looked right at me, smiled, that's it." Linkkila struggled to put a magazine into his weapon, but never managed to fire it. In just seconds the truck crashed through the sandbags at the sentry post directly in front of BLT headquarters and into the lobby. An instant later the driver detonated a massive bomb with explosive force of 12,000 pounds of TNT.[62]

From that moment on explosives experts began to speak of conventional weapons of mass destruction. The force of the blast pulverized the concrete-reinforced building. Photographs snapped an instant after the explosion from miles away captured images of a black column of smoke and dust rising into the clear Beirut sky. The shock jolted Colonel Geraghty and his executive officer from their sleep in the adjacent Marine Amphibious Unit headquarters. They awoke to a nightmare—"a fog of debris . . . a deathly silence"—and the sudden realization that "the BLT building, the headquarters, was gone."[63] And Geraghty's Marines were gone: 241 Marines and sailors died buried in tons of concrete. It was slaughter. Minutes after the explosion tore through the Marine headquarters, another suicide bomber struck the headquarters of French paratroopers assigned to the MNF. That attack killed fifty-eight French soldiers. A month earlier, an armada of U.S. warships laid down a withering five-hour barrage of naval gun fire on Muslim and Druze positions in the Shouf without altering the course of the battle for Lebanon's future. Now, in just seconds, a lone suicide mujahid had devastated the Marine's "presence" in Lebanon. It was a kill ratio of 241:1.

The attack on the Marines at the Beirut International Airport inevitably destroyed Geraghty's career of service to United States. A Department of Defense commission, chaired by retired Navy admiral Robert Long, established to investigate the attack, excoriated the Marine, concluding Geraghty "shares the responsibility for the catastrophic losses" because, among other things, he had moved a quarter of the Marines at the airport into the BLT headquarters.[64] The commission tepidly blamed the administration's decision-making—"U.S. decisions as regards Lebanon over the past fifteen months . . . may have been taken without clear recognition that these initial conditions had dramatically changed and that the expansion of our military involvement in Lebanon greatly increased the risk to, and adversely impacted upon the security of, the USMNF"—but it did not specifically criticize the commander in chief's errors in judgment.[65]

Reagan later wrote that "I wanted to accept full responsibility for the tragedy [because] I was the one who sent them there."[66] But if the president now recognized the consequences of his specific decisions regarding Lebanon, he was oblivious to the consequences of his covert policy of arming the Lebanese mujahideen's brethren in Afghanistan. The idea that the call to jihad against an infidel invader—Soviet or American—unified Muslims throughout the entire Muslim world did not enter U.S. policy-makers' collective consciousness. It would be a decade before a U.S. president would realize the enemy of America's enemy was America's enemy too. The realization could have come much sooner—less than a month after the slaughter of the Marines in Beirut, America's new enemy struck again in Kuwait.

The Al-Dawa Seventeen

On 12 December, Shi'a militants belonging to Hizb al-Dawa al-Islamiyya, the Islamic Call Party, mounted coordinated attacks against their enemies in Kuwait City. In just over ninety minutes, bombs exploded at the U.S. and French embassies, the air traffic control tower at the national airport, Kuwait's principal petroleum refinery, and a housing complex for employees of the defense contractor, the Raytheon corporation. It was a complex and well-coordinated operation whose resemblance to the simultaneous attacks on the U.S. and French MNF contingents in Lebanon indicated the same forces were at work. Simultaneous vehicle bomb attacks were a new tactic, but the operation was larger in scale with twice the number of targets. And, al-Dawa struck at symbols of the Kuwaiti regime, as well as the forces of foreign occupation. The bombs that exploded in Beirut and Kuwait City were identical to the conventional weapons of mass destruction Imad Mugniyah devised for the attack on the Marines—weapons-grade high explosives packed around 45 gas cylinders. The death toll could have been even more catastrophic than the Beirut attacks, but they claimed relatively few casualties—six dead and more than eighty wounded—only because the gas cylinders failed to ignite.[67]

Kuwaiti authorities arrested seventeen al-Dawa militants soon after the attacks. Al-Dawa was an Iraqi Shi'a organization dedicated to the overthrow Saddam Hussein's secular Baath regime in Iraq. Like Hizb'allah in Lebanon, al-Dawa received its support from Iran.[68] The Iraqi dictator ruthlessly suppressed Iraq's Shi'a, who constituted some 60 percent of Iraq's population. Saddam's first decrees against al-Dawa came in 1969, a full decade before Khomeini's revolution in Iran. Saddam Hussein ordered the arrest of al-Dawa's spiritual leader, Muhammad Bakr al-Sadr, no fewer than five times between 1972 and 1979. Al-Sadr's stature deterred Saddam from simply killing the Shi'a cleric, but Iraqi security forces executed hundreds of Shi'a in a series of pogroms. Then, in April 1980, al-Dawa assassinated a senior Baath leader and nearly assassinated

another, Tariq Aziz, the deputy prime minister, who in 1983 would celebrate the restoration of U.S.-Iraq diplomatic relations with Ronald
Reagan in the Oval Office. Saddam had reached the limit of his tolerance. After the attacks, Saddam ordered the arrest and execution of al-
Sadr and his sister. That only intensified al-Dawa's hatred of him. In July
1982, al-Dawa nearly killed Saddam Hussein outside Baghdad during a
two-hour firefight with his security detail. (Saddam Hussein was hanged
on 30 December 2006, three years after his capture by U.S. troops, for
ordering the executions of 148 Shi'a in retaliation for that attempt on
his life.)

With the Kuwait City attacks, the royal family realized it confronted
the same threat Hosni Mubarak confronted in the aftermath of Sadat's
assassination. The Egyptian security forces were already seizing Egyptian
Islamic Jihad militants in massive security sweeps when al-Dawa exploded its bombs. The Kuwaiti authorities also took a hard line, sentencing the men to death for the December attacks. The al-Dawa Seventeen,
as the condemned men came to be called, would not die on the gallows.
Ironically, they escaped prison during Iraq's invasion of Kuwait in 1990.
But while they sat awaiting execution, the al-Dawa Seventeen's Lebanese
brethren would rise to their defense. To liberate them, Lebanese Hiz-
b'allah would seize Americans and hold them under the threat of execution. One of the Seventeen, Mustafa Youssef Badr al-Din, was the cousin
of Hizb'allah's archterrorist, Imad Mugniyah.[69] For Mugniyah, Hizb'allah's archterrorist, the cause of the al-Dawa Seventeen was personal.
America's ordeal in Lebanon was just beginning.

Chapter 7

America Will Never Make Concessions to Terrorists

Ronald Reagan began 1984 without fear that the disasters that befell the Americans in Lebanon in 1983 would ruin his chances for reelection in November. The electorate did not blame errors of presidential judgment for the bombings of the U.S. embassy in April or the slaughter of the Marines in October. More controversial were the administration's policies in Central America, where the United States was arming the Contra rebels in Nicaragua and a brutally repressive government in El Salvador. Reagan's Central American and Middle Eastern policies eventually collided, and much of his second term was consumed by the Iran-Contra scandal after the administration's sale of arms to Iran in exchange for American hostages in Lebanon and the transfer of the profits to the Contras became public. Militant Islam confounded the Reagan administration. The president apparently did not recognize the folly of arming Arab and Afghan mujahideen in Afghanistan while Arab mujahideen were killing and kidnapping Americans in Lebanon and Kuwait. The consequences were catastrophic. Until Reagan intervened in Lebanon after Israel's invasion, terrorists rarely targeted Americans. The murders of U.S. diplomats in Khartoum in 1973 and in Lebanon in 1975 were exceptions. But terrorist attacks against Americans and American interests became frequent during the Reagan years. There were multiple threats. Hizb'allah seized American hostages in Beirut, hijacked American airliners, and bombed the embassy for a second time. Terrorists belonging to Abu Nidal's terrorist-for-hire organization commandeered American airliners, murdered American hostages, and killed Americans in airline terminals. Remnants of Wadi Haddad's terror organization bombed American commercial airliners in flight. And Muammar Qaddafi propelled himself into America's consciousness as the personification of state-sponsored terrorism. Ronald Reagan groped for a policy to subdue these terrorist threats. But Reagan's controversially triumphant presidency ended with a horrific blow against Americans when Muammar Qaddafi, whom Reagan tried to strike dead in April 1986, struck back in December 1988.

The First Hostages

As 1984 began, Ronald Reagan's instincts about Beirut turned from fight to flight. The suicide attacks against the U.S. embassy and the Marine contingent of the ultinational orce killed nearly 300 Americans. Another 27 Marines died in separate incidents from hostile fire while trying to manifest America's presence in Lebanon. A disheartened Reagan finally ordered the Marines out of Lebanon on 26 February, an action that future terrorists would mistake as a sign of U.S. moral weakness. But the withdrawal did not end the hostility toward Americans, it merely shifted its attention. Now Hizb'allah turned against America's citizens instead of its soldiers.

On 18 January 1984, two Hizb'allah militants murdered Malcolm Kerr, president of the American University of Beirut and father of an NBA star, in his office. Shi'a militants had had Kerr and other prominent Americans under surveillance for some time before Shi'a clerics issued the fatwa condemning him to death.[1] Over the next few years U.S. administrators at the prestigious American University in the Lebanese capital would become the prey of Hizb'allah. Kerr had replaced David Dodge, whom Islamic Amal had kidnapped on 19 July 1982, shortly after the Israeli invasion.[2] Dodge's captors released him a year later, in July 1983, just as the Marines were being drawn into Lebanon's sectarian violence. Kerr's murder was the first sign of what would become a violent campaign to force Americans to abandon Lebanon. But after Kerr's murder Hizb'allah returned to abduction.

On 11 February, three weeks after Kerr's murder and a week before the Marine withdrawal, Hizb'allah abducted Frank Regier, an American professor at the American University, and Christian Joubert, a French citizen.[3] Their captivity would last just over a year, until Amal militiamen rescued them on 15 April 1984.[4] Hizb'allah's decision to abduct rather than kill Regier and Joubert signaled a change of objectives. Hizb'allah abducted them in order to gain the release of the al-Dawa prisoners who were set to stand trial in March for the bombings in Kuwait the previous December. Imad Mugniyah, chief of Hizb'allah's terror operations, planned the abductions. For Mugniyah the cause of the al-Dawa defendants was familial as well as confessional: one of the prisoners, Mustafa Youssef Badr al-Din, was Mugniyah's brother-in-law. To Mugniyah's way of thinking, U.S. pressure on Kuwaiti authorities was the key to the safe release of the Shi'a militants. With the trial of the al-Dawa defendants set to begin in March, more abductions were inevitable.

On 7 March, Hizb'allah abducted Jeremy Levin, who managed to escape nearly a year later in February 1985. On 16 March, Mugniyah abducted the man who would be his single most important hostage, William Buckley, as he left his apartment in West Beirut. The Party of God abducted a fourth American, Benjamin Weir, on 8 May, after a Kuwaiti court found seventeen of the al-Dawa defendants guilty and sentenced six of them to death. Levin, Buckley, and Weir were symbolic of America's presence in Lebanon, but in different ways. Levin was the Cable Network News (CNN) bureau chief in Beirut. Weir, a Presbyterian minister who for years had resided in Muslim West Beirut, was taken because he was a Christian ministering in a multiconfessional nation that the Shi'a claimed for Islam. Weir's captivity lasted more than fifteen months, until mid-September 1985, when Hizb'allah released him at the behest of Iran's ayatollahs after the Reagan administration secretly sold weapons to Iran to gain release of the U.S. hostages. William Buckley was altogether different. He was not in Lebanon to report the news or preach the gospel—he was there to spy.

William Buckley, whose official title was conciliar officer in the U.S. embassy, was the CIA station chief in Lebanon. He had taken over after the Hizb'allah suicide bombing of the U.S. embassy killed nine CIA officers, including station chief Robert Ames, the previous April. A former lieutenant colonel in the army, Buckley had a distinguished career. A company commander during the Korean conflict, Buckley became a member of the Army Special Forces attached to the South Vietnamese army during the Vietnam War. He had served with the CIA before, from 1955 to 1957 and again in 1965.[5] The Iranians discovered Buckley's identity from documents seized after militant students stormed the U.S. embassy in Tehran in November 1979, and the Iranian Revolutionary Guards in Lebanon almost certainly were involved in planning Buckley's abduction. Hizb'allah transported him to the Iranian Revolutionary Guards contingent in the Bekaa Valley; they eventually returned him to Hizb'allah in Beirut.[6] Buckley survived a year before torture and cruel and inhumane treatment killed him.

Hizb'allah would take Americans and Europeans hostage in waves of abductions between 1984 and the end of the decade. Hizb'allah had discovered a new terror tactic. This new dynamic—interminable captivity under perpetual threat of death—was different from airline hijackings or other hostage situations. The victims simply disappeared into the labyrinth of ethnicities and creeds that in better times made Beirut a symbol of cosmopolitan tolerance. The only proof of life came via videotapes of individual hostages reading prepared statements that invariably repeated the abductors' demands and threats. The hostage crisis unnerved the Reagan administration.

Reagan was determined to assert U.S. interests in Lebanon, despite his order to evacuate the Marines and this new danger to Americans. But Hizb'allah was equally determined to drive the Americans away. The hostage-taking was intended to make Lebanon too dangerous for the Americans. The possibility of bartering them for the al- Dawa prisoners was another benefit. So, while Hizb'allah could be expected to take more hostages, it could also be expected to inflict more casualties. At the end of September 1984, Hizb'allah mounted a suicide bombing that nearly struck down the U.S. and British envoys in Lebanon.

In the first week of September, the United States vetoed a UN Security Council resolution that criticized Israel for the IDF treatment of civilians in southern Lebanon. Hizb'allah vowed to punish the United States for its refusal even to admonish Israel. On 20 September, a suicide bomber drove a Chevrolet van laden with explosives to the U.S. embassy annex on the outskirts of Beirut. The United States no longer had an embassy in Lebanon; Hizb'allah had destroyed it in April of the previous year. The annex was a makeshift symbol of America's increasingly painful presence. The attack was well timed. British ambassador David Miers was meeting with his U.S. counterpart, Reginald Bartholomew, when the suicide bomber arrived at a security checkpoint on an access road near the embassy annex. An alert member of Miers's security detail opened fire on the van as it raced toward the building, killing the bomber and sending the van veering into a parked vehicle. The truck bomb exploded on impact. The embassy escaped the full force of the blast, but the explosion killed twenty, including two Americans, a soldier and a sailor, who were assigned to the defense attaché's office. Ambassador Bartholomew was injured along with twenty other Americans and more than fifty Lebanese. Hizb'allah claimed responsibility for the attack and renewed a vow to drive all Americans from Lebanese soil.[7]

A third major terror attack on Americans in Beirut did not influence the American electorate's perception of Ronald Reagan's stewardship of U.S. security. Reagan won reelection in November in a landslide. Exactly one month later, on 3 December 1984, Hizb'allah seized another American on the streets of Beirut. Peter Kilburn was the librarian at the American University. Kilburn's disappearance was a mystery. Some of his colleagues believed the sixty-three-year-old Kilburn, who was known to be ill, had wandered off. No one connected him with the other U.S. hostages until April 1986, when he was found shot to death in a field outside Beirut.

The Hijacking of Kuwait Airways Flight 221

The day after Kilburn's disappearance, four Hizb'allah terrorists boarded Kuwaiti Airways flight 221 in Karachi. Witnesses who survived the six-day ordeal remember the men standing on the tarmac near the rear of the aircraft while airline officials processed passengers through the doors at the front. No one guarded the aircraft and no one searched the passengers. The four were armed with pistols, grenades, and other explosives, although no one has ever learned whether they carried the weapons though security in Beirut where the x-ray machines and metal detectors were out of service, or whether they got the weapons in Dubai.

A few minutes into the flight, two terrorists broke into the cockpit, one of them pressed a grenade against the pilot's neck, and ordered him to divert to Tehran. Hizb'allah now had 162 hostages, six of them Americans. Three of them—Charles Hegna, William Stanford, and Charles Kaper—worked for the Agency for International Development in Karachi. This was not a random hijacking, and it was not incidental that the terrorists diverted the plane to Tehran. Hizb'allah was a creature of the Iranian revolution, and Hizb'allah and Tehran shared common objectives: the release of the al- Dawa Seventeen and punishment of the United States. Those objectives drove the dynamic of the hijacking of Kuwati Airways 221 for the next six days.

Immediately after the jet touched down in Tehran, the terrorists forced Charles Hegna to the cockpit at gunpoint and made him kneel. The pilots remembered Hegna praying. Then one of the terrorists took him to the galley, pressed a pistol into his abdomen, shot him, and threw him out onto the tarmac below. Hegna agonized there for nearly half an hour before the terrorists allowed Iranian authorities to rush him to a hospital. Hegna died in Tehran a few days later. After murdering Hegna, the terrorists released 44 of the passengers, all women and children. Two of them were Americans. But they still held Stanford, Kaper, and another American, John Costa. The terrorists tortured each of them.[8]

Two agonizingly long days passed before there was any movement on the hijacking. And then the news was not good. On 6 December, the terrorists brought William Stanford to the door of the jet and forced him at gunpoint to read a statement. It began with the claim that the men who had already murdered one hostage held no enmity toward anyone and that they intended to frighten no one. Their only concern was for their "enchained brothers in Kuwait." The statement ended with the proclamation of their "hopes for martyrdom."[9] After the statement, a terrorist murdered Stanford. Three more days passed before the resolution of the hijacking. On 9 December, the terrorists shot out the passenger cabin windows, grounding the plane. They announced their intention to blow up the jet, martyring themselves and murdering the remaining hostages, and began chanting their final prayers. But instead, a few hours later they summoned ground crew personnel to clean the plane. The men who boarded the plane were Iranian commandos who seized the terrorists without a struggle: the takedown was an arranged surrender. The Iranian revolutionary government has never prosecuted the murderers of Charles Hegna and William Stanford.

Ronald Reagan took the oath of office for a second time a month later. By then, Hizb'allah had seized another U.S. hostage. On 8 January 1985, Hizb'allah abducted Father Lawrence Jenco, a Roman Catholic priest who, like Benjamin Weir, was in Lebanon out of religious conviction. Reagan did not utter a single word about the hostages, or about terrorism, in his second inaugural address at the end of January or his State of the Union address in February. But there was deep frustration in the White House, the Pentagon, and the CIA over the U.S. impotence to defend Americans from terrorist attacks.

On 1 November 1984, six weeks after Hizb'allah bombed the U.S. embassy annex in Beirut, Reagan had put his name to National Security Decision Directive 149, "Support to Govt of Lebanon in Planning for Counter Terrorism Operations." The directive remains entirely classified. An earlier directive, dated 1 February 1984, authorized the Pentagon to provide "counter-terrorism/counter-insurgency training" to the Lebanese Armed Forces and to deploy "a company-size unit of Special Operations Forces to act as trainers." Two of the next three paragraphs are still classified.[10] The president found himself under pressure from officials in his own administration who counseled "fighting terrorists with terrorism" and "wanted to follow [Israeli prime minister] Menachem Begin's slogan of 'an eye for an eye'."[11] Reagan claims to have rejected the proposition because, three years earlier in December 1981, he had signed Executive Order 12333 directing that "no person employed by or acting on behalf of the United States Government shall engage in, or conspire to engage in, assassination." Why the president felt it was necessary to mention the ban on assassinations in his memoir may have something to do with a deadly car bombing in the spring of 1985.

Fighting Terrorists with Terrorism

On 8 March 1985, a massive car bomb exploded in southern Beirut, shearing off the front of an apartment building. The bomb was meant to kill Sheikh Fadlallah, the spiritual guide of Hizb'allah. The sheikh survived, but the blast killed 85 and wounded more than 200 people. Lebanon's Shi'a blamed the Reagan administration for the bombing and draped a banner over the ruins of the apartment building that read "Made in America." No one has ever proven the allegation, but there are those who believe that William Casey, director of the CIA, enlisted Saudi intelligence to carry out the attack on Fadlallah.[12]

Terry Anderson covered the attempt on Fadlallah's life for the Associated Press and tried to interview the sheikh the day after the bombing.[13] He was denied the interview. Instead, on 16 March, Hizb'allah abducted him in retaliation for the attempt on Fadlallah. Anderson's was the first of three more abductions.

On 28 May, six weeks after Anderson's abduction, Hizb'allah abducted David Jacobsen, CEO of the American University in Beirut Hospital. On 9 June, Hizb'allah abducted Thomas Sutherland, acting dean of the School of Agriculture at the American University. Hizb'allah's terrorists took Anderson and Jacobsen to the clandestine location where they held Buckley, Jenco, and Jacobsen. They took Sutherland to another location where they held Benjamin Weir.

The beginning of Anderson's, Jacobsen's and Sutherland's captivity was the end of Buckley's. By early June, the conditions of William Buckley's confinement had destroyed his body. Anderson and Jacobsen, who were being held down the hall from Buckley, heard the CIA station chief die. Buckley was delirious with fever, coughing, and babbling. Anderson's and Jacobsen's recollection of Buckley's final words were similar, "Oh God, I've lasted a year, and now my body is going"; "I don't know what has happened to my body, thirty days ago I was so strong." Then Buckley's broken body gave out. Anderson and Jacobsen heard their captors drag Buckley's body away.[14] Hizb'allah announced that it had executed the CIA station chief in October 1985 in retaliation for an Israeli air attack on PLO headquarters in Tunis. The CIA did not confirm Buckley's death until January 1987.[15]

By the summer of 1985, Reagan's presidency was darkened by the same shadow that had hung over Carter's—Americans in captivity. There were six of them: Peter Kilburn, Terry Anderson, David Jacobsen, Thomas Sutherland, Benjamin Weir, and Lawrence Jenco. William Buckley was dead, but the CIA did not know this. Then, suddenly, there were scores more.

The Hijacking of TWA Flight 847

On 14 June 1985, two Lebanese men, Hassan Izz al-Din and Ali Youness, boarded TWA flight 847 in Athens for the flight to Rome. A third man, Ali Atwa, tried to board the overbooked flight. All three belonged to Hizb'allah. Atwa demanded the right to board the flight. His protests aroused the suspicions of Greek authorities, who later arrested him. Twenty minutes into the flight to Rome, Izz al-Din and Youness rushed to the restrooms, where Hizb'allah militants working with the ground crew somewhere along the flight's itinerary had somehow managed to conceal hand grenades and a 9mm pistol. They stormed the cockpit and ordered Captain John Testrake to fly to Beirut. Hizb'allah now held 153 passengers and crew hostage, 100 of them Americans; 39 would remain hostages in Beirut for seventeen days and one would die there.

The hijacking of TWA 847 captured extraordinary media attention—much more than that of Kuwaiti Airlines flight 221 the previous December—because of the extraordinary media presence in wartorn Beirut. The sounds and images of the hijacking dominated news coverage for the next two weeks, beginning with Captain Testrake's first desperate radio transmissions from the cockpit on approach to the airport in Beirut. Lebanese authorities refused Testrake's request to land in Beirut. There had been two hijackings in the previous two weeks, and the burned out fuselages of the jets still littered the taxiways. Testrake pleaded with the control tower: "He has pulled a hand grenade pin and is ready to blow up the plane if he has to. . . . We must land, I repeat, we must land in Beirut. . . . They are beating the passengers, they are threatening to kill the passengers. . . . We want fuel now, immediately." Then the voice of one of the hijackers came over the radio, "the plane is booby-trapped. If any one approaches, we will blow it up. Either refueling the plane or blowing it up. No alternative."[16]

Captain Testrake's appeals convinced the Lebanese to allow the plane to land. On the ground in Beirut, the terrorists released 19 passengers and then demanded to speak with representatives of Nabih Berri's Amal movement. Amal refused to be drawn into the crisis at first. With that, the two terrorists ordered the jet to cross the Mediterranean to Algiers. They released 21 more hostages in the Algerian capital, then, after five hours on the ground, ordered the plane back to Beirut, where it arrived for a second time late on the first night of the ordeal. When Lebanese authorities tried to deny permission to land a second time, one of the hijackers came on the radio with a startling threat: "We are suicide terrorists . . . we will crash the plane into your control tower, or to fly it to Baabda and crash it into the Presidential Palace!" The hijacker's threat, made nearly two decades before the 9/11 atrocity, belie any U.S. official claims that no one ever anticipated terrorists would contemplate using an aircraft as a weapon of mass destruction: as of 15 June 1985, counterterrorism officials in the United States had forewarning.

TWA flight 847 was on the ground in Beirut again. For a second time, the Hizb'allah terrorists demanded to speak with an Amal representative. And for a second time, Amal refused to confer. The terrorists' reaction to Amal's refusal was to kill. "He just killed a passenger, he just killed a passenger!" With that transmission, Captain Testrake announced the death of a U.S. sailor, Robert Stethem. Stethem, just twenty-three years old, was a navy deep-sea diver who, like Hegna and Stanford, in Iran seven months earlier, paid with his life for his service to the United States. The terrorists brutally beat Stethem before shooting him to death at point-blank range. The murder was revenge for the 8 March car bombing intended to kill Hizb'allah's Sheikh Fadlallah. "Did you forget the Bir al- Abed massacre?" Stethem's killer demanded when Lebanese officials protested the murder of the American. The terrorists threw Stethem's body to the tarmac. Two full hours passed before they allowed Red Cross representatives to retrieve the body.

The hijacking took a confusing twist after Stethem's murder. Around midnight, two Amal representatives boarded the Boeing 727. Soon after, the terrorists demanded that the Lebanese authorities cut electricity to the lights illuminating the remote area of the airport where the plane sat. The Lebanese authorities complied, and under cover of darkness a squad of armed men boarded the jet. What began as a hijacking by two men now became an armed standoff involving fifteen. At dawn the hijackers ordered the plane to fly to Algiers yet again, the third Mediterranean crossing in two days. Captain Testrake put the plane down late that morning. In Algiers the hijackers released three more hostages, but also demanded the release of Ali Atwa, the third terrorist whom Greek authorities had arrested on the day of the hijacking. After the murder of Stethem, the Greek authorities had to take seriously the threat to murder the Greek citizens aboard the flight, including one of Greece's most popular singers. Ali Atwa joined the hijackers later in the day, two days after he was supposed to have helped commandeer the jet. The terrorists released another 58 passengers after Atwa climbed aboard. On Saturday 16 June, the hijackers ordered the fatigued flight crew to fly back to Beirut, where they released all but 39 of the hostages.

The hijacking of TWA 847 changed dramatically that day. After midnight, Amal militiamen from Nabih Berri's Amal boarded the plane and took custody of all but four of the hostages with Jewish-sounding names, whom Hizb'allah removed to a makeshift prison in the Shi'a neighborhoods surrounding the airport. Captain Testrake, his copilot, and flight engineer remained on board. The terror of the first days of the hijacking was over, and now the hostages fell into a limbo. At a press conference, Berri announced that he was now holding the hostages.

The hijacking of TWA 847 sent the Reagan White House into crisis mode and raised tensions between the United States and Israel. Israel's actions in Lebanon always had lethal consequences for Americans. Hizb'allah's terror campaign against Americans came in retaliation for the U.S. alliance with Israeli interests. Now, three years after Israel launched Operation Peace for Galilee, Hizb'allah took U.S. hostages aboard TWA 847 to leverage U.S. pressure on Israel. The IDF were in the midst of a phased withdrawal from positions in southern Lebanon. As they withdrew, they took more than 1,100 Shi'a men prisoner. In early April, the IDF transferred more than 700 of the Shi'a across the border to Atlit, an Israeli prison south of Haifa. The State Department immediately expressed concern about the transfer in a carefully worded statement that "it appears Israel's actions are inconsistent with provisions of the fourth Geneva Convention."[17] Three months later, the Shi'a took action to compel Reagan to bring pressure on Israel.

President Reagan returned to the White House from Camp David to monitor the crisis and, after convening a meeting of his National Security Council, ordered Delta Force commandos to position themselves for a possible hostage rescue. But the president knew he had few good options. So he talked tough: "Let me further make it plain to the assassins in Beirut and their accomplices, wherever they may be, that America will never make concessions to terrorists—to do so would only invite more terrorism nor will we ask nor pressure any other government to do so. Once we head down that path there would be no end to it, no end to the suffering of innocent people, no end to the bloody ransom all civilized nations must pay."[18] In fact, the president found himself appealing to Israel to make concessions, and to Syria, a state that sponsored terrorism in Lebanon, to mediate. Soon he would find himself agreeing to concessions to America's most menacing terrorist threat—Iran.

After taking custody of most of the hostages, Nabih Berri publicly called on Reagan to force the Israelis to release the Shi'a, whom he called "Israel's hostages." On the fourth day of the crisis, Berri framed the contours of the solution: "If your government asks Israel to do this one little thing . . . release these innocent people from your jail, this problem, it will be resolved in twenty-four hours." For better or worse, Berri represented the administration's only real hope of a resolution to the crisis. That was what the director of the CIA told the president. "Bill Casey," the president wrote in his diary, "feels we must come up with a fig leaf for Berri or releasing the hostages would cause his assassination by fanatics."[19] Berri, leader of Amal and Lebanese state minister for southern Lebanon, was under challenge from the radical Hizb'allah. There may have been collusion between Amal and Hizb'allah in the hijacking. Now the burden was on Berri to win the release of the Shi'a who were held in an Israeli prison.

The Israelis sharpened Reagan's dilemma. A week into the crisis, on 20 June, he noted that "The Israelis are not being helpful. They have gone public with the statement that they would release their prisoners if we asked them to . . . by going public with a statement that the U.S. should ask them to release the Shiites, loused things up by establishing a linkage we insist does not exist." In fact, the administration was attempting to forge that linkage. The Israelis did release 31 Shi'a prisoners, but insisted that the release was preordained. Berri rejected the gesture. The hostages themselves would have something to say about this. On the twelfth day of the crisis—the day of Robert Stethem's funeral— five of the hostages appeared at a press conference. One of them read a statement: "We do sincerely pray that the governments involved in this problem can put aside fear, anger and insult in the process of rectifying injustices that have been committed to date."[20]

It was obvious that only a secret Israeli pledge to parcel out the release of Shi'a prisoners could break the impasse. With that, Syrian president Hafez al-Asad, who viewed Lebanon as the territory of a Greater Syria, decided to intercede. On 29 June, Amal militiamen gave the U.S. hostages a farewell party at a seaside restaurant, then moved them to a Red Cross facility. Plans were in place to transport the hostages overland from Beirut to Damascus. But Hizb'allah still held four U.S. hostages in a separate location. As Reagan put it, "apparently neither Mr. Berri or Asad could spring the missing four from the bastardly Hizballah." For whatever reason, the Hizb'allah delivered the other four Americans on 30 July. After a four-hour journey under the guard of Amal militiamen and Syrian special forces, the Americans arrived in the Syrian capital. Two days later they landed at Andrews Air Force Base, where the president and the first lady welcomed them home.

The president had more strong words. "Hijacking is a crime, kidnapping is a crime, murder is a crime," he said. "There are promises to keep . . . there will be no forgetting, killers must be brought to justice." The president proved unable to keep that promise—twenty years after the hijacking of TWA 847 and the murder of Robert Stethem, the young sailor's killers are still at large; their names appear on the FBI's list of most wanted terrorists, along with Imad Mugniyah, the man behind the hijacking of TWA 847. President Reagan privately expressed frustration that seven Americans "were still held captive in Lebanon" and his determination to "bring them home." But for those seven Americans, the administration's failure to negotiate the release of all the Americans came as a betrayal.[21]

The fate of the hostages left behind in Beirut after the return of the TWA hostages weighed on Ronald Reagan, who later admitted to spending "many, many hours late at night wondering how we could rescue the hostages, trying to sleep while images of those lonely Americans rolled past my mind." Reagan viewed the safe return of the Americans as a presidential duty and began his morning national security briefings with a single question, "Any progress on getting those hostages out of Lebanon?"[22] The president's preoccupation with the hostages in Lebanon blurred the vision of his national security advisors, Robert McFarlane and later John Poindexter, who worked the problem in a way that clashed with Reagan's core belief that "we couldn't negotiate with kidnappers [because] that would simply encourage terrorists to take more hostages."[23] In fact, Reagan approved his national security advisors' plans to negotiate with the Iranians to secure the release of Americans held by the Lebanese. Reagan's predictions proved true—Hizb'allah inevitably seized more U.S. hostages.

Arms for Hostages

In July, soon after the resolution of the TWA 841 crisis, Ronald Reagan entered Bethesda Naval Hospital for a routine physical examination. He was discharged a few days later, after surgeons removed polyps from his colon. Three days after the surgery, Reagan's national security advisor, Robert McFarlane, approached him with a scheme to transform America's hostile relations with Iran and to gain the release of U.S hostages in Lebanon. A year earlier, McFarlane, as special envoy to Lebanon, had advised Reagan to order naval guns to fire in support the Lebanese army in its skirmish with Druze forces in the Shouf; the slaughter of the Marines at the airport came as a consequence. McFarlane had advised the president badly and was offering bad advice again. Reagan's mental and physical condition may have clouded his judgment, but for more than a year Reagan would commit the same error of judgment again and again.

As Reagan remembers it, McFarlane approached him with information about a secret Israeli overture to "a group of moderate, politically influential Iranians," who, as "disenchanted members of Iran's government, wanted to establish a quiet relationship with U.S. leaders as a prelude to establishing formal relations." The most exciting piece of news was that these disenchanted moderates "had offered to persuade the Hizballah terrorists to release our seven hostages" in Lebanon. The United States, to bolster the position of the Iranians, needed only to allow Israel to transfer stocks of U.S- manufactured TOW anti-tank weapons from Israeli stockpiles to the Iranians. Said the former president, "and that is how the Iran-Contra affair got started."[24] The president did not appear to ponder how moderate members of the Iranian government could ever convince the radical members of Hizb'allah to release U.S. hostages.

In fact, the Reagan administration would be not dealing with disenchanted moderate members of the government of the Islamic Republic of Iran, but principally with an Iranian arms merchant, Manucher Ghorbanifar, who had no standing in the revolutionary government in Tehran. The CIA knew Ghorbanifar well—and distrusted him. But the National Security Council staff placed full confidence in him. The secretaries of state and defense objected to the scheme to transfer weapons to Iran to curry favor with the mullahs, and they would later raise serious questions about its legality. But CIA director Casey adamantly supported it. Sometime late in July, Reagan approved the first transfer of U.S.-manufactured weapons from Israeli stockpiles to Iranian forces with the understanding that the United States would replenish the Israeli inventory.

On 20 August 1985, an Israeli aircraft secretly transported 96 TOW anti-tank weapons to Iran. The gesture did not gain the release of any U.S. hostages. Nonetheless, a month later Reagan approved another arms deal in the hope of gaining the freedom of a hostage. McFarlane sent word that if the Iranians could prevail on Hizb'allah to release only one U.S. hostage, that hostage should be William Buckley, the CIA station chief whom Hizb'allah abducted the previous March. The CIA had not discovered that Buckley was already dead. On 14 September, the Jewish state secretly shipped another 408 TOWs to the Islamic republic. The next day, Hizb'allah released Benjamin Weir, the Presbyterian minister taken in May 1984. The administration had effectively purchased the freedom of a hostage.

The administration could not publicly disclose that it had bartered weapons for the freedom of an American, so it became imperative to find a cover story to explain Weir's release. Enter Terry Waite, the envoy of the archbishop of Canterbury. Two weeks after Weir's release, Waite appeared beside Weir at a press conference in New York and disclosed that the archbishop of Canterbury had authorized Waite to mediate on behalf of the hostages some sixteen months earlier, in May 1984, after Weir's family contacted Waite.

Waite was the Archbishop of Canterbury's envoy to trouble spots. In May 1984, senior representatives of the American Presbyterian Church put Waite in contact with senior administration officials. Exactly a year later, in May 1985, Waite met with Donald Gregg, Vice President George Bush's national security advisor, who arranged for Waite to meet Lieutenant Colonel Oliver North. North, a member of the National Security Council staff, had become the administration's point man for its covert and illegal operations in Nicaragua and later Iran. For North and the men around him, Terry Waite was heaven sent and his symbolic efforts to mediate the hostage crisis provided the administration cover for the secret arms-for-hostages negotiations. North and Waite met some twenty times over the next eighteen months, at each critical moment of the administration's efforts to work a deal with the Iranians. Waite's contacts with North would have terrible personal consequences for him. After the administration's covert dealings with Iran became public in late 1986, in January 1987, Hizb'allah took Waite hostage and held him for 1,763 days.[25]

The release of Weir was confirmation enough for the advocates in the administration of the arms deals that secret overtures to Iranian moderates could free Americans from captivity and even transform U.S.-Iranian relations. But before the Americans and Israelis could negotiate another deal with the Iranians, Palestinian terrorists struck.

On 25 September 1985, a Palestinian terror squad attacked an Israeli yacht tied up in Larnaca, Cyprus, killing three Israelis. Khalil al-Wazir, aka Abu Jihad, Fatah's military commander, organized the operation. It was an act of desperation by a beleaguered organization. Five years earlier, after Arafat's triumphant address before the UN General Assembly, the Fatah-dominated PLO had reached the zenith of its influence. But the Israeli invasion of Lebanon in 1982 had driven the PLO from Beirut to Tripoli, farther up Lebanon's Mediterranean coast. Then, a mutiny within the ranks of Fatah in 1983 badly damaged Arafat's organization. Syria, for its own strategic reasons, backed the Fatah rebels against Arafat. In the broader context of the ongoing violence in Lebanon, Palestinians were again killing each other in a miniature civil war. The violence subsided a few days before Christmas 1983, when the PLO agreed to evacuate Tripoli under U.S. protection from Israeli attack. The PLO was driven out of Lebanon. Arafat set up headquarters in Tunis across the sea, but not out of reach of the Israelis [26]

This was the context for the murders in Larnaca. Abu Jihad ordered the operation because he believed the three murdered Israelis were Mossad agents spying on Palestinian movements across the Mediterranean. The Mossad would eventually strike down Abu Jihad for this, and for his efforts to coordinate the intifada uprising in the Occupied Territories. But Israel had a more immediate response. On 1 October, the Israeli Air Force blasted Arafat's compound in Tunis. The air raid killed 58 Palestinians and 14 Tunisians, and provoked a series of retaliatory attacks that invariably left innocent victims. Hizb'allah—using the name Islamic Jihad—announced the execution of William Buckley in retaliation for the Israeli attack; Buckley, in fact, died from the cumulative effect of his mistreatment months earlier. Then came another act of terror.

The *Achille Lauro* Affair

Early on the morning of 7 October 1985, a week after the Israeli air strike, four terrorists seized the Italian cruise ship *Achille Lauro* after it sailed from Alexandria, Egypt. The men belonged to one of the three factions proclaiming itself the Palestine Liberation Front. The PLF was a splinter of Ahmed Jabril's PFLP-General Command, which had broken away from George Habash's PFLP in 1970. In reality, three separate factions took the name Palestine Liberation Front, each reflecting the widening internal rifts within the PLO between pro-Arafat, pro-Syrian, and pro-Libyan tendencies. The men who seized the *Achille Lauro* on the high seas belonged to the faction headed by Mohammed Zeidan, known as Abu Abbas.[27] The connection between Arafat and Abu Abbas, who sat on Arafat's PLO executive committee, would later complicate the PLO chairman's effort to portray himself as a diplomat worthy of a dialogue with the United States even after Arafat formally renounced terrorism at the end of 1988.

The act of piracy aboard an Italian ocean liner off the Egyptian coast would have wide repercussions—for the PLO, for Egyptian-U.S. relations, and even for relations between the United States and Italy, its NATO ally. After commandeering the ship, the hijackers ordered it to proceed to the Syrian port of Tartus. Hafez al-Asad, warned by the Reagan administration to avoid involvement, denied the hijackers' demands to put into the Syrian port. The terrorists reacted by murdering an American, Leon Klinghoffer, an elderly Jew who was confined to a wheelchair. It was a cruel murder: after shooting Klinghoffer at point blank range, the terrorists forced other passengers to hurl his body overboard. They threatened more executions unless Israel complied with their sole demand: the release of more than fifty Palestinian prisoners in Israeli custody.

The crisis forced the principal parties to take action. Ronald Reagan, who was preparing for a summit meeting with Soviet president Mikhail Gorbachev, ordered Navy Seal and Army Delta Force commandos to position themselves for an armed rescue. Egypt, embarrassed because the *Achille Lauro* was sailing between the Egyptian cities of Alexandria and Port Said, hurried to mediate. Arafat, concerned that the incident was damaging to him, also rushed to intercede. Arafat persuaded Abu Abbas, whose men had seized the ship, to order the terrorists to bring the *Achille Lauro* back to Port Said and surrender to Egyptian authorities.[28] The formula was not new. The Egyptians would take custody of the Palestinians and provide them with safe conduct to Tunisia, where Arafat would subject them to PLO discipline for the unruly act. The formula had worked in 1974, when Abu Iyad mediated the end of the British Airways hijacking. Something similar happened in 1973 when the Sudanese president granted clemency to the killers of George Curtis Moore and Cleo Noel. It is not known whether Arafat and Egyptian president Hosni Mubarak knew about Klinghoffer's murder when they worked out the surrender, but it probably would not have made a difference to them. It made all the difference to Ronald Reagan.

On 8 October the *Achille Lauro* pulled into Port Said, where the terrorists released their hostages and turned themselves over to Palestinian justice. Speaking to reporters at O'Hare International Airport in Chicago two days later, Ronald Reagan expressed disappointment that the terrorists "had been allowed to depart Egypt . . . to parts unknown," but he attempted to absolve the Egyptians. Asked if he was angry with Egyptian president Mubarak, he could only say that "apparently the Egyptians did not know that a hostage had been murdered." Reagan could not say whether there was evidence of PLO involvement in the crime, but he was adamant that the PLO should turn the hijackers over to "whichever country should have proper jurisdiction."[29]

Reagan did not say so, but he surely believed the terrorists belonged in U.S. jurisdiction. Nor did he let on that he was aware that the terrorists had not yet left Egypt, as the Egyptian authorities had implied. In fact, the Egyptians planned to move the four terrorists to Tunisia that night. On the night of 10 October, the men who had commandeered the *Achille Lauro* and murdered Leon Klinghoffer boarded an Egyptian airliner for the short flight to Tunisia. Abu Abbas was with them. The jet was over the Mediterranean when four U.S. navy fighters from the USS *Saratoga* intercepted it and forced it to divert to the NATO base at Sigonella, Sicily, where U.S. Special Forces were waiting for it. It was an audacious operation that offered a rare opportunity for the United States to bring terrorists to justice for the murder of an American. But it was not to be. On the ground in Sicily, Italian forces confronted the Americans and demanded custody of the Palestinians. Sicily is Italian soil, so the Americans could not prevent the Italians from taking custody of the men who had hijacked an Italian ship before they had killed a U.S. citizen. The Italians dutifully arrested the four hijackers but allowed Abu Abbas to fly to Yugoslavia and eventually to Tunis. Ronald Reagan masked his disappointment with Italian prime minister Betino Craxi's refusal to arrest Abbas: "I think he also worried about the political ramifications that he would face if hijackers of an Italian ship were released to us." Then, to the press, the president put terrorists on notice, "you can run but you can't hide."[30]

The *Achille Lauro* hijacking was the first act of terror in retaliation for the Israeli raid on the PLO headquarters. That it came from an Arafat ally was not surprising. The next operations were those of Arafat's mortal enemy, Abu Nidal. The first of those came less than two months later.

Abu Nidal's Atrocities

On 23 November, three Palestinians belonging to the Abu Nidal organization hijacked Egypt Air flight 648 from Athens to Cairo, soon after takeoff from the Greek capital. There were 90 passengers and crew aboard. The hijacking was a bloody affair. As in the hijackings of Kuwait

Airways flight 221 and TWA 847 in December 1984 and June 1985, the hijackers singled out Americans for death. The hijacking itself was violent. Egypt was by now placing sky marshals aboard some of its flights; one of them shot and killed one of the hijackers before being wounded himself. Then Omar Mohammed Rezaq took charge of the operation and ordered the plane to fly to Malta. There Rezaq collected passports for the purpose of learning the nationalities of his hostages—and he began shooting them. His first two victims were Israelis. Rezaq shot them at close range but, miraculously, one of them survived. Rezaq threw their bodies to the tarmac in a now familiar indignity to innocent victims. Then he turned on Americans. Rezaq shot at one American, Patrick Baker. The bullet grazed his head but did not kill him. Later he shot and killed Scarlett Rogenkamp, a civilian employee of the United States Air Force. Rogenkamp became the fifth American killed by terrorist hijackers in just eleven months—William Stanford, Charles Hegna, Leon Klinghoffer, and Robert Stetham. Finally Rezaq shot Jackie Pflug in the head, but miraculously she also survived.[31]

The next evening, with negotiations stalled and the threat of more killing hanging over the passengers, Egyptian Special Forces attempted a hostage rescue. It ended in disaster. The commandos stormed the plane and began firing indiscriminately; worse, the flash-bang grenades exploded into flames, and 59 passengers were killed. Rezaq was wounded in the rescue attempt, but survived. The Egyptian authorities tried and convicted him, but Rezaq served only seven years of a twenty-five-year sentence for the crimes. The FBI eventually arrested him in Nigeria, where he had fled following his release. A U.S. court subsequently convicted Rezaq for the murder of Rogenkamp, rejecting his attorneys' pleas that, as a survivor of the horrific massacres at Sabra and Shatila in 1982, post-traumatic stress mitigated Rezaq's criminal culpability.

A month later, Abu Nidal struck in the heart of Europe. On 27 December, two squads of terrorists calling themselves the Martyrs of Palestine attacked the El Al, TWA, and Pan Am ticket counters at the international airports in Rome and Vienna with grenades and automatic rifles. In Vienna, four terrorists killed three and wounded thirty before Austrian police shot one of the terrorists to death and captured the others. The carnage in Rome's Leonardo Da Vinci airport was reminiscent of the December 1973 killing rampage of Abd al-Ghafur's National Arab Youth for the Liberation of Palestine that left twenty-nine dead. This time the terrorists killed eleven passengers, including five Americans— Natasha Simpson, Donald Maland, John Buonocore, Frederick Gage, and Elena Tommarello—before Israeli security personnel and Italian authorities returned fire, killing three of the terrorists. Simpson, the daughter of the Associate Press editor in Rome, was the youngest victim, age eleven; Tommarello, the oldest, age sixty-seven.

The terrorists deliberately targeted the children. Natasha Simpson's death was especially brutal. According to witnesses, one of the terrorists felled the eleven-year-old with a burst of fire from his Kalashnikov, then took aim at her head before turning his weapon on Natasha's brother and other children standing nearby. In all, six children were wounded in Rome, the youngest a nine-month-old. Another witness was certain the Martyrs of Palestine intended to kill children, "I saw one of the terrorists throw a grenade and I saw the look in his eyes. When he shot into the crowd he was trying to kill children."[32] The attackers proclaimed their intention to harm innocents in a document found on the survivor of the Rome massacre. "As you have violated our land, our honor, our people, we in exchange will violate everything, even your children, to make you feel the sadness of our children. The tears we have shed will be exchanged for blood."[33]

The CIA and the Iran Initiative

At the end of 1985, the United States confronted separate terrorist threats: secular Palestinian nationalist terror represented principally by Abu Nidal and sponsored by Libya and Syria; and sacred Islamist terror represented principally by Hizb'allah and backed by Iran. The Reagan administration's reaction to these threats was incoherent. It pursued military options against Libya while it stumbled into a policy of appeasement with Iran. Worse still, in 1986, the CIA's covert support for the Islamic jihad against the Soviets in Afghanistan was approaching its zenith—the Reagan administration was arming, feeding, and financing the spiritual brethren of the jihadists who were bloodying America in Lebanon.

In mid-November, President Reagan authorized another arms-for-hostages exchange involving sale of 80 HAWKs to Iran. But the November weapons shipment would turn into a fiasco.[34] Customs officials in Portugal blocked the departure of the Israeli cargo plane transporting the weapons to a rogue state in violation of a U.S.-imposed embargo on Iran. That forced the CIA to deliver the weapons to Iran aboard an aircraft belonging to a secretly run CIA company. The plane arrived in Tehran on 24 November—the day after the Egypt Air hijacking—with only 18 weapons on board, not the 80 the Iranians demanded. The Iranians rejected the shipment; Hizb'allah released no hostages. But even the November fiasco did not convince Ronald Reagan to terminate the arms-for-hostages deals. Instead, Reagan attempted to give an ill-advised and illegal operation legal cover.

The involvement of the CIA made the November arms transfer a covert operation that by law required presidential "finding" and congressional notification. Reagan signed the presidential "finding" in December, a week after the debacle. The December finding authorized the provision of "munitions" to the "government of Iran which is taking steps to facilitate the release of American hostages." It said nothing about improvement of relations with Iran, or about overtures made by Iranian dissidents—President Reagan had authorized a straight arms-for-hostages deal. More serious was the president's direct orders regarding the notification of Congress: "I direct the director of Central Intelligence not to brief the Congress of the United States" as provided by law, "until such time as I may direct otherwise." The president did not direct otherwise for nearly a year. Admiral John Poindexter, who had replaced MacFarlane as national security advisor two days before Reagan signed the retroactive finding, destroyed the presidential finding a year later in November 1986, after the Iran-Contra scandal broke, fearing correctly that the document's language about weapons transfers in exchange for hostages would be politically embarrassing to the president.[35]

In the final weeks of December 1985 and into January of the new year—after the Rome and Vienna atrocities—Ronald Reagan met with his senior advisors to discuss the prudence and the legality of proceeding with a covert operation that had secured the release of only one U.S. hostage but had brought the administration into conflict with the law and the president's own declaratory policy regarding negotiations with terrorist states and the arms embargo on Iran.

On 7 January, after a meeting with Vice President George Bush, the secretaries of defense and state, the attorney general, the national security advisor, and the director of the CIA, Reagan decided to push ahead with yet another arms sale to Iran, despite the opposition of the secretaries of state and defense, and the secretary of defense's belief that the sales would be illegal. The attorney general assured the president that an illegal weapons sale could be made legal by the simple act of signing a presidential finding that declared the act to be in the national security interest of the United States. The president signed that finding on 17 January. The United States transferred another 500 TOW missiles to Iran on 18 February, and another 500 weapons ten days later. President Reagan had authorized the sale of a thousand lethal weapons, but Hizb'allah did not free a single American hostage. Incredibly, the administration did not lose faith in the initiative. Despite having only one hostage to show after six months of secret arms deals, the administration decided to send representatives directly to Tehran to confer with the mythical Iranian moderates.[36] The secret mission to Tehran came in May and actually provoked another round of hostage taking. Before any of that occurred, the Reagan administration struck out against Libya.

Qaddafi and Terror

On 8 January 1986, the day after President Reagan met with his senior cabinet officials to discuss the Iran initiative, he signed National Security Decision Directive 205, which declared the president's finding that Libya's support for international terrorism constituted "an unusual and extraordinary threat to the national security of the United States." The directive specifically attributed the Rome and Vienna attacks to Libya; Qaddafi publicly had called the attacks "noble." The president then ordered the Pentagon to heighten "the readiness of U.S. forces to conduct military action" against Libya and dispatched an aircraft carrier battle group to prowl the Gulf of Sidra. But Libya attacked first.[37]

On 2 April, a bomb exploded aboard TWA 840 from Rome to Athens during the plane's descent into the Greek capital. The explosion tore a 9-by-3-foot hole in the fuselage and killed four Americans—Alberto Espinoza and three generations of a single Greek-American family, Demetra Stylianopoulis, her daughter Maria Klug, and her nine-month-old granddaughter, Demetra Klug. It was a horrible death. The four were sucked out of the cabin by the plane's sudden depressurization. The plane was severely damaged, but the pilot managed to land it safely. Within hours of the attack, a group calling itself the Ezzedine Kassam Unit of the Arab Revolutionary Cells claimed responsibility for the bombing and justified it as a reaction to the provocations of the U.S. navy off the Libyan coast. U.S. investigators rapidly developed information about May Elias Mansour, a Lebanese man who U.S. intelligence believed belonged to the Special Operations Group, commanded by a Fatah dissident, Abdullah Abd al-Hamid Labib, and who took the nom de guerre of Colonel Hawari. The Americans also suspected Mohammed Rashid, because of the similarities between TWA bombing and the bombing of Pan Am flight 830 during the plane's decent into Honolulu in August 1982. Rashid was the bomber of Pan Am 830.[38]

Three days later, terrorists struck at another U.S. target. On 5 April, Verena Hauesler-Chanaa, a middle-aged German woman married to a Palestinian, carried a powerful bomb into La Belle discotheque in West Berlin in her handbag. The explosion tore through the crowded discotheque wounding nearly two hundred, mostly U.S. military personnel. The bomb killed two, a U.S. solider and a Turkish woman. American intelligence rapidly traced the attack to Libya; a West German court later convinced a Libyan diplomat, Musbah Eter, of complicity in the crime, along with Verena Hauesler-Chanaa and her husband.[39]

The Reagan administration's response to the La Belle bombing was Operation El Dorado Canyon. In the late hours of 14 April 1986, Navy A-6 fighter-bombers flying off the USS *America* and USS *Coral Sea* and Air Force F-111 fighter-bombers flying out of the Royal Air Force Base at Lakenheath, England, raided Libya. It was an immense operation: more than one hundred aircraft, including fighter-bombers, aerial tankers, interceptors, and electronic jamming aircraft were involved. The 38 strike aircraft struck 5 separate targets in Tripoli and Benghazi, including military barracks and airfields and one of Muammar Qaddafi's residences. They dropped some 60 tons of explosives during the twelve-minute raid, killing 32 and wounding nearly one hundred others. One Air Force F-111 and its two-man crew were lost.[40]

Three days after the Libyan raid, a group calling itself the Arab Revolutionary Cells executed Peter Kilburn, the librarian at the American University of Beirut abducted by Hizb'allah in December 1984, and three Britons. Philip Padfield and John Leigh Douglass, both educators at the American University, had been abducted on 28 March, days before Operation El Dorado Canyon, and were found shot to death with Kilburn. Two weeks later, on 28 April, a group calling itself the Revolutionary Organization of Socialist Muslims delivered a videotape of the lynching of Alec Collett, abducted by Hizb'allah in March 1985, nine days after the abduction of Terry Anderson. Collett, a journalist, was working on assignment for UN Relief and Works Agency to monitor conditions of Palestinians in Lebanon's refugee camps.[41]

The Arab Revolutionary Cells and the Revolutionary Organization of Socialist Muslims were almost certainly fictitious names. It is widely believed that Qaddafi purchased the four men from Hizb'allah in order to execute them in retaliation for the raid on Libya. Despite the murder of four hostages, including an American, Caspar Weinberger, Reagan's secretary of defense, considered the bombing raid a significant victory. Operation El Dorado Canyon, he said, "drove Qaddafi underground, so that nothing was heard from him effectively for two or three years."[42] It was two years precisely; in 1988, Muammar Qaddafi retaliated with the most lethal terrorist attack since the Marine barracks bombing.

The Secret Mission to Iran

Operation El Dorado Canyon was meant to punish Qaddafi for his sponsorship of Abu Nidal's terror, but only weeks after the raid on Libya, Reagan sent emissaries to Iran to negotiate a deal with the sponsor of Hizb'allah. In May, Reagan authorized a delegation to visit Tehran. Robert McFarlane, the former national security advisor, led the delegation, which included Lieutenant Colonel Oliver North, a CIA officer fluent in

Farsi, and the counterterrorism advisor to the Israeli prime minister. Weeks of planning had gone into the secret mission, which was supposed to produce the release of all U.S hostages in Beirut and a thaw in the frozen relations between the United States and the Islamic Republic of Iran. The delegation arrived on the morning of 25 May aboard an Israeli aircraft with false markings carrying a pallet of spare parts for HAWK missiles. This was to be the first in a series of exactly timed deliveries of some 240 spare parts for the HAWKs and hostage releases. But over the next seventy-two hours the Americans learned they had been acting under a delusion: there would be no meeting with senior Iranian ministers as promised, and there would be no release of all the U.S. hostages as promised. Indeed, the Iranians with whom the U.S. delegation met shocked them with the news that the Iranians did not have control of the U.S. hostages thousands of miles away in Beirut. McFarlane, North, and the others left on the morning of 28 May without securing the release of a single U.S. hostage. In fact, they narrowly avoided becoming hostages themselves. And the Iranians took possession of the weapons parts the Americans had brought with them.

As Reagan administration officials pondered their next moves to free the hostages, the Iranians seized the initiative by depositing funds in secret accounts to pay for the spare HAWK parts that were to have been delivered in May, and then pressured Hizb'allah into releasing a U.S. hostage to restart the arms-for-hostages arrangements. On 26 July Hizb'allah freed Father Lawrence Jenco, the Roman Catholic priest seized in January 1985. When Jenco arrived in Damascus as a free man, Terry Waite was there to greet him.

The envoy of the Anglican Church interpreted Jenco's release as affirmation of his own efforts to persuade the Kuwaitis to treat the al-Dawa prisoners humanely. But it was Oliver North who arranged for Waite to travel to Damascus to be present when Jenco arrived to maintain the fiction that the release of another cleric (Weir was a Presbyterian minister, Jenco a Roman Catholic priest) was the result of Waite's intervention on behalf of the Anglican Church. Waite appeared standing beside Jenco in newswire photographs.[43]

President Reagan did not believe that Waite's intercession delivered Jenco into freedom; he thought Jenco's release was "the direct result of Bud McFarlane's Iranian mission in May." So, four days after Jenco's release the president authorized what he described as "a small additional shipment of spare missile parts to the Iranian military as a demonstration of goodwill and gratitude."[44] In fact, the shipment of 240 HAWK missile parts on 8 August just closed the American end of the deal cut before McFarlane's trip to Iran. Iran still did not make good on its end of the bargain to secure the release of all the U.S. hostages. Rather, Hizb'allah would seize three more U.S. hostages in the coming weeks.

Abu Nidal—Again

Just at this moment, terrorists from Abu Nidal's organization seized more Americans aboard a U.S. passenger jet. On 5 September, Zaid Hassan Abd Latif Safarini and three other men wearing uniforms of Pakistani security personnel and driving an official van rushed across the tarmac of Karachi's international airport to a Pan Am 747 preparing for departure. Armed with assault rifles, grenades, and plastic explosives strapped to their waists, the men rushed aboard the jet. They seized two flight attendants at gunpoint and ordered the jet's doors closed. One of the attendants alerted the flight crew to the hijacking, and the crew escaped. Like the Abu Nidal organization's hijacking of the Egypt Air flight the previous November, this one would end violently.

Pan Am flight 73 was scheduled to fly to Frankfurt and ultimately to New York. There were 389 passengers and crew aboard when the terrorists seized it, more than 70 of them U.S. citizens.[45] This operation had nothing to do with America's activities in Lebanon—Abu Nidal ordered it to compel Israeli and Cypriot authorities to release some of his men captured during previous terror operations.

Safarini's mission failed the moment the flight crew escaped from the cockpit. But he had hostages. Safarini ordered the flight attendants to gather passports. He was looking for Americans. He began issuing demands to Pakistani authorities standing on the tarmac beneath the jet. His immediate demand was for a flight crew. He took a hostage, Rajesh Kumar, to the door in the first class cabin. Kumar, who had just become a U.S. citizen, was about to die for possessing a U.S. passport. Holding Kumar by the neck in the doorway of the jet, Safarini shot him in the head in the presence of the flight attendants and the Pakistani negotiator.

The standoff lasted seventeen hours. As evening fell, the jet's auxiliary power failed and the cabin went dark. Safarini and the terrorists moved all the hostages to the center of the passenger cabin, opened fire with their assault rifles, and hurled as many as six grenades. They murdered 21, including another American national, Surenda Patel. The youngest victim was just seven years old, the oldest eighty-one. Another 200 were wounded, including 73 Americans, before the survivors escaped through emergency exists. All the terrorists survived. Safarini, who wore an explosive belt around his waist, ordered one of his men to fire a round into the belt. The shot seriously wounded him but did not detonate the explosives. Safarini was arrested in a hospital where he was being treated for his wounds.

Safarini was one of only a few terrorists the Americans ever brought to justice. In 1988, a Pakistan court convicted him, the three other terrorists, and an accomplice and sentenced them to death, but another court commuted their sentences to life. In 2000, Pakistani authorities released all five men. On 28 September 2001, only two weeks after the 9/11 attacks, the FBI captured Safarini and brought him to the United States. In December 2003, after more than two years of legal proceedings concerned principally with the availability of the death penalty in the case, Safarini pled guilty to 95 counts that included murder, conspiracy to commit murder, and conspiracy to commit offenses against the United States. He was sentenced to three consecutive life sentences, plus an additional twenty-five years.[46]

The day after the slaughter on Pan Am flight 73, Abu Nidal terrorists opened fire in a synagogue in Istanbul, killing two worshipers. The Karachi and Istanbul atrocities convinced Syrian president Hafez al-Asad to expel Abu Nidal, just as Iraq's Saddam Hussein had done three years earlier. Abu Nidal moved on to his next state sponsor, Muammar Qaddafi's Libya.

More Arms, More Hostages

Four days after the massacre aboard Pan Am flight 73 in Karachi, Hizb'allah began seizing more Americans in Beirut. Hizb'allah took three Americans hostage between 9 September and 21 October 1986: Frank Reed, director of the Lebanese International School, Joseph Cicippio, an administrator at the American University, and Edwin Tracy, a freelance writer. President Reagan took comfort in an intelligence report that "not the same faction of Hisballah but another terrorist group" seized the men; he simply could not see that the previous arms transfers whetted the kidnappers' thirst for more hostages, so he could see no reason to abandon the arms-for-hostages swaps.[47] In the final week of October, after the abduction of Reed, Cicippio, and Tracy, Reagan approved the sale of another 500 TOW missiles to Iran. The transfer took place on 28 October. Within the week, on 2 November, Hizb'allah released David Jacobsen after eighteen months of captivity. Reagan believed Jacobsen's release was "new evidence that the Iran initiative was working," but refused to comment publicly on the captors' vague indication that they were responding to "unspecified American overtures." In fact, in his memoir Reagan omits any reference to the very specific overture that produced Jacobsen's release—the 28 October transfer of 500 TOW missiles.[48] He seemed to believe that Terry Anderson and Thomas Sutherland would follow Jacobsen into freedom within twenty-four hours. The president's narrative about Jacobsen's release makes no mention of the fate of Reed, Cicippio, and Tracy.

Terry Waite was on the scene to welcome David Jacobsen back to freedom. Oliver North arranged Waite's travel, just as he arranged his trip to Damascus in July when Hizb'allah released Father Jenco. But this time Waite traveled with North aboard a chartered jet to Cyprus, and then aboard a U.S. military helicopter from Cyprus to Beirut, where journalists photographed the men together. From that moment on, Terry Waite—the envoy of the Anglican Church's good faith effort to mediate and the decoy for the Reagan administration's covert operation to appease Iran—was a marked man.[49]

Jacobsen's release marked the culmination and collapse of the Reagan administration's covert operations on both the Iranian and Nicaraguan fronts. A month before Jacobsen's release, the Sandinista Popular Army shot down a CIA-owned aircraft illegally delivering supplies to the U.S.-backed Contra rebels in Nicaragua, and captured an American under CIA contract. Reagan publicly lied about the administration's covert support for the Contra rebels, which Congress had prohibited in a law Reagan had signed. Things went from bad to worse. The day after Jacobsen's release, a small newspaper in Beirut published a story about McFarlane and North's supposedly secret mission to Tehran in May and the entire arms-for-hostages arrangements. Reagan lied about this too, denying Israel's involvement in the operation and asserting that all the weapons transferred to the Islamic Republic of Iran could fit aboard a single Boeing 747. Later, the Special Council appointed to investigate possible high crimes and misdemeanors of Reagan administration officials related to the Iran-Contra affair discovered that administration officials, including the national security advisor, had destroyed incriminating documents and that North had diverted some of the money from the weapons sales to Iran to the Contra rebels; thus the Iran-Contra scandal.

Hizb'allah released no more Americans for four years. Instead, it seized more hostages. On 20 January 1987, eight days after he arrived in Beirut, Hizb'allah abducted Terry Waite. The abduction was inevitable. North had manipulated the naïve good intentions of the Anglican envoy to conceal the administration's covert operations under the cover of a humanitarian effort to save lives, and the deception cost Waite his freedom. Indeed, Hizb'allah—still calling itself Islamic Jihad—announced it seized Waite because he had failed in his promises to deliver weapons to Iran and to gain the freedom of the al-Dawa Seventeen. Waite understood the risks. Colleagues who perceived that the exposure of the Reagan administration's arms-for-hostages exchanges endangered him advised him not to return to Beirut. But Waite, who would remain captive until mid-November 1991, apparently accepted the risk to prove his integrity and independence. After his release he admitted that he felt "devastated by the political actions" of the U.S. government, actions he considered "duplicitous."[50]

On 24 January, four days after Waite's abduction, Hizb'allah seized three more American academics teaching at the American University of Beirut: Jesse Turner, Robert Polhill, and Alann Steen. When Reagan signed off on the arms-for-hostages project in the summer of 1985, Hizb'allah held seven U.S. hostages: Kilburn, Weir, Jenco, Buckley, Anderson, Jacobsen, and Sutherland. In January 1987, after eighteen months of secret negotiations with Iran, Hizb'allah held eight American hostages: Anderson, Sutherland, Reed, Cicippio, Tracy, Turner, Polhill, and Steen. The president had traded thousands of lethal weapons for the lives of three hostages; Hizb'allah had killed two Americans and seized five more. They would languish there for four years, until after Reagan left office.

In a new strategy, the Reagan administration, and the Bush administration that succeeded it, opted to devalue the hostages to deprive Hizb'allah of its bargaining advantages. The new strategy did not hasten the release of the hostages. Hizb'allah freed Polhill and Reed at the end of April 1990, after Lebanon's sectarian civil war burned out and the belligerents agreed to the Saudi-brokered Ta'if accords. Hizb'allah did not release Tracy until 19 August 1991, seventeen days after Saddam Hussein ordered his forces to invade Kuwait. Hizb'allah freed Waite and the remaining U.S. hostages between October and December. Terry Anderson, the Associated Press bureau chief, was the last to walk free, on 4 December—after seven years in captivity—the longest of any of the Western hostages in Lebanon. There was a bitter irony in the release of the hostages. Hizb'allah abducted the hostages to gain the freedom of the al-Dawa Seventeen, and released them after the men who had executed the terror bombings of December 1983 walked to freedom. But the al-Dawa Seventeen escaped as a consequence of Saddam Hussein's invasion of Kuwait.

The Iran-Contra scandal consumed much of Reagan's penultimate year in office. In March 1987, the president publicly accepted the report of the Tower Commission, a named in December to provide him with a full accounting of what went wrong, as the president said, "on my watch," And he came close to admitting the truth about the arms-for-hostages dealings: "A few months ago I told the American people I did not trade arms for hostages. My heart and my best intentions still tell me that's true, but the facts and the evidence tell me it is not."[51] A Congressional Committee investigating Iran-Contra began hearings about possible high crimes and misdemeanors in May and issued its report on 18 November. And by the summer of 1988, Lawrence Walsh, the Independent Counsel for Iran-Contra Matters appointed by the Justice Department in March 1987, had issued indictments. Walsh would win criminal convictions in courts of law. The president's national security advisor, Robert McFarlane pled guilty to lying to Congress in March 1988; a court convicted John Poindexter, who succeeded McFarlane, on five criminal counts in April 1990. A court convicted Oliver North on three counts in May 1989.[52] It was the inglorious end to a set of covert operations set in motion by the president's instincts about the nation's security.

Arafat Renounces Terror

Over the previous three years, beginning with Hizb'allah's suicide bombing of the U.S. embassy in Beirut in April 1983, the management of terror incidents virtually had become a primary White House function. Then, suddenly, major terror attacks against Americans and U.S. interests ceased for two full years. There were only a few, sporadic terror incidents involving U.S. servicemen in Greece, Spain, and West Germany throughout 1987, although one of those incidents—the sabotage of a rail line in West Germany—would generate suspicions about the involvement of the PFLP-General Command in a horrific terror incident that closed out the decade of the 1980s. The aerial bombardment of Libya temporarily deterred Muammar Qaddafi from permitting Abu Nidal to strike at Americans. Qaddafi's forbearance ended a few days before Christmas 1998. Then too, America's lower profile in the Lebanese conflict took Americans out of the line of fire. In fact, major terrorist acts diminished overall. Abu Nidal mounted only three incidents in 1987 and eleven in 1988, including the attempt to seize the Greek cruise ship, *The City of Poros*, on 11 July 1988. The operation failed, but not before Abu Nidal killers murdered eleven, including one American, and wounded 98 others. It could have been much worse, because a car laden with explosives detonated prematurely before it could damage the ship. Greek and U.S. authorities have always speculated that the purpose of the *City of Poros* operation was to prevent Greek authorities from extraditing Mohamed Rashid, the bomber of Pan Am flight 830 in August 1982 and possibly TWA 840 in April 1986, to the United States.[53]

Meanwhile, the dynamic of one of the principal causes of terror—the Palestinian-Israeli conflict—changed dramatically. The Israeli invasion of Lebanon in 1982, and the internecine fighting that ensued, drove the PLO from Lebanon across the sea to Tunisia. The departure of the PLO left Palestinians living under Israeli occupation in the occupied West

Bank and Gaza to defend their own interests. Life under occupation provided the material for the spontaneous combustion of a mass uprising. On 8 December 1987, an Israeli military truck accidentally struck and killed four Palestinian workers at a check point in Gaza. The next day, Israeli soldiers shot and killed a Palestinian while running down young Palestinians throwing rocks. These incidents sparked what became known as the Intifada. It would last until 1993, when Yasser Arafat returned from exile to Palestine to stand for election as the president of the Palestinian National Authority.

The Intifada was an explosion that did more that any act of terror to affect change in the Palestinian-Israeli conflict. The IDF had crushed the armies of the Arab states encircling the Jewish state and had expelled the PLO from Lebanon. But Israeli soldiers could not suppress a sustained rebellion by angry, unarmed Palestinians. A series of harsh tactics—the breaking of arms and destruction of family homes as collective punishment for participation in the uprising—created unmanageable public relations problems for the Israeli authorities. For the PLO in exile in Tunisia, the Intifada represented both a challenge and an opportunity. Because it was spontaneous, the Intifada challenged the absolutist control Arafat demanded over the resistance to Israeli occupation. But because the anger behind the Intifada was incandescent, it gave Arafat the opportunity to direct it. Sensing the opportunity, Arafat ordered his military chief, Khalil al-Wazir, Abu Jihad, to take control of the hitherto spontaneous mass uprising. The Israelis took action to prevent that from happening. On 16 April 1988, Israeli Sayaret Matkal commandos went ashore near the Tunisian village of Hammam el-Shat on the Mediterranean coast and assassinated Abu Jihad in his bed while he slept beside his wife.

The commando raid came fifteen years to the week after Lieutenant Colonel Ehud Barak led his Sayaret Matkal commandos in Operation Youth of Spring in central Beirut, which killed three senior PLO officials in 1973. Barak, a future prime minister, participated directly in Operation Youth of Spring. This time, Barak now a major general, commanded the operation from offshore.[54] Twelve years in the future, Yasser Arafat would come face to face with Prime Minister Barak to negotiate the final status agreement between the Palestinians and Israelis in the waning days of the Clinton administration.

The assassination of Abu Jihad, one of Fatah's founders, deepened Arafat's isolation. The PLO's corrupt bureaucracy was far removed from the action in occupied territory and it was rapidly appearing irrelevant to the political future of the Palestinian people. Arafat had to say or do something. Yitzak Shamir, who was serving as Israeli prime minister for a second time, also found himself under pressure from the United States to move a semblance of a peace process forward. In March 1988, Secretary of State George Shultz addressed a letter to Shamir proposing negotiations between the Israelis and a joint Jordanian-Palestinian delegation.[55] But Arafat's dilemma was dire: his only hope was that a change in the winds of U.S. politics would change his fortunes.

On the first Tuesday in November 1988, Americans elected Vice President George Herbert Walker Bush to be the forty-first president of the United States. Bush could be expected to carry on the Reagan legacy, although without the charisma that made Reagan iconic. The United States had nearly become lost in the turmoil in the Middle East. But as the Reagan presidency came to an end and the Bush presidency was about to begin, a U.S.-mediated dialogue between the Palestinians and Israelis suddenly became possible.

On 15 November 1988, Yasser Arafat, at the close of the Palestinian National Council meeting, issued a Palestinian declaration of independence.[56] Exactly a month later, he addressed the UN General Assembly in Geneva. The Reagan administration denied Arafat a visa to enter the United States in an effort to force Arafat to accept, in Reagan's words, America's "conditions for a substantive dialogue." The General Assembly simply convened in Switzerland. Irritated, Arafat reacted by revealing the secret security arrangement his late security chief, Ali Hassan Salameh, had negotiated between the PLO and the CIA after Arafat's triumphal address to the UN General Assembly in 1974.[57] But ultimately the refusal to grant the chairman of the PLO entry into the United States prompted Arafat to accept America's conditions for dialogue. In a press conference after his address before the General Assembly, Arafat conceded Israel's right "to live in peace and security, according to Resolutions 242 and 338." Henry Kissinger once denounced the sacramental language and mystical ambiguities of UN Security Council Resolution 242, but now, by uttering the sacramental language, Arafat moved closer to the promise of U.S. support for a diplomatic initiative. The Reagan administration rightly demanded more, so Arafat said this: "We totally and absolutely renounce all forms of terrorism."[58] Coming only seven months after Israeli commandos killed Khalil al-Wazir, one of Arafat's oldest and most trusted partners, the renunciation of terrorism was astounding. A decade later, Arafat, as president of the Palestinian National Authority, would have the opportunity to prove the sincerity of his renunciation of terror. He would fail.

In the past, peace overtures produced terrorist acts. In the weeks before and after Arafat's first address to the UN General Assembly in New York, Palestinian dissidents hijacked airliners or destroyed them in flight. Two weeks after Arafat's address to the General Assembly in

Geneva, terrorists destroyed another jet in the skies. But this time the desire for revenge, not the rejection of peace, was the motive.

Pan Am 103

Four days before Christmas 1988, 259 passengers and crew boarded Pam Am flight 103 at London's Heathrow Airport for a flight to New York. Of these, 189 were Americans, 35 of them students from Syracuse University. The Boeing 747—"Clipper Maid of the Sea"—was aloft at 6:25 P.M. At 7:00 P.M., the captain informed air traffic control that he had leveled off at 31,000 feet, and the copilot requested clearance to cross the Atlantic. It was the Maid of the Sea's final transmission. One minute later, the bomb that killed the men, women, and children aboard Pan Am flight 103 exploded.

Alan Topp saw the images of Pan Am flight 103's destruction on his radar screen at Scotland's Shanwick Oceanic Control air traffic control center. Pan Am 103's transponder signal vanished. Instead of the signature of a huge Boeing 747, radar tracked three, four, then five images, and finally hundreds of bright squares scattered over a square mile. The moment Pan Am 103 disappeared from radar, it appeared in the skies over Lockerbie, Scotland, as a "white and orange flash," then a "glowing object" falling in a "burning arc" as fragments of the aircraft, and the bodies of the passengers, crashed into Lockerbie like burning "meteors."[59]

The bomb that destroyed Pan Am 103 was concealed in a Toshiba cassette recorder, placed in a brown Samsonite suitcase, and loaded into a baggage container in a forward cargo hold on the left side of the Clipper Maid of the Seas. A few ounces of SEMTEX military-grade plastic explosive blew a 25-inch hole through the baggage container and through the thin skin of the plane's fuselage. The rupture of the pressurized hull of the jet traveling more than 600 miles an hour 31,000 feet above the earth caused sudden depressurization and sent a shock wave along the fuselage that ripped the plane apart in seconds. The flight deck and the first class and business sections of the two-deck Boeing 747 tore off from the main passenger cabin taking one of the jet's huge engines with it, the wing assembly separated from the fuselage, the tail section fell away, and passengers tumbled out of the disintegrating jet into inner space. The burning meteors of Pan Am 103 crashed to earth over hundreds of miles of Scotland for more than two minutes. The massive wings crashed through a row of townhouses, igniting thousands of pounds of jet fuel, gouging a crater 50 feet deep and 150 feet long—and obliterating two families, eleven people. The meteors of debris ignited fires in Lockerbie that burned through the night. The sabotage of Pan Am 103 rendered more than 800 square miles of Scotland a vast crime scene. Fragments of the plane became pieces of evidence. victims' bodies lay around Lockerbie, some of them for days, until forensic technicians could document their recovery.

After a two-year hiatus, terrorism had again scorched America's sense of invulnerability. The sabotage of Pan Am 103 was the third sabotage of an aircraft in the Middle East's worsening history of terrorism: The death toll (270) exceeded the combined tolls of Swiss Air flight 330 in 1970 (47) and TWA 841 in 1974 (70), as well as the Israeli shootdown of the Libyan airliner in 1970 (106), and approached that of the simultaneous suicide attacks on the Marine and French Multinational Force compounds in Beirut in 1983 (299). The United States had never lost so many to a terror attack on unarmed civilians.

Authorities in the United States and the United Kingdom suspected an act of terror from the moment the news of the crash of Pan Am 103 reached them, and within days investigators found the evidence that proved sabotage: a 20-square-inch section of the skin of the fuselage showing signs of "pitting and sooting," peeled away in a "starburst pattern" indicating "a high-energy event," an explosion.[60] By then, the CIA had received claims of responsibility. In fact, the agency had received warning of the bombing of a Pan Am flight weeks before the destruction of the Maid of the Seas. The CIA reported the claims the day after the disaster. Two organizations, Islamic Jihad and the Guardians of the Islamic Revolution, boasted of the murders. Islamic Jihad—the front for Hizb'allah—had become the most ferocious U.S. terror threat. Hizb'allah bombed buildings and hijacked aircraft; sabotage of airplanes in flight was not one of its tactics. But there was another possible connection. Four U.S. intelligence agents were aboard the Maid of the Seas. Matthew Gannon was the CIA's deputy station chief in Beirut; Major Chuck McKee was attached to the Defense Intelligence Agency; the other two, Ronald Lariviere and Daniel O'Conner, were bodyguards. Gannon and McKee may have been returning from a mission to locate Hizb'allah's U.S. hostages in Beirut; Hizb'allah could have silenced them in the act of punishing the United States.[61]

The CIA gave more credibility to the claim of the scantily known Guardians of the Islamic Revolution. More alarming was the acknowledgment that "an anonymous caller told a U.S. diplomatic facility that a bombing attempt would be made against a Pan Am aircraft flying from Frankfurt, West Germany, to the United States."[62] The State Department dutifully conveyed this "Helsinki Warning" to the Federal Aviation Administration and to Pan Am, but the U.S. government never warned Pan Am passengers. This revelation turned the grief of the Pan Am 103 families into outrage because the flight originated in Frankfurt, and investigators would eventually prove the bomb came aboard the Maid of the Seas in Frankfurt. The fact that U.S. authorities later concluded that Helsinki warning was a hoax did not obscure the fact that U.S. officials opted not to disrupt air travel by posting a public warning about the threat to destroy a passenger airliner in flight, although the State Department posted the warning at European diplomatic facilities for State Department employees. Worse still, U.S. authorities knew, because West German authorities informed them, that just two months before the sabotage of Pan Am 103, West German police as part of its Autumn Leaves operation had discovered SEMTEX bombs with barometric pressure triggers in a terrorist safe house.[63]

In October, West German counterterrorism units raided a safe house belonging to a PFLP-General Command cell. Ahmed Jabril's PFLP-General Command was still capable of sporadic acts of terror in 1988. The previous summer, its terrorists planted a bomb on railroad tracks in a failed effort to derail a train carrying munitions to a U.S. military base in West Germany. The PFLP-General Command was the first Palestinian terror organization to destroy a passenger jet in flight, Swiss Air flight 330 in February 1970, almost nineteen years earlier. West German authorities had the cell under surveillance with the cooperation of a Jordanian who infiltrated it for Jordanian intelligence. The operation, codenamed Autumn Leaves, culminated in October with the raid on the safe house where the German police discovered SEMTEX bombs concealed in Toshiba cassette recorders, with barometric pressure triggers designed to destroy planes in flight.

But then there was the question of a motive. Yasser Arafat's self-serving repudiation of terrorism in October in an effort to appease the Reagan administration was the kind of overture that, in the past, motivated Palestinian rejectionists to commit atrocities; the bombing of TWA flight 841 in October 1974 was one of them. The claims by Islamic Jihad and the Guardians of the Islamic Revolution pointed to Iran, whose enmity toward the United States virtually defined the terrorist threat in the 1980s. Beyond the Islamic Republic's theological depiction of the United States as the Great Satan, Iran had another motive for revenge. On 4 July 1988, a U.S. warship patrolling the Persian Gulf, the USS *Vincennes*, fired a surface-to-air-missile at an approaching jet that the ship's captain feared was an attacking Iranian warplane. The incident came during the final phases of the Iran-Iraq War, when fighter jets of both Iran and Iraq were attacking tankers transporting crude oil through the gulf; in March 1987, Iraqi warplanes attacked a U.S. warship, the USS *Stark*, killing 37 sailors in an incident the United States also determined to be an accident. The *Vincennes* incident was another tragic mistake; the *Vincennes* shot down a civilian airliner, Iran Air flight

655, with 290 passengers and crew aboard the Airbus A300, twenty more than those killed on Pan Am 103.[64] Within a few months, CIA analysts began to connect the Islamic Republic of Iran to the secular PFLP-General Command, on the theory that Iran had contracted with the group to destroy Pan Am 103. Iran had the obvious motive, and West German authorities had discovered the PFLP-General Command's bomb-making capabilities in the Autumn Leaves investigation.[65]

In fact, Muammar Qaddafi's desire for revenge for Operation El Dorado Canyon in April 1986 was behind the mass murder in the skies above Lockerbie. Investigators searching for components of the improvised explosive device that destroyed Pan Am 103 discovered the critical piece of evidence that proved the complicity of Libya's Jamahariya Security Organization (JSO) in January 1989: a tiny fragment of circuit board burned into a shard of a shirt purchased in a Maltese clothing store. In June 1990, an FBI explosives expert identified the circuit board as a fragment of a sophisticated timer that a Swiss company sold in batches to Libyan intelligence agents. The Maltese shopkeeper remembered the man who randomly purchased the charred shirt and other items of charred clothing contaminated with explosive residue— clothing the bomber had packed in the Samsonite suitcase with the Toshiba cassette recorder that contained the SEMTEX explosives. Investigators were able to trace the suitcase back to Air Malta flight 180 to Frankfurt, where baggage handlers placed it on Pan Am flight 103A to London and then flight 103 to New York. No one at Malta's Luqa Airport, Frankfurt's International Airport, or Heathrow Airport became suspicious of a suitcase without a passenger.[66]

Nearly two years passed before authorities in Scotland and Washington were able to identify publicly two Libyans as suspects—Abdel Basset Ali al-Megrahi and Al-Amin Khalifa Fhimah—in indictments issued on 13 November 1991.[67] The indictments alleged that al-Megrahi was a Libyan intelligence agent; Fhimah managed Air Libya operations at Malta's Luqa Airport. By the time the indictments came down, George H. W. Bush, who was completing the second year of his presidency, had led a grand coalition in war to expel Iraqi forces from Kuwait. But Bush did not order the Defense Department to punish Libya for the murder of 189 Americans aboard Pan Am 103, as Ronald Reagan had done in 1986 in retaliation for the murder of five Americans in the Rome airport massacre or of one American in the La Belle discotheque bombing. Instead, Bush, whom the families of the victims of Pan Am 103 came to resent for his apparent lack of concern, chose to assign America's response to the second worst terror attack against Americans to the departments of Justice and State.

After issuing the indictments, authorities in both the United Kingdom and the United States sent démarches to Libya demanding the extradition of al-Megrahi and Fhimah for trial in Scotland or the United States. Qaddafi rejected the demand as vehemently as he denied Libya's culpability. In his final year in office, Bush opted for UN sanctions to compel Qaddafi to relent. In January 1992, the UN Security Council passed Security Council Resolution 731, deploring Libya's refusal to cooperate in the investigation of Pan Am 103. In March, the Council passed Resolution 748, imposing severe restrictions on air travel to Libya in an effort to isolate Qaddafi. The Bush administration never pressed the Security Council to impose the one sanction that would hurt Qaddafi most: an embargo on Libyan oil. President Clinton's State Department was more aggressive. In November 1993, the Security Council approved a U.S.-sponsored resolution, Resolution 883, authorizing the freezing of Libyan assets and prohibiting imports of Libyan oil.

By then, nearly four years after the crash of Pan Am 103, a new, supremely more lethal terrorist enemy had already attacked the World Trade Center for the first time. Qaddafi endured the United Nations sanctions for six years, until December 1998, when he first began to hint that he would negotiate the conditions for the extradition of al-Megrahi and Fhimah during a meeting with Secretary General Kofi Annan. That same month, a U.S. appeals court ruled that international law gave the families of Qaddafi's victims the right to sue Libya for the crime. On 16 December 1998, painfully close to the tenth anniversary of the bombing, the Libyan People's Congress dutifully ratified Qaddafi's agreement to extradite al-Megrahi and Fhimah to the Netherlands, a neutral country, for trial in a Scottish court under Scottish rules of evidence and criminal procedure. The trial began at Camp Zeist, the Netherlands, in May 2000.

The criminal prosecution of the Pan Am 103 defendants offered the smallest measure of justice owed to the families of the victims. Al-Megrahi, an agent with Qaddafi's JSO, stood accused of planting the bomb; Fhimah was in the dock for aiding and abetting the crime. But the court did not adjudicate Qaddafi's personal culpability, and Bush's refusal to order military retaliation sealed Qaddafi's impunity. When the trial concluded on 31 January 2001, just days after Bush's son took the presidential oath of office, this small measure of justice was reduced by half. Although the court convicted al-Megrahi of murder, it acquitted Fhimah. An appellate chamber denied al-Megrahi's appeal on 14 March 2002, after the 9/11 attacks replaced the destruction of Pan Am 103 as the worst act of terror against civilians in the history of terror.

President George W. Bush had even less desire than his father to punish Qaddafi, despite his administration's rhetoric about the moral imperative for regime change in states that sponsored terror and sought weapons of mass destruction—rhetoric that led to Operation Iraqi Freedom in March 2002. In August 2003, Libya agreed to pay $4 million in compensation to each of the families of the victims of Pan Am 103. The tacit admission of guilt gave the governments of the United States and the United Kingdom the cover they needed to permit Libyan oil flow into the world market. The Bush administration's April 2001 energy task force, chaired by Vice President Dick Cheney, former CEO of the Halliburton Corporation, had apparently advocated this commercial rapprochement with Qaddafi.[68] On 12 September 2003, the day after the second anniversary of the 9/11 attacks, the UN Security Council unanimously approved the resolution lifting economic sanctions on Libya at the behest of the United States. On 24 March 2004, British Prime Minister Tony Blair paid Qaddafi a state visit in the hope of forging "a new relationship" with Libya. It was a controversial overture, coming only weeks after the terror bombings of trains in Madrid. But Blair apparently believed that a state visit was an appropriate reward for Qaddafi's decision to abandon terrorism and to dismantle Libya's faltering weapons of mass destruction programs the previous December. But the allure of Libyan petroleum also drew Blair to Tripoli: during the visit, the Anglo-Dutch Shell Corporation announced an agreement with the Libyan government to drill for the estimated $60 billion worth of natural gas off the Libyan coast.[69]

The destruction of Pan Am 103 marked the end of two decades of terror inspired by secular ideologies that drove the Israeli-Palestinian and Israeli-Arab conflicts, and a decade of terror inspired by a jihadist interpretation of Islamic theology. The Islamist terrorist threat inflicted grievous harm on the United States in Beirut, but the threat seemed confined to the madness of Lebanon's sectarian violence. U.S. Cold War strategists saw jihadists as allies, not enemies, in Afghanistan. But the Arab-Afghans, whom the Reagan administration armed to fight the common Soviet enemy in Afghanistan, saw in the United States a mortal enemy deserving of punishment. Their jihad against the United States would reach America's shores early in final decade of the twentieth century—and it would come to define America's national security dilemma in the first decade of the new millennium.

Chapter 8

The Real Enemy Is America

George Herbert Walker Bush took the oath of office in January 1989 as investigators collected the wreckage of Pan Am 103 strewn over the Scottish countryside. When he left office four years later, he could speak confidently about the advent of "a new world order freer from the threat of terror." The archterrorists of the past had fallen into the hands of authorities or had faded into obscurity: Carlos the Jackal had fled to Khartoum, where French authorities finally arrested him in 1994; Abu Nidal descended into paranoia after murdering his primary rival in the Palestinian liberation movement just before the first Gulf War in 1991, and returned to Baghdad, where the Iraqi secret police murdered him just before the second Gulf War in 2002; and Imad Mugniyah, the chief of Hizb'allah's murderous operations, apparently vanished after the release of the last U.S. hostages in Beirut at the end of 1991. There was not a major terror attack against Americans or American interests during the four years of Bush's presidency.

Historical forces that had been operating for decades produced momentous geopolitical changes. The Soviet Union completed its humiliating withdrawal from Afghanistan, and the Berlin Wall fell in 1989, and the Soviet Union imploded two years later. The sectarian violence in Lebanon burned out, and the last American hostage went free. A bankrupt PLO reluctantly recognized Israel's right to exist and entered into U.S.-mediated talks that eventually produced imperfect peace agreements between Palestinians and Jews. And, the Iran-Iraq War ground to a halt without either Saddam Hussein's Baathi Iraq, or Ayatollah Khomeini's Islamic Republic of Iran, having conquered a mile of enemy territory.

The new world order was illusory. Conflicts flared in the Balkans and the Horn of Africa drawing U.S. forces into perplexing ethnic struggles. Saddam Hussein miscalculated the degree of the United States' tolerance for his misadventures and sent Iraqi forces to conquer Kuwait's oil fields in 1990. George Bush presided over America's swift war to expel Iraqi forces from Kuwait the following year, but the terms of Iraq's surrender agreement left Saddam Hussein in power as a menace to U.S.

interests and regional security. The political benefits of the triumph in the Gulf War vanished by the time Americans went to the polls in 1992, and the electorate punished Bush for the dismal state of the domestic economy.

William Jefferson "Bill" Clinton became president in 1993 and inherited the burden to enforce United Nations sanctions on Iraq and to manage escalating crises in Bosnia and Somalia. More ominously, militant Muslims who had rushed to Afghanistan to expel the Soviet invaders heard a call to global jihad against the United States after the Soviet withdrawal. As the United States focused attention on Iraq and a cruel war in Yugoslavia, Arab volunteers to the Afghan jihad took the struggle against apostasy back to their native lands, and Osama bin Laden began to meticulously construct Al Qaeda—the Base—for a global jihadist movement. The Clinton administration was agonizingly slow to recognize the emergence of the threat of Islamist terror. Terrorists struck on U.S. soil twice in Clinton's first weeks in office: against CIA headquarters in Langley and the World Trade Center in New York, and they bombed U.S. military installations in Saudi Arabia in 1995 and 1996. Late in the summer of 1996, on the eve of another presidential election, Osama bin Laden declared war against the United States.

Desert Storm

The Reagan administration bolstered Saddam Hussein's secular Baathi regime in Iraq as a counterweight to the Ayatollah Khomeini's Shi'a theocracy in Iran beginning in the early phases of the Iran-Iraq War. The administration had evidence of Iraq's chemical weapons attacks against Iranian forces as early as 1982, but chose to cultivate relations with Saddam's Iraq anyway, compromising America's moral standing on the issue of weapons of mass destruction, WMD. In March 1988, Saddam Hussein entrusted a cousin, Ali Hassan al-Majid, to resolve Iraq's Kurdish question by poisoning Kurdish villages. The Iraqi air force attacked the villages of Halabja on 16 March and Guptapa on 3 May with a lethal combination of mustard and nerve gases. Some 5,000 men, women, and children died in Halabja alone. The gassing of the Kurdish villages was genocidal, but Reagan did not consider the atrocities serious enough to disrupt United States commercial relations with Iraq; neither did his successor. George Bush, who came to office less than a year after Halabja, doubled Commodity Credit Corporation credits to Iraq to $1 billion per year to permit Saddam to purchase grain and foodstuffs from U.S. farmers.[1]

Saddam desperately needed the credits. The eight-year war with Iran left Iraq bankrupt and hundreds of thousands of Iraqis dead. The price of oil aggravated matters. Saddam complained bitterly that Kuwait's oil production exceeded its quota, and he saw in this a conspiracy to drive down the price of oil and to drive him from power. On 17 July, Saddam threatened an invasion of Kuwait unless Kuwait curtailed its oil production. Saddam met with U.S. ambassador April Glaspie on 25 July, and came away with the misimpression that the Bush administration would not punish him if he moved against Kuwait. Saddam ordered Iraqi forces into Kuwait on 2 August.

The day of the invasion, the UN Security Council unanimously adopted Resolution 660 condemning it. Over the next few weeks, the Security Council adopted no fewer than 12 resolutions, imposing economic sanctions on Iraq and nullifying Iraq's annexation of Kuwait. The Security Council's demands culminated in resolution 678 on 29 November authorizing member states to use "all necessary means . . . to restore international peace and security in the area." The Security Council imposed a 15 January deadline for Iraq's compliance.

President Bush reacted to the invasion by deploying U.S. forces to Saudi Arabia on 8 August, two days after Secretary of Defense Dick Cheney met with Saudi King Fahd to outline a U.S. proposal to defend the kingdom. On 20 August, Bush signed National Security Directive 45, which explained that the president had deployed troops to the region to defend Saudi Arabia and other regional allies, as well as to enforce the Security Council's resolutions. By the end of August, the number of U.S. forces in the region reached 300,000. On 21 October, Colin Powell, chairman of the Joint Chiefs of Staff, briefed Saudi officials on plans for offensive operations against Iraqi forces.[2] Two weeks later, President Bush dispatched another 150,000 troops to the region.

In an address to Congress—ironically, on 11 September—Bush warned the American people that "Saddam Hussein is literally trying to wipe a country off the face of the Earth." The president spoke of "vital issues of principal," but what was really at stake was a vital resource, oil. "We cannot permit a resource so vital," said the president, "to be dominated by one so ruthless." The president saw the defeat of Iraqi aggression in sweeping geopolitical terms. The restoration of Kuwait's sovereignty, he said, could lead to the emergence of a "new world order . . . a new era, freer from the threat of terror, stronger in the pursuit of justice, and more secure in the quest for peace."[3]

The Security Council ultimatum of 29 November authorized the use of force after 15 January. Over the next six weeks, the United States completed the buildup of its own forces and assembled a 26-nation coalition of member states that included forces from ten Arab and Muslim nations. Congress authorized the use of U.S. armed forces on 12 January, three days before the UN deadline. The "Persian Gulf War Resolution" passed by relatively narrow margins in both houses (250 to 183 in the House, 52 to 47 in the Senate), but it gave the president the authority to lead a grand alliance to liberate Kuwait.

The United States let a full day pass after Saddam's failure to comply with the ultimatum before attacking. In the predawn hours of 17 January, the United States began an intensive thirty-nine day air assault on Iraqi positions in Kuwait, and Iraq's command, control, and communications facilities in Iraq. The ground assault began on 24 February. It was swift and lethal. In one hundred hours of ground combat the U.S.-led forces encircled, entrapped, and destroyed a substantial part of Saddam's armed forces in Kuwait. Bush ordered a halt to offensive operations effective on 28 February. Ninety-nine Americans and an unknown number of Iraqis died in Operation Desert Storm. The destruction of Iraq's military machine was great, but it was not total and the bulk of Saddam's most loyal forces escaped. When news that Bush had halted offensive operations reached him, Saddam's mood changed from desperation to elation, according to one of his senior intelligence officers. "We won," Saddam exclaimed.[4]

The ceasefire prevented the wanton slaughter of a defeated enemy, but it left Saddam Hussein's regime in power. On 3 March, General Norman Schwarzkopf, commander of allied forces in Iraq, dictated the terms of surrender to Iraqi generals at the Iraqi border village of Safwan. Inexplicably, Schwarzkopf granted Iraq permission to fly attack helicopters over rebellious Shi'a villages in southern Iraq. It was an error that would have murderous consequences, because President Bush had recklessly called on the Shi'a to rise up against Saddam. U.S. forces in Kuwait stood idly by as Saddam's Republican Guards ruthlessly crushed the Shi'a rebellion with helicopter gun ships.[5]

UN Security Council Resolution 686, adopted on 2 March, codified the terms of surrender Schwarzkopf dictated at Safwan. But the Security Council went further when it adopted Resolution 687 on 3 April and Resolution 688 two days later, demanding that Iraq "not use, acquire, or develop weapons of mass destruction." The resolutions demanded that Iraq destroy all chemical and biological weapons stockpiles as well as ballistic missiles with a range greater than 150 kilometers under the supervision of a UN Special Commission, and that Iraq cease efforts "to acquire or develop nuclear weapons." The Security Council demanded Iraq's unconditional acceptance of these terms.

These would be the first of a dozen resolutions the Security Council hurled at Iraq over the next decade at the insistence of the administrations of three U.S. presidents. Within six months of the adoption of Resolution 687, the Security Council would find itself compelled to adopt Resolution 707, condemning Iraq for "serious violations" of Resolution

687. The Security Council would condemn or deplore Iraqi noncompliance, or its repression of the civilian population, at regular intervals: once in 1994, twice in 1996, twice 1997, three times in 1998, and once in 1999. All of this was prelude to the resolutions the Security Council adopted after the 9/11 attacks—and to Operation Iraqi Freedom in 2003.

As the United States was dictating surrender terms to Iraq's Baathist regime, the Afghan mujahideen, and their Arab brethren were preparing to topple Afghanistan's communist regime. The situations in Iraq and Afghanistan had practically nothing to do with one another—except in the minds of the mujahideen, who defeated the Soviets and who saw the deployment of U.S. forces in the Arabian Peninsula as an offense against God.

The Solid Base

In February 1988, Mikhail Gorbachev publicly announced his intention to withdraw the bloodied Red Army from Afghanistan. The last column of Soviet forces left the country exactly one year later, on 15 February 1989, five months after Saddam Hussein and Ayatollah Khomeini halted the insanity of the Iran-Iraq War, and eighteen months before Saddam recklessly invaded Kuwait. But, the retreat of the Red Army did not mark an end to the conflict in Afghanistan. The regime of Mohammad Najibullah, Moscow's protégé, held out against the mujihadeen until 1992, four months after the Soviet Union imploded. Then rival Pashtun, Tajik, and Uzbek tribal chieftains turned against one another and turned what had been a jihad against a foreign invasion into fratricide.[6] Afghanistan did not have a semblance of peace until 1996 when the ultra fundamentalist Taliban movement seized Kabul and imposed a harsh Islamic order on much of the country, and even then Tajik and Uzbek fighters resisted Taliban rule.

The beginning of the Soviet withdrawal was a moment of reckoning for the Arab mujahideen who journeyed to Afghanistan to fight the Soviets, and for the men who managed the logistics of the jihad. Osama bin Laden, wealthy heir to a Saudi construction company empire, rushed to Afghanistan soon after the 1979 Soviet invasion. There, in 1984, he and Abdallah Azzam, a Palestinian cleric, established the Beit al- Answar— House of the Supporters—to receive the foreign fighters who came to Afghanistan to fulfill their religious duty, and the Services Bureau— Maktab al-Khidamat, MAK—a global network of offices to recruit and finance them. The MAK had offices in as many as nine U.S. cities, including Washington, D.C., and New York. Like the terror organization it spawned, the MAK had a global presence.

Azzam, whom the mujahideen revered as their emir, eclipsed bin

Laden. Born in Jenin, Palestine, in 1941, Azzam was older than bin Laden by some sixteen years. During the 1967 Six Day War, Azzam fought against the Israelis only to see Israel conquer the site of Islam's third holiest site, in Jerusalem. After the Six Day War, Azzam earned his doctorate in Islamic jurisprudence from Al-Azhar University, Egypt's, and Islam's, preeminent institution of higher learning. He taught at King Abdul Azziz University in Saudi Arabia when Osama bin Laden was a student there. Azzam spoke with compelling religious authority and had authored a book, *The Defense of Lands*, which elevated jihad against occupation by infidels as the supreme personal duty for Muslims. Azzam became the jihad's itinerate preacher. His sermons—including sermons in Texas, Oklahoma City, and in Brooklyn's Al-Farouq Mosque, which housed MAK's New York branch, the Al-Kifah Refugee Services Center—generated men and money for the war in Afghanistan.[7]

The Soviet withdrawal did not pacify Azzam, who believed the Arab mujahideen had the religious duty to fight alongside their Afghan brothers until they consecrated an Islamic state. Then, as Azzam interpreted it, the mujahideen would be duty-bound to reclaim Muslim territory in the Soviet Republics of Central Asia, the Philippines, and above all else, Palestine. Every Muslim, he proclaimed, "should unsheathe his sword and fight to liberate Palestine." In April 1988, the same month the Soviet Union formally agreed to begin the gradual withdrawal of all Soviet forces from Afghanistan, Azzam urged Muslims to create the Solid Base—Al Qaeda al-Sulbah—of a network of mujahideen to defend other Muslim lands.[8]

Azzam was the jihad's theologian, bin Laden its logistician. Bin Laden's genius was in the management of the training and financing of the Arab mujahideen. He shared Azzam's belief that jihad was the supreme obligation of Muslims, but he soon came to interpret the obligation to demand more than just the reclamation of land from infidels. And, bin Laden was impatient to transform the Services Bureau into the Solid Base of a mujahideen network that Azzam prophesied. As early as 1986, bin Laden began training Arab mujahideen in a camp in eastern Afghanistan—Masadah, the Lions' Lair—to fight independently of the Afghan mujahideen. Azzam resented it.[9] The schism between Azzam and bin Laden was inherently doctrinal. Bin Laden had fallen under the influence of Egyptian militants who had given the world the first glimpse of the coming Islamic militancy when they executed Anwar Sadat in 1981, and whose interpretation of jihad was more radical than Azzam's.

Ayman al-Zawahiri, a founder of Egypt's Jama'a al-Jihad—the Jihad Group—was the most influential. Al-Zawahiri, a surgeon, met bin Laden in 1980 when he went briefly to Afghanistan to offer medical care to the mujahideen. He was back in Cairo in October 1981 when militants of the Jihad Group assassinated Sadat. Al-Zawahiri endured three years of abuse in an Egyptian prison for his involvement with militant Islam. By 1985 he was back in Afghanistan, where he would influence bin Laden's thinking and become his most trusted advisor and confidant.

Sheikh Omar Abdel Rahman also traveled to Afghanistan in 1985. Rahman, like Azzam, was a cleric who was educated at Egypt's Al-Azhar University. As the spiritual mentor of both the Jihad Group and its companion, the Jama'a al-Islamiyya—the Islamic Group—Rahman also suffered the wrath of Egyptian authorities after Sadat's assassination. Rahman, like Azzam, spoke with authority on the subject of jihad, but his interpretation defied Azzam's orthodoxy. Azzam interpreted jihad as a divine injunction to expel infidels from Muslim lands. Rahman discerned in the Qur'an a duty to destroy apostate regimes, like Egypt's. As an Egyptian, Rahman yearned for the liberation of Egypt from apostasy as ardently as Azzam yearned for the liberation of Palestine from Zionism. Azzam thought this dangerous. Not long before his violent death, Azzam criticized the Egyptians, and others, who began "issuing fatwas against this leader and that government."[10]

Rahman found justification in the Qur'an for jihad against the United States, as well. Rahman briefly returned to Egypt then, in 1990, he immigrated to New York where some of his militant followers were already undergoing paramilitary training.[11] Rahman's sermons in Brooklyn's Al-Farouq Mosque, the home to the Services Bureau's New York operations, and later at the Al-Salaam Mosque in New Jersey, inspired acts of terror in the New York area. Federal authorities arrested the Egyptian cleric in June 1993, five months after a terror cell attempted to destroy the World Trade Center. A federal court convicted Rahman on the charge related to the first attack on the World Trade Center in 1993 and conspiracy plots to destroy tunnels in the New York area in 1995. The court sentenced him to life imprisonment in January 1996. The sentence did not silence Rahman, who smuggled from prison a fatwa calling on "Muslims everywhere" to attack Americans mercilessly, "destroy their embassies, attack their interests, sink their ships, and shoot down their planes, kill them on land, at sea, and in the air. Kill them wherever you find them."[12]

Bin Laden had already organized a transnational terror network to destroy America's embassies, sink its ships, and crash its planes when Rahman gave religious sanction to the murder of Americans. Sometime in September 1988, as the Soviet Union began to draw down its forces in Afghanistan, bin Laden began to build up Al Qaeda. The Services Bureau had recruited, trained, and sent into combat thousands of volunteers from throughout the Muslim world. From these bin Laden could select the most capable and militant volunteers to become the flesh and bones of Al Qaeda. Bin Laden, a Saudi, became Al Qaeda's emir, but he entrusted terrorists from Egypt's Islamic Group and Jihad Group to form Al Qaeda's nucleus. Al-Zawahiri took a prominent place on Al Qaeda's consultative council, or Shura, and on its Fatwa Committee. Amin Ali al-Rashid, aka Abu Ubaidah al-Banjshiri, commanded Al Qaeda's military operations.[13]

Azzam objected to bin Laden's diversion of men and money from the Afghan jihad, but he probably would not have stood in bin Laden's path. He never had that chance. On 24 November 1989, a massive car bomb killed Azzam and two of his sons outside a mosque in Peshawar, Pakistan. Bin Laden lamented Azzam's death, but after the assassination, bin Laden emerged from Azzam's shadow.[14]

Bin Laden was in Saudi Arabia when assassins killed Azzam. Three weeks before Azzam's assassination, Saudi officials summoned bin Laden home at the behest of Benazir Bhutto, Pakistan's first female prime minister, who had declared bin Laden persona non grata. Bhutto had reason to fear the influence of militant Islam. She became Pakistan's prime minister in December 1988, four months after the death of military president Zia-ul-Haq in a mysterious plane crash hastened the return of a fragile democracy. Bhutto's father, Zulfikar Ali Bhutto, had been Pakistan's last democratically elected prime minister, until General Zia, an ardent Islamist, deposed him in a 1977 coup and hanged him two years later. Bin Laden's expulsion from Pakistan was a matter of political, and perhaps personal, survival for Bhutto.

Bin Laden posed an even more serious threat to the Saudi royal family, because of his status as an emir of the mujahideen among ordinary Saudis and his interpretation of jihad as the duty to dethrone apostate regimes. Conservative clerics, who were beginning to publicly condemn the conduct of the royal family, began to invite bin Laden to their mosques for Friday prayers. Fearing bin Laden might endorse the condemnations of the House of Saud, Saudi officials put bin Laden under surveillance, restricted his foreign travel, and threatened him with arrest.[15] Then Iraq invaded Kuwait.

The invasion terrified the Saudi royal family, which shared the Bush administration's fears that Saddam really coveted Saudi Arabia's oil fields. King Fahd did not hesitate to accept the U.S. proposal to defend the kingdom with hundreds of thousands of troops, backed by armor, artillery, and an air armada. Bin Laden, who detested Saddam's secular Baathi regime, urged the royal family to allow him to bring his lightly armed mujihadeen from Afghanistan to repel an Iraqi invasion. It was an absurd proposition.[16] The guerrilla tactics of the Arab mujahideen in the mountains of Afghanistan could not defeat Iraqi armored formations on the flat deserts of the Arabian Peninsula. The Saudi royal family wisely rejected bin Laden's proposal. Bin Laden saw the deployment of U.S. forces in the birthplace of Islam as an abomination that hastened his conversion to the belief that the House of Saud had fallen into apostasy and that the United States was the mortal enemy of Islam.

Bin Laden left Saudi Arabia for Pakistan in April 1991, immediately after the Gulf War, to escape the restrictions the Saudi government imposed on him and to take command of his nascent Al Qaeda organization.[17] He arrived on the Pakistan-Afghanistan border region just as the Afghan mujahideen were preparing to launch a major offensive. Najibullah's communist regime had managed to survive more than a year without the Red Army, but only because Moscow continued to pour money and weapons into Afghanistan to prevent the triumph of militant Islam on the Soviet Union's southern frontier. The 1991 offensive was meant to inflict the final wound on the communist regime, but when it failed bin Laden abandoned Afghanistan for the Sudan, which was in the midst of an Islamic revolution.[18]

In June 1989, General Omar Hassan al-Bashir led a cadre of Islamist officers in a coup d'etat, which abruptly terminated a four-year struggle to create the semblance of a democracy that began after the collapse of the Nimeiry regime in 1985. The military coups in the Middle East in mid-century—in Egypt, Iraq, and Syria—were invariably secular, and Islamists suffered under the secular pan-Arab nationalist regimes. All that had changed. Bashir's Islamist coup, like Zia's in Pakistan in 1977, was a sign of the triumph of political Islam over the secular, Arab nationalist ideology.

General Bashir led the coup, but Hassan al-Turabi was its guiding force. Born in 1932, Turabi was educated in London and Paris. In 1964, after he became dean of the country's most influential college of law, Turabi began organizing an Islamist challenge to the Nimeiry regime under the banner of the National Islamic Front.[19] Like Iran's Khomeini, Turabi exerted a religious influence over the politics of his country, and he believed that the Sudan could be the birthplace of a regional Islamic revival. Recognizing the militant spirit of that revival in bin Laden, Turabi invited him to Khartoum. Bin Laden actually began moving Al Qaeda militants there as early as 1989.[20]

Bin Laden spent five years in the Sudan. He started several business ventures in Khartoum, and he constructed a highway from Khartoum to Port Sudan on the Red Sea under contract with the Sudanese government. But his real purpose for being in the Sudan was to construct Al Qaeda as the base of a global jihad by solidifying alliances with other jihadist groups from around the Muslim world. By the time Sudanese authorities compelled him to leave Khartoum in May 1996, bin Laden had established an Al Qaeda presence in a number of countries, woven a global network of front charities, using the Services Bureau as his paradigm, and negotiated collaborative arrangements with twenty or more Islamist militant organizations from the Middle East, Asia, and Africa. And, he began planning attacks on U.S. facilities abroad.[21]

These were tumultuous years. Bin Laden discerned signs of an American and Zionist crusade against Islam in events in the Middle East, East Africa, and Europe. He saw the feeble United Nations efforts to broker a peace settlement in Afghanistan as an attempt to deny the mujahideen the right to establish an Islamic state. The United States abandonment of Afghanistan after the collapse of the Soviet Union proved to him that the Americans assisted the mujahideen in Afghanistan "not for the sake of Almighty God but out of fear for their thrones from the Soviet advance."[22] America's interminable military presence in Saudi Arabia long after the liberation of Kuwait revealed to him that America's true motive was to plunder Saudi Arabia's petroleum and petrodollars. The U.S. enforcement of UN sanctions on Iraq to punish Saddam Hussein's refusal to comply with the Security Council resolutions confirmed for him America's desire to oppress Iraq's Muslims. The failure of the United Nations and NATO to halt the Orthodox Christian Serbs' slaughter of Bosnian Muslims in Yugoslavia convinced him of the Christian West's complicity in genocide. And then there was the U.S. intervention in Somalia in 1992.

In December 1992, the United Nations Security Council adopted Resolution 794 sanctioning a humanitarian intervention in Somalia to save a starving people from a war-induced famine. President Bush, who could see no strategic value in a desperately poor, failing state in the Horn of Africa, waited until the very last weeks of his presidency to order 28,000 U.S. soldiers and Marines to Somalia. Troops from sixteen nations, including six Muslim nations, participated in Operation Restore Hope. But bin Laden saw this as U.S. aggression rather than humanitarian intervention, and he vowed to resist it.

The same month U.S. troops began deploying in Somalia, terrorists bombed hotels in Yemen, where U.S. officers stayed before deployment. The blasts killed two tourists, but no Americans.[23] Bin Laden sent Al Qaeda's military commanders, Abu Ubaidah and Mohammed Atef, and other Al Qaeda operatives, including operatives who would later bomb the U.S. embassies in Kenya and Tanzania in 1998, to Mogadishu to train the fighters of Mohammed Fara Aideed's National Islamic Front in the tactics that had negated the Soviet Union's military superiority in Afghanistan. In June 1993, members of Aideed's militia ambushed a Pakistani contingent during an operation to confiscate the militia's weapons, killing twenty-one Pakistanis. In August, Aideed's fighters laid an ambush that killed four U.S. soldiers. In reaction, Bill Clinton, who inherited Operation Restore Hope from George Bush, authorized U.S. Special Operations Forces to capture, or kill, Aideed. On 3 October 1993, Somali fighters killed eighteen U.S. Army Rangers and elite Delta Force commandos during an operation to capture Aideed's top lieutenants in Mogadishu. The Mogadishu incident convinced President Clinton to pull U.S. forces out of Somalia to cut America's losses. There may have been no Al Qaeda participation in the incident, but to bin Laden's mind it confirmed what Hizb'allah had proven a decade earlier in Beirut when Ronald Reagan was in the White House: the United States did not have the moral character to stand and fight.

Hizb'allah's resistance to America's presence in Beirut virtually defined the terror threat in the 1980s. Hizb'allah's megabombs destroyed the U.S. embassy, the embassy annex, and the Marine compound in Beirut in 1982 and 1983. So, bin Laden, who was solidifying alliances with militant Sunni Muslim organizations around the world, had operational reasons for reaching out to Imad Mugniyah, the Shi'a Hizb'allah chieftain, and Hizb'allah's sponsor, Shi'a Iran.

Mugniyah appeared to have vanished after the release of the U.S. hostages in Lebanon in 1991, the year bin Laden arrived in the Sudan, but he was still very active against the Israeli occupation of southern Lebanon a full decade after Menachem Begin mounted Operation Peace for Galilee. And, Mugniyah's terror had global reach. On 17 March 1992, a truck bomb exploded in front of the Israeli Embassy in Buenos Aires, killing 29 and wounding 242. This was Hizb'allah's retaliation for Israel's assassination of Sheikh Abbas Musawi, a Hizb'allah cleric, in Lebanon. The Iranian embassy in Argentina facilitated the attacks. Two years later, in December 1994, a more lethal truck bomb destroyed the Jewish Cultural Center in the Argentine capital, killing 86.[24]

Hizb'allah's mastery of the mass-casualty attack made it an important contact for Al Qaeda. Mugniyah and bin Laden—the man who personified Islamic terror against Americans in the 1980s and the man who would come to embody it two decades later—met in Khartoum to negotiate an arrangement. Hizb'allah began training Al Qaeda operatives in Lebanon's Bekaa Valley sometime after 1991.[25] The new world order freer from the threat of terror President Bush envisioned before leaving office was about to end. Truck bombs, like the one's Hizb'allah used to kill Americans in Lebanon, began killing Americans—in New York in 1993, in Saudi Arabia in 1995 and 1996, and in Kenya and Tanzania in 1998.

The Liberation Army, Fifth Battalion

On 1 September 1992, as Bill Clinton and George Bush campaigned for the hearts and minds the U.S. electorate, Ahmad Ajaj and Ramzi Yousef arrived at New York's JFK Airport on a flight from Pakistan. Ajaj, a Palestinian residing in Houston, was returning from Pakistan, where he had traveled six months earlier to train in bin Laden's Khalden camp in Afghanistan. Immigration and Naturalization Service officers detained Ajaj for possession of a false passport and confiscated documents and bomb- making manuals and videos. One document bore the title "Facing the Enemies of God Terrorism is a Religious Duty and Force is Necessary." One of the videos captured images of the bombing of a U.S. embassy.[26] INS agents also detained Ramzi Ahmad Yousef because his Iraqi passport lacked a valid U.S. visa. But Yousef cleverly appealed for political asylum from Saddam Hussein's regime. When the INS released him on his own recognizance pending an official hearing, Yousef disappeared into New York.

In New York, Yousef made contact with a small group of Egyptian, Palestinian, and Jordanian militants who were devoted to Sheikh Omar Abdel Rahman and to jihad. Two of the men, Mahmud Abouhalima and Ibrahim el-Gabrowny, had trained in one of Al Qaeda's camps. A third, Billal Alkaisi, trained others in those camps. All the men said their prayers at Al-Farouq Mosque in Brooklyn, and later at the Al-Salaam Mosque in New Jersey where Sheikh Omar Abdel Rahman raised the call to jihad against the United States. The Al-Farouq Mosque was the home of the Al-Kifah Refugee Services Center, an affiliate of bin Laden's Services Bureau. U.S. authorities blindly permitted Al-Kifah Refugee Services to raise money for a foreign war in the 1980s. But, by 1992, three years after the Soviet withdrawal from Afghanistan, the FBI's Joint Terrorism Task Force (JTTF) in New York had some of the men around Omar Abdel Rahman under surveillance, because of their connections with an Egyptian man convicted in connection with the slaying of Meir Kahane, the militant leader of the Jewish Defense League, in New York in 1990, and to militant Black Muslims. For a brief spell, the FBI even had an informant in the group. But somehow Ramzi escaped the JTTF's attention.

The man who entered the United States under the alias of Ramzi Yousef was born in Kuwait as Abdul Basit Karim to a Pakistani father and a mother of Palestinian ancestry. Born in 1968, the year the PFLP initiated the modern age of terror, Yousef represented a new generation of terrorists. Yousef was supremely dangerous. He spoke English, which gave him an advantage in the United States. He possessed technical aptitude. He had studied electronics at the Swansea Institute in Wales, and then studied explosives in bin Laden's Khaldan camp in Afghanistan. There Yousef met Ahmad Ajaj, and the two men decided to punish the United States for its fealty to Israel.[27]

Yousef arrived in New York in September to make contact with the cell around Omar Abdel Rahman. At the end of November, after Bill

Clinton won the presidency, Yousef began purchasing chemicals—urea nitrite as the main charge, aluminum power as an accelerant, hydrogen gas for a secondary blast—for a 1,500-pound bomb. He began constructing it in a New Jersey apartment and a storage facility in January after Clinton took the oath of office.[28] It would take him more than a month, until the end of February, to complete the bomb and execute the attack. But before Yousef could act, another angry Pakistani acted out his hatred.

Early in the morning of 25 January 1993, five days after Clinton's inauguration, Mir Aimal Kansi appeared outside the entrance to the CIA headquarters armed with an assault rifle. He walked along the stopped cars of CIA employees and raked them with gunfire, killing two and wounding three before fleeing the scene of the murders and the country. Federal authorities put a bounty on Kansi. The FBI searched for Kansi for more than four years before capturing him in Pakistan in June 1997. Five years later, in November 2002, the State of Virginia put Kansi to death.[29]

Nineteen days after Kansi's rampage outside CIA headquarters, on 15 February, Ramzi Yousef and Mohammed Salameh, another conspirator, reconnoitered the World Trade Center to select a location for the bomb. Eight days later, Salameh rented a Ryder Ford Econoline van, and two days after that Yousef and his accomplices completed the bomb, loaded it onto the van, and then drove it from New Jersey to Brooklyn. The next morning, 26 February, Yousef and Eyad Ismoil, a Jordanian accomplice, drove the Ryder van to the World Trade Center. They parked it in the B-2 level of the garage beneath the Vista Hotel in the massive World Trade Center complex, near a vital support column in Tower One. Then Yousef lit a fuse to allow himself time to escape in a car driven by one of the conspirators. Yousef had come to murder Americans, not to martyr himself.

At seventeen minutes past noon, Yousef's truck bomb exploded. The blast instantly killed six World Trade Center employees eating lunch in an underground lunchroom—John DiGiovani, Robert Kirkpatrick, Stephan Knapp, William Macko, Wilfredo Mercado, and Monica Smith—and injured more than 1,000. The explosion tore through reinforced concrete two levels above and three levels below the epicenter of the explosion on B-2, devastated B-2, tore open a 150-square-foot crater, and destroyed 200 vehicles, including a presidential limousine that the Secret Service kept in the World Trade Center. Above, the blast tore a 400-square-foot hole in the Vista Hotel's Liberty Ballroom and blew out its windows. One level below, the blast gouged a 1,500-square-foot hole in the garage ramp. The force reached three levels below, collapsing a section of the ceiling of the PATH commuter station. Dense smoke rushed upward through Tower One.[30] It was a devastating blast, but the attack was a failure. Ramzi Yousef had wanted the bomb to collapse Tower One into Tower Two and kill tens of thousands of Americans. He killed six.

The day after the attack, Nidal Ayyad, a Palestinian involved in the conspiracy, sent a communiqué to the *New York Times* claiming the attack in the name of the Liberation Army, Fifth Battalion. The attack came near the second anniversary of Iraq's defeat in Operation Desert Storm, but the communiqué did not mention Iraq: "This action was done in response for (sic) the American political, economical and military support to Israel." No one had ever heard of the fictional Liberation Army, but behind the fiction was the reality of many thousands of Muslims, like the men radicalized in Brooklyn's Al- Farouq Mosque, who hated the United States. The communiqué boasted of more than 150 "suicidal soldiers" ready to execute "missions against military and civilian targets in the United States."[31]

In a radio address on his economic plan the day after the bombing, President Clinton promised the U.S. public that he would put the full resources of the federal government into an investigation to discover "who was involved and why this happened." He never mentioned the word terrorism, but he acknowledged that "thousands were struck with fear in their hearts" when Ramzi Yousef's 1,500-pound bomb exploded beneath the World Trade Center. Clinton was reassuring. "Feeling safe," he said, "is an essential part of being secure," a curious inversion of the logic that being secure is essential to feeling safe. Three days later, the president still was not prepared to say that the detonation of a massive bomb in the World Trade Center was an act of terrorism. "I am very concerned about it," the president assured the public, "but I think it is also important that we not overreact to it."[32] The president's concern about overreaction to an obvious terrorist act on American soil would guide his administration's counterterrorism policy for the next three years. Few in the administration, or in the intelligence community, appeared ready to accept the possibility that there really were "suicide soldiers" ready to strike military and civilian targets in the United States.

True to the president's promise, the FBI was able to identify Ramzi Yousef and the others involved in the World Trade Center bombing. Yousef and two others had fled the country. But eventually federal authorities convicted seven conspirators for the attack, including Yousef and Omar Abdel Rahman. Sheikh Rahman's religious sanction for the attack was as critical to the World Trade Center conspiracy as was Yousef's bomb-making. In fact, Rahman continued to incite violence, and those around him planned a new wave of terror attacks: the assassination of Egyptian President Hosni Mubarak during a visit to New York the month after the World Trade Center attack, and the bombing of the Lincoln and Holland tunnels, UN headquarters, and Federal Building in Manhattan. But the World Trade Center bombing exposed the cell. On 24 June, the FBI arrested Rahman and nine others before they could carry out the new wave of attacks. The government eventually convicted all ten. A federal court convicted Sheikh Omar Abdel Rahman in 1995 for seditious conspiracy against the United States and sentenced him to life in prison.[33] The conviction deepened his contempt. From prison the blind cleric surreptitiously issued his fatwa exhorting Muslims to kill Americans "on land, at sea and in the air. Kill them wherever you find them."

Ramzi Yousef was obsessed with killing Americans long before Omar Abdel Rahman issued his prison fatwa. Yousef evaded capture for two years after the World Trade Center bombing. He fled to his native Pakistan the day of the attack, and in 1994 set up operations in the Philippines. Yousef came to New York to kill Americans in the tens of thousands on land. After the failure of World Trade Center attack, Yousef conspired to kill thousands of Americans in the air.

In the Philippines Yousef rendezvoused with two men, Wali Khan Amin Shah and Khalid Sheikh Mohammed. Shah, alias Usama Asmurai, a wounded veteran of the Afghan jihad, was one of the men bin Laden entrusted to establish Al Qaeda's presence in the Philippines; bin Laden's brother-in-law Mohammed Jamal al-Khalifa was the other.[34] Khalid Sheikh Mohammed was Ramzi Yousef's uncle, and like his nephew, was determined to harm the United States. Mohammed had actually attended college in the United States. In 1987, a year after graduating from a North Carolina state college with a degree in mechanical engineering, Mohammed traveled to Pakistan to train in one of bin Laden's camps. But Mohammed never fought the Soviets. Instead, he operated a service organization for Arab mujihadeen moving through Pakistan to the battlefields of Afghanistan during the final phase of the jihad against the Najibullah regime. Mohammed left Pakistan for Qatar in 1992, the same year his nephew arrived in the United States to bomb the World Trade Center, ostensibly to work for the Qatar government. But Mohammed somehow found the money to travel around the world to places where Muslim militants were organizing for jihad. In 1994 those travels took Mohammad to the Philippines to join with Ramzi Yousef to organize another mass casualty terror operation.[35]

In November 1994, exactly two years after Yousef began purchasing urea nitrite in New Jersey to destroy the World Trade Center, Yousef began purchasing nitroglycerine in Manila for a dozen miniature bombs to destroy airliners in flight. Middle Eastern terrorists had sabotaged commercial airliners in flight before: Ahmed Jabril's PFLP-GC destroyed

Swiss Air flight 330 in 1970; Abd al-Ghafur's National Arab Youth for the Liberation of Palestine destroyed TWA 841 in 1974; Muammar Qadaffi's intelligence service destroyed Pan Am 103 in 1988. In total those bombs killed 381 passengers and crew members. Ramzi Yousef planned to kill ten times that. His Operation Bojinka was a plan to destroy twelve U.S.-flag airliners, eleven bound for the United States, in the skies over the Pacific over two days—twelve transoceanic airliners each carrying nearly 300 passengers. Yousef intended to randomly murder nearly 3,500 human beings.[36]

The destruction of Pan Am 103 in 1988 alerted aviation officials to the danger of a bomb in the luggage compartment of a commercial airliner. To defeat airport security, Yousef planned for terrorists to carry bomb components—nitroglycerine in bottles of contact lens solution, batteries in the heels of shoes, Casio watches converted into timing devices—in their carry-on luggage. Each terrorist would assemble a bomb, place it beneath his seat, set the timer, and then deplane during a stopover. A decade earlier, Mohammed Rashid had bombed a Pan Am flight out of Tokyo to Honolulu this very same way.

On the night of 1 December 1994, Yousef and Wali Khan planted a bomb in a Manila theater to test it. The bomb exploded, but did not kill anyone. Ten days later, Yousef boarded Philippine Airlines flight 434 from Manila to Tokyo. He deplaned during a stopover in Cebu after assembling a bomb and placing it beneath his seat.It killed a Japanese citizen, Haruki Ikegami, but it did not destroy the plane.

Operation Bojinka was in the advanced stage of planning when a clumsy accident forced Yousef to abandon the operation and flee the Philippines. Yousef had designed, fabricated, and tested bombs. Yousef, Mohammed, Wali Khan, and Abdul Hakim Murad, who had joined the conspiracy, had collected detailed information about transoceanic flights. Yousef and Mohammed actually boarded flights to Hong Kong and South Korea to observe in-flight procedures.[37] Then, On 6 January, Yousef and Murad were mixing the chemicals for the Bojinka bombs in a Manila apartment when they accidentally ignited a chemical fire. Both fled the scene. Police entered the apartment and discovered a bomb factory.

Philippine authorities arrested Murad the night of the fire when he returned to the apartment to retrieve Yousef's laptop computer. They arrested Wali Khan days later. Ramizi Yousef fled the Philippines, but he had left tracks. FBI and State Department Diplomatic Security Service agents captured Ramzi Yousef in Islamabad on 7 February 1995, just two weeks before the second anniversary of the World Trade Center attack.

Yousef confessed to the crime to FBI agents during the twenty-hour flight from Pakistan to the United States—"I masterminded the explosion"—and explained that he wanted to compel the United States to abandon Israel. But Yousef revealed more than that. He had conducted surveillance for a possible assassination of President Clinton during a state visit to the Philippines in November 1994, and had considered assassinating the pope during his visit in January 1995. Encrypted files on the laptop computer the Philippine police seized in Manila revealed the terrifying breadth of the Bojinka plot. Yousef and Murad boasted about these conspiracies to interrogators. Murad revealed even more: five years before the 9/11 attacks, he and Yousef were already thinking about crashing an airplane into CIA headquarters. Ramzi Yousef gave authorities a glimpse of the existence of a global jihadist movement during his interrogation. He admitted that he knew the names of Mohammed Jamal al-Khalifa and Osama bin Laden. But he denied that he acted under a superior's orders. He was not a member of a militant Muslim organization. He was a militant Muslim acting on his own sense of duty to Islam. That is all Yousef, who now enjoyed the Miranda privilege against self-incrimination, would tell the FBI.[38]

Yousef killed six Americans and one Japanese. He might have killed tens of thousands more if he had had a battalion of suicide soldiers, more funding, and a solid base. Bin Laden possessed these, but he was just beginning to fund and plan terror operations when Yousef was planning and executing his. Bin Laden did not order the World Trade Center attack or Operation Bojinka; Yousef's Liberation Army, Fifth Battalion's operations were not Al Qaeda operations.[39] Actually, it was Yousef who inspired the 9/11 attacks. The year after the FBI captured Yousef, the year bin Laden declared war against the United States, Khalid Sheikh Mohammed, who was safely in Qatar when U.S. authorities captured his nephew, appealed to bin Laden to fund another attack on the World Trade Center—an attack that would have the suicide soldiers and the funding of the Base.

The Most Generous Solution

In January 1993, as Ramzi Yousef was secretly making a bomb in New Jersey for an attack on the United States in the name of the Palestinians, Palestinians were secretly making peace overtures to the Israelis in Oslo. By September, Palestinian and Israeli leaders had agreed to a Declaration of Principles in the White House Rose Garden. This was the first of a series of agreements that eventually led to the creation of the Palestinian National Authority and to Arafat's triumphal return to Palestine as the Authority's president.

Ironically, Iraq's invasion of Kuwait was the catalyst for the revival of the peace process, just as it was a catalyst for bin Laden's jihad. Yasser

Arafat had drawn closer to Saddam's regime in Baghdad before Iraq's attempt to annex Kuwait. Dependent on Saddam's financing, Arafat imprudently backed Iraq. Saddam reciprocated by disingenuously attempting to link Iraq's compliance with UN resolutions demanding its withdrawal from Kuwait to Israel's compliance with UN resolutions demanding its withdrawal from the occupied territories. Arafat, as chairman, carried the weight of the official PLO, but there was opposition to support for Iraq within the PLO leadership and within Fatah. Abu Iyad's opposition was potentially the most consequential.

Salah Khalef, aka Abu Iyad, was the most senior and influential of the Fatah's surviving founders, besides Arafat himself. Arafat, Abu Iyad, and Abu Jihad created Fatah more than three decades earlier. Israeli commandos led by the future Israeli prime minister Ehud Barak killed Abu Jihad, Fatah's military chieftain, in 1988. Abu Iyad was Fatah's intelligence chieftain and the man behind Black September's terror rampage twenty years earlier. Abu Iyad had clashed with Arafat over strategy in years past. Now, they clashed over policy toward Iraq. Abu Iyad saw the error of alienating other powerful Arab states by embracing Saddam, so he endorsed the war to expel Iraqi forces from Kuwait. It was Abu Iyad's final pronouncement as a leader of the Palestinian nationalist movement.

On 17 January, as the first bombs of the U.S. air war against Iraq fell on Baghdad, one of Abu Iyad's bodyguards suddenly turned his weapon on Iyad and killed him and two of his deputies in his office in Tunis.[40] The assassination was the inevitable end of the life of the archterrorist who was behind the murder of Israeli athletes in Munich and U.S. diplomats in Khartoum and who justified terrorism by resorting to semantics. "I do not confuse revolutionary violence, which is a political act" Abu Iyad wrote in his autobiography, "with terrorism, which is not." The assassination was also Abu Nidal's final act of terror. Sabri Khalil al-Banna, aka Abu Nidal, had dreamed of the elimination of Abu Iyad, his primary rival in the Palestinian national movement, ever since he founded his Fatah-Revolutionary Council with Iraqi support in 1974. Abu Nidal boasted of being the world's most dangerous terrorist, "the ghost who walks through the night," but he began and ended his career as a hired assassin for Saddam Hussein. The assassination of Abu Iyad was neither political nor revolutionary: it was the act of a psychopath to satisfy a dictator's thirst for vengeance. Abu Nidal descended into paranoia after the assassination of Abu Iyad and eventually sought refuge in Baghdad after the first Gulf War. Saddam had him killed in 2002 as Operation Iraqi Freedom approached.

The death of Abu Iyad did not alter the strategic equation. Saudi Arabia and the other Gulf states slashed their subsidies to the PLO to punish Arafat, as Abu Iyad foresaw, after Operation Desert Storm took its inevitable course.[41] The depletion of the PLO treasury left the chairman with few options. In March, immediately after U.S. forces vanquished the Iraqis, President Bush called for a peace conference to resolve the Arab-Israeli conflict. This was the president's good faith effort to turn the rhetoric about a new world order into reality. In a sign of weakness, Arafat agreed to send Palestinians representatives to the peace conference as members of the Jordanian delegation when the conference began in Madrid at the end of October 1991.

The Madrid conference gave the peace process new life. Official talks continued in other European venues and in Washington after Bill Clinton replaced Bush in the White House and Itzak Rabin replaced Itzak Shamir as Israeli prime minister. Rabin was the real force behind the new peace process. In a bold gesture, the former general authorized secret, unofficial discussions between Israelis and Palestinians in Oslo, Norway. Israelis and Palestinians met there on 20 January 1993, the very moment Ramzi Yousef was mixing the chemicals for the World Trade Center bomb. The secret phase of the Oslo talks culminated in August with the conclusion of the Oslo Agreement. Israel's only concession was its recognition of the PLO as the representative of the Palestinian people, close enough to the Arab League's 1973 Algiers Declaration to placate the PLO chairman. With that, negotiations moved into the open and gained momentum. Bill Clinton, who correctly realized that the conclusion of a real and lasting peace between the Israelis and the Palestinians could be his presidential legacy, seized the initiative. By September 1993, Clinton had his first major foreign policy triumph when prime minister Rabin and chairman Arafat stood beside him in the White House Rose Garden. On 13 September, Rabin and Arafat signed the Declaration of Principles of Interim Self-Government Arrangements.

An era of secular Palestinian terror seemed to have ended with a handshake between Arafat and Rabin in the Rose Garden. Twenty-three years earlier to the week, the PFLP staged its spectacular Skyjack Sunday operation to disrupt a minor cease-fire agreement between Israel and Egypt. Palestinian Rejectionists reacted to virtually every peace overture with some act of terror throughout the 1970s and well into the 1980s, until circumstances compelled Arafat to renounce terrorism in 1988. Arafat's and Rabin's handshake sealed the end of that era.

But the agreement's awkward title captured the limits of what the Israelis would permit: limited Palestinian administration of some government functions in some of the territory the Israelis had seized twenty-seven years before. It took a year for negotiators to transform the principles of self-government into substance. In May 1994, Rabin and Arafat put their names to the Cairo Agreement in the Egyptian capital. The agreement granted the Palestinians limited autonomy over the Gaza strip and the West Bank town of Jerico. In July, Arafat triumphantly arrived in Gaza as a national hero, but in reality he had no more authority than a provincial governor.[42] Two decades earlier, Arafat stood triumphantly before the UN General Assembly and invited Jews to live together with Palestinians in peace and without discrimination in a democratic Palestine. This was the "most generous solution," Arafat could imagine. Now it was Arafat who was dependent on Israeli generosity.

As president of the Palestine National Authority, Arafat would negotiate a series of agreements over the remainder of the decade in the hope of solving the ambiguous status of the Palestinians by gaining them a state. But the dynamics of Israeli politics changed after an Israeli zealot assassinated Rabin on 4 November 1995, and the more hard-line Likud party regained control of the Israeli government. Arafat, under unrelenting pressure from Clinton, would conclude minor agreements with Israeli prime ministers who embodied the historic hostility between the Palestinians and the Jews: Yitzhak Rabin, the commander of Israeli forces during the Six Day War; Binyamin Netanyahu, the brother of the only Israeli killed in the fabled Entebbe hostage rescue in July 1976; and Ehud Barak, once the leader of Israel's elite Sayaret Matkal comandos, who led the Youth of Spring assault in the heart of Beirut that killed three senior members of PLO in 1973 and commanded the 1988 operation that killed Arafat's trusted military chieftain, Abu Jihad. But a just and lasting peace remained elusive. Clinton brought Israeli and Palestinian negotiators together at Camp David in the final days of his administration in the hope of achieving a final status agreement that would have created a Palestinian state beside Israel. But Arafat, President Clinton later lamented, "just couldn't bring himself to say yes."[43]

The failure of the final status agreement talks created the conditions for a resumption of violence. Then, on 28 September 2000, in the midst of his campaign to become prime minister, Ariel Sharon, who as defense minister directed Israel's 1982 invasion of Lebanon, visited the Temple Mount, the site of the remnants of the biblical Temple, accompanied by nearly one thousand armed Israeli police. It was a provocation. Muslims revere the place as Haram al-Shariff, the site of the Al-Aksa Mosque, one of the holiest places of Islam. The next day Palestinian civilians began to hurl rocks at Israeli soldiers. The Israelis responded with bullets, killing four. This was the origin of the second Intifada—the Al-Aksa Intifada. The Israelis have always contended that Arafat, who had gained politically from the first Intifada, somehow planned this new uprising.[44] But after the Palestinians erupted, radical Islamic organizations— Hamas, which the late Abdallah Azzan helped create, and Palestinian

Islamic Jihad—directed the fury of the Palestinians. Another generation would have to wait for peace.

Declaration of War

As the FBI and CIA pursued Ramzi Yousef, the Clinton administration pursued peace agreements to end the decades-old conflict between the Palestinians and Israelis and a terrible war between Croats, Serbs, and Bosnians that erupted in Yugoslavia, the same year, Yousef attacked New York. In September 1995, the Israelis and Palestinians signed an Interim Agreement on the West Bank and Gaza that extended Palestinian autonomy into the West Bank. In November, Croatian, Serbian, and Bosnian leaders signed the Dayton Peace Accords at Wright-Patterson Air Force Base in Ohio after tense negotiations that verged on collapse any number of times. President Clinton could justifiably boast of these diplomatic breakthroughs.

There were no major terror attacks against the United States in the two years between the attack on the World Trade Center in February 1993 and the capture of Ramzi Yousef in February 1995. This fact seemed to vindicate Clinton, who had warned Americans against overreaction in the aftermath of bombing of the World Trade Center. Things might have been very different had Yousef executed Operation Bojinka. But now U.S. authorities had him in custody, and a U.S. attorney was vigorously prosecuting Omar Abdel Rahman and other militant Muslims in a New York courtroom for the World Trade Center attack and the "Landmarks" conspiracy. The chance discovery of the Bojinka conspiracy in January 1995 might have alerted U.S. counterterrorism officials to the existence of a radically more lethal terror threat, but the plot appeared to be the psychopathic fantasy of a lone terrorist. That perception was dangerous.

In fact, there were explosions of jihadist terror in Asia, North Africa, Europe, the Arabian Peninsula, and even the Americas. In the Philippines, the Abu Sayyef organization began a series of bombings, kidnappings, and armed assaults culminating in April 1994 with an attack on a remote town in the archipelago, where militants killed more than 60. In August, Moroccan militants staged the first of what they intended to be a series of attacks against foreign tourists and killed two in a Marrakesh hotel. In December 1994, as Yousef was testing his miniature bombs for Bokinka, a Hizb'allah truck bomb killed 89 in Buenos Aires, the second lethal attack in the Argentine capital in less than two years as Hizb'allah's ongoing struggle to expel Israeli forces from southern Lebanon went international.

That same month, four terrorists belonging to the Algerian Armed

Islamic Group (GIA) hijacked Air France flight 8969 after departure from Algiers and flew it to Marseilles, where they demanded that airport personnel refuel the huge Airbus. They murdered three French passengers before French counterterror commandos stormed the jet and killed them. The takedown averted a much greater tragedy. The hijackers were on a martyrdom operation to crash the jet into the Eiffel Tower. The FBI and the intelligence community were now aware of two plots to use hijacked aircraft as weapons of mass destruction; Murad, Yousef's accomplice, confessed to one; the December 1994 GIA incident in Paris was the other.[45]

Throughout the summer and fall of 1995, the GIA carried out a series of bombings to punish the French government for its support of the Algerian government in its campaign to suppress militant Islam. Bombs exploded in the Paris Metro station three times, once in July and twice in October, killing twelve and wounding hundreds. The 25 July attack, the most deadly, killed ten and wounded more than one hundred.[46] So, by early 1995, there were signs of Islamic militancy across the Islamic world from Algeria to Saudi Arabia. The attacks in Paris proved that jihadists regarded the friends of their enemies to be enemies. Then came another act of terror on American soil.

On 19 April, Timothy McVeigh, a veteran of Operation Desert Storm, parked a Ryder rental truck packed with 5,000 pounds of ammonium nitrate and fuel oil directly in front of the Murrah Federal Building in Oklahoma City. Just after 9:00 A.M., a thunderous explosion sheered off the front of the building. The attack, the worst ever on U.S. soil, killed 168, 19 of them children playing in a day-care center in the federal building.[47] The bombing had the look and feel of the World Trade Center attack two years earlier and the Hizb'allah attack in Buenos Aires the previous December. But there was no connection to Al Qaeda or militant Islam. Timothy McVeigh was a White Supremacist, not an Islamic fundamentalist. McVeigh killed to punish the Federal government for the death of 76 members of a religious cult, 27 of them children, when the FBI attempted to storm the compound of the Branch Davidians in Waco, Texas. 19 April marked the second anniversary of the fiery end of a two-month siege that began on 28 February 1993, only two days after Ramzi Yousef bombed the World Trade Center. McVeigh's only connection to militant Islam was the anti-Semitism White Supremacy shared with militant Islam.[48]

The Oklahoma City atrocity, like the bombing of the World Trade Center three years earlier, revealed the vulnerability of the American homeland. A month later, members of Aum Shinrikyo, a Japanese religious cult, attacked a Tokyo subway with Sirin gas, killing 12 and injuring three times that many. The Tokyo incident, like the attack in Oklahoma

City, exposed the vulnerability of open societies to terrorist attack. But now there was the specter of weapons of mass destruction becoming weapons of terror. President Clinton, who had warned against overreaction to terrorism two years earlier, directed the intelligence community to provide him with an estimate of the threat.

Militant Islam posed the gravest danger, but in the early months of 1995 counterterrorism officials barely grasped its dimensions. Ramzi Yousef's activities compelled the intelligence community to probe deeper. The FBI, the lead agency in the World Trade Center bombing, produced an analysis that called attention to "a new generation of terrorists . . . with access to a worldwide network of support." The CIA reached similar conclusions.[49] By summer, the intelligence community had produced a comprehensive National Intelligence Estimate about the emerging pattern of global terrorism that warned of "increasing domestic threat posed by foreign terrorists." There were special risks for the symbols of U.S. political and economic power: the White House and the Capitol in Washington, and Wall Street in New York. But the discovery of the Bojinka conspiracy forced analysts to take a hard look at the vulnerability of civilian aviation. The conclusions were disturbing: "Our review of the evidence obtained thus far about the plot uncovered in Manila in early 1995, suggests the conspirators were guided in their selection of the method and venue of attack by carefully studying security procedures in place in the region. If terrorists operating in this country are similarly methodical, they will identify serious vulnerabilities in the security system for domestic flights."[50]

The intelligence community's estimate elicited a presidential directive. On 25 June Clinton signed Presidential Decision Directive 39, "U.S. Policy on Counterterrorism." Its premise reflected the conclusion of the intelligence community that terrorism, whether domestic or international, represented "a potential threat to national security." To counter that threat, the United States would "identify groups or states that sponsor or support terrorism, isolate them, and extract a heavy price for their actions." PDD 39 mentioned preemption, but it emphasized deterrence and the reduction of America's vulnerabilities at home and abroad. The president instructed the CIA to conduct an "aggressive program of intelligence collection and analysis, counterintelligence and covert action." The day after the president signed the directive, the threat of terrorism to American interests became apparent again.

On 26 June, militants of the Egyptian Jihad Group nearly assassinated president Hosni Mubarak in an ambush of his motorcade with automatic weapons and rocket propelled grenades during a state visit to Addis Ababa, Ethiopia. The ambush sparked a campaign of attacks by Egyptian Islamists against Egyptian embassies and tourists visiting the land of the Pharaohs, culminating in the massacre of tourists in Luxor in 1997. Ayman al-Zawahiri, now the emir of the Egyptian Jihad Group, was behind the assassination attempt.[51] Zawahiri had personally suffered the wrath of the Mubarak government after the assassination of Sadat twelve years earlier, but the motivation for the ambush was political, not personal. Islamic militants condemned America's staunchest allies in the Middle East—the Mubarak regime and the House of Saud—as godless, and they abhorred the United States for sustaining them. This was the impetus of the emerging pattern of global terrorism that the intelligence community was just beginning to discern.

Egyptian and Ethiopian authorities were able to trace the plot to kill Mubarak to the Islamic Group and the Sudan. But the intelligence community was becoming increasingly cognizant that bin Laden lurked in the shadows of the attempt on Mubarak and other terror operations as the principal financier of a host of terror groups operating in a widening radius from the Sudan.[52] Soon, bin Laden would become the focus of much of the CIA's "aggressive program of intelligence collection, analysis, and covert action" as per Clinton's June directive.

The Saudi royal family had tried to rid itself of bin Laden, the man who had once been the kingdom's honored son. The Saudi government banished bin Laden in 1991, seized his assets in 1992, and finally revoked his Saudi citizenship in 1994. Saudi security services may have been involved in one of several attempts to assassinate bin Laden in Khartoum, although the long-time head of Saudi intelligence ridiculed the accusation: "we would have done it better."[53] Bin Laden took these chastisements as further evidence of the Saudi regime's descent into illegitimacy. Only weeks after the attempt on Mubarak, on 11 July, bin Laden published an open letter to King Fahd denouncing the "atrocities" the Saudi monarch and his "clan perpetrated against God and his religion." The king's subservience to the United States was the greatest of these atrocities. King Fahd, bin Laden charged, had tolerated Saudi Arabia's transformation into a U.S. "protectorate to be defiled by soldiers of the Cross with their soiled feet in order to protect your crumbling throne," and had acquiesced as the U.S. armed forces, operating from bases in Saudi Arabia to pursue its policy of "annihilation of the Iraqi army and the Muslim people of Iraq." The Saudi government's allegiance to infidels against Muslims had the effect of "nullifying its validity before God." Bin Laden urged the king to abdicate, then warned that if King Fahd tried to cling to power, bin Laden and other pious Muslims would seek God's help to be "loyal to our pledge of vengeance for His religion."[54]

Bin Laden's letter apparently did not alarm U.S. officials in the kingdom. Five months earlier, President Clinton directed the CIA to undertake an aggressive program of intelligence collection and analyses to identify terrorist organizations, and he directed the Department of Defense and other cabinet departments to reduce vulnerabilities to terror attacks at home and abroad. But, U.S. intelligence saw no evidence of "large, organized terrorist groups" operating in the kingdom and estimated that the risk of the terrorist incident was "very low." Notably, bin Laden did not openly threaten violence against the regime or the soldiers of the Cross in his letter to King Fahd. In fact, he had already taken the decision to arm dissidents to the Saudi regime for attacks against Americans.[55] There were two lethal attacks against Americans in Saudi Arabia in the span of seven months between 1995 and 1996. The first came in the second week of November in the Saudi capital, Riyadh.

On 13 November, two men parked a small truck in front of the Office of the Program Manager-Saudi Arabian National Guard in Riyadh, where U.S. military advisors and private contractors trained officers of the Saudi Arabian National Guard. The men armed a bomb then fled. At 11:40 A.M., 250 pounds of military grade explosives detonated. The blast sheared off the front of the building, killed five Americans and two Indian nationals, and wounded 34 others. The Saudi authorities rushed to bring the attackers to justice in order to demonstrate the regime's firm control. Police arrested four men in connection with the attack, televised their confessions, and then beheaded them in May 1996. The men admitted only that bin Laden inspired them, although three of them had fought in Afghanistan.[56] They said nothing about financing or about membership in Al Qaeda. They revealed no more about bin Laden than Ramzi Yousef revealed after his capture that February.

The second attack came seven months later, in June 1996. There were warnings. In January, the U.S. embassy in Riyadh publicly warned Americans visiting Saudi Arabia about the threat of attacks against institutions identified with U.S. interests. In March, the Defense Intelligence Agency learned that "a large quantity of explosives was being smuggled into Saudi Arabia during the month-long Hajj pilgrimage to Mecca between April and May." On 28 June, Saudi authorities seized 85 pounds of explosives in a car at the Jordanian border and arrested the driver. A week later, Saudi security services arrested three other men. All four were Shi'a, and all belonged to the Saudi branch of Hizb'allah, Hizb'allah Al-Hijaz. The arrests gave Saudi and U.S. intelligence solid evidence of a conspiracy to attack U.S. military personnel "during or immediately after the Hajj."[57]

U.S. intelligence officers briefed the commander of the 4404th Fighter Wing about those threats in March. The airmen of the 4404th, based at the King Abdul Azziz air base in Dharhan, were the most visible and vulnerable U.S. military personnel in the kingdom. In fact, the airmen's situation in 1996 was eerily similar to the situation of the Marines at the Beirut International Airport in 1983. The Marines deployed in Lebanon to protect Muslims after the massacres in Sabra and Shatila camps. The airmen deployed in Saudi Arabia to enforce the no-fly zone over southern Iraq to protect Iraq's Shi'a Muslims after Saddam Hussein's Republican Guard crushed the Shi'a uprising in 1991. But to Hizb'allah, the purpose of the Marines' presence in Lebanon was to reinforce the Israeli occupation; to Saudi Hizb'allah, the purpose of the airmen's presence in Saudi Arabia was to menace Shi'a Iran. And there was another similarity between the situation of the Marines and the airmen. Both were dangerously exposed to an act of terror. Hundreds of the Marines in Beirut had been billeted in a six-story building adjacent to an open parking lotwhen a Hizb'allah suicide attacker drove a truck laden with explosives into the building.

The airmen in at Abdel Azziz airbase were billeted in the Khobar Towers complex. Building 131 sat adjacent to an open parking lot on the eastern parameter of the complex. Just after 10:00 P.M. on 25 June, terrorists drove a huge fuel tanker into the parking lot, backed it up to a concrete barrier a few yards from Building 131, armed the bomb, and fled in a car. Sentries on the roof had only minutes to alert the airmen in the top three floors before the huge bomb exploded. The blast, with the force of 5,000 pounds of TNT, tore off the front of Building 131, damaged six buildings, and blew out windows in the wide radius of the explosion. Hurling glass and debris killed nineteen Americans and wounded more than 200.[58]

The Saudi regime reacted to the Dharhan attack just as to the Riyadh attack seven months earlier by attempting to suppress politically dangerous truths about internal dissent and the existence of groups capable of mounting lethal terrorist attacks in the kingdom. Security forces were able to apprehend some of the men involved in the conspiracy. In fact, the four men that the Saudis arrested in March and April actually belonged to the same Saudi Hizb'allah cell that carried out the attacks. But the Saudi government refused to grant the FBI access to the bombing suspects fearing that a probing interrogation would yield evidence of the involvement of Iran, and possibly bin Laden.[59]

Bin Laden never claimed credit for either the Riyadh or Dharhan attack. But he openly praised the men who carried them out: "I hold in great esteem and respect these great men because they removed the brand of shame from the forehead of our [Islamic] nation." He also acknowledged that he instigated the attack: "I would like to say that this is obvious."[60] In fact, U.S. intelligence was able to determine that that the Khobar Towers bombing was an Iranian operation. The men who planned and executed it trained in Hizb'allah camps in Lebanon, Syria, and Iran. The explosives originated in Lebanon. A Lebanese member of Hizb'allah personally converted the fuel tanker into a mobile bomb for his Saudi accomplices. An Iranian intelligence officer supervised the operation from inception to execution. The Hizb'allah cell had conducted surveillance of U.S. facilities in the kingdom for more than two years, until it identified the Khobar Towers complex as its target.[61]

Bin Laden's and Al Qaeda's participation in the plot remains a mystery, but it could have been substantial.[62] Iran and bin Laden had different reasons for attacking Americans in the Saudi kingdom. Iran knew that the presence of U.S. forces thwarted its aspirations for hegemony in the Persian Gulf. Bin Laden believed that the Soldiers of the Cross defiled Islam's most sacred land. So, both Iran and Al Qaeda had reason to dream that the Clinton administration would flee the danger of more terror attacks in Saudi Arabia just as the Reagan administration had fled Lebanon a decade earlier.

After the Khobar Towers attack, bin Laden warned that the bombings were signs of anger at the Saudi royal family's corruption and America's oppression of Muslims. Bin Laden was in back in Afghanistan when Saudi Hizb'allah bombed the Khobar Towers. In May, Sudanese authorities expelled bin Laden and his men under withering pressure from Egypt's Mubarak, who had narrowly survived an assassination attempt the previous June. Egyptian intelligence had tracked the conspiracy back to Khartoum, Al-Zawahiri's Jihad Group, and bin Laden. The Sudanese knew that the National Front regime could not survive the retribution of its powerful neighbor, so it prudently sent bin Laden away. Bin Laden left Khartoum for Afghanistan the same month Saudi authorities beheaded the men who carried out the Riyadh attack and a month before Saudi Hizb'allah bombed the Khobar Towers in Dhahran. For bin Laden, Saudi Arabia was now the locus of a global jihad, but the Egyptian militants who composed the core of Al Qaeda did not forsake Egypt. Only six days after the Khobar Towers bombing that killed 19 Americans, an Egyptian Jihad Group cell detonated a car bomb in front of the Egyptian embassy in Islamabad, Pakistan, killing 16.[63]

In July, bin Laden granted an interview to a British journalist. He vented that bombings coming seven months apart was evidence of "the huge anger of the Saudi people against America." "The Saudis," he said "know their real enemy is America."[64] A week after the interview, on 17 July, TWA flight 800 disintegrated only minutes after it took off from JFK airport in New York; 230 people died in the crash of the Boeing 747. The FBI investigated the crash of TWA 800 as a probable act of terrorism because of similarities with the destruction of Pan Am 103 in 1988. Twenty days later, a small bomb exploded in Centennial Park in Atlanta during the summer Olympic Games, killing one. Neither was an attack

by Islamic militants. A spark in a fuel tank, not a bomb, destroyed TWA
880; the Atlanta Olympics bombing was the act of a lone American
fanatic. But these incidents put the Clinton administration on edge
about a wave of terror.

On 23 August, as the presidential raced heated up in the United
States, bin Laden published a "Declaration of War against the Americans who Occupy the Land of the Two Holy Mosques."[65] He warned of
"volcanic eruption" of popular anger against the corruption of the
Saudi royal family and U.S. aggression against Muslims everywhere as
the leader of a "Zionist-Crusader alliance." "The greatest of these
aggressions" was the occupation of "the land of the two holy mosques."
These were the same grievances bin Laden had articulated more than a
year earlier in his open letter to King Fahd when he urged the king to
abdicate. Now he was raising the call to jihad, because he wrote, "after
Belief, there is no more important duty than pushing the American
enemy out of the holy land." The declaration urged Saudi men to rebel,
Saudi women to boycott U.S. goods, and the Saudi National Guard to
mutiny. Bin Laden's declaration eloquently blended analyses of current
affairs with verses from the Qur'an in what was a classic call for revolutionary guerrilla war. The volcano of popular resentment against the
regime and the Americans did not erupt. This did not disillusion bin
Laden—he had declared war on the United States, and now he would
wage it.

Chapter 9

Kill Them on the Land, the Sea, and in the Air

In 1996 Bill Clinton became the first Democrat to win reelection since Franklin Delano Roosevelt, the Democratic Party's icon, earned a second term a half century earlier. Clinton's second term would be troubled, despite his domestic and foreign policy achievements: the elimination of a crushing fiscal deficit run up by the two previous Republican administrations, the peace agreements between the Israelis and Palestinians in 1993, and a peace agreement that ended the vicious civil war in Bosnia in 1995. The Republicans, who seized control of both the House and the Senate in the 1994 midterm elections, attacked the Democratic president with acrimony that was poisonous even for Washington. The revelation in early 1998 of Clinton's dalliance with a young intern gave conservatives the opportunity they coveted to try to force the president from office. The House impeached him in December 1998; the Senate put the president on trial in January and acquitted him in February 1999.

While the American public was caught up in the presidential scandal, Osama bin Laden pressed ahead with his plans for a low intensity war against the United States. Terrorists killed U.S. airmen in Saudi Arabia in June, only six months before the presidential elections in 1996. It was the second deadly attack against Americans in the Saudi Arabian Peninsula in the span of seven months. Bin Laden openly declared war against the United States in August that year. Then in February 1998, a month after the revelation of the president's affair in the Oval Office, bin Laden called on Muslims everywhere to kill Americans as a religious obligation. In August, Al Qaeda cells bombed the United States embassies in Kenya and Tanzania; Clinton retaliated by bombing Al Qaeda training camps in Afghanistan. But although the United States was under attack by an enemy that declared war on America twice in as many years, congressional Republics relentlessly pushed for the impeachment and trial of the commander in chief.

As the third millennium of the Christian era approached, bin Laden ordered his militants to strike at the United States in the name of Islam. In 1999, the Jordanian intelligence service thwarted a series of attacks in Jordan; an alert customs official prevented another in Los Angeles. But, Al Qaeda managed to strike out against the United States just weeks before the presidential elections in 2000.

Virtual War

Bin Laden's declaration of war was hubris: states declare war, not stateless terrorist organizations. But, bin Laden pretended to speak in the name of the entire Muslim nation with the expectation that his call to jihad commanded the authority of a senior Islamic imam. Bin Laden did not command that religious authority, but he commanded an organization that had proven its ability to raise money, recruit fighters, and to facilitate attacks. The Clinton administration took bin Laden's declaration of war seriously.

The CIA and Al Qaeda moved in each other's shadow. The CIA developed plans to capture or kill bin Laden; bin Laden developed plans to kill Americans. In the summer of 1995, Clinton had signed Presidential Decision Directive 39 directing the CIA to undertake an aggressive program of intelligence collection and analysis and covert operations. The presidential directive was not specifically directed at bin Laden; the CIA knew precious little about bin Laden's operational involvement in terrorist acts over the previous years. The bombings of the World Trade Center and the Murrah Federal Building and the nerve gas attack in the Tokyo subway provided the impetus for PDD 39. In fact, Clinton's directive was the first to warn of the danger of terrorists obtaining weapons of mass destruction. But, bin Laden's name surfaced so many times in so many investigations that the CIA opted to create a special unit devoted to him. The Bin Laden Issues Station within the CIA's Counterterrorism Center, codenamed Alec, opened in January 1996. Unlike the agency's traditional stations operating in embassies around world, the Bin Laden unit was a "virtual station."[1]

The CIA was aware that bin Laden financed the terror operations of Egyptian, Yemeni, Libyan, and Algerian militants as early as 1993. Three years later, its appreciation of bin Laden's involvement had not changed much. One Counterterrorism Center assessment, made public in 1996, described bin Laden as "one of the most significant financial sponsors of Islamic extremist activities in the world" who "provided financial support to militants actively opposed to moderate Islamic governments and the West," by leveraging his personal wealth as well as "pious donations" from wealthy Muslims. CIA described bin Laden as the head of an "Islamic Salvation Foundation." The Counterterrorism Center was still not familiar with the name Al Qaeda, the Base, and saw bin Laden's sponsorship of extremism through the provisions of grants from a malevolent foundation.[2] In the spring of 1996, the Bin Laden unit's sense of the bin Laden threat was largely intuitive. What Station Alec needed was someone on the inside.

Then, after bin Laden moved from the Sudan to Afghanistan, and after the Khobar Tower attack, Jamal Ahmed al-Fadl arrived at a U.S. embassy in Eritrea seeking protection from Al Qaeda and told a frightening tale. Al-Fadl had been present at the creation of Al Qaeda. A Yemeni who emigrated to the United States in 1986, al-Fadl was recruited into the Afghan jihad at the Al-Farouq Mosque in Brooklyn, the home of Azzam's and bin Laden's Services Bureau. Al-Fadl went to Afghanistan in 1988, just as Abdallah Azzam and bin Laden began to quarrel over the future of the jihad. When bin Laden created Al Qaeda, al-Fadl became one of its very first foot soldiers. In 1989, bin Laden dispatched him to the Sudan to prepare for the way for Al Qaeda's transplantation.[3]

Al-Fadl's information came as a revelation to the analysts of the Bin Laden unit who were trying to assemble the pixels of fragmentary intelligence into a coherent picture of bin Laden's activities. Al-Fadl described Al Qaeda's Shura council and its committee structure, and he identified its senior leaders: bin Laden, Al Qaeda's emir; al-Zawahiri, head of its Fatwa committee; Abu Ubaidah, the head of the military committee; his deputy, Abu Hafs al-Masry, aka Mohammed Atef; and others. Al-Fadl shattered the CIA's earlier assessment about the activities of what the agency knew as bin Laden's Islamic Salvation Foundation: Al Qaeda, the Base, was not a foundation that just funded and instigated terror, it had a military committee that was actively planning terror operations. Most alarming was al-Fadl's revelation that bin Laden had instructed him to find and purchase uranium for a nuclear weapon or a dirty bomb. This confirmed Clinton's instinct, put into writing in PDD 39 the previous June, that the acquisition of weapons of mass destruction by terrorists represented the worst case scenario in an increasingly perilous new world order.

Al-Fadl's revelations sent counterterrorism officials in the White House into a state of "enduring anxiety." The anxiety seeped into the Bin Laden unit, which took a new look at bin Laden's involvement in terror and "found connections everywhere." The new assessment of bin Laden and Al Qaeda made preemption imperative.[4]

After a year of operation, the men and women of Station Alec began thinking about a covert operation to capture bin Laden. The CIA worked through the spring and summer of 1997 to devise an initial plan. It would take the remainder of the year for the unit and the CIA Directorate of Operations to coordinate enough of the moving pieces of the plan to confidently present it to the White House for preliminary approval. The plan called for commandos to capture bin Laden in Afghanistan at an isolated location called Tarnak Farms near the airport outside Kabul, where bin Laden and his entourage sometimes stayed. This should have been an operation for U.S. Special Forces, but the CIA's plan called for Afghan warriors, who had their own reasons to kill bin Laden, to carry out the raid on Tarnak Farms.[5] The possibility that the Afghans would inadvertently kill bin Laden—or women and children who lived in Tarnak Farms—almost paralyzed those planning the operation, because of legal prohibitions against assassination dating back to the Ford administration. According to Clinton's national security advisor, Sandy Berger, who was the liaison between the White House and the CIA, the White House granted the CIA the legal authority to kill bin Laden. Neither George Tenet, the CIA director, nor the CIA case officers in the field were ever certain of that.[6]

The CIA did the heavy lifting to make the plan workable between May 1997, when it began to take shape, and the beginning of 1998. On 13 February (Coincidently, as bin Laden and Aymin al-Zawahiri were putting the final rhetorical flourishes on a fatwa calling on Muslims everywhere to kill Americans.) Tenet briefed Berger on the capture plan. Over the next three months, the CIA's agents in the field drilled the Afghan commandos. By mid-May, government attorneys in Washington had drafted legal language sanctioning a covert operation on the other side of the globe. Two days later, the CIA and the Afghans ran through the operation one last time. But the authorization to proceed never came.

On 29 May, Tenet ordered the CIA operatives in the field to stand down. Senior officials in the National Security Council Counterterrorism Security Group as well the CIA's Counterterrorism Center concluded the probability of success—only one in three, according to the CIA operatives who scored the final rehearsal—were too meager to justify the risks. Even some of the most intense bin Laden hunters, like Richard Clarke, who headed up the Counterterrorism Security Group, counseled against proceeding. That was enough for the Clinton's national security advisor. Sandy Berger told Tenet to shut the operation down without ever briefing the president about it.[7]

Bin Laden's Fatwa

Bin Laden declared war against America in August 1996, but Al Qaeda could not manage an act of war for two years. Al Qaeda was weakened when bin Laden arrived in Afghanistan. The Sudanese had seized the assets of the business bin Laden founded to support his men, their families, and his operations after they expelled him in May 1996. The seizure did not exhaust bin Laden's resources, but it depleted them substantially. The situation in Afghanistan complicated matters. The struggle for the soul of the nation had entered yet another phase when bin Laden arrived. In Kabul, the government of president Burhanuddin Rabbani and his defense minister and son-in-law, Ahmed Shah Massoud, was crumbling under the pressure of an insurgency spearheaded, principally, by Gulbuddin Hekmatyar's forces. Four years after the collapse of the Najibullah regime, the rivalry between Hekmatyar and Massoud still held Afghanistan hostage.

But now there was a new force, the Taliban, a movement of ultra pious Muslims who moved from the religious schools, madrasas, to the battlefield with a zeal inspired by a literal interpretation of the Qur'an. Pakistan, concerned that the chaos in Afghanistan shut down the trade routes to Central Asia, threw its support to the Taliban and the movement's leader, Mullah Omar. Bin Laden would also have to choose sides. His personal sacrifices during the anti-Soviet phase of Afghanistan's conflict earned him the admiration of many of the commanders of the country's armed factions. But bin Laden and Mullah Omar gravitated to each other. When the Taliban launched its offensive to seize Kabul in late September 1996, a month after bin Laden's declaration of war against the United States, bin Laden dug into his financial reserves and invested millions of dollars to ensure the Taliban's victory.[8]

Afghanistan became a safe haven for bin Laden and Al Qaeda after the Taliban seized Kabul. Al Qaeda camps began to churn out terrorists with the specialized skills of urban warfare. Recruitment was global. Thousands passed through Al Qaeda's camps. Bin Laden and his lieutenants, Aymin al-Zawahiri, Abu Ubaidah, the military commander, his deputy, Mohammed Atef, and Abu Zubaydah, the commander of Al Qaeda's most active terrorist training camp, began vetting plans to attack the United States. One plan bore the unmistakable likeness of Hizb'allah: the simultaneous bombing of U.S. embassies as the symbols of America's global presence and the nests of its spies. Another plan involved attacks against a U.S. airport and against Christians and Jews in Jordan visiting holy sites on the eve of the new millennium of the Christian era. Another called for an attack on a U.S. warship during a port call on the Arabian Peninsula. The most audacious plan revived Ramzi Yousef's Bojinka conspiracy to kill thousands of Americans aboard airliners, but contorted it into a plan to kill thousands of Americans *with* airliners. Bin Laden simultaneously set in motion the operations to destroy a U.S. warship and to crash U.S. airliners in a spectacular mass casualty attack.[9] This kind of destruction demanded moral justification.

On 23 February 1988, a statement from "The World Islamic Front for Jihad against Jews and Crusaders" appeared in print in the Al-Quds al-Arabi newspaper in London bearing five names. Aymin al-Zawahiri signed it as emir of the Egypt's Jihad Group. The leader of Egypt's other prominent terror organization, the Islamic Group, and representatives of lesser-known Islamist groups from Pakistan and Bangladesh endorsed the statement as well. Osama bin Laden's name appeared above the others but without mentioning an affiliation to any organization. The phrase Al Qaeda did not appear. The World Islamic Front for Jihad against Jews and Crusaders seemed to be a new beast. In fact, the statement was principally the work of Al Qaeda's fatwa committee, al-Zawahiriri, the committee's chair, and Osama bin Laden.[10]

Bin Laden issued the statement as a ruling of Islamic law, a fatwa. It was reprehensible: "In compliance with God's order, the ruling to kill the Americans and their allies—civilians and military—is an individual duty for every Muslim who can do it in any country in which it is possible to do it." It was God's order, they proclaimed, to kill Americans in order to liberate the Al-Aksa Mosque in Jerusalem and the holy mosque in Mecca from Jews and Crusaders and to expel their armies "out of all the lands of Islam."[11]

The threat against American civilians was new and ominous. His August 1996 Declaration of War against the Americans did not threaten civilians. But bin Laden's thinking was evolving in that direction. In March 1997, bin Laden told CNN journalists Peter Arnett and Peter Bergen that "we declared jihad against the U.S. government, because the U.S. government is unjust, criminal, and tyrannical." The jihad, he said "is directed against the U.S. soldiers" in Saudi Arabia. But bin Laden warned, "even though American civilians are not targeted in our plan, they must leave. We do not guarantee their safety."[12] Now bin Laden not only refused to guarantee the safety of U.S. civilians in Saudi Arabia, he called for their murder everywhere.

Bin Laden's fatwa was tantamount to an incitement to genocide. "We—with God's help—call on every Muslim who believes in God and wishes to be rewarded to comply with God's order to kill the Americans and plunder their money wherever and whenever they find it."[13] Fifty years earlier, the international community adopted the Genocide Convention and criminalized direct and public incitement to acts intended "to destroy—in whole or in part—any national, ethnic, racial, or religious group." Indonesia and the United Arab Emirates were the only important Muslim states to shun ratification of the convention. Saudi Arabia and Egypt were among the first nations in the world to endorse the Genocide Convention's pledge "to liberate mankind from such an odious scourge."[14] But bin Laden, a Saudi, and al-Zawahiri, an Egyptian, believed the Qur'an justified the indiscriminate murder of Americans everywhere in order to expel the Crusader army from Muslim lands.

The fatwa exhorted Muslims to kill Americans, but beneath it was the genocidal intent to destroy the Jews. After a press conference on 26 May, bin Laden repeated his threat ABC's John Miller: "We do not differentiate between those dressed in military uniforms and civilians; they are all targets in this fatwa." Bin Laden was blunter in his answers to his followers: "The enmity between us and the Jew goes far back in time and is deep rooted. There is no question that war between the two of us is inevitable."

Then bin Laden invoked a saying of the Prophet Mohammed: "judgment day shall not come until the Muslims fight the Jews, whereas the Jews will hide behind trees and stones, and the tree and the stone will speak and say 'Muslim, behind me is a Jew come and kill him.'"

Bin Laden's enmity of the United States was deeply rooted in the anti-Semitism of militant Islam. Al Qaeda had declared jihad against the Americans not only because they commanded the Crusader alliance that occupied the land of the holy mosques, but also because they "help the Jews occupy Muslim land."[15]

The February 1998 fatwa did not bear Sheikh Omar Abdel Rahman's name; the blind sheikh was serving a life sentence in the United States for sedition in connection with the first attacks by Islamist militants in the United States five years earlier. But the fatwa radiated Rahman's influence. Rahman continued to inspire terrorism from his prison cell; his acolytes massacred fifty-four Western tourists visiting the archeological ruins in Luxor, Egypt, in November 1997, in order to avenge Rahman's incarceration. And, somehow Rahman managed to issue his own fatwa from prison calling on "Muslims everywhere" to kill Americans "wherever you find them." Bin Laden's fatwa used Rahman's specific language, and bin Laden's plans would conform to Rahman's specific injunctions about attacking Americans: "destroy their embassies . . . sink their ships and shoot down their planes." This was not coincidental. Two of Omar Abdel Rahman's sons were present at the May 1998 press conference where bin Laden repeated his threat to kill all Americans, and Al Qaeda distributed laminated cards with Rahman's image and his fatwa to kill Americans "on land, at sea, and in the air."[16]

Destroy Their Embassies

Six months after the fatwa to kill Americans appeared in print, and three months after bin Laden's press conference, Al Qaeda cells destroyed two U.S. embassies in East Africa. Two of the men bin Laden called on to make those attacks happen were naturalized U.S. citizens.

Ali Mohamed began conducting surveillance of U.S. embassies in East Africa in 1993. An Egyptian, Mohamed served in his country's armed forces and eventually rose to the rank of major before his discharge in 1984. That year, Mohamed approached the CIA in Cairo to offer himself as an asset. He had important skills. He was a soldier and he was multilingual. Arabic was his mother tongue, but he also spoke English, French, and Hebrew. The CIA broke with Mohamed and placed him on a terrorist watch list after the agency discovered he had made contact with a Hizb'allah cell in Germany. But Mohamed managed to slip through the porous U.S. immigration bureaucracy. He immigrated to the United States in 1985, married an American, became a naturalized citizen, and became a sergeant in the elite Green Beret and an advisor on militant Islam at the John F. Kennedy Special Warfare Center at Fort Bragg. In 1988, Ali Mohamed made his first unauthorized trips to Afghanistan where he made contact with Al Qaeda. He left the U.S. Army a year later.

That is when the FBI took an interest in him. Agents interviewed him for the first time in 1989. Five years later, in 1994, the FBI interviewed him again in connection with the prosecution of Omar Abdel Rahman, prior to the blind sheikh's trial in the World Trade Center and New York landmark conspiracy prosecutions. Mohamed lied about what he knew, especially about bin Laden. What Ali Mohamed concealed from U.S. investigators was that by 1991 he was a member of Al Qaeda in whose hands Osama bin Laden placed his own life.

In 1991, Mohamed helped arrange the transplantation of Al Qaeda to the Sudan; he and another Al Qaeda member, Anas al-Liby, began the surveillance of the U.S. embassies in Kenya and Tanzania in 1993 on bin Laden's orders; in 1994, after an attempt on bin Laden's life, he assumed command of the training of bin Laden's bodyguards. It was Ali Mohamed who arranged security for the terror summit between bin Laden and Imad Mugniyah, chief of Hizb'allah's terror operations; it was Ali Mohamed who arranged for Aymin al-Zawahiri's clandestine visits to the United States in the mid-1990s.[17]

Another man bin Laden called on to organize attacks on Americans was Wadi el- Hage. Hage was born into a Christian family in Lebanon, but he converted to Islam as a young man. He immigrated to the United States in 1978 at the age of eighteen and like Ali Mohamed, became a U.S. citizen and married an American. Sometime in 1986, at the height of the anti-Soviet jihad, Hage took his new family to Pakistan to work for Abdallah Azzam's—and bin Laden's—Services Bureau. For a brief time in 1987, he directed the Bureau's New York office, the Al-Khifa Center. When bin Laden moved to the Sudan, Hage went with him as his personal secretary. In 1994, bin Laden sent him to Nairobi to establish a cell under the cover of an Islamic charity. Hage traveled frequently between

Kenya and the United States, where he communicated with Al Qaeda operatives in Florida, Oregon, Texas, and California. His contact in California was Ali Mohamed.[18]

Bin Laden dispatched Al Qaeda's senior military men, Abu Ubaidah and Mohammed Atef, to Kenya to meet with Hage regularly. But it took three years before the Kenyan cells were ready for action. Bin Laden's expulsion from the Sudan in May 1996 was one disruption, the drowning death of Abu Ubaidah in ferry accident in Lake Victoria a few months later was another. But at the beginning of 1997, six months after he issued his declaration of war against the United States, bin Laden summoned Hage to Peshawar, Pakistan. Bin Laden had decided to attack Americans. In fact, bin Laden had already selected men for a martyrdom operation. Hage went back to Kenya with an order to "militarize the cell."[19]

The U.S. embassy had some suspicions about Hage's activities. On 21 August, the FBI and Kenyan authorities raided the office of Hage's Islamic charity, an Al Qaeda front, in Nairobi, and seized documents and a computer. The seizure was potentially the most significant intelligence coup since the Philippine authorities stumbled upon Ramzi Yousef's laptop computer in Manila two and a half years earlier. The most incriminating document was a letter to Al Qaeda's "honored and wise supreme command." The FBI raid was proof of the letter's urgent message: "The cell members in East Africa are in great danger."

Bin Laden's public statements, beginning with his August 1996 declaration of war against the United States, had created the danger. The moment the members of the East African cell heard the declaration of war, said the letter, "We understood that there is a war on and the situation is dangerous and that anybody who is associated with the Hajj regardless of their position and their nationality are at risk." The Hajj was the honorific title for bin Laden.

The author of the letter was Fazul Abdullah Mohamed, aka "Harun," a native of the Comoros Islands in the Indian Ocean. Harun was another ideal Al Qaeda member: multilingual, technically adept, pious, and eager to wage jihad. But now he was concerned that Al Qaeda's supreme command was planning an operation somewhere that would endanger the cell's security by heightening the vigilance of hostile intelligence services. "So we are asking you . . . to tell us that there is a possible danger that may take place in a while due to a certain decision so we can prepare ourselves." What Harun did not realize was that bin Laden had taken the decision to militarize Harun's own cell.[20]

Hage fled Kenya after the raid. Inexplicably, he returned to the United States where the FBI interviewed him a month after the raid in Nairobi. Hage lied repeatedly about bin Laden in his interview, Ubaidah's drowning, the fatwa to kill Americans, the names and pseudonyms of Al Qaeda operatives, and other information that would have cracked the East Africa cell. Later, he perjured himself before a grand jury investigating the crime his cell was planning. The FBI believed that the raid on Hage's office "dissipated alleged threats" against Americans. But the Nairobi raid only delayed the attack.[21]

The Al Qaeda cells were secure. Hage had fled, but there were men to take his place. One was Mohamed Sadeek Odeh, a Jordanian, who had established a separate Al Qaeda cell in Mombasa around the time Hage established his in Nairobi. Harun was another replacement. It was Harun who had warned Al Qaeda's high command about surveillance by the Americans. Harun managed to escape detection and took over for Hage. The fact was, despite the raid on Hage's office, Al Qaeda was able to move operatives in and out of Kenya and Tanzania to organize attacks on Americans with frightening ease. Three of those operatives came to martyr themselves.

Bin Laden personally selected Mohamed Al-'Owhali for the mission. Al-'Owhali, like Ali Mohamed and Wadih el-Hage, had lived in the Christian West. He was born in England to affluent and religious Saudi parents. His piety drove him to enlist in the Jihad in 1996. In Afghanistan, al-'Owhali appealed to bin Laden to select him for a mission and, bin Laden granted him his wish. Al-'Owhali was present at the May 1998 press conference in Afghanistan where bin Laden repeated his threat to kill U.S. citizens. In June, al-'Owhali taped a martyrdom video. Two months later, he traveled to Kenya to kill Americans and himself.

Jihad Mohammad Ali al-Makki made his martyrdom video at the same time al- 'Owhali made his. Jihad Ali, who identified himself by the pseudonym Azzam, was to be al-'Owhali's comrade in Nairobi. Militancy ran in his family. His uncle, Abd al-Rahim al-Nashiri, was Al Qaeda's regional commander in the Arabian Peninsula; al-Nashiri was already planning an operation to sink a U.S. ship when his nephew was preparing to destroy a U.S. embassy. Hamdan Khalif Alal, known as Ahmed the German because of his fair hair, was the third martyr. His mission was in Dar es Salaam. This would be Al Qaeda's first martyrdom attack.[22]

On 7 August 1998, Azzam, al-'Owhali, and Hamdan Alal carried out operations Kaaba and Al-Aqsa—named for the mosques in Mecca and Jerusalem—within minutes of each other in two East African capitals hundreds of miles apart. It was eight years to the day that U.S. forces began deploying in Saudi Arabia for Operation Desert Shield, and inevitably, Operation Desert Storm. That date marked the final passage in bin Laden's conversion to the belief that the United States was the mortal enemy of Islam and that the Saudi regime was its slave. The codename for the operations—Al-Kaaba and Al-Aqsa—expressed bin

Laden's outrage at the two greatest atrocities of the Crusaders and Jews, U.S. occupation of Saudi Arabia and the Jews' very presence in Jerusalem.

Just before ten thirty, Azzam and al-'Owhali drove up to a checkpoint at the rear the U.S. embassy at a busy intersection in Nairobi and demanded access to the underground parking garage. When the Kenyan sentries denied them entry, al-'Owhali leaped from the Toyota Dyna truck and hurled a flash grenade at the guards to force them to raise the gate to the garage. Azzam fired shots from a handgun at the embassy. But the guards held their ground. In that instant al-'Owhali's belief in the glory of martyrdom failed him and he fled. Azzam detonated the bomb. The blast crumbled the building's rear façade and killed forty-two, twelve Americans and thirty Kenyans working at the embassy. The destruction was far worse across the street where the concussion shattered the windows of an office building. Most of the 213 persons murdered and the nearly 4,000 maimed were Kenyans. Minutes later and hundreds of miles away in Tanzania, Hamdan Alal, Ahmed the German, drove a Nissan Atlas truck to the perimeter of the U.S. embassy in Dar es Salaam, once the site of the Israeli embassy, and detonated his bomb. A water tanker truck parked in front of the embassy absorbed most of the blast, saving countless lives. The attack took the lives of 11 Tanzanians, and injured 85 others, including scores of Americans, two seriously.

It had been fifteen years since years since Hizb'allah destroyed the U.S. embassy and the Marine Battalion Landing Team headquarters in Beirut with truck bombs like the ones that exploded in Nairobi and Dar es Salaam. The April 1983 attack on the U.S. embassy in Beirut killed more Americans, 17, and struck down the CIA's chief Middle East intelligence analyst and eight of his operatives; the October mass-casualty attack killed 241 U.S. Marines. Operations Kaaba and Al-Aqsa fit the Hizb'allah pattern but took fewer American lives. Bin Laden may have convinced the suicide bombers that it was God's order to kill Americans, but more Africans than Americans died in Operations Kaaba and Al-Aqsa, by a factor of twenty.

The intelligence community did not have "credible intelligence that provided immediate or tactical warning" of the embassy attacks. But it immediately discovered Al Qaeda's complicity in them. Suspicious customs officials detained Mohamed Odeh, the man who directed the Al Qaeda cell in Kenya, when he arrived aboard a flight to Karachi the day of the attack. Pakistani authorities did not have to coerce a confession from Odeh: he believed participation in the jihad against the Americans was his duty as a good Muslim, like attending mosque for prayers, making the annual hajj to Mecca, or giving alms to the poor, so he boasted of his complicity. The situation was different for Mohamed al-'Owhali, who had to live with the shame that his faith failed him moments before Azzam detonated the Nairobi bomb. U.S. and Kenyan officials arrested al-'Owhali in Kenya days after the attack in a clinic where he was recuperating from the wounds he suffered when the shockwave blew over him as he ran from the scene. Much of what U.S. authorities know about the embassy attacks comes from the interrogations of Odeh and al-'Owhali.[23]

Infinite Resolve

The day after the attacks, President Clinton promised to "pursue terrorists until the cases are solved and justice is done."[24] The president spoke about terrorists in the plural, but the reality was that the threat of terrorism to the United States was singular. In the 1980s, the Reagan administration confronted terrorists inspired by conflicting ideologies: Palestinian nationalist terror represented principally by Abu Nidal and lesser Palestinian factions backed by Libya, Syrian, and Iraq; and Islamist terror represented principally by Hizb'allah in Lebanon. Now, terror inspired by Islam was the mortal danger to Americans. Bin Laden personified that threat. The CIA and the Pentagon had been hunting bin Laden for nearly two years when Al Qaeda struck in Africa. The murder of U.S. Foreign Service officers compelled Clinton to strike back. Two weeks after Al Qaeda carried out operations Al-Kaaba and Al-Aqsa, Clinton gave the order to execute Operation Infinite Reach.

Infinite Reach was the high tech United States retaliation for the low tech Al Qaeda attacks in Africa. Three weeks after the embassy attacks, on 20 August, President Clinton ordered the U.S. warships in the northern Arabian Sea and Red Sea to launch cruise missiles against a network of six Al Qaeda camps near Khost, Afghanistan, and a pharmaceutical factory in Khartoum. In all 75 cruise missiles flew off the warships. The missiles pulverized the Al Qaeda's camps and killed as many as 60 militants, mostly Pakistanis training for the interminable conflict between Pakistan and India for sovereignty over the Kashmir. But bin Laden was not harmed. The CIA and the Pentagon launched the attacks on the twentieth because of intelligence that bin Laden would be in one of the camps meeting with senior Al Qaeda leaders. Bin Laden may have left the area during the two hours it took for the missiles to reach their target; he may have never been anywhere near Khost at all.

Clinton ordered the attack on the al-Shifa pharmaceutical plant in Khartoum out of an abundance of caution about weapons of mass destruction becoming weapons of terror. The president's Decision Directive in June 1995 was explicit about that threat. Al-Shifa rose to the top of the Pentagon's target list because the CIA suspected that it produced VX, a deadly nerve agent. After the Tokyo subway Serin gas attacks, and after Jamal al-Fadl's revelations about bin Laden's pursuit of WMD, Clinton could not dismiss the possibility that bin Laden had invested in a primitive chemical weapons program in the city where he lived and that he had planned terror operations against Americans for five years.[25]

When the smoke cleared from Operation Infinite Reach, the president had to fend off charges that he ordered the attacks to divert attention from the scandal of his affair with a young intern, Monica Lewinsky. Later, after the 9/11 attacks, former administration officials had to defend themselves against charges that they, and the president, went weak on bin Laden and Al Qaeda after the cruise missile strikes. The reality is more complex. The president did not waver in his determination to kill Al Qaeda's emir. Throughout the remainder of his presidency, he pressed the CIA and the Pentagon to insert CIA paramilitaries or Army Special Forces into Afghanistan to eliminate bin Laden.[26] Operation Infinite Reach gave way to Operation Infinite Resolve. Infinite Resolve was not a specific operation; it was a standing order for the Pentagon to develop plans to capture or kill bin Laden and for the CIA to produce the actionable, real-time intelligence that would put bin Laden in the Pentagon's crosshairs. The insertion of Special Operation Forces into Afghanistan to snatch bin Laden was a conceivable option, but the logistical complexities daunted even the chairman of the Joint Chiefs of Staff, Hugh Shelton, the first member of the Special Operations Forces to hold that position. Military operations, Shelton commented, were "not magic."[27]

The only realistic option to kill bin Laden was another cruise missile strike. The Washington lawyers' preoccupation about inadvertently killing bin Laden in an operation to capture him disappeared after the Africa attacks. Now the only concern was to avoid excessive collateral damaging—killing too many women and children—when the warheads exploded around bin Laden. But the CIA never got a clear sighting of bin Laden. The agency had intelligence about bin Laden's location in December 1998 and again in February and May 1999, but Tenet, the DCI, Sandy Berger, the NSA, and Richard Clarke, the NSC's counterterrorism coordinator, did not have enough confidence in the intelligence to order submarines to launch their missiles. This enraged Michael Scheuer, the head of the Bin Laden unit. Scheuer left the unit in frustration about the reticence of his superiors. Days before the fifth anniversary of 9/11, Scheuer lashed out. "America is suffering today," Scheuer said, "from Mr. Clinton's failure, complete and utter failure, to use the ten occasions the CIA provided him to kill Bin Laden . . . Bin Laden's innards, sir, should be splattered over the deserts of southern Afghanistan. The only reason he is alive today is because President Clinton and his national security advisors refused to press the button." Scheuer laid the blame for bin Laden's survival squarely on the shoulders of "Bill, Dick, and Sandy."[28]

The time and distance factors offered bin Laden relative protection from death by cruise missile. Flying at subsonic speed, 400 miles per hour, cruise missiles coming from the Arabian Sea took two hours to arrive on target in Afghanistan. By one estimate, bin Laden was present in one of the camps near Khost when Clinton ordered Operation Infinite Reach on 20 August, but he left before the warheads demolished it. Killing bin Laden would take "boots on the ground" in Afghanistan in sufficient numbers to find, entrap, and kill him. In 1998, the U.S. public was in no mood for even limited casualties in a raid in Afghanistan to kill a man whose name no one knew, and who was responsible for the deaths of fewer than two dozen Americans—not after the October 1993 fiasco in Mogadishu that cost the lives of eighteen U.S. rangers and Delta Force commandos in a flawed operation to capture one obscure man. Things were different after 9/11. President George Bush, who replaced Clinton eight months before the 9/11 tragedy, had an opportunity to kill bin Laden. Exactly one month after the attacks in New York and Washington, Bush launched Operation Enduring Freedom. By November, Special Operations Forces and CIA paramilitaries had closed in around bin Laden in the Tora Bora Mountains. But bin Laden escaped, because, according to the CIA operative on the ground, the White House and the Pentagon refused the request for the insertion of another 600 Army Rangers. The Bush administration's planning for the coming war in Iraq suffocated the efforts to kill bin Laden.[29]

Sink Their Ships

Al Qaeda's fingerprints were on previous attacks, in New York in 1993 and Saudi Arabia in 1995 and 1996, but it appears that the August 1998 embassy attacks were Al Qaeda's first fully independent terror operations. It was critical that Al Qaeda sustain operational rhythm. Thirty years earlier, Wadi Haddad, the master of the PFLP's terror operations, launched his assault on civilian aviation. Haddad's PFLP fedayeen staged attacks at almost predictable intervals over a decade. The credibility of bin Laden's 1998 fatwa depended on the ability of Al Qaeda mujahideen to sustain the attack on Americans. Al Qaeda had plans in motion.

Near the end of the year, two veterans of Al Qaeda's Khalden camp proposed an attack in the spirit of bin Laden's fatwa to kill Americans wherever pious Muslims could kill them. One of the men, Raed Hijaz, was a U.S. citizen born in California to Palestinian parents. Hijaz's allegiance was to militant Islam. The other man, Khadr Abu Hosher, was also a Palestinian. Their plan was to murder Americans in near-simultaneous attacks on a luxury hotel in Amman, Jordan, a border crossing between Israel and Jordan, and two Christian holy sites in the country. The Egyptian Islamic Group had introduced the tactic of attacking tourists visiting archeological or holy sites; the massacre of seventy tourists in Luxor, Egypt, was the bloodiest of several attacks. The idea, the men later boasted, that "the bodies will pile up in sacks."

The plan impressed Abu Zubaydah, the commandant of Al Qaeda's Khalden camp, and Zubaydah quickly gave his, and bin Laden's, blessing to it. The operation took a year to put together and the timing was critical. Al Qaeda planned for the next wave of attacks to come at the dawn of the third millennium of the Christian era. In November, Hijaz and Abu Hoshar left Afghanistan for Jordan via Syria. Fourteen other terrorists were waiting to the carry out the first of Al Qaeda's Millennium attacks. They would have been devastating. The Al Qaeda cell had amassed enough chemicals in an Amman safe house to manufacture explosives with the destructive power of sixteen tons of TNT. It was a huge conspiracy nearing execution. But the Jordanian intelligence service has a long history of detecting terror plots, dating back to Black September's ill- fated 1973 attempt to storm the U.S. embassy and the prime minister's offices. The General Intelligence Department kept terror suspects under surveillance and intercepted their telephone communications. On 30 November, the Jordanians intercepted a cryptic message from Abu Zubaydah to Khadr Abu Hosher—"the time for training is over"—and swept up the members of the Al Qaeda cell.[30]

Exactly one month later, on 14 December, customs officials arrested Ahmed Ressam in Port Angeles, Washington. Ressam, an Algerian, arrived aboard a ferry from Vancouver with some 130 pounds of explosives in the trunk of his car. He had come to detonate a bomb at the Los Angeles International Airport. His story was like the story of the Egyptians around Omar Abdel Rahman who joined in Ramzi Yousef's conspiracy to bomb the World Trade Center six years earlier. Ressam immigrated to Canada in 1994 and appealed for asylum when Canadian customs officials discovered irregularities in his passport. Ramzi Yousef told this same lie when he arrived in New York in 1992. Ressam's story was plausible; in 1994, Algeria was torn by a savage war between security forces and Islamist organizations, like the fanatical GIA, which had planned to crash a loaded passenger jet into the Eiffel Tower the same year Ressam arrived in Montreal. So Canadian authorities took him at his word.

Ressam was not a terrorist when he arrived in Canada. Like the Egyptian émigrés in New York, his radicalization was incremental. By 1998, he had decided to make the pilgrimage to Afghanistan to be trained for the jihad in his native Algeria. In March 1998, Ressam arrived at Abu Zubaydah's Khalden camp to train with a large group of Algerians. It was the same camp where Yousef went to for advanced terror training in the late 1980s, and where the men who planed the Millennium attacks in Amman had trained. The six months of training were rigorous and covered the tradecraft of terrorism, security, surveillance, assassinations explosives, and urban warfare. Ressam went to Afghanistan to train for the jihad in Algeria. But when he left the camp in September 1999, he was determined to take the jihad to the Americans. The influence of the Egyptian Omar Abdel Rahman made the difference. Ressam told U.S. interrogators that the mujahideen at Khalden were given a laminated copy of a photograph of Rahman with the text of the blind sheikh's fatwa calling on Muslims, as Ressam paraphrased it, to "fight Americans and hit their interests everywhere." Ressam carried with it him the United States.

In early 1999, Ressam left Afghanistan for Canada to rendezvous with five Algerians to attack vulnerable locations in the United States. When the State Department rejected the visa applications for the other men, Ressam decided to carry out an attack without them. He had settled on the Los Angeles Airport. He planned to rendezvous with his only contact in the United States, Abdelghni Meskini, another Algerian, who was already living in Seattle., but first he had to cross the boarder.[31]

Bin Laden did not bless Ressam's independent operation, because a bombing on U.S. soil at the dawn of the new millennium would endanger a conspiracy, already in motion, to conduct a catastrophic, mass-casualty attack in the United States. Ressam informed Abu Zubadah in Afghanistan about his plot. Zubaydah enjoined Ressam from claiming the attack in the name of Al Qaeda, but did not instruct him to call it off.

The conspiracy to attack the airport on the millennium failed when an alert customs officer, Diana Dean, became suspicious of Ressam and ordered him to open the trunk of his car. A single customs official's alertness prevented Ressam's plan. But the United States was supremely vulnerable. Just as Ressam was attempting to enter the United States to attack it from within, two Al Qaeda terrorists were preparing to enter the United States on valid U.S. visas to learn how to pilot commercial jetliners. They arrived, ironically at Los Angeles Airport, exactly one month after Ressam's plot to bomb it failed.

The U.S. intelligence community had no specific intelligence about Al Qaeda's plots to slaughter Americans in Jordan or Los Angeles until the Jordanians intercepted Abu Zubaydah's phone call in the Middle East and a customs official became suspicious of Ressam at a remote border crossing in the Pacific Northwest. It had no intelligence whatsoever about a plot to sink a U.S. warship in the Port of Yemen until years after the first attempt failed and a second succeeded.

On 5 January 2000, Al Qaeda suicide terrorists put a small boat laden with explosives into the water in the Port of Aden, where the USS *The Sullivans* had put down anchor. Their mission was to pull aside the destroyer, detonate the bomb, and sink the ship. The mission failed when the boat sank under the weight of the explosives. The U.S. navy was never aware of the attempt to sink one of its most modern destroyers, nor was the CIA. The next day, the terrorists retrieved the partially submerged boat, dried out the explosives, and waited for another opportunity to strike. It came eight months later.

The passage of months meant nothing for bin Laden, who believed Al Qaeda was engaged in a millennial struggle against the forces of disbelief. Patience was one of Al Qaeda's most formidable weapons. From conception to execution the attack on the U.S. embassies in Africa took five years. The millennium attacks had been in planning for more than a year. So, had the plot to sink a U.S. vessel.

In fact, some of the men behind the failed attack on the USS *The Sullivans* in Yemen had connections to the embassy attacks in Africa. Abd al-Rahim al-Nashiri first approached bin Laden with the idea to sink a U.S. warship in late 1998, after his cousin, "Azzam," detonated the bomb and killed himself in Nairobi. Mushim Musa Matawalli Attwah, "Abdel Rahman," fabricated the bombs that destroyed the embassies in Nairobi and Dar es Salaam. The embassy attacks demonstrated his skills as a bomb-maker. But now Abdel Rahman had to build a bomb to more exacting specifications. It had to be compact enough to be carried aboard a small fiberglass skiff—the weight of the bomb was the undoing of the plot against the USS *The Sullivans*—and powerful enough to blast through the armored hull of a modern warship. The failure of the previous attack actually gave Abdel Rahman the time to design a more destructive bomb, one with a shaped charge that would direct the full force of the blast into the side of the next U.S. warship to wander into harm's way. The USS *Cole* would be that ship.

In the second week of October 2000, the USS *Cole*, a 505 foot-long Arleigh Burke class destroyer, made the passage through the Suez Canal and put into the Port of Aden to take on fuel before proceeding to the Persian Gulf to intimidate Saddam Hussein. The *Cole*'s refueling stop at Port of Aden was as much a diplomatic gesture as an operational necessity. The U.S. warships that prowled the Persian Gulf had to take on fuel somewhere in the region. The commander of the Central Command, General Anthony Zinni, later told the Senate Armed Services Committee that he considered Yemen to be a calculated risk. The country was known to harbor terrorists, but the alternatives, Saudi Arabia, Jordan, and Somalia, were not risk-free. Terrorists had killed twenty-four Americans in separate incidents in Saudi Arabia in 1995 and 1996, and the Jordanian intelligence service had just defused a major terror plot in Jordan. Zinni knew Somalia was off-limits; he had been the ground commander in Somalia seven years earlier, when the 18 Army Rangers and Delta Force operators fell in the Black Hawk Down incident in October 1993. The Marine general was about to lose that many sailors.

The diplomatic considerations were as important as the operational ones. The United States was struggling to improve diplomatic relations with the recently reunified country. U.S. ambassador Barbara Bodine worked this angle hard. The appearance of formidable U.S. warships in Yemeni waters was not the ideal gesture of good will, but the military-to-military contacts were as important to the State Department as they were to the Pentagon. Ambassador Bodine gave priority to her diplomatic charge to smooth relations with Yemen, even after an attack against Americans, when the FBI arrived to conduct its investigations.

The sailors aboard the USS *Cole* had the mission to enforce the United Nations and United States sanctions on Iraq by interdicting contraband materials entering and leaving Iraq and supporting the pilots who policed the no-fly zone in the south. Their mission was the same as that of the airmen of the 4404th Fighter Wing that came under attack at Khobar Towers five years earlier. Nineteen Americans were killed in June 1995 when Saudi Hizb'allah bombed the Khobar Towers complex. Al Qaeda's attack on the USS *Cole* would be just as lethal.

Late in the morning of 12 October a small boat pulled beside the *Cole*. The ship had nearly taken on a full load of fuel; it would be ready to put to sea within the hour. The two men who steered the skiff out to the *Cole*—Hassan al-Khamri and Ibrahim al-Thawar, aka Nibras—had waited months for their martyrdom, so when they came to the ship, they stood at attention an instant before they detonated their bomb. It was "a horrific weapon," said Admiral Harold Gehman, who was appointed to an official board of inquiry charged with investigating the attack. The blast killed 17 sailors and maimed another 39 and opened a gaping, 40-by-60-foot wound in the destroyer's port side. The *Cole* was open to the sea, and the ship flooded. The overpressure of the blast contorted the ship's structure near the point of detonation and knocked out most of her internal systems. When Admiral Gehman inspected the *Cole*, he found the main deck of the ship "physically transplaced." The eight feet of space between the main deck and the deck above it, he marveled, "is just not there anymore."

The wound inflicted on the *Cole* nearly sank her, but the crew kept the destroyer afloat. Even so, the attack was a spectacular triumph for Al

Qaeda. And, bin Laden had intended for it to be a spectacle. One of the conspirators, Fahd al-Quso, was supposed to have videotaped the attack from the same apartment overlooking the port where the Al Qaeda cell monitored shipping and patiently awaited the arrival of an U.S- flag vessel. Bin Laden intended to post the video on the Internet as a recruitment piece, but al-Quso arrived to the apartment too late to capture the images of the near destruction of the *Cole*.[32]

The FBI immediately dispatched a team of investigators to develop evidence of complicity in the bombing. It was painstaking forensic work. The *Cole* was in danger of sinking. That was one complication. The interference of Yemeni authorities was another. Most frustrating for the FBI special agents was the attitude of the U.S. ambassador, whose deference to the host country's sensitivities, particularly when it came to interrogating suspects, slowed the investigation. And time was critical. Time was running out on the Clinton presidency. Clinton could not retaliate until investigators told him who deserved retaliation.[33]

There is another dimension to the *Cole* investigation. Within weeks of the attack, an Arabic-speaking FBI agent detailed to the investigation managed to interview Fahd al- Quso, whom Yemeni authorities had captured. Al-Quso revealed details of the conspiracy; his most important revelation was that Tawiq bin Attash helped direct the attack from inception to execution. It was critical intelligence, because ten months before the *Cole* attack, Attash had rendezvoused in Malaysia and Thailand with the men who carried out the *Cole* attack and two Al Qaeda terrorists who were moving forward the plan to attack Americans on U.S. soil with hijacked airliners. Tawiq bin Attash was the true identity of the man the CIA knew as Khallad, a veteran mujahid who had lost a leg in the jihad. The analysts in the CIA's Bin Laden unit called him a "major league killer." The CIA learned Khallad's true identity within a month of the attack; it was aware he was a member of an "operational cadre" that rendezvoused in Kuala Lumpur and Bangkok in December 1999. Malasyian authorities photographed him and al-Quso and other men; Thai authorities informed the Americans that one of the Al Qaeda cadre had a U.S. visa and that another had already traveled to the United States in January 2000. The tragedy in all this was that the CIA never informed the FBI that terrorists who met with the bomber of the *Cole* entered the United States ten months before the *Cole* attack and nineteen months before 9/11.

Twenty-five days after the attack on a U.S. warship in the waters off the Arabian Peninsula, Americans went to the polls to elect a new president. Bin Laden had already set in motion a plan to kill Americans on American soil. By the time George W. Bush took the oath of office in January, the men bin Laden selected and entrusted with the mission to attack New York and Washington, D.C., had already been living in the United States for nearly a year.

Chapter 10

Today, Our Nation Saw Evil

George W. Bush entered the White House in January 2001 after the most controversial election in four decades. Twenty-five days before the November elections, Al Qaeda suicide bombers aboard a small skiff blasted a hole in the USS *Cole* in a Yemeni port, killing seventeen U.S. sailors. President Clinton, who was fixated on a final peace agreement between the Israelis and Palestinians in the waning days of his presidency, did not retaliate for the *Cole* attack because the CIA could not give him proof positive of bin Laden's hand in it. President Bush opted not to retaliate either, or even to pursue bin Laden. Bush gave higher priority to the deployment of a ballistic missile defense against an imaginary future threat than to the real and present danger of Al Qaeda.

As the Bush administration moved to implement its agenda in the first year of the new millennium, Al Qaeda cells in the United States made the final preparations for the most lethal acts of terror in history. Reports of an impending Al Qaeda attack, most of them vague, inundated the CIA during the spring and summer. The Agency was aware that known Al Qaeda terrorists had entered the United States in the weeks after the millennium crisis, but for reasons that have never been adequately explained, it did nothing to alert the FBI or other federal agencies charged to protect the homeland. President Bush's lack of a sense of urgency about the Al Qaeda threat slowed an already slow federal bureaucracy. The director of the CIA and the director of the Agency's Counterterrorism Center personally warned the president's national security advisor in July that an attack could occur with no warning. In August, while he was on vacation at his Texas ranch, the CIA briefed Bush on bin Laden's determination to strike in the United States. But the president failed to take action because he did not deem the intelligence that came to him about a probable act of terror to be actionable. Bush's negligence was catastrophic: Bin Laden struck the United States thirty-seven days later.

The Operation

Khalid Sheikh Mohammed joined Al Qaeda a decade after its birth in Afghanistan. He had resisted joining for three years after he first approached bin Laden with an idea for a cataclysmic attack on the United States in 1996, but then he came to the realization that he needed Al Qaeda's funding, logistical support, and martyrs. Mohammed had dreamt about a mass casualty attack against Americans perhaps as early as 1987 when he graduated from an American college and trekked to Afghanistan to enlist in the jihad. Until the East Africa embassy bombings, Mohammed had come as close to any militant Muslim, except his nephew, to answering Omar Abdel Rahman's and bin Laden's call to kill Americans anywhere and everywhere. Mohammed had helped finance his nephew Ramzi Yousef's 1993 attack on the World Trade Center and conspired with him to destroy U.S. planes over the Pacific in the years after the World Trade Center attack. But when Plan Bojinka—or the Manila Air Plot, as U.S. prosecutors called it—collapsed, Mohammed fled to Qatar to regroup. The FBI's capture of his nephew in Pakistan only deepened Mohammed's desire to convert U.S. planes into weapons of mass destruction.

Mohammed proposed some version of what would become the 9/11 attack to bin Laden as early as 1996.[1] Bin Laden rebuffed him, not because his idea did not hold the promise of immense destruction, but because Al Qaeda's emir demanded allegiance to Al Qaeda and a personal oath of loyalty, bayat, to him. Mohammed held out until the end of 1998, after bin Laden's fatwa and the African embassy bombings. By then, Khalid Sheikh Mohammed recognized their mutual interests: bin Laden, to mount a spectacular attack on U.S. soil as the culmination of a series of blows that began with the bombings in Africa; Mohammed, to realize his nephew's dreams of bringing down the Twin Towers of the World Trade Center and destroying U.S. planes in flight.

In the spring of 1999, bin Laden summoned him to Kandahar for a conference. Mohammed Atef, Al Qaeda's military commander, had already endorsed the concept. Atef understood the military logic behind sustained attacks and the escalation of violence. The embassy attacks were the beginning, not the end, of an epochal struggle. Atef was willing to consider new tactics. Al Qaeda's attacks imitated Hizb'allah's operations. Al Qaeda had provided material or logistic support to the 1995 and 1996 vehicle bombings in the Arabian Peninsula, and it had conducted its first fully independent attacks in Kenya and Tanzania only a few months earlier, in August 1998. Atef studied the alternative of hijacking operations, but rejected air piracy because, historically, terrorists hijacked planes to negotiate the release of captured comrades not to inflict casualties on the enemy. But Khalid Sheikh Mohammed's operational concept was radically different: hijacking planes was an expedient to acquire weapons of mass destruction. But for Mohammed Atef and Osama bin Laden, Khalid Sheikh Mohammed's proposal came as an epiphany.

So, in spring 1999, Al Qaeda was planning major operations in different quadrants of the globe. The conspiracy to slaughter Christian pilgrims in Jordan on the eve of the Christian millennium was one. Another was a plot to sink a U.S. warship in the waters surrounding the Arabian Peninsula, a plot that culminated in the attack on the *Cole* in October 2000. A third was to crash airliners into monuments of American power.

Bin Laden personally selected the men for the warship operation and what Al Qaeda would call, straightforwardly, the Planes Operation.[2] In fact, bin Laden selected one man, Tawfiq bin Attash, aka Khalled, for both operations. Khalled would help direct the *Cole* operation; his reward was to be martyrdom in the Planes Operation. Three other men impressed bin Laden as worthy mujahideen: Khalid al-Midhar and Nawaf al-Hamzi, both Saudi nationals, and Abu Bara, a Yemeni. All four were veterans of the jihad. Khalled, who went to Afghanistan at the age of fifteen, had lost a leg fighting against the Northern Alliance Forces of Ahmed Shah Masoud, the Taliban's mortal enemy. But, these men needed specialized training for their new mission: they had to learn to fly large commercial airliners, and they had to learn English to complete flight training in schools in the United States. In fact, Khalled and Abu Bara never acquired visas to enter the United States. Al-Midhar and al-Hamzi, who easily acquired visas because they were Saudi nationals, managed to enter the United States, but they never learned passable English and so never passed flight training. Instead, on 9/11 their mission was to kill the flight crew and subdue the passengers.

As the millennium approached, the U.S. intelligence community was tracking Al Qaeda operatives with presidential authority to disrupt its activities and to kill its emir. So, any a lapse of security could have been fatal, and Al Qaeda made one. In the first week of January 2000, five of the men selected for the Ship and the Planes operations rendezvoused in South Asia. Khalled, al-Hamzi, al-Midhar, and Abu Bara met briefly in Kuala Lumpur, Malaysia, and then moved on to Bangkok, Thailand. Khalled went to Kuala Lumpur to be fitted for a new prosthesis for the leg he had lost in jihad. He also came to probe security aboard U.S. commercial airliners flying out of Asia to the United States. At this stage in the evolution of the Planes Operation, bin Laden and Atef were still considering two waves of suicide hijackings: the first aboard jets arriving on the West Coast, the second, aboard planes departing from East Coast airports. Because Khalled could not obtain a U.S. visa, bin Laden and Atef assigned him, and presumably Abu Bara, to the Asian component of the Planes Operation. In fact, on the first day of the new millenium, Khalled boarded a U.S. airliner on a flight to Hong Kong carrying a box cutter to probe airport security. Khalid Sheikh Mohammed had cased some of these flights exactly six years earlier when he and his nephew were planning to place miniature bombs aboard them. Eventually, bin Laden canceled the Asian component of the operation and instructed Khalled to focus his energies on the destruction of a U.S. warship.

Nawaf al-Hamzi and Khalid al-Midhar, who had already passed through specialized training for the Planes Operation in Afghanistan, traveled to Kuala Lumpur for a final briefing before beginning the next phase of their mission. They were the vanguard of the East Coast component of the Planes Operation. But Midhar's presence nearly disrupted the conspiracy. For months the National Security Agency, NSA, had been monitoring telephone calls in and out of a home belonging to Khalid al-Midhar's father-in-law in Yemen. When Khalled left the message instructing Khalid al-Midhar and Nawaf al-Hamzi to travel to Kuala Lumpur, the NSA was listening. The NSA informed the CIA in direct terms that a meeting of an "operational cadre" was set to take place in Kuala Lumpur the first week of January. A CIA cable back to headquarters concluded, correctly, that "Nawaf's travel may be in support of a terrorist mission."[3]

The intelligence was vital, but partial and perplexing. The NSA could provide the CIA names, but first names only. Khalid, Nawaf, and Salem. The CIA managed to discover Khalid al-Midhar's full name even before he arrived in Malaysia and tracked him to a hotel room in Dubai, where al-Midhar stayed briefly en route to Malaysia. CIA agents broke into his room and photographed his passport. The Agency had al-Midhar under surveillance the moment he arrived in Kuala Lumpur. But there was confusion. The CIA did not know whether Khalid al-Midhar and Khalled, whose real name was Tawfiq bin Attash, were one and the same person; it would not learn that for a full year, until after the *Cole* attack. The Agency did not learn the full names of Nawaf and Salem al-Hamzi until March 2000, after Nawaf al-Hamzi and Khalid al-Midhar had already entered the United States; Nawaf al-Hamzi's younger brother, Salem, entered in the summer of 2001. Actually, the NSA already had al-Hamzi's full name, but did not disclose it to the CIA until much later.

The CIA's Bin Laden unit had an extraordinary opportunity to disrupt not one, but two Al Qaeda operations, in January 2000. U.S. intelligence did not know this, but the operation to sink a U.S. warship, the USS *The Sullivans*, in Yemeni waters, was planned for the first week of the new year. And, the first of the 9/11 terrorists were preparing to infiltrate the United States. The CIA had the opportunity to discover the connection between Al Qaeda and the Jamaah Islamiah, the Indonesian Islamic Group, whose leader, Hambali, facilitated the meeting. Malaysian intelligence, the Special Branch, placed Khalled, al-Midhar, al-Hamzi, and Abu Bara under surveillance at the behest of the CIA, and took high quality surveillance photographs of them, photographs that might have led to the arrest of two of the 9/11 hijackers in the summer of 2001. But, there was no audio recording of their meetings.

It was at this point that Khalled made an error that could have compromised the attack on the *Cole*, which was still nearly a year away. On 8 January, after he had probed airline security on the flight to Hong Kong, Khalled traveled to Bangkok, Thailand. Al-Midhar and al-Hamzi followed him. In the Thai capital, Khalled rendezvoused with two other men, Ibrahim al-Thawar, aka Nibras, and Fahd al-Quso. Khalled had come to debrief them. Three days earlier, Nibras and al-Quso had attempted to sink the USS *The Sullivans* in the Port of Yemen. The attack failed when the skiff sank under the weight of the explosives. Here were two sets of Al Qaeda operational cadre in the same city at the same time planning different attacks. Al-Midhar and al-Hamzi did not meet with Nibras and al-Quso, but Khalled met with all four men.

Khalled's lapses in operational security were offset by gaps in CIA surveillance. The CIA did not monitor the men's movements in Bangkok. It never caught sight of Khalled with Nibras and al-Quso, and it lost sight of al-Midhar and al-Hamzi altogether. Eight months later, Nibras martyred himself in the attack on the USS *Cole*; Khalled directed that operation, al-Quso participated in it. But in March, Thai authorities informed the CIA that Nawaf was Nawaf al-Hamzi and that he had traveled to the United States on a valid U.S. visa on 15 January. The CIA field office apparently did not share this information with the CIA Counterterrorism Center, or the Bin Laden Unit, until March in a cable with the annotation "Action Required: None." The CIA also learned that al-Midhar had a U.S. visa. If the Agency had examined the flight manifest, it would have learned that al-Midhar entered the United States on the same flight with al-Hamzi. In fact, the CIA never informed the FBI or any other domestic agency about the presence of one, and possibly two, known Al Qaeda terrorist in the United States. The FBI did not learn about that al-Midhar and al-Hamzi had come to the United States until late August 2001.[4]

The value of intelligence the CIA possessed about al-Hamzi and al-Midhar in January 2000 increased exponentially in January 2001. The investigation in the attack on the *Cole* was progressing, despite the obstacles that Yemeni authorities sometimes hurled in the investigators' path. The Yemenis had detained two of the conspirators. One of them, Fahd al-Quso, admitted to an FBI interrogator that Khalled had directed the *Cole* operation, that he, al-Quso, participated in it, and that he had met with Khalled in Thailand the previous January. There was another source of critical information, an informant whom both the FBI and CIA considered an asset. The source identified Khalled in one of the surveillance photographs Malaysian authorities had taken at the CIA's behest. He identified Khalled, but not al-Midhar.

This was a revelation to the CIA. The Agency now knew that Tawfiq bin Attash, aka Khalled, was not Khalid al-Midhar, and it had definitive confirmation that al-Midhar and al-Hamzi were Al Qaeda terrorists because of their association with Khalled, the mastermind of the *Cole* attack. But, the CIA still did not reveal this information to the FBI or instruct the State Department to place al-Midhar and al-Hamzi on its terror watch list, an action it could have taken a year earlier when the Agency knew that al-Hamzi had entered the United States and that al-Midhar probably entered the country with him. The failure was consequential. The FBI had the authority to place al-Midhar and al-Hamzi under surveillance in the United States, authority that the CIA did not possess. The FBI might even have penetrated the conspiracy, because, as it turns out, al-Midhar and al-Hamzi had frequent contacts with a reliable FBI informant in San Diego. The State Department could have alerted Customs officials to prevent the men from reentering. In fact, by January 2001, al-Midhar had already left the United States; he returned on Independence Day 2001. Al-Midhar and al-Hamzi's names never made it on the official terror watch list until August, less than a month before they, and Hamzi's younger brother Salem, hijacked the jet that pierced the side of the Pentagon.[5]

Al-Midhar and al-Hamzi landed at LAX in January 2000 around the time Ahmed Ressam was to have bombed it, but they were they lost in Los Angeles without functional English. Al Qaeda operatives may have assisted them, although this has never been proven. Within weeks, Omar al-Bayoumi, a Saudi student living in San Diego, encountered the men in a halal restaurant in Culver City and urged them to relocate to San Diego. Bayoumi assisted the men in various ways. This could have been the gesture of a Muslim to fellow Muslims, or something more. In San Diego, al-Midhar and al-Hamzi encountered a number of Muslims, who, like them, were strangers in a strange land. One of the men, Anwar Aulaqi, a Yemeni, was the imam of a San Diego-area mosque. His encounters with the two Al Qaeda terrorists raise even greater suspicions that Al Qaeda operatives in the United States may have prepared the way for the 9/11 attacks; Aulaqi relocated from San Diego to Falls Church, Virginia, at the end of 2000. The next spring, Nawaf al-Hamzi, and another 9/11 terrorist, Hani Hanjour, met up with Aulaqi in Falls

Church at another mosque where, coincidently or not, Aulaqi had become the imam.[6]

It is not known whether al-Midhar and al-Hamzi met with Al Qaeda operatives lurking in the United States. It is known that they encountered a trusted FBI informant who had long provided the Bureau information about militant Muslims. The man never became suspicious of al-Midhar and al-Hamzi, who impressed him only as pious Muslims. The FBI special agent who handled the informant did not learn about the presence of al-Midhar and al-Hamzi in the San Diego area until after 9/11. That information "would have made a huge difference," he later told members of the House and Senate Intelligence Committees. "We would have immediately opened an investigation. We had the predicate for an investigation if we had that information. We would immediately go out and canvas the sources and try to find out where these people were . . . and we could have done it within a few days. They were so close."[7]

Al-Midhar and al-Hamzi, who came to the United States to learn how to fly, contacted area flight schools, but they were poor candidates for flight training. Neither man seriously attempted to learn to fly after May. In June, al-Midhar left the United States, leaving al-Hamzi behind. Al-Midhar would not return for more than a year, until 4 July, when the U.S. intelligence community was struggling to make sense of recurring threats about a spectacular Al Qaeda attack. Al-Midhar's departure infuriated Khalid Sheikh Mohammed, because it was a security breach that jeopardized the operation. He had no reason to worry. A man the CIA knew to be one of an Al Qaeda "operational cadre" was able to enter, leave, and reenter the United States.

Just as al-Midhar departed the United States, three more Al Qaeda terrorists entered the country on valid U.S. visas to attend flight schools. Mohammed Atta, Marwan al-Shehhi, and Ziad Jarrah had been friends for years. These three and another man, Ramzi Binalshibh, had met in Germany as students and became radicalized in a Hamburg mosque whose imam was a veteran of the Afghan jihad.[8]

Atta, born in Cairo in September 1968 at the dawn of the contemporary age of terror, was the oldest, ten years older than the youngest. He came from a successful middle-class Egyptian family that expected much from him. Atta earned a degree in architectural engineering from the University of Cairo before traveling to Hamburg in 1992 for graduate studies. By 1995, he identified himself with militant Islam. This was the year Atta met Ramzi Binalshibh, a Yemeni, who arrived in Germany the same year as Atta. The two men attended the same Hamburg mosque and articulated the same virulent anti-Semitism that had once animated Nazi Germany. Their friendship was enduring. Marwan al-Shehhi and

Ziad Jarrah arrived in Germany in 1996, the year of bin Laden's declaration of war against the United States. Shehhi was a full ten years younger than Mohammed Atta. Born in the United Arab Emirates, Shehhi was a soldier. He passed through basic training and then won a military scholarship to pursue technical training in Germany. He met Atta and Binalshibh in 1998, the year of bin Laden's fatwa calling on Muslims to kill Americans. Ziad Jarrah came to Germany from Lebanon that same year to study dentistry before shifting to aviation engineering.[9]

These four men—an Egyptian, a Yemeni, an Emirati, and a Lebanese—embodied Al Qaeda's transnational appeal. With their opportunity for a university education in Europe, each could have lived a respectable middle-class life, married, and had children. But Europe suffocated them. Two full decades after Osama bin Laden left Saudi Arabia to wage jihad against the Russians in Afghanistan, these four men left Germany to fight the Russians in Chechnya. Ramzi Binalshibh, who is the only one of the four to live to tell about it—the FBI captured him in Pakistan on the first anniversary of the 9/11 attacks—told U.S. interrogators that en route to Chechnya aboard a train, the four had a random encounter with someone named Khalid al-Masri. Al-Masri overheard them speaking Arabic, engaged them in conversation, and learned of their desire for martyrdom. Then and there al-Masri urged them to travel to an Al Qaeda camp in Afghanistan instead of Chechnya. The chance encounter changed their lives. Al-Masri put Binalshibh in contact with an Al Qaeda recruiter, Mohamedou Ould Slahi, who arranged for the men's travel and training in Afghanistan.

This random encounter also had future consequences for a German national whose misfortune was also to have the name of Khalid al-Masri. In early 2003, the CIA abducted one Khalid al-Masri, who was vacationing in Macedonia, and took him to a clandestine prisoner camp in Afghanistan. It was a case of mistaken identity that has raised disturbing questions about the CIA's longstanding practice of "extraordinary rendition," and possibly torture and abuse in the war on terror. Al-Masri later filed a civil suit in a U.S. court naming George Tenet as a defendant.[10]

Atta, Binalshibh, Shehhi, and Jarrah entered Afghanistan through Pakistan in December 1999, just as the men bin Laden had selected for the Planes Operation, Nawaf al-Hamzi and Khalid al-Midhar, were preparing to travel to the United States through Thailand. Osama bin Laden and Mohammed Atef personally took the measure of the men when they arrived in an Al Qaeda training camp and found them worthy for the Planes Operation. They possessed technical aptitude and fidelity to the cause of jihad. Bin Laden himself selected Mohammed Atta, who spoke some English, to be the tactical commander of the Planes Operation. Mohammed Atef and Abu Zubaydah supervised their terrorist training. In January 2000, Al Qaeda recorded a video tape of Mohammed Attah and Ziad Jarrah reading their last will and testament; it was their martyrdom video. Then, they returned to Hamburg to seek U.S. visas before traveling to the United States to train in U.S. flight schools.[11] U.S. authorities denied Binalshibh a visa and thus the opportunity to martyr himself. Binalshibh instead became the critical liaison between Khalid Sheikh Mohammed and Mohammed Atta in the Planes Operation. But, the State Department did grant visas to Atta, Shehhi, and Jarrah. The three arrived separately in the United States in the span of a month between the end of May and end of June 2000. They began flight training in different flight schools in Florida in July. All three earned single-engine private pilot licenses a few days before Christmas and immediately began learning how to fly large commercial jets on flight simulators.

That same month, December, another Al Qaeda pilot arrived in California. Hani Hanjour did not have to learn to fly jets because he already had a commercial pilot's license. Hanjour, a Saudi, went to Afghanistan to enlist in the jihad in his late teens, after the Soviet withdrawal. In 1991, he traveled to the United States to study English at the University of Arizona in Tucson. His stay was brief, but five years later, in 1996, he went back to Arizona to learn to fly in the Phoenix area, where for some reason a number of militant Muslims resided and trained as pilots. The FBI would later become suspicious about the desire of so many young Muslims whose names turned up in counterterrorism investigations to learn to fly. On the eve of the 9/11 attack, one special agent drafted a memorandum to his superiors recommending a canvassing of Arab men enrolled in flight schools, but nothing came of the "Phoenix electronic communication."

In the spring of 1999, just as Osama bin Laden was meeting with Khalid Sheikh Mohammed to announce his decision to move forward with the Planes Operation, the Federal Aviation Administration granted Hanjour a pilot's license. A year later, Hanjour appeared in Al Qaeda's Faruq camp in Afghanistan. It is not known whether Hanjour was already sworn to Al Qaeda, or even whether he had been an Al Qaeda member when he first entered the United States in 1991. What is known is that when bin Laden learned that Hanjour was a pilot, he selected him for martyrdom.[12]

All four men who seized the flight controls of U.S. passenger jets on 9/11 were in the United States at the close of 2000. In January, Mohammed Atta, their commander, left the United States for Germany for a face-to-face briefing with Ramzi Binalshibh, the liaison with Khalid Sheikh Mohammed, Mohammed Atef, and bin Laden. He returned to the United States on 10 January, ten days before George W. Bush took the oath of office.

Al Qaeda Is Present in America

George W. Bush did not mention terrorism in his first inaugural address on 20 January 2001, although he pledged to strengthen America's defenses and to "confront weapons of mass destruction, so that a new century is spared new horrors." And, he had a warning for America's enemies including, implicitly, terrorists. "We will defend our allies and our interests," he announced, "We will meet aggression and bad faith with resolve and strength." Bush did not mention terrorism, but it was a real and present danger. Bin Laden personified that danger. Prior to the inaugural, the director of the CIA, George Tenet, personally briefed the president-elect about Al Qaeda, and he told him that President Clinton had given the Agency the legal "authorities" to kill bin Laden prior to the inaugural. Bush assured Tenet that under his administration the CIA would have those same authorities.[13]

But Bush failed to comprehend the immediacy of the threat. He has admitted it. "There was a significant difference in my attitude after September 11," he told journalist Bob Woodward. Bush knew, he said, that bin Laden was "a menace" and that "he was responsible for the bombings that had killed Americans." Bush had already granted the CIA the same legal authorities to hunt down bin Laden that Clinton had given the Agency. He was, he said, "prepared to look at a plan that would bring him to justice and would have given the order to do just that." Bush had no qualms about killing bin Laden, but he did not consider it urgent to kill him. "I didn't feel the same sense of urgency, and my blood was not boiling."[14]

President Bush did not explain why his blood was not boiling when he entered the White House. Al Qaeda had murdered seventeen U.S. sailors aboard the USS *Cole* just twenty-five days before the presidential election. President Clinton did not retaliate for the *Cole* attack; he was intensely engaged in last minute negotiations that he hoped would achieve an historic final settlement to Palestinian-Israeli conflict. Neither the CIA nor the FBI could assure him that Al Qaeda was behind the *Cole* attack, and so Clinton sheathed the sword of military retaliation. The intelligence community had settled the question of Al Qaeda's complicity in the death of the sailors aboard the *Cole* by the time Bush took office. Bush opted not to retaliate either, despite his inaugural pledge to "meet aggression and bad faith with resolve and strength." He wanted to see a comprehensive plan to bring bin Laden to justice, because he did not want to "swat flies," according to his national security advisor, Condoleezza Rice.[15] Actually, a plan was already on Rice's desk, but it would take eight months for the new administration to adopt it.

Rice, the former provost of Stanford and member of the elder Bush's NSC staff, was the person charged with coordinating the streams of information and advice flowing to the president from the statutory members of the NSC, the "principals." The team was a mixture of the old and the new. George Tenet stayed on as director of Central Intelligence. Donald Rumsfeld, the new secretary of defense, had served in that post before during the Ford administration. The FBI was in flux. Louis Freeh remained director but only until mid-June, when threats of imminent terror attacks began reach alarming levels. Thomas Pickard ran the Bureau as acting director during the critical summer months before 9/11. Robert Mueller did not formally become director until 4 September, the very same day the NSC deputy secretaries met to discuss the threat of Al Qaeda, and exactly one week before 9/11. John Ashcroft, Bush's appointment to direct the Department of Justice, was responsible for oversight of the FBI. But Pickard, who briefed Ashcroft on terrorism first as deputy director and then as the acting director, came away with the impression that Ashcroft was not much concerned about terrorism.[16]

Clinton's staff had put Rice on notice about Al Qaeda in the transition briefings. Sandy Berger, Rice's predecessor, specifically warned Rice that she could expect to spend more time on Al Qaeda than any other single issue. Bill Clinton said this same thing to George Bush as he prepared to hand over the reins of power. Tenet and his deputy director for operations told Bush and Dick Cheney, the vice president-elect, that bin Laden's Al Qaeda posed an immediate threat, days before the two men took their oaths of office. Richard Clarke, the coordinator for counterterrorism at the NSC, put his anxieties into a transition memo.[17]

Clarke enjoyed virtual cabinet status in the Clinton White House when they met to discuss terrorism. Clarke routinely briefed Clinton in the Oval Office. So, Clarke was accustomed to having the principals, and the president, listen when the intelligence told him that a terror attack was in the works. This was how the Clinton White House managed the millennium crisis a year earlier. The Bush administration would manage things differently. Rice kept Clarke on as coordinator for counterterrorism, but with a lower profile than he had enjoyed in the Clinton White House. Gone too was his direct access to the president. Clarke never briefed Bush on terrorism, not even during the summer of 2001 as the intelligence reporting about an imminent attacks reached "a crescendo," in Clarke's words, and the "system was blinking red," in Tenet's. Clarke was no longer invited to sit with the principals when they met to discuss terrorism. But he believed the principals urgently had to reach a consensus about Al Qaeda. On 25 January, five days after Bush took the oath of office, Clarke sent Rice a three-page memorandum informing her exactly why "we *urgently* need such a principals level review on the Al Qida network." Clarke began by reminding Rice—"as we noted in our briefings to you"—"al Qida (sic) is not some narrow, little terrorist issue that needs to be included in broader regional policy."[18]

Clarke urged the principals to ask and answer a critical question, "Do the principals agree that the al Qida network poses a first order threat to U.S. interests?" Clarke and the others who worked on the bin Laden problem in the Clinton administration had already answered that question for themselves in the affirmative. In the waning months of the Clinton administration, both the CIA's Counterterrorism Center and Clarke's Counterterrorism Security Group drew up comprehensive strategies to eliminate the threat. The CTC dubbed its plan Blue Sky. Clarke's team adapted it. By December, Clarke's staff had a thirteen-page strategy paper outlining the plan to take the fight to bin Laden by arming the warriors of Ahmed Shah Massoud's Northern Alliance to fight the Taliban in Afghanistan and by arming the Predator reconnaissance drone with Hell Fire missiles capable of striking down bin Laden and his lieutenants via satellite.

Clarke attached the paper, "Strategy for Eliminating the Threat from the Jihadist Networks of Al-Qida [sic]: Status and Prospects," to the memorandum he sent to Rice in January. The language could not have been more foreboding. "The al Qida network is well financed, has trained tens of thousands of Jihadists, and has a cell structure in over forty nations. It is also actively seeking to develop and acquire weapons of mass destruction." The reference to WMD should have caught the attention of the president, who had pledged to confront weapons of mass destruction in his inaugural speech, and who would later make preventing terrorists from acquiring WMD a justification for the invasion of Iraq in the spring of 2003. The paper was explicit about Al Qaeda's determination to strike in the United States. One section was titled "direct attacks on the U.S." Another section began with the pronouncement that "al Qida is present in the United States," a statement supported by the confession of Ali Mohammed, the former Green Beret who doubled as a senior member of bin Laden's security detail, "that an extensive network of al Qida 'sleeper' agents currently exists in the U.S."[19]

The jolting statement that Al Qaeda was present in the United States might have prompted the national security advisor to advise the administration to take some immediate action. But, Rice just did not see the urgency of informing the president that Al Qaeda had sleeper agents in the country. "I don't remember whether I discussed this with the president," she testified later, "I don't remember the Al Qaeda cells as being something that we were told to do something about." Rice did not remember telling the president, but Thomas Pickard, the deputy director of the FBI, remembered telling the vice president that Al Qaeda was present in the country. "He was surprised," Pickard said later, but Cheney asked no questions and made no recommendations. After the 9/11 attacks, Robert Mueller, the FBI director, told Bush that the Bureau had placed more than 300 persons living in the United States on the terror watch list. "I was floored," Bush told Bob Woodward, "It's an incredible number."[20]

Nor did Condoleezza Rice share Clarke's sense of urgency about the need for a meeting of the principals to validate the Counterterrorism Security Group's professional judgment that Al Qaeda posed a first order threat to the nation's security. Rice insisted that the deputy secretaries properly frame the issues before the principals met to set policy. But Rice delayed bringing the deputies together to discuss Al Qaeda for more than three months, until 30 April; the principals would not meet to discuss Al Qaeda until 4 September, more than seven months after Clarke requested an urgent meeting, and only a week before Al Qaeda attacked Americans on American soil.

Stephan Hadley, Rice's deputy who would succeed her as national security advisor in Bush's second term, chaired the meeting. The deputies met as the intelligence community frantically toiled to separate the wheat from the chaff in reports of impending attacks. Threat reporting began to surge soon after Bush's inauguration. By April, the NSA, which was pulling communications between Al Qaeda operatives from the airwaves, had intercepted the first conversations with oblique hints about a "spectacular" attack. The NSA would intercept nearly thirty communications warning of spectacular attacks or the approach of the "zero hour" or something similarly ominous in the months leading up to 9/11. But, this was not a meeting about the warnings of an attack. Bush had conveyed his desire for a comprehensive strategy to confront Al Qaeda. So when the deputies deliberated, the warnings about an imminent Al Qaeda attack were lost in a tangle of important, but less urgent, regional issues. Lost was the opportunity to energize the entire U.S. intelligence and law enforcement communities in a unified effort to prevent a spectacular attack that counterterrorism officials sensed was coming in weeks, or possibly even days.[21]

The three-month delay in organizing a deputies' meeting deepened Clarke's belief that the Bush administration considered terrorism important, but not urgent. He felt this from the moment of his first briefings during the transition. Clarke eventually asked for a new assignment because, he said, the administration was "unprepared to act as though there's an urgent problem." The delay in organizing an urgent meeting of the principals had real consequences for counterterrorism. "The difficulty in obtaining the first Cabinet level (Principals) policy meeting on terrorism and the limited Principals' involvement sent unfortunate signals to the bureaucracy about the Administration's attitude toward the al Qida threat." Clarke actually stayed on as the national counterterrorism coordinator and ably managed the CSG's emergency response on 9/11; he moved on to his new assignment, cyber-security, in October. Clarke was not the only counterterrorism official to despair over the new administration's slow reaction to reports of threats. Two CTC officials, one of them a senior CIA analyst, also considered tendering their resignations or leaking stories to the press around the end of May in order to focus attention on the peril. Their boss, George Tenet, believed the White House "grasped the sense of urgency he was communicating," but analysts who put in long hours sifting through the intelligence desperately wanted White House leadership.[22]

The volume of reports about a possible attack strained the intelligence community's analytical capability. None of the threat reporting revealed the contours of a specific attack. Most of it indicated an attack in Saudi Arabia or possibly Israel. But there was reason to be alert to an attack on U.S. soil. Ramzi Yousef's 1993 attack on the World Trade Center and New York Landmarks conspiracy were evidence that jihadists desired to strike in the United States; the discovery of an attempt to bomb LAX in 1999, a little more than a year before the Electoral College gave Bush the presidency, was further proof. Then, in May, an informant told the FBI that Al Qaeda planned to mount attacks in Boston and New York, as well as London. Later that month, an anonymous call to a U.S. embassy warned of an attack with explosives on U.S. soil. Neither report turned out to be credible, although it took some time for analysts to make that determination. That same month, the intelligence community began to pick up indications of a plot to hijack a commercial airliner to secure the release of Omar Abdel Rahman from a U.S. prison. The intelligence community had heard reports of hijackings to free Rahman before, as early as 1998; the CIA briefed the president on those specific reports on 6 August. At the end of the month, the trial of four of the men complicit in the African embassy bombings began in New York under tight security; an act of terror to disrupt the proceedings seemed a real possibility.

More alarming were the electronic intercepts of communications from Abu Zubaydah that hinted at impending attacks. Zubaydah ran Al Qaeda's principal terror training camp and supervised the operations of the men who passed through it. Intercepts of Abu Zubaydah's coded messages prevented the millennium attacks in Jordan. On 4 June, the deputy director of the Counterterrorism Center told the House Select Intelligence Committee that he worried "that we are on the verge of more attacks that are going to be larger and more deadly." He was explicit about the possibility of attacks with weapons of mass destruction. Then a new bin Laden threat seeped out. "There will be attacks against American and Israeli interests," he told a Pakistani journalist, "in the next several weeks." This was ominous. Bin Laden spoke about an impending attack only weeks before the 1998 East African embassy attacks. Two weeks after bin Laden's warning, Khalid Sheikh Mohammed's name surfaced in a CIA analytical report. Mohammed had been high on the CIA's terrorist list ever since the Agency had connected him to Ramzi Youssef and the attack in New York eight years earlier. The report made only a single reference to Mohammed, but it specifically alluded to an attack in the United States: Mohammed was thought to be recruiting mujahideen for operations in the United States with "colleagues who are already there." This was confirmation of the assertion in Counterterrorism Security Group's December policy paper that Al Qaeda was present in the United States. In fact, by the second week in June, fourteen more Al Qaeda terrorists had entered the United States; these were the men trained to terrorize the flight crews and passengers into submission on 9/11. Everything indicated something soon and something spectacular. But the administration had its doubters. Donald Rumsefeld, the secretary of defense, and Paul Wolfowitz, his deputy, speculated that surge in the chatter about impending attacks might be an Al Qaeda ruse to flood the intelligence community's early warning system and to assess the government's reaction. The CIA counterterrorism analysts rushed to refute Rumsfeld's speculation. On 30 June, the Agency circulated a top secret executive intelligence briefing among senior administration officials warning "Bin Laden Threats are Real."[23]

A number of reports hinted at attacks on aviation, probably hijackings. The threat reporting about attacks against civilian aviation threw the intelligence community off balance. All the attacks over the past decade were vehicle bomb attacks in the likeness of Hizb'allah. Hijackings did not fit the Al Qaeda profile. Terrorists hijacked jets to compel governments to release imprisoned comrades, not to inflict mass casualties. The reporting about the possibility of a hijacking to free the blind sheikh conformed to the historical paradigm. But, there were indications that terrorists were beginning to think about passenger jets as weapons; the Algerian Armed Islamic Group had actually tried to slam a passenger jet into the Eiffel Tower in 1994. FBI interrogators knew that Ramzi Yousef, who had attempted to destroy a dozen passenger airliners in flight, had thought about crashing a plane into CIA headquarters. At least one FAA notice raised, but discounted, the possibility of a spectacular suicide hijacking during the summer of 2001.[24]

There was a more recent incident than the Armed Islamic Group's 1994 hijacking in the skies over France. On 31 October 1999, the copilot of Egypt Air flight 990 seized the controls of the Boeing 767 after takeoff from New York's JFK airport when the pilot left the cockpit and slammed the jet into the Nantucket Sound, killing himself and the other 216 souls on board. The cockpit voice data recording captured him chanting "I put my faith in God."[25] The FAA is reasonably certain that the copilot's actions caused the crash of the Egypt Air flight, but the motivation behind them remains a mystery. But then there was another mysterious, although not fatal, incident. One month later, in November 1999, two Saudi nationals twice attempted to enter the cockpit of an Air West flight. After landing, the authorities questioned the men, who innocently claimed to have mistaken the door to the cockpit for the door to the lavatory, and released them. The FBI later developed evidence that both men had jihadist connections; one of them tried to reenter the United States only a month before the 9/11 attacks.

A suicide operation aboard a jet was within the realm of the possible. In fact, the FAA and Secret Service actually simulated a suicide attack on the White House as early 1985. The president's life is the responsibility of Secret Service. In 1985, at the dawn of the era of Hizb'allah's suicide terror in the name of Islam, the Secret Service's upper echelon wanted to know whether the Presidential Protective Detail could protect the president from a pilot on a suicide mission to destroy the White House. The scenario was eerily similar to the actual 9/11 attack. FAA officials in Virginia warn the Secret Service about an aircraft intrusion into P-56, the restricted airspace that radiates seventeen miles out from the Washington Monument almost directly behind the White House. The Secret Service has only minutes to rush the president to safety in a bunker beneath the presidential residence. The president's life depended on the instantaneousness of the FAA's warning and the Secret Service's actions. The exercise, which the Secret Service videotaped, left the agents doubting their ability to perform their duty to protect the president from a suicide attack from the skies.[26]

The Wall

On 11 June CIA analysts and FBI agents met in New York. The meeting was one real opportunity to prevent the 9/11 atrocity. There would be others moments in July and August when senior administration officials, and the president himself, could have awakened to the danger. But this meeting came before one of the 9/11 hijackers, who was out of the country, reentered the United States to kill Americans. The CIA knew who he and what he was. What was tragic about this tense meeting was the confusion about the legal restrictions—"the wall"—that blocked the exchange of information between the CIA and the FBI, and even between agents in the Bureau's criminal and intelligence sections.

The meeting was the idea of a senior CIA officer with the Counterterrorism Center, Tom Wilshire, who was assigned to the FBI's International Terrorism Operations Center. This kind of liaison was intended to promote information sharing. In May, as the background noise about an imminent attack began to rise to frightening decibels, Wilshire began to worry that the meeting in Malaysia between Khalled, al-Midhar, and al-Hamzi was an omen. He knew Khalled was "a major league killer," a fact confirmed by the *Cole* investigation. He knew about Khalid al-Midhar, and he suspected, correctly, that by tracking Fahd al-Quso's travels he could expose an impending terror operation. "Something bad was definitely up" is the way Wilshire phrased it. In fact, al-Quso had traveled in Malaysia in January 2000 carrying large sums of cash, some of it to purchase the tickets for al-Midhar's and al-Hamzi's flight to the United States. So, Wilshire put in a request to the Counterterrorism Center for the surveillance photographs of the meeting in Kuala Lumpur, and he and another CIA analyst began to reexamine the intelligence already in the CTC's possession. Wilshire wanted, he informed the CTC, to "find a photo of the second Cole bomber"—Khalled. But beyond that, he was interested in understanding more about the activities of Khalid al-Midhar's companions during the Kuala Lumpur meeting, because he thought they were "couriers of a sort, who traveled between [the Far East] and Los Angeles." Wilshire called al-Midhar's companions "Hamzi" and "Salah." Wilshire was confused about some facts. Only one of the men he thought were al-Midhar's companions, "Hamzi"—Nawaf al-Hamzi—had traveled to the United States. The man he referred to as "Salah" was actually Khalled, the mastermind of the *Cole* attack; Salah, like Khalled, was simply another one of Tawfiq bin Attash's aliases. But, Khalled had not traveled from the Far East to Los Angeles with al-Hamzi; Khalid al-Midhar himself had made that trip.

Wilshire believed that the FBI analysts and agents assigned to the *Cole* investigation had answers that could confirm his suspicions. One of them, Margarette Gillespie, was an FBI analyst assigned to the CIA's Counterterrorism Center. Wilshire sought her out. So, here was a CIA analyst from the CTC assigned to the FBI's International Terrorism Operations Center, asking for the collaboration of an FBI analyst assigned to the CIA's Counterterrorism Center. On 11 June, Wilshire sent Gillespie, Dina Corsi, an FBI analyst, and another CIA analyst to

New York to meet with FBI criminal investigators. The New York agents
were tasked with developing evidence of criminal responsibility for the
murder of seventeen Americans aboard the *Cole* in October 2000. Wilshire's agenda was to prevent another attack against Americans, somewhere, sometime in 2001. Gillespie carried with her the surveillance
photographs of the Kuala Lumpur meeting.

The law governing the exchange of information between the CIA and
the FBI, and between the FBI's own criminal and intelligence divisions,
negated whatever good may have come from the meeting. At the crucial
moment of the hours-long meeting, Gillespie displayed three surveillance photographs to the FBI's *Cole* investigators. The images of al-
Midhar and al-Hamzi were in one of them. The CIA wanted to know
whether the FBI could identify them, and whether al-Quso, the man who
confessed to FBI interrogators everything he knew about Khalled's and
Al Qaeda's involvement in the *Cole* operation, appeared in the photographs. Gillespie also had a photograph of Khalled, but she did not show
it to the FBI agents.

The FBI agents had questions of their own.

"Why were you looking at this guy?

"You couldn't have been following everybody around the Millennium. What was the reason behind this?"

"Why were they taken?"

"Where were they taken?"

"Where are the rest of the photographs?"

Gillespie knew the answers to none of these questions, but the CIA
analyst who sat silently through the meeting knew the answers to all of
them. He said nothing, believing that he did not have the authority to
share the information with the FBI investigators. The only piece of information the FBI investigators took away from the meeting was the name
of Khalid al-Midhar, but nothing that could have helped the FBI to track
him down: a date of birth, the Saudi equivalent of his social security
number, or the fact that he possessed a U.S. visa. Gillespie, who as an
FBI analyst must have agonized over the restrictions imposed on her and
her colleagues from the bureau, could say only that "the information
could not be passed." [27]

The answer to one of those questions about the photographs—"why
were they taken?"—was critically important. The CIA had asked the
Malaysian intelligence service to take the surveillance photographs in
January 2000 because of the NSA electronic intercepts of phone calls to
and from a home in Yemen. That home belonged to Khalid al-Midhar's
father-in-law. The FBI itself was already aware that Al Qaeda operatives
relayed information through that location; in fact, the FBI had turned
up that information in the course of the *Cole* investigation. The answer

to that question could have led the FBI to discover the presence of Al Qaeda terrorists in the United States; al-Midhar made eight calls to that Yemeni number from the apartment he shared with Nawaf al-Hamzi in San Diego.[28]

This was not the end of it. Wilshire encouraged Gillespie and Corsi to probe for some of the answers. Corsi poured over the information in the terrorist data base on her free time throughout July and August. On 22 August, Gillespie and Corsi met with INS officials who informed them that al-Midhar had entered, left, and reentered the United States; al-Hamzi had entered and there was no documentation that he ever left. This was critical information that the CIA could have shared with the FBI in June, or in January, or in January 2001 for that matter. Al-Midhar and al-Hamzi had visas. Had the Bureau known this, even as late as the June meeting in New York, events might have transpired differently. Al-Midhar, who had left the United States in June 2000, did not return until Independence Day. Had Customs officials been watching for him, they might have detained him immediately upon arrival. Had the FBI field office in San Diego been aware that al-Midhar and al-Hamzi arrived in January 2000, agents could easily have found them and questioned them, or placed an informant inside the conspiracy. In fact, both Al Qaeda terrorists interacted with a reliable FBI informant during their first weeks in the country.

Gillespie and Corsi began their search for al-Midhar and al-Hamzi in the United States then and there and almost immediately crashed into the wall that separated criminal investigations and intelligence gathering even within the FBI. At the end of August—incidentally, after FBI agents in Minneapolis detained Zacarias Moussaoui, an Al Qaeda operative who aroused suspicion by pursuing flight training—Corsi flashed an e-mail to the New York office asking for help in locating al-Midhar as "a risk to the national security." The director of New York office, which took the lead in the Bureau's counterterrorism intelligence, decided that this strictly an intelligence matter, off limits to the FBI's criminal investigators. FBI headquarters in Washington concurred. But one special agent, Steve Bongardt, whose involvement in the *Cole* criminal investigation gave him a special interest in the information about al-Midhar, requested more information. By the end of August, it was almost certainly too late to prevent the 9/11 attacks; the nineteen hijackers had moved into place and were making final preparations. But what happened between these FBI colleagues was something of a parable of intelligence community's failures: Corsi flashed another message to Bongardt demanding that he delete the original e-mail communication referring to al-Midhar and forget he had even seen it.

Corsi was obeying orders from superiors in Washington who dictated that criminal agents could even not be present during an interview with al-Midhar, assuming the FBI managed to locate him. But, FBI headquarters directed, "if at such time as information is developed indicating the existence of a substantial federal crime, that information will be passed over the wall." The directive from headquarters was predicated on a misreading of the law regulating the exchange of information between the Bureau's intelligence and criminal sections; in fact, FBI criminal investigators possessed all the legal authority they needed to have access to al-Midhar, because the FBI was already conducting a criminal investigation into the *Cole* attack and al-Midhar appeared in a surveillance photograph with Khalled, a man the FBI knew to be an accomplice in the crime. Steve Bongardt reacted to the directive with revulsion. "Someday someone will die," he wrote back, "and wall or not—the public will not understand why we were not more effective." That day was fast approaching.[29]

Khalid al-Midhar reentered the United States on Independence Day. All nineteen of the men who carried out the 9/11 attacks were now in the United States. The very next day, 5 July, Richard Clarke summoned officials from the FAA, INS, Customs, the Coast Guard, and Secret Service to a briefing. The FBI and the CIA sent counterterrorism officials. Clarke tried to be forceful, but the participants left the briefing confused about their authorization to share the information with those with the greatest need to know: the officials at airports, borders, and ports. Only the president could have dispelled doubts about their authorization to share information and to take preemptive measures to protect the United States from attack. The administration took some prudent measures aimed at protecting Americans abroad. Vice President Cheney put in a call to Saudi crown prince Abdallah to ask him to instruct Saudi security forces to disrupt potential terror operations in the kingdom. But the president was still not seized by a sense of urgency to take control of his administration's crisis management. [30]

Three days after Clarke's hastily arranged meeting, Mohammed Atta left the United States to meet Ramzi Binalshibh in Madrid. It was Atta's second trip out of the United States. He would return on 19 July. Binalshihb was carrying instructions from bin Laden. Bin Laden, his worries that U.S. authorities would discover the conspiracy growing with each passing day, wanted Atta to strike soon. All nineteen conspirators were already in the United States. The FBI was sure to discover the infiltration of so many Al Qaeda operatives. One of suicide pilots, Ziad Jarrah, was exhibiting signs of moral weakness. Jarrah maintained a romantic relationship with a German woman of Turkish descent whom he met in Hamburg. Confusion about the true object of Jarrah's true devotion—a woman or jihad in the way of God—could imperil the operation. Jarrah traveled in and out of the United States to visit her. Jarrah's confusion prompted Khalid Sheikh Mohammed to send money to Zacarias Moussaoui, a French national of Moroccan descent who was already in the United States, to pursue flight simulator training as a possible replacement for Jarrah. That almost proved to be the fatal error: the INS arrested Moussaoui at the behest of the FBI a month before 9/11.[31]

Bin Laden had another instruction for Atta: destroy the White House. Bin Laden comprehended the reasons why Khalid Sheikh Mohammed, and Ramzi Yousef before him, desired the destruction of the World Trade Center's Twin Towers: mass casualties, financial chaos, and symbolism. The towers were profane monuments to U.S. affluence and arrogance. The destruction of the Capitol was important because it was the seat of America's representative democracy. But the White House was supremely important to Bin Laden. Bin Laden may have wanted to inflict a head wound to the U.S. government in retaliation for America's attempt to decapitate Al Qaeda in the summer of 1998. Atta told his friend Binalshibh that he would need another six weeks, at a minimum, to execute the Planes Operation. He was reluctant to promise the destruction of the White House. Atta knew that it was improbable that any of the pilots could navigate a large commercial airliner into the White House because of its size and location. Atta was personally committed to attacking the World Trade Center. He assigned Hani Hanjour, the most experienced pilot, to attack the Pentagon. He gave Jarrah, the most unreliable of the four pilots, to strike another location in the nation's capital, probably the Capitol Building. Binalshibh reported all this back to Khalid Sheikh Mohammed and bin Laden.

On 10 July, five days after Clarke convened the meeting of domestic agencies, George Tenet, the director of the CIA, and Cofer Black, the director of the CIA's Counterterrorism Center, made an impromptu visit to the White House to confront Condoleezza Rice. Tenet and Black carried with them a classified CIA briefing paper on Al Qaeda. The Agency's conclusions—"based on the review of all source reporting over the last five months"—came down to four terse, declarative statements.

Al Qaeda will launch a significant terrorist attacks against U.S. and/or Israeli interests in the coming weeks.

The attack will be spectacular and designed to inflict mass casualties against U.S. facilities or interests.

Preparations have been made.

Attack will occur with little or no warning.[32]

The intelligence did not disclose the time or place or the modality of an attack, but this constituted a strategic warning: preparation had been made for a spectacular, mass- casualty attack that would come without warning in coming weeks. Tenet and Black felt compelled to personally deliver this warning to the national security advisor. The director of the CIA and his counterterrorism chieftain had come to convince the president's national security advisor to convince the president finally to take charge of a national security crisis. Rice was no more impressed by Tenet and Black's warnings about an imminent attack than she was by Clarke's warning, more than seven months earlier, about the presence of Al Qaeda sleeper agents in the country. Just as Rice did not remember telling the president about the presence of Al Qaeda on U.S. soil back in January, she did not recall telling the president that the director of the CIA had warned her of an imminent attack in July. If fact, Rice did not even recall that the 10 July meeting even took place. Her failure to tell the president, and Tenet's failure to speak those four declarative sentences directly to the president, would have consequences in August when the president received a very different CIA briefing on bin Laden's intentions.

Coincidently, that same day, Kenneth Williams, an FBI special agent in Phoenix sent an e-mail to FBI headquarters in the nation's capital and to the Bureau's New York office. Williams was tasked with counterterrorism, and he had anxieties. The special agents in the Phoenix office had observed that "an inordinate number of individuals of investigative interest" have, or are, attending flight schools in the United States. Williams's memo was explicit about the possibility that bin Laden was behind the coordinated effort "to establish a cadre of individuals who will one day be working in the civil aviation community." These were not mere conjectures. Williams had a confidential source, and the agents in the FBI's Phoenix office were actively conducting surveillance of "individuals of investigative interest": ten men from at least six Muslim countries. "These individuals," Williams warned, "will be in a position in the future to conduct terrorist activity against civil aviation targets." [33]

The Phoenix office had concluded that it was no mere coincidence that so many Muslim men trained to fly in Arizona, because "significant" bin Laden associates have lived in Arizona. Williams reminded headquarters that Wadi el-Hage, who had recently been convicted in connection with East Africa embassy bombings, had lived in Tucson. The principal subject of the Phoenix office investigation, Zakaria Mustapha Soubras, was known for his militancy. Soubras brazenly told FBI agents, who questioned him in April and again in May 2000, that the U.S. embassies in Kenya and Tanzania were "legitimate military targets of Islam." What caught the FBI's attention was that Soubras was also a student at Embry Riddle University in Prescott, Arizona, a school that specialized in aviation and aeronautical engineering.

Ghassan al-Sharbi, another person of interest to the Phoenix FBI, also studied at Embry Riddle. Sharbi may have become an Al Qaeda militant after he left the United States for Afghanistan in the summer of 2000; he may have already been in Al Qaeda when he studied in Prescot. What is certain is that he was in Al Qaeda. The CIA captured him in Pakistan with Abu Zubaydah, the commandant of bin Laden's principal training camp, in March 2002.[34] The FBI confirmed Sharbi's connection to Al Qaeda after the 9/11 hijackings. But the Phoenix office already had good reasons to be concerned about hijackings, or other "terrorist activity against civilian aviation," in July 2001. Phoenix agents observed Soubras under surveillance with two men, Hamdan al-Shalawi and Muhammed al-Qudhaieed, who attempted to intrude into the cockpit of an America West jet during a flight in November 1999. Both were students in Arizona and both, it was learned later, trained in Al Qaeda camps. The America West incident did not raise special concerns at the time, although it occurred only a month after the suicidal copilot of an Egypt Air flight crashed a plane full of passengers into the sea of the United States East Coast. But U.S. authorities prudently placed both men on a watch list. In August 2001, one of them applied for a visa to return to the United States; the State Department denied the request.[35]

And then there was Hani Hajour, although it is not clear whether Williams named him in the memo. Hanjour learned to fly in Arizona in 1999. After Hanjour reentered the United States in early December 2000 to participate in the 9/11 operation, he traveled to Mesa, Arizona, with Nawaf al-Hamzi to practice his flying skills on a commercial jet flight simulator. He stayed in Mesa through March, when he left for the East Coast to make his final preparations before 9/11. He may have had contacts with Soubras, the principal subject of the Phoenix offices investigation.[36]

The Phoenix office was on to something. Williams copied the memo to the FBI's New York field office, but New York did not leap at this information or his recommendations. Williams's recommendation—that the FBI begin canvassing all flight schools in the United States to confirm that an inordinate number of Arab males with possible jihadist inclinations—was wildly impracticable. Agents in New York were not alarmed by the information because, remarkably, "the agents knew that persons connected to al-Qa'ida had already received training in the United States."[37] It was assumed only that bin Laden needed pilots to transport him and his mujahideen. But this too was a lost opportunity. In June, CIA analysts met with FBI's *Cole* investigators in New York and revealed the name of Khalid al-Midhar to them. Al-Mihdhar had entered the United States with Nawaf al-Hamzi. Hani Hanjour, the suicide pilot trained in Arizona, traveled to Mesa, Arizona, with al-Hamzi, and reen-rolled in an Arizona flight school.

Then another piece of the puzzle fell into place. On 16 August, about month after Ken Williams circulated the Phoenix memo, the INS arrested a French citizen of Moroccan descent at the request of the FBI field office in Minneapolis. Moussaoui passed through Al Qaeda's Khalden camp in early 1998. Khalid Sheikh Mohammed recruited him and sent him to the United States to fly at the beginning of 2001, more than a year after he had sent Atta, Shehhi, and Jarrah, three of the operation pilots who were already in the United States learning to fly; Hani Hanjour arrived in December. Mohammed may have wanted to execute a second wave of attacks. Mousssaoui arrived in the first week of February 2001 and went directly to Norman, Oklahoma, where he took pilot training from the end of February through the end of May. In July, Moussaoui put down a large payment for flight simulator training to learn to fly Boeing 747s.

Around this time, Ziad Jarrah left the United States for Germany on a one-way ticket. Khalid Sheikh Mohammed monitored the operation as best he could from Pakistan by communicating with Atta through Ramzi Binalshibh. So, Mohammed was aware of Ziad Jarrah's inner turmoil and the tensions between the Lebanese-born Jarrah and the Egyptian-born Atta, seven years Jarrah's senior. Jarrah was in love with a German citizen living in Germany, and his love tempted him to abandon the conspiracy. Jarrah flew to Hamburg, where he had first met Atta, Shehhi, and Binalshibh, to visit her. And, he met with Binalshibh, who eventually persuaded to return to the United States for the glories of martyrdom.

Jarrah's sudden departure for Germany led Mohammed to consider Moussaoui as Jarrah's replacement. Binalshibh almost immediately wired Moussaoui $15,000 for flight simulator training at a Pan Am facility in Minneapolis. But Moussaoui acted stupidly. He paid a large sum of money, more than $8,000 for simulator training, but admitted to his instructor that he was not interested in pursuing a commercial pilot's license. The suspicious instructor alerted the FBI's Minneapolis office, which urged the INS to detain Moussaoui for overstaying his visa.

The FBI in Minneapolis moved against Moussaoui because his aberrant interest in flight training aroused the same suspicions that prompted Ken Williams in the Phoenix office to draft his memo. But nothing came of this either. The Minneapolis field office immediately appealed to FBI headquarters to apply for a warrant under the Foreign Intelligence Surveillance Act to scour Moussaoui's computer hard drive. But Washington declined the request citing an absence of probable cause of a criminal conspiracy, even though a routine search for information on Moussaoui revealed that French intelligence had placed him on a terror watch list. FBI headquarters' inaction infuriated the Minneapolis agents, who applied for a criminal warrant on the morning of Tuesday 11 September, even as the attacks were underway, citing the same evidence of probable cause as contained in previous requests. Eight months after 9/11, Coleen Rowely, one of the Minneapolis agents, vented her anger at FBI headquarters, which publicly minimized the significance of the Moussaoui arrest. By now, she was aware that the Phoenix office had alerted FBI headquarters to the possibility that Al Qaeda was sending terrorists to train to fly in order to be in a position to conduct terrorist activities against civilian aviation. "The agents in Minneapolis," she wrote, "who were closest to the action and in the best position to gauge the situation locally, did fully appreciate the terrorist risk/danger posed by Moussaoui and his possible co-conspirators even prior to September 11th. Even without knowledge of the Phoenix communication (and any number of other additional intelligence communications that FBIHQ personnel were privy to in their central coordination roles), the Minneapolis agents appreciated the risk."[38]

The President's Briefing

The sudden appearance of the director of the CIA and the director of the Counter Terrorism Center at the White House on 10 July did not electrify the Bush administration. Rice asked Tenet to repeat the briefing to Donald Rumsfeld and John Ashcroft, the attorney general, but there is no evidence that Tenet conveyed the Agency's dire warning to either the secretary of defense or the attorney general. The national security advisor did not take any extraordinary measures.[39] The president himself took no action. A week later, Bush traveled to Genoa, Italy, for the G-8 Summit, where Italian officials took the extraordinary measure of deploying surface-to-air missiles to defend against a terrorist intrusion into the airspace above the heads of the world's wealthiest states. When Bush returned to the United States, he went on a working vacation at his ranch in Crawford, Texas. There, on 6 August, the CIA briefed him again on Al Qaeda's determination to strike on U.S. soil.[40]

The CIA's presidential daily briefing was routine in the Bush White House. This was the thirty-seventh PDB specifically concerned with the threat of Al Qaeda, a number that validated the former president's admonition that Bush would spend more of his time dealing with bin Laden than any other single national security concern. And, that day's presidential briefing came when a surge of threat reporting saturated the intelligence community. There was a clear and present danger of an Al Qaeda attack. The analysts who prepared the briefing wanted to convey the urgency of the situation and the imminence of the threat of an

Al Qaeda attack on U.S. soil. The title of the briefing of the 6 August Presidential Daily Brief, "Bin Laden Determined to Strike in U.S.," captured that message.[41]

The president misinterpreted the briefing as a recitation of past events. The briefing summarized intelligence reports or even media reports dating back to 1997 and 1998. Ressam's failed effort to attack LAX in 1999—"which may have been part of Bin Ladin's (sic) first serious attempt to implement a terrorist strike in the U.S."—was the most recent event. These may have been events in the past, but they came in the recent past. The briefing warned the president that bin Laden "prepares operations years in advance and is not deterred by setbacks," presumably like the arrest of Ressam during the millennium. It repeated the warning Clarke conveyed to Rice in January that "Al Qa'ida members—including some who are U.S. citizens—have resided in or traveled to the U.S. for years, and the group apparently maintains a support structure that could aid attacks." It warned the president that the FBI had developed information that "indicated patterns of suspicious activity in this country consistent with preparations for hijackings," information that was similar to threats dating back to 1998, hinting at an Al Qaeda operation "to hijack a U.S. aircraft to regain the release of the 'blind Shaykh' 'Umar 'Abd al-Rahman."

But the 6 August briefing did not have the force of the 10 July briefing that Tenet and Black personally gave to Rice, warning that all the intelligence indicated that Al Qaeda had already made preparations for a spectacular, mass-casualty terrorist attack against U.S. interests in the coming weeks with little or no warning. Rice was not in Crawford on 6 August, but she defended the president's inaction. "There was nothing actionable in this," Rice testified later. "It was historical information based on old reporting. There was no new threat information, and it did not, in fact, warn of any coming attacks inside the United States."[42]

Worse, the briefing gave misleading assurances to the president that the FBI was alert to the threat and that the Bureau was conducting "approximately 70 full field investigations through the United States that it considers Bin Laden-related." The number was an estimate that included minor investigations on a number of individuals, suspicious fund-raising activities, and even a background check on a deceased man. In fact, neither the FBI nor the Department of Justice gave instructions to the FBI's field offices to heighten surveillance of possible Al Qaeda sleeper cells in the United States. FBI headquarters in Washington and the New York office had dismissed the 10 July Phoenix memo. When the Minneapolis office detained Zacaria Moussaoui, ten days after this briefing in Crawford, the FBI in Washington failed to see Moussaoui's activities in light of an impending threat. John Ashcroft, who as attorney general was charged with oversight of the FBI, blamed this on the "wall"—the legal restrictions blocking the flow of information between intelligence analysts and criminal investigators. "Before September 11, government was blinded by this wall," he said. "We did not know an attack was coming because for nearly a decade our government had blinded itself to its enemies." But Ashcroft's own failings were as consequential. The acting director of the FBI, Thomas Pickard, remembers Ashcroft telling him that he did not want to hear about reports of threats after August. Ashcroft denies the charge, but admitted he made the "dangerous assumption" that FBI was acting in all due diligence. Ashcroft did not take any specific or special action to ensure that the FBI or the INS would counter a possible domestic attack.[43]

The president himself did not pursue the matter after 6 August. He did not confer with the attorney general or even with the director of the CIA about Al Qaeda. He gave no special instructions.[44] The analysts who drafted the PDB may have hoped that the historical narrative would compel the president to see the surge of threat reporting in a new and more sinister light. But even then, Bush "did not feel the same sense of urgency" that he would seize him a month later.

Cofer Black, the director of the CTC, knew that intelligence about bin Laden's determination to strike the United States was not merely historical information, it was a clear and present danger. Nine days after the briefing in Crawford, Black gave a classified presentation to his counterterrorism colleagues at the Pentagon. "We are going to get struck soon," he said with a terrible sense of certainty, "many Americans are going to die, and it could be in the U.S." The very next day, the FBI detained Zacarias Moussaoui in Minneapolis.[45]

The NSC cabinet principals finally met to discuss Al Qaeda in the context of a broad review of regional policy on 4 September. It had been seven months since Richard Clarke wrote to Rice requesting an urgent cabinet-level meeting, four months since the deputies first met to frame the issues, two months since the director of the CIA and the director of the CIA Counterterrorism Center personally warned Rice of a mass-casualty attack, and a month since the CIA briefed the president on bin Laden's determination to strike in the United States. The principals had met thirty times to discuss policy in the president's first eight months in office, including a meeting on 7 Frbruary, only two weeks into the new administration, to discuss Iraq. In front of the principals was the deputies' draft of National Security Presidential Directive 9. The deputies had completed the draft in June. In its basic contours, NSPD-9 was substantially the same as the strategy Clarke had presented to Rice in January.[46]

President Bush signed eight prior National Security Presidential Directives, but none of the president's directives directed the energies of the U.S. government on Al Qaeda. Ironically, the month after the 11 September attacks, Bush signed his ninth National Security Presidential Directive, NSPD-9, "Defeating the Terrorism Threat to the United States," which in its basic contours was substantially the same as the strategy Clarke's team drafted in December and presented to Rice in January.[47]

It had taken seven months for the senior Bush administration officials to meet to decide on a course of action to counter Al Qaeda. Rice believed that the deputies had painstakingly framed a comprehensive strategy, and she took comfort in the fact that President Bush's ninth national security directive was "the very first major national security policy directive of the Bush administration—not Russia, not missile defense, not Iraq, but the elimination of al Qaeda." Clarke believed it had taken the better part of the administration's first year in office to ratify the policy the Clinton administration had left on Bush's desk, and even then, the administration was "left waiting for the big attack, with lots of casualties, after which some major U.S. retaliation will be in order." The same day the principals met, Clarke fired off another note to Rice. "Decision makers should imagine themselves on a future day," he wrote Rice, "when the [Counterterrorism Security Group] has not succeeded in stopping al Qida attacks and hundreds of Americans lay dead in several countries, including the U.S."[48]

That future day when Americans lay dead in the United States was only a week away. There would be thousands, not hundreds, of dead.

Tuesday, 11 September 2001

Early on the morning of the second Tuesday of September, Al Qaeda terrorists boarded flights in Boston, Newark, and the nation's capital. There were nineteen of them. Two of them, Khalid al-Midhar and Nawaf al-Hamzi, first came to the United States almost twenty months earlier, in January 2000; the CIA knew their names, their fidelity to Al Qaeda, and their presence in the country. Three others, Mohammed Atta, Marwan al- Shehhi and Ziad Jarrah, arrived that summer. Another, Hani Hanjour, came just before New Year's. The remainder arrived in the summer of 2001. All were in the United States, hiding in plain sight, by Independence Day.

In Boston, Mohammed Atta and four others boarded American flight 11; Marwan al-Shehhi and four others boarded United flight 175. In Newark, Ziad Jarrah and three others took their seats on United flight 93. In the nation's capital, Hani Hanjour and the remaining four terrorists boarded American flight 77. There were 246 passengers and crew aboard those flights. The murder of those 246 alone would surpass the number of Americans—241 sailors and Marines—whom Hizb'allah murdered in 1983 in the worst terrorist attack against Americans, until that Tuesday morning.[49]

Bin Laden's attack on the United States began at 8:15 A.M., when the terrorists commandeered American flight 11; thirty minutes later, they seized United flight 175; ten minutes after that, at 8:51, they seized American flight 77. The terrorists aboard United flight 93 did not manage to commandeer that flight until nearly 9:30, seventy-five minutes after the first hijacking. Air traffic controllers came slowly to the realization that terrorists were conducting multiple, simultaneous hijackings in the skies over America's eastern seaboard. There was nothing like it in the history of air piracy in the United States. Thirty-one years earlier to the week, Palestinian terrorists simultaneously hijacked three jets in the skies over Europe and nearly seized a fourth. But Tuesday 11 September 11 2001 was nothing like Skyjack Sunday in 1970 either. The terrorists aboard these four flights had not seized the jets to take hostages, they seized the jets to acquire terribly destructive weapons. There was one similarity. Now, as then, the passengers and crew defeated the purpose of the hijackers aboard one of the jets.

Al Qaeda's attack in New York and Washington lasted 148 minutes. Mohammed Atta crashed American flight 11, carrying 87 passengers and crew and five terrorists, into the North Tower of the World Trade Center at 8:45; Marwan al-Shehhi guided United 175, with its sixty passengers and crew into the South Tower seventeen minutes later, at 9:03. In an instant, ten terrorists murdered 147 people aboard two commercial airliners and an incalculable number of people in the impact zone in the Towers. Thirty-four minutes later, Hani Hanjour, flying American flight 77 at virtually ground level, crashed the plane into the Pentagon. With him were Khalid al-Midhar and Nawaf al-Hamzi, men whom the CIA knew to be terrorists and knew to be in the United States since January 2000. Nawaf al-Hamzi's younger brother and two other terrorists were aboard with the 59 passengers and crew. The attack on the Pentagon killed all 59 passengers and crew aboard the plane and 175 servicemen and -women.

United flight 93 departed from Newark only minutes before Atta flew American flight 11 into the North Tower, in plain sight of the Newark airport. But the terrorists aboard the plane did not seize it until after Shehhi crashed United fight 175 into the second Twin Tower, and only minutes before Hanjour crashed American 77 into the Pentagon. The plane was over eastern Ohio before the hijacking. By then everyone in the United States and all forty passengers and crew aboard the plane knew that the United States was under attack, even before Ziad Jarrah turned the jet to the southeast, toward Washington, D.C.

The scenario was graver than the FAA and Secret Service had even imagined when, in 1985, the agencies simulated a suicide attack like this one against the White House. The president was not there: he was reading to elementary school students in Sarasota, Florida, that morning. But the Secret Service did evacuate the White House at 9:45 A.M., eight minutes after the strike on the Pentagon across the Potomac. American flight 77 had departed Washington Dulles. It was over eastern Ohio when the terrorists overpowered the flight crew and the jet disappeared from radar. The FAA warned the Secret Service that an inbound jet, flying nearly 500 miles per hour, had intruded into the P-56 airspace, just five minutes before the impact on the Pentagon. Now, United 93 was inbound for the nation's capital. It too had been over eastern Ohio when the terrorists took control of the plane and put Ziad Jarrah at the flight controls just before 9:30. Seventeen minutes later, the FAA in Washington informed the Secret Service that the plane was "twenty-nine minutes out of Washington, D.C." The Secret Service evacuated the White House.

Ziad Jarrah never piloted flight 93 to its target, probably the Capitol Building. The passengers and crew, aware by now that terrorists had seized three other planes and crashed them into buildings in New York and Washington, knew that the assurances Jarrah broadcast over the intercom—we "are going back to the airport to have our demands" heard—were false. The passengers resisted. They were moments away from breaking into the cockpit when Jarrah put the jet into a steep dive. United flight 93 crashed in a rural field in Pennsylvania at 10:03. Al Qaeda's attacks on New York and Washington came to an end 148 minutes after they began. The resistance of the passengers and crew of United 93 saved innumerable lives, and saved a symbol of American freedom.

But the killing did not end. Two minutes after United 93 crashed in Pennsylvania, the molten South Tower of the World Trade Center came crashing down in Manhattan. Twenty-three minutes after that, the North Tower collapsed. Thousands perished in the ruins. In all, Al Qaeda murdered 2,819 on that Tuesday morning.

Osama bin Laden rejoiced when he saw these images of the collapsing towers. "There is America," he said. "Its greatest buildings were destroyed. Thank god for that. There is America, filled with fear from its north to its south, from its east to its west. Thank god for that."[50]

That night a somber but fiercely resolute President Bush returned to the nation's capital where he addressed the American people. His blood was now boiling. George Bush was haunted by the same images that caused bin Laden to rejoice. "Pictures of airplanes flying into buildings, fires burning, huge structures collapsing," he said "have filled us with disbelief, terrible sadness, and a quiet, unyielding anger." The president comprehended that the United States was at war with an implacable enemy who believed falsely that an act of mass murder was obedience to God. The president discerned the truth of these acts.

"Today, our nation saw evil."[51]

Epilogue

President Bush addressed a joint session of Congress on the night of 20 September, 2001, as rescue workers sifted through a million tons of debris at ground zero, once the site of the World Trade Center. "On September the 11th, enemies of freedom committed an act of war" the president said. Bush alluded to the attack on Pearl Harbor, and like FDR, who addressed a joint session of Congress the day after the attack on the American fleet in Hawaii in 1941, Bush stated the obvious: America was at war. But, unlike FDR, he did not ask Congress to declare one. "Our war on terror begins with al Qaeda, but it does not end there. It will not end until every terrorist group of global reach has been found, stopped and defeated."

Bush, who confessed his "blood was not boiling" before September 11, said that he now had a sense of urgency and purpose. "Whether we bring our enemies to justice or justice to our enemies, justice will be done." He dictated an ultimatum to the Taliban regime harboring bin Laden in Afghanistan: "They will hand over the terrorists, or they will share their fate." Then he put the world on notice: "from this day forward, any nation that continues to harbor or support terrorism will be regarded by the United States as a hostile regime." But the president warned Americans that the war on terror would be a "lengthy campaign, unlike any other we have seen." George W. Bush, the evangelical Christian president, saw this confrontation just as Osama bin Laden, the Muslim emir of Al Qaeda, saw it, as a confrontation with evil: "Freedom and fear, justice and cruelty, have always been at war, and we know that God is not neutral between them."

Never before had a nation, not even Israel, declared a global war on terror, although Al Qaeda was not the first terrorist organization of global reach. The secular Palestinian terror organizations—PFLP and its splinters, Black September, Abu Nidal, and others—constructed a network that facilitated terror operations in Europe, North Africa, and Asia as well as the Middle East through the 1970s and well into the 1980s. They could move men, money, and weapons across national frontiers and plan lethal operations in safe houses in strategic European capitals. Germans, Japanese, and Latin Americans devoted to the myth of a global Socialist revolution joined Palestinian nationalist organizations that militated for a territorial state rather than a revolutionary world order. The Arab "confrontation" states—principally Iraq, Syria, and Libya—plied the terror organizations with money and staked their political legitimacy on the rejection of peace through terror. The Soviet Union and the Soviet bloc states—principally East Germany and Czechoslovakia—aided and abetted them in the name of solidarity with peoples waging wars of national liberation, although the true motivation was the Soviet bloc's strategic Cold War interest in menacing the United States and its North Atlantic Treaty Organization (NATO) allies. State sponsorship brought the advantages of money, weapons, false documents, safe havens, and even cautious diplomatic support, but when the strategic interests of the confrontation states and the Soviet Union shifted, terror organizations found themselves operating under debilitating constraints.

Al Qaeda is mystifyingly different, because it acquired a global reach without a state sponsor. The Sudan provided Al Qaeda safe haven, but when Al Qaeda organized an attempt on the Egyptian president's life from Khartoum in 1995, the Sudanese expelled Al Qaeda and seized bin Laden's funds. The Taliban in Afghanistan initially welcomed bin Laden as an emir among the Arab mujahideen who had fought against the Soviets, and allowed Al Qaeda to operate terrorist camps on Afghan territory, but the Taliban did not materially support Al Qaeda's operations. The Taliban had to reassess bin Laden's value to the regime after Operation Infinite Reach, the cruise missile attack on Al Qaeda camps in Afghanistan in retaliation for the East Africa embassy bombings in August 1998. Mullah Omar, the Taliban's spiritual leader, forbade bin Laden from uttering public pronouncements that would provoke a more serious U.S. military retaliation. Bin Laden ignored Mullah Omar's admonitions and organized the 11 September 2001 attacks—the Planes Operation—on Afghan soil. So, on the eve of the 9/11 atrocities, bin Laden sent assassins to kill Ahmed Shah Massoud, the charismatic commander of the Northern Alliance and the Taliban's most formidable foe, in a cunning gesture to placate the Taliban. Mullah Omar defied the U.S. ultimatum to deliver bin Laden to American justice—and suffered the consequences.

Al Qaeda does not depend on state sponsorship, so bin Laden is not beholden to any state. Al Qaeda's one true advantage is the devotion of numbers of Islam's more than one billion adherents. Only a fraction of Muslims gravitate to militant Islam, but those who answered the call to jihad share a blinding fanaticism that the young far-left Marxists who sought thrills in terror operations in the 1970s rarely displayed. Bin Laden and his lieutenants worked to string together a network of terror organizations in regions from Chechnya to Indonesia, anywhere Muslims believed infidels or apostates oppressed them. Al Qaeda established a secret presence in Europe: in Germany, where three of the men who organized and executed the 9/11 attacks had met, and in Spain and the United Kingdom where Islamic militants committed horrifying massacres in 2004 and 2005. This was the network of terror organizations with global reach which President Bush vowed to destroy.

On the fourth Sunday after the attacks in New York and Washington, Al Jazeera television broadcast a videotape of bin Laden that had been recorded sometime earlier. He rejoiced in the carnage: "There is America, filled with fear from its north to its south, from its east to its west. Thank god for that." He raised the call to jihad. "In the aftermath of that event," said bin Laden, "and now that senior U.S. officials have spoken, beginning with Bush, the head of the world's infidels . . . every Muslim should rush to defend his religion."[1]

In a sheer coincidence, that same day, 7 October, the president addressed the American people to announce that the U.S. military had launched Operation Enduring Freedom to displace the Taliban regime and destroy Al Qaeda. But the president declared that the war on terror would not be confined to Afghanistan. "Today we focus on Afghanistan, but the battle is broader. Every nation has a choice to make. In this conflict, there is no neutral ground."[2] In fact, the administration was already considering another war in another nation.

Operation Enduring Freedom was swift and lethal. Northern Alliance forces, advancing behind devastating American air attacks, routed the Taliban in only weeks. Three days before Christmas—one hundred and one days after the 9/11 attacks and seventy-eight days after the first bombs fell on Afghanistan—General Tommy Franks, commander of the U.S. Central Command (CENTCOM), flew into Kabul to attend the inauguration of an interim Afghan government. The rout of the Taliban and Al Qaeda was astonishing, but it was incomplete. Bin Laden and Aymin Al-Zawahiri narrowly escaped. and nearly five years after 9/11 they remain at large. However, history might have taken a different course.

On the last day of November, more than two months into Operation Enduring Freedom, a small team of CIA paramilitaries—codenamed Jawbreaker—located bin Laden and directed a ferocious aerial bombardment of Al Qaeda positions in the White Mountains in Afghanistan's Tora Bora region. "The planes poured lava on us," bin Laden said after he narrowly survived the assault. Two weeks into the operation, Jawbreaker had trapped bin Laden in a kill zone measuring only a few square kilometers. Bin Laden's only options were to stand, fight, and die, or flee through the rugged mountain range to the tribal area of

Pakistan. He chose to flee. Jawbreaker's commander repeatedly pleaded for the deployment of a small contingent of army Rangers to seal the mountain passes leading to Pakistan; General Franks denied the requests, and opted to give Afghani warlords the task of closing the escape routes. In mid-December, bin Laden assembled his surviving fighters, begged them for forgiveness for leading them to disaster, led them in prayer, and slipped away.[3]

Bin Laden appeared on a videotape two days after the inauguration of the interim Afghani government to prove to his acolytes that he had survived. He released another tape on 11 February, mocking the U.S. "failure" in Tora Bora: "The U.S. forces dared not break into our positions," he said, "despite the unprecedented massive bombing. . . . Is there any clearer evidence of their cowardice, fear, and lies regarding their legends about their alleged power?" He was already preparing for another confrontation with the United States: "We are following up with great interest and extreme concern the crusaders' preparations for war to occupy a former capital of Islam."[4] It was an allusion to Baghdad. Bin Laden was perceptive. President George Bush, on the advice of senior advisors and their deputies—including Vice President Cheney, who had served as secretary of defense under Bush senior—had already resolved to rectify what they believed was the elder Bush's most grievous error: leaving Saddam Hussein in power in Iraq after the Gulf War in 1991.

Bin Laden and Al-Zawahiri escaped, but Operation Enduring Freedom inflicted great harm on Al Qaeda. The U.S. military killed hundreds of Al Qaeda and Taliban and took more than seven hundred prisoners of war, or "unlawful enemy combatants" as the administration has controversially classified them. The swift victory deprived Al Qaeda of its sanctuary and destroyed the Taliban regime. The Americans killed Mohammed Atef, the chief of Al Qaeda's military operations, in an air strike in November 2001. In the coming months and years the CIA and FBI, working with the Pakistani intelligence service and other intelligence services, would capture important Al Qaeda figures.

The CIA captured Ibn al-Sheikh al-Libi, who trained Al Qaeda terrorists at the Khalden camp, in Pakistan in November 2001, and delivered him to the Egyptian intelligence service. Under torture, al-Libi revealed that Saddam Hussein had provided chemical weapons training to Al Qaeda terrorists in Iraq. The information was false, but President Bush alluded to it in his 2003 State of the Union address as a justification for the invasion of Iraq two months later.[5]

Al-Libi's capture led to the capture of his superior, Abu Zubaydah, in March 2002. Zubaydah had been long sought; intercepts of Zubaydah's conversations had led to the disruption of the Millennium attacks in Jordon. The FBI seized Ramzi Binalshibh on the first anniversary of 9/11.

Binalshibh was a member of the Hamburg cell along with Mohammed Atta and Ziad Jarah, who piloted planes on 9/11; he would have been the twentieth hijacker, but the Department of State refused to grant him a U.S. visa. In March 2003, the FBI tracked Khalid Sheikh Mohammed to a hotel in Pakistan. Mohammed's zeal to harm Americans began years before he swore fealty to bin Laden and Al Qaeda. He provided material support to his nephew—Ramzi Yousef's—attack on the World Trade Center in 1993; he conspired with Yousef to destroy American airliners in flight in the Bojinka plot in 1995; he originated the Planes Operation and persuaded bin Laden of its strategic value. Except for bin Laden and Al-Zawahiri, no one was more central to Al Qaeda's terror operations.

Other Al Qaeda figures had been fugitives from the Clinton era. Abd al- Rahim Nashiri, whom the Americans captured in November 2002, was a critical actor in the attack on the USS *Cole* attacks; his cousin was the suicide bomber who attacked the U.S. embassy in Kenya in 1998. Tawfiq bin Attash, aka Khalled, who directed the USS *Cole* attack, fell into U.S. hands in April 2003. His capture was especially bittersweet. The CIA had photographs of Khalled meeting with two of the 9/11 hijackers, Khalid al-Midhar and Nawaf al-Hamzi, who the Agency learned had entered the United States in January 2000; it is entirely possible that, possessing such information, the CIA and FBI could have disrupted the Planes Operation. In October 2004, the CIA apprehended Mushim Musa Matawalli Attwah, the man who fabricated the bombs that exploded in front of the American embassies in Kenya and Tanzania in August 1998, and that nearly sank the USS *Cole*.

These men were among the fourteen high value "ghost detainees" whom the CIA shuffled between secret "black sites" in Eastern Europe and the Middle East on "ghost flights" aboard CIA aircraft. This practice of extraordinary rendition would be among the most controversial in the war on terror. President Bush, under intense pressure after the revelation of the black sites and secret flights, ordered the transfer of the fourteen to Guantanamo Bay, Cuba, just five days before the fifth anniversary of the 9/11 attacks.[6]

These arrests were important metrics of progress in the war on terror. More significantly, there has not been another act of terror on American soil in the five years since 9/11. Vigilant intelligence and law enforcement agencies denied Al Qaeda the freedom to execute attacks in the United States. Americans were also vigilant. In December 2001, passengers on an American Airlines flight from Paris to New York subdued Richard Reid before he could detonate a bomb concealed in the heel of his shoe. The attempt to sabotage the jet over the Atlantic resembled the failed Bojinka plot Ramzi Yousef and Khalid Sheikh Mohammed had set in motion in 1995; in the summer of 2006 British authorities intercepted a conspiracy to replicate Bojinka aboard multiple passenger jets en route to the United States.

Notwithstanding these setbacks, the spectacle of 9/11—Khalid Sheikh Mohammed called it Holy Tuesday—aroused Muslims, in bin Laden's words, to defend their religion. In January 2002, Al Qaeda militants abducted and beheaded Daniel Pearl, an American journalist with the *Wall Street Journal* in Pakistan; Khalid Sheikh Mohammed may have killed Pearl with his own hands. Islamic militants bombed a Christian church in Islamabad in March, killing five, including two U.S. citizens. In April, terrorists detonated a fuel truck outside a synagogue in Djerba, Tunisia, killing nineteen, including fourteen German Jews, and wounding many others. In May, a suicide bomber killed seventeen French sailors traveling by bus in Karachi, Pakistan. In June, a car bomb exploded outside the U.S. consulate in Karachi, killing eleven innocent Pakistanis. On 5 October, a small skiff blasted a hole in hull of a French oil tanker, the SS *Limburg*, off the coast of Yemen in an attack like the one that nearly sank the USS *Cole* almost exactly two years earlier; the ship remained afloat, but one seaman drowned. Six days later, militants belonging to the Jamaah Islamiah (JI) in Indonesia conducted coordinated multiple bombings of a nightclub in Bali, killing 202, including more than 80 Australians. Sixteen days after that, Al Qaeda operatives murdered a U.S. diplomat, Laurence Foley, in Amman, Jordan. A month after the Bali attack, suicide bombers attacked a tourist resort frequented by Israelis in Mombasa, Kenya, killing thirteen and wounding scores of others. In the same operation, the terrorists fired shoulder-held surface-to-air missiles at an Israeli charter airliner; the SAMs missed their mark, but the attack evinced Al Qaeda's capabilities. Al Qaeda had struck in Kenya before, when it bombed the US embassy in Nairobi in 1998, and one of the men involved in that attack, Fazul Abdullah Mohammed, aka Harun, may have been behind the Mombasa attack.

In March 2003, after a year of drum-beating, the Bush administration launched Operation Iraqi Freedom to disarm Saddam Hussein and liberate Iraq. There was a surge of terrorist attacks after the president prematurely declared the end of major combat operations in Iraq on 1 May aboard the USS *Abraham Lincoln*. Twelve days after the president's declaration, terrorists belonging to Al Qaeda in Saudi Arabia assaulted a housing complex for foreign nationals in Riyadh, killing thirty-four, nine of them Americans. Four days later, suicide bombers attacked multiple sites in Casablanca, Morocco, killing forty-four. On 5 August, the JI struck a second time in Indonesia, bombing the Marriott Hotel in Jakarta, killing 16, all but one of them Indonesians. Six days later, the CIA, working with Thai authorities, captured the JI leader, Riduan Isamuddin, aka Hambali, in Bangkok, striking a blow to the organization's ability to conduct terror operations in the world's most populous Muslim country. But in the remaining months of 2004, Islamic terrorists struck in three other Muslim countries. In October, terrorists struck the Hilton hotel in the Egyptian resort city Taba, in the Sinai, killing thirty-one. On 8 November, Al Qaeda in Saudi Arabia launched another major attack in Riyadh, killing seventeen, five of them children. Then came two attacks in rapid succession in Istanbul, Turkey: bombings of two mosques on 15 November killed twenty; attacks on the British Consulate and the British-owned HSBC bank five days later killed more than thirty.

Al Qaeda's jihad reached into Western Europe in the spring of 2004. On 11 March, terrorists exploded bombs on trains during the busy morning commute in Madrid, Spain. The suicide bombings killed 191 and wounded thousands. The Spanish government defied Spanish public opinion by sending a small contingent of troops to support Operation Iraqi Freedom; the 3/11 attacks, the deadliest in a country that had endured decades of terrorism of the Basque separatist group, ETA, were acts of retribution for Spain's alliance with the United States. Terrorists struck at foreign tourists in Cairo, Egypt, twice in April, on the seventh and again on the thirtieth. No one was killed, but this time the attacks were in the capital, rather than at tourist sites in the remote Sinai. There was yet another deadly attack in Khobar, Saudi Arabia, at the end of May, which claimed twenty-two more innocent lives.

The pattern is obvious. Jihadists have attacked Western tourists in Muslim lands, in countries whose governments they considered corrupt, or in countries whose governments were allied with the United States in the wars in Afghanistan and Iraq. No government has been more staunchly allied to U.S. policy in the Middle East than Tony Blair's New Labor government in the United Kingdom. On 7 July 2005, as Blair hosted the G-8 Summit in Scotland, four suicide bombers attacked the London Underground. The attack, which resembled the Madrid railway bombings, killed fifty-two and wounded hundreds of morning commuters. Two weeks later, another set of suicide bombers attempted to slaughter commuters, but their explosive packs failed to explode. Apart from the carnage, the July attacks were shocking because the suicide bombers were all British citizens of Pakistani descent. In September, Al Qaeda released a videotape of two of the attackers, who proclaimed that their true allegiance was to Islam rather than to the country where their parents had emigrated.

Exactly three weeks after the atrocity in London, terrorists executed multiple, near simultaneous bombings in the Egyptian resort of Sharm el Sheikh on the Gulf of Aqaba. It was the second major terrorist attack in Egypt. The attacks killed sixty-three and left hundreds of others wounded. In November, terrorists simultaneously struck three hotels in Amman, Jordan, in attacks that maimed more than one hundred and and killed sixty, including guests at a wedding party. Some of those same hotels had been targeted in the Millennium plot at the end of 1999. The man behind the slaughter in Amman, Abu Musab al-Zarqawi, a Jordanian, had become the world's most dangerous terrorist by the time of the Amman attacks. In the summer of 2003, only weeks after President Bush declared the end to major combat operations, Zarqawi's Jama'at al Tawhid wal-Jihdad—the Monotheism and Jihad Group—introduced suicide bombings in Iraq. In August, suicide bombers attacked the Jordanian embassy and the United Nations headquarters in Baghdad; the attacks killed more than thirty, including the head of the UN mission, Sergio Viera del Mello, and twenty-one of this staff. This was the beginning of an offensive to drive U.S. forces from Iraq and to provoke a civil war between Sunni and Shi'a by attacking Shi'a shrines. By the time al Zarqawi ordered the bombing of the Golden Mosque, the site of the Shi'a Askariya shrine in Samarra, in February 2006, he had renamed his organization Al Qaeda in Mesopotamia, signaling the formal amalgamation into bin Laden's Base. Zarqawi was killed in an air strike in June, but his Al Qaeda in Mesopotamia has survived his death.

Al Qaeda has reconstituted itself. Bin Laden and al Zawahiri, apparently operating in the tribal areas in Northwest Pakistan, continue to release a stream of videos inciting terror. A new cadre of Al Qaeda leaders have replaced those whom the United States captured or killed, and regional Al Qaeda branches have declared their existence. Al Zarqawi's Al Qaeda in Mesopotamia is one; another, Al Qaeda in the Islamic Maghreb, arose in Algeria from the remnants of the Salafist Group for Preaching and Combat, one of the early Jihadist organizations formed in Afghanistan during the anti-Soviet Jihad more than two decades earlier. In the spring of 2007, Al Qaeda in the Islamic Maghreb conducted a series of suicide attacks in Algiers, one near the office of the prime minister, which killed thirty-three; the attacks coincided with similar attacks in Morocco.

In the first five years after 9/11, the Islamist terror network amassed more than 800 victims in attacks in the Middle East, Central and South Asia, North and West Africa, and Europe. This sustained terror campaign far surpasses that waged by Palestinian nationalist terror organizations in the 1970s and 1980s in terms of their frequency, geographic dispersion, and lethality. The attacks of the 1990s were harbingers of this new terror, but those attacks were sporadic and fewer organizations, indeed only a very few organizations, were conducting terror operations then. Al Qaeda has revolutionalized terror. Bin Laden has succeeded in creating a Base as the vanguard of a global Islamist movement of relatively autonomous cells waging jihad. And, bin Laden's greatest wish has been granted him: America is being bled in an apparently interminable conflict in a land that was once the location of the Caliphate of Islam.

The invasion of Iraq in March 2003 altered the dynamic of the war on terror. The Bush administration began planning a war to remove Saddam Hussein from power within weeks of Al Qaeda's devastating attacks on New York and Washington.[7] CENTCOM, which was already engaged in Afghanistan, strained to work out the battle plan for what became Operation Iraqi Freedom for more than a year. Throughout 2002, the president and members of his cabinet, the vice president, members of his staff, and other senior administration officials set out to make the case for war. Critical to the administration's thinking was the nexus between rogue states, terror organizations, and WMD, and the prudent belief that, after 9/11, dangers could not be allowed to gather until a threat became imminent. Iraq under Saddam Hussein, which together with Iran and North Korea belonged, in the words of the president, to an "axis of evil," was the most menacing rogue state.

In his State of the Union address in January 2003, less than two months before the invasion of Iraq, the president stated—and perhaps overstated—the case for war:

> Before September the 11th, many in the world believed that Saddam Hussein could be contained. But chemical agents, lethal viruses and shadowy terrorist networks are not easily contained. Imagine those 19 hijackers with other weapons and other plans —this time armed by Saddam Hussein. It would take one vial, one canister, one crate slipped into this country to bring a day of horror like none we have ever known. We will do everything in our power to make sure that that day never comes.[8]

So many influential members of the Bush administration ascribed to the view that the nation's security interests demanded the removal of the Saddam Hussein regime that war was virtually inevitable after 9/11. These neoconservative "Vulcans"—as they have come to be known— began militating for a war to promote regime change in the Middle East, beginning in Baghdad, during the decade after the first Gulf War. The advent of the administration of George W. Bush gave them the historic opportunity to make that happen. That the administration was obsessed with Saddam Hussein was obvious. Indeed, national security advisor Condolleezza Rice chaired a principals meeting to discuss Iraq on 7 February 2001, less than two weeks into the new administration, even though counterterrorism officials on her own NSC were urgently appealing for a principals meeting to discuss Al Qaeda; Rice put off the meeting to discuss Al Qaeda until 4 September.[9]

The controversies surrounding the war in Iraq are well known. The serious intelligence failures regarding WMD, the apparent lack of transparency in the pronouncements of the president, vice president, and senior officials in the run-up to the war, the administration's wildly optimistic assumptions about the small occupation force's ability to secure and stabilize Iraq after the fall of Baghdad, the Pentagon's adamant refusal to acknowledge the existence of an insurgency in the months after the invasion, and so on cost the Republican party control over both houses of Congress in the November 2006 elections and seriously damaged President Bush's credibility with the American people. The facts on the ground are beyond dispute: as the number of U.S. troops killed in action in Iraq to pacify the former capital of Islam, in bin Laden's words, climbs toward 4,000, U.S. forces find themselves ensnared in a tenacious insurgency conducted by both Iraqis and foreign jihadists aligned with Al Qaeda, and entangled in a sectarian war between Sunni and Shi'a militias.

President Bush and senior administration officials have taken to calling the invasion of Iraq the opening of the "central front" in the war on terrorism; critics argue that Operation Iraqi Freedom was a reckless diversion of intelligence and military resources away from the real war on terror. There is truth in both perspectives. Certainly, the president's declarations about Iraq as the central front in the war on terror have become self-fulfilling prophecies. A leaked and then declassified 2006 National Security Estimate—the consensus judgment, "estimate," of the entire U.S. intelligence community—captured it this way:

The Iraq jihad is shaping a new generation of terrorist leaders and operatives; perceived jihadist success there would inspire more fighters to continue the struggle elsewhere.

The Iraq conflict has become the "cause celebre" for jihadists, breeding a deep resentment of US involvement in the Muslim world and cultivating supporters for the global jihadist movement. Should jihadists leaving Iraq perceive themselves, and be perceived, to have failed, we judge fewer fighters will be inspired to carry on the fight.[10]

Thus, the war in Iraq is shaping a new generation of terrorists, deepening resentment of the U.S. in the Muslim world, and cultivating the global jihadist movement the president vowed to defeat, but failure in Iraq would inspire even more jihadists to take up the struggle, while victory there would discourage others from carrying on the fight. This is a classic dilemma from which there is no easy escape.

The seventh anniversary of the 9/11 atrocity will have passed when Americans elect their next president. Whoever he or she may be, the forty-fourth president's national security priorities have already been set: extrication of U.S. combat forces from a minimally secure and stable

Iraq, and prosecution of the global war on terrorism. As to the war on terror, progress—and ultimately "victory"—will depend on three conditions. First, U.S. and other intelligence and law enforcement agencies must continue to thwart terror conspiracies, like the conspiracy to destroy airliners discovered in the United Kingdom in summer 2006, or the plot to kill American soldiers at Fort Dix, New Jersey, disrupted in the spring 2007. Second, the U.S. and its allies must sustain momentum in what is essentially a low intensity war of attrition by capturing or killing terrorists. The third condition is not within the power of the United States or its allies to achieve: ultimately, Islamist terror will ebb only when the most influential Muslim clerics rule that terrorism contravenes Qu'ranic principles of warfare. Only then will the belief be abandoned that the slaughter of innocent civilians is jihad in the way of Allah and that suicide in the act of murdering others bestows the glories of martyrdom.

John F. Kennedy once described the struggle against Communism as "a long twilight struggle." This is an apt description of the war against terrorism. To repeat President Bush's words, "Freedom and fear, justice and cruelty, have always been at war, and we know that God is not neutral between them."

Notes

Introduction

1. Rome Statute of the International Criminal Court, articles 6–8; similarly, Article 3, Common to the Geneva Conventions of 1949 strictly prohibits specific acts against "persons taking no active part in hostilities," including murder, torture, and the taking of hostages.

2. Convention on the Prevention and Punishment of the Crime of Genocide, articles 2–3.

Chapter 1. No One Heard Our Screams or Our Suffering

1. Lyndon B. Johnson, *The Vantage Point: Perspectives of the Presidency, 1963–1969* (New York: Holt, Rinehart, 1971), 287, 301.

2. See Michael B. Oren, *Six Days of War: June 1967 and the Making of the Modern Middle East* (Oxford: Oxford University Press, 2002); William Quandt, *Peace Process: American Diplomacy and the Arab-Israeli Conflict Since 1967* (Berkeley: University of California Press, 1993), chap. 2.

3. Tom Segev, *1949: The First Israelis* (New York: Henry Holt, 1986), chap. 2.

4. Said K. Aburish, *Arafat: From Defender to Dictator* (New York: Bloomsbury, 1998); Alan Hart, *Arafat: A Political Biography* (Bloomington: Indiana University Press, 1989); Andrew Gowers and Tony Walker, *Behind the Myth: Yasser Arafat and the Palestinian Revolution* (New York: Olive Branch Press, 1992).

5. Aburish, *Arafat*, 40; Yezid Sayigh, *Armed Struggle and the Search for the State: The Palestinian National Movement, 1949–1993* (New York: Oxford University Press, 1997), 87; Helena Cobban, *The Palestinian Liberation Organization: People, Power and Politics* (Cambridge: Cambridge University Press, 1984), 23.

6. Ely Karmon, "Fatah and the Popular Front for the Liberation of Palestine: International Terrorism Strategies (1968–1990)," International Policy Institute for Counter-Terrorism, November 2002, 2.

7. Sayigh, *Armed Struggle*, 94–95; Cobban, *The Palestine Liberation Organization*, 28–29.

8. Sayigh, *Armed Struggle*, 71–80; Gowers and Walker, *Behind the Myth*, 7.

9. Peter St. John, *Air Piracy, Airport Security, and International Terrorism: Winning the War Against Hijackers* (New York: Quorum Books, 1991), 22; Neil Livingstone and David Halevy, *Inside the P.L.O.: Covert Units, Secret Funds, and the War Against Israel and the United States* (New York: William Morrow, 1990), 204–5. Livingstone and Halevy suggest the PFLP suspected general and future prime minister Ariel Sharon may have been onboard.

10. Livingstone and Halevy, *Inside the PLO*, 205.

11. "Algeria Releases 10 Israelis of 22 on Hijacked El Al Jet," *New York Times*, 27 July 1968 (hereafter *NYT*).

12. John M. Lee, "Hijacking Mastermind Is No. 2 in the Popular Front," *NYT*, 13 September 1972.

13. St. John, *Air Piracy*, 21; Karmon, "Fatah and the Popular Front for the Liberation of Palestine," 7.

14. Ian Black and Benny Morris, *Israel's Secret Wars: A History of Israel's Intelligence Services* (New York: Grove Press, 1991), 269.

15. John L. Hess, "Swiss Curb Entry of Arabs and Ask Air Safety Talks," *NYT*, 23 February 1970, A1.

16. Hess, "Swiss Curb Entry of Arabs"; "Swiss Government Investigates Sabotage," *NYT*, 22 February 1972.

17. "Guerrilla Groups Deny Crash Role," *NYT*, 23 February 1970; Karmon, "Fatah and the Popular Front," 7.

18. Livingstone and Halevy, *Inside the PLO*, 217.

19. Quandt, *Peace Process*, chap. 4; Henry Kissinger, *White House Years* (Boston: Little, Brown, 1979), chaps 10, 14; Richard Nixon, *RN: The Memoirs of Richard Nixon* (New York: Grosset and Dunlap, 1978), 476–85.

20. Nixon, *RN*, 478; Kissinger, *White House Years*, 347.

21. St. John, *Air Piracy*, 25.

22. "4 Jets Hijacked, One, a 747 Is Blown Up," *NYT*, 7 September 1970; "Arabs Hold 150 Hostage in Seized Jets in Desert," *NYT*, 8 September 1970; Eric Pace, "Life on Jets Held In Desert Is Harsh," *NYT*, 9 September 1970; Linda Charlton, "Desert Jet Deadline Is Extended," *NYT*, 10 September 1970; "5 Nations Reject Terms for Freeing of Hostages," *NYT*, 11 September 1970; Linda Charlton, "Arabs Release Some Passengers," *NYT*, 12 September 1970; "London Is Willing to Free Hijacker, " *NYT*, 12 September 1970; John L Hess, "Arabs Blow Up 3 Jets in Desert," *NYT*, 13 September 1970; "Israel and Arabs Stiffen Positions on Hostage Deal," *NYT*, 16 September 1970.

23. Nixon, *RN*, 483; Kissinger, *White House Years*, 601.

24. Bernard Weintraub, "BOAC Jet Joins Others in Jordan," *NYT*, September 9 1970, 1.

25. "Transcripts: The Guerrillas Story," BBC, UK Confidential, 1 January 2001; "Black September: Tough Negotiations," BBC, UK Confidential, 1 January 2001.

26. Aburish, *Arafat*, 115.

27. Ibid.

28. Abu Iyad and Eric Rouleau, *My Home, My Land: A Narrative of the Palestinian Struggle* (New York: Times Books, 1978), 97.

Chapter 2. Revolutionary Violence Is a Political Act, Terrorism Is Not

1. Sayigh, *Armed Struggle*, 306–12; Aburish, *Arafat*, 20–128; Gowers and Walker, *Behind the Myth*, 86–101; Hart, *Arafat*, 337–63; Christopher Dobson, *Black September: Its Short, Violent History* (London: Robert Hale, 1975), chap. 2; Karmon, "Fatah and the Popular Front"; Livingstone and Halevy, *Inside the P.L.O.*, 103–6.

2. Iyad and Rouleau, *My Home, My Land*, 98.

3. Livingstone and Halevy, *Inside the P.L.O.*, 106; Gowers and Walker, *Behind the Myth*, 87.

4. Hart, *Arafat*, 339.

5. David Ignatius, "The Secret History of U.S.-PLO Terror Talks," *Washington Post*, 4 December 1988; Ignatius, "Penetrating Terrorist Networks," Washington-

post.com, 16 September 2001; Korn, *Assassination in Khartoum*, 44–45, 237–42; Livingstone and Halevy, *Inside the P.L.O.*, 109–12.

6. Livingstone and Halevy, *Inside the P.L.O.*, 106.

7. "Hijackers in Aden Free All Passengers, Including Kennedy," *NYT*, 22 February 1972.

8. "Bonn Paid Hijackers $5-Million Ransom," *NYT*, 25 February 1972; St. John, *Air Piracy*, 25.

9. "Bonn Paid Hijackers."

10. Livingstone and Halevy, *Inside the P.L.O.*, 205–6; Sayigh, *Armed Struggle*, 308.

11. Sayigh, *Armed Struggle*, 308; Black and Morris, *Israel's Secret Wars*, 269.

12. "4 Armed Arab Hijackers Hold Jet and 101 Hostages in Israel," *NYT*, 8 May 1972.

13. Published sources are inconsistent on the identity of the commander of the operation. Sayigh (*Armed Struggle and the Search for State*, 308) and Livingstone and Halevy (*Inside the P.L.O.*, 206) name Ali Taha. The PFLP in a communiqué at the end of the month named him as well ("3 with Guns and Grenades Slay 25 at Israeli Airport," *NYT*, 31 May 1972). Simon Reeve, *One Day in September: The Full Story of the 1972 Munich Olympics Massacre and the Israeli Revenge Operation "Wrath of God"* (New York: Arcade, 2000), 36–37, identifies the two male hijackers as Ahmed Awad and Abdel Atrash. Ian Black and Benny Morris (*Israeli's Secret Wars*, 269) identify the commander as Ali Abu Sneineh, but give identical biographical details as Livingstone and Halevy. Korn, *Assassination in Khartoum* (Bloomington: Indiana University Press, 1993), 47, using different transliteration, also identifies Kamal Rifaat as Ali Abu Sanina.

14. "4 Armed Arab Hijackers," *NYT*, 8 May 1972.

15. PBS History Channel documentary "Revenge!"; Livingstone and Halevy, *Inside the P.L.O.*, 204.

16. "Israelis Kill 2 Hijackers and Free 100 on Airliner," *NYT*, 9 May 1972.

17. Black and Morris, *Israel's Secret Wars*, 268.

18. St. John, *Air Piracy*, 26; Rex A. Hudson, Marilyn Majeska with Andrea M. Savada and Helen C. Metz, *The Sociology and Psychology of Terrorism: Who Becomes a Terrorist and Why: The 1999 Government Report on Profiling Terrorists* (Guilford, Conn.: Lyons Press, 1999), 115–16.

19. "3 with Guns and Grenades Slay 24 at Israeli Airport," *NYT*, 31 May 1972.

20. Lebanon Releases Member in Japanese Red Army," Arabic News.com, 22 March 2000.

21. Black and Morris, *Israel's Secret Wars*, 272; Sayigh, *Armed Struggle and the Search for State*, 309–10.

22. Iyad and Rouleau, *My Home, My Land*, 106.

23. Ibid.

24. "When the Terror Began," Special Report, *Time*, 25 August 2002. Iyad and Rouleau (*My Home, My Land*, 107) imply Black September began planning the operation in January, with the selection of the commanders whom they identify as Che Guevara and Mussalha; presumably these are "Issa" and "Tony." Iyad and Rouleau do not admit to any direct responsibility for Munich, and do not mention Abu Daoud by name or a rendezvous in Rome in July. Abu Daoud's 1999 book *Palestine: de Jérusalem à Munich* gives a more candid account. Other sources, including the documentary film *One Day in September* and Simon Reeve's book of the same title, describe the July meeting in Rome.

25. Segev, *The First Israelis*, 59.

26. "When the Terror Began."

27. Reeve, *One Day in September*, 83.

28. St. John, *Air Piracy*, 27.

29. History Channel documentary, "Revenge!"; Reeve, *One Day in September*, 160; Alexander Calahan, "The Israeli Response to the 1972 Munich Olympic Massacre and the Development of Independent Covert Action Teams," Master's thesis, Marine Corps Command and Staff College, 1995; Black and Morris, *Israel's Secret Wars*, 272–75; George Jonas, *Vengeance: The True Story of an Israeli Counter-Terrorist Team* (New York: Simon and Schuster, 1984); Aaron J. Klein, *Striking Back: The 1972 Munich Olympics Massacre and Israel's Deadly Response* (New York: Random House, 2005).

30. Alexander Wolff, "The Mastermind," Sports Illustrated.com, CNNSI.com, 26 August 2002.

31. Black and Morris, *Israel's Secret Wars*, 273.

32. Korn, *Assassination in Khartoum*, 49–50.

Chapter 3. Much Blood Will Flow, Not All of It Ours

1. Black and Morris, *Israel's Secret Wars*, 273; Jonas, *Vengeance*, chap. 7.

2. Sayigh, *Armed Struggle*, 311; Dobson, *Black September*, 119.

3. Iyad and Rouleau, *My Home, My Land*, 99.

4. Livingstone and Halevy, *Inside the P.L.O.*, 106; Korn, *Assassination in Khartoum*, 51. Hart asserts that it was Abu Iyad, obeying Arafat's orders, who betrayed Abu Daoud in order to sabotage the operation. *Arafat*, 359.

5. Korn, *Assassination in Khartoum*, 1–5; Dobson, *Black September*, 118–26.

6. Korn, *Assassination in Khartoum*, 150. Notably, Nixon does not mention the Khartoum incident in his presidential memoir.

7. Livingstone and Halevy (*Inside the PLO*, 279–80), citing an unnamed former high-ranking intelligence official report intercepted conversations between Abu Iyad, Ali Hassan Salameh and, finally, Arafat, during the Khartoum operation in which the three repeat the code word Nahr al-Bard (Cold River) and interpret this to be the order to kill the diplomats. Notably, Arafat repeats the phrase *after* the murder of the diplomats. George Jonas ("Arafat's Past Comes Back to Haunt Him," *National Post*, 1 January 2002) cites a former National Security Agency official, James Welsh, who claims only that the NSA intercepted a transmission on 28 February 1973, the day before the seizure of the Saudi embassy, between Arafat and Abu Jihad (not Abu Iyad), in which the Fatah leaders discussed "Operation Nahr al-Bard." The *Wall Street Journal* picked up the story on 10 January 2002. The Israelis have never produced the tape.

8. Sayigh, *Armed Struggle*, 308; Aburish, *Arafat*, 123–24.

9. Livingstone and Halevy, *Inside the P.L.O.*, 36–37; History Channel documentary "Revenge"; CBS news magazine *60 Minutes II*, "An Eye for an Eye," 20 November 2001.

10. *60 Minutes II*, "An Eye for an Eye."

11. Iyad and Rouleau, *My Home, My Land*, 115–16.

12. Hart, *Arafat*, 362; Sayigh, *Armed Struggle*, 311.

13. Iyad and Rouleau, *My Home, My Land*, 188; In the interview aired in the History Channel's documentary "Revenge!" Barak claims the operation lasted thirty minutes. Livingstone and Halevy describe a pitched battle in which "several Israel commandos were killed and wounded." *Inside the P.L.O.*, 38.

14. Calahan, "The Israeli Response to the 1972 Munich Olympics Massacre," 14.

15. David Yallop, *Tracking the Jackal: The Search for Carlos, the World's Most Wanted Man* (New York: Random House, 1993), 65.

16. Dobson, *Black September*, 161.

17. Aburish, *Arafat*, 124.

18. Calahan, "The Israeli Response to the 1972 Munich Olympic Massacre"; Black and Morris, *Israel's Secret Wars*, 275–77; History Channel documentary, "Revenge!"

19. *60 Minutes II*, "An Eye for an Eye."

20. "Norway Solves Riddle of Mossad Killing," *The Guardian*, 2 March 2000. Two years later, Norwegian authorities issued a warrant for the arrest of Mike Harari, commander of the assassination squad that killed Bouchiki. In 1999, a Norwegian special commission issued the report of a special investigation that absolved Norwegian authorities of complicity. That same year, the prosecutors dropped the charges against Harari, citing the practical impossibility of ever bringing the former Mossad agent to justice.

21. Dobson, *Black September*, 161–62, 166–67.

22. Livingstone and Halevy, *Inside the PLO*, 147; Sayigh, *Armed Struggle*, 311.

23. Patrick Seale, *Abu Nidal: A Gun for Hire* (New York: Random House, 1992), 91.

24. Henry Kamm, "Gunmen Hold 15 Hostages in Saudi Embassy in Paris," *NYT*, 6 September 1973; Juan de Onis, "Freeing of Arab Is Sought Again," *NYT*, 7 September 1973; Juan de Onis, "Terrorists Free Hostages and Surrender in Kuwait," *NYT*, 8 September 1973.

25. Iyad and Rouleau, *My Home, My Land*, 105.

26. Seale, *Abu Nidal*, 92. Abu Iyad does not mention the incident. He hardly mentions Abu Nidal, whom he recruited and protected, at all. Mahmoud Abbas, or Abu Mazen, was indeed a moderate. In 2003, Yasser Arafat, president of the PLO, appointed Abu Mazen prime minister at the insistence of the United States and Israel.

27. Kissinger, *White House Years*, 1292, 1295; Quandt, *Peace Process*, 149. Black and Morris offer an alternative explanation for these overtures: that Egypt was engaged in an elaborate strategic deception. *Israel's Secret Wars*, 299.

28. Nixon, *RN*, 920–21.

29. Ibid., 939

30. Iyad and Rouleau, *My Home, My Land*, 126.

31. Hart, *Arafat*, 398.

32. David Ignatius, "The Secret History of U.S.-PLO Talks," *Washington Post*, 4 December 1988.

33. Korn, *Assassination in Khartoum*, 242.

34. Ignatius, "The Secret History of U.S.-PLO Talks."

35. Gowers and Walker, *Behind the Myth*, 398.

36. David Ignatius, "Penetrating Terrorist Networks," Washingtonpost.com, 16 September 2001.

37. "Palestinians Demand the Release of 2 Held in Greece," *NYT*, 18 December 1973; Paul Hofmann, "Grenade Attack in Rome," *NYT*, 18 December 1973; "Pilot-Athens Tower Talk," *NYT*, 17 December 1973; Israel Shenker, "Arab Hijackers Land in Kuwait; 11 Hostages Freed," *NYT*, 18 December 1973. "Athens Killing Described," *NYT*, 19 December 1973.

Chapter 4. Peace Would Be the End of All Our Hopes

1. Henry Kissinger, *Years of Renewal* (New York: Simon and Schuster, 1999), 358.
2. Sayigh, *Armed Struggle*, 339, 356; Quandt, *Peace Process*, 205; Aburish, *Arafat*, 140.
3. Iyad and Rouleau, *My Home, My Land*, 133, 144.
4. Sayigh, *Armed Struggle*, 337.
5. National Transportation Safety Board, "Aircraft Accident Report: Trans World Airlines Inc. Boeing 707–331B, N8734 in the Ionian Sea, September 8, 1974" (Report NTSB-AAR-75-7); "U.S.-Bound Plane with 88 Crashes in Sea Off Greece," *NYT*, 9 September 1974.
6. Sayigh, *Armed Struggle*, 355; According to Seale, Khalil al-Wazir (Abu Jihad) gave the orders. Seale, *Abu Nidal*, 102.
7. Seale, *Abu Nidal*, 104.
8. Iyad and Rouleau, *My Home, My Land*, 148
9. Kissinger, *Years of Renewal*, 383.
10. "Palestinians Planning to Review Policy on Terrorism," *NYT*, 23 November 1974.
11. David Ignatius, "The Secret History of U.S.-PLO Terror Talks," *Washington Post*, 4 December 1988; Sayigh, *Armed Struggle*, 395; Korn, *Murder in Khartoum*, 243; Gowers and Walker, *Arafat*, 163.
12. Korn, *Assassination in Khartoum*, 243; Livingstone and Halevy, *Inside the P.L.O.*, 111.
13. *60 Minutes II*, "An Eye for an Eye."
14. Calahan, "The Israeli Response to the 1972 Munich Olympic Massacre," 17.
15. Seale, *Abu Nidal*, 102.
16. Iyad and Rouleau, *My Home, My Land*, 150.
17. "Jet Hijacked at Dubai Puts Down in Libya," *NYT*, 22 November 1974; "Hijackers Demand Release of 13 Guerrillas in Cairo," *NYT*, 23 November 1974; "Hijackers of Jet Kill a Passenger at Tunis But Release 13 Hostages," *NYT* s, 24 November 1974; "Tunis to Grant Asylum to Arabs Who Seized Plane," New York Times, 25 November 1975.
18. Iyad and Rouleau, *My Home, My Land*, 157.
19. John Follain, *Jackal: The Complete Story of the Legendary Terrorist, Carlos the Jackal* (New York: Arcade, 1998), 126.
20. Yallop, *Tracking the Jackal*, 76; Follain, *Jackal*, 48; Patrick Bellamy, "Carlos the Jackal: Trail of Terror," www.crimelibrary.com
21. Yallop, *Tracking the Jackal*, 98; Follain, *Jackal*, 53.
22. Yallop, *Tracking the Jackal*, 98.
23. Ibid., 121.
24. Gerald Ford, *A Time to Heal: The Autobiography of Gerald Ford* (New York: Berkley Books, 1980), 238.
25. Quandt, *Peace Process*, 242, Sayigh, *Armed Struggle*, 368.
26. Sayigh, *Armed Struggle*, 359.
27. Ibid., 361, 369.
28. Sayigh, *Armed Struggle*, 365; Gowers and Walker, *Behind the Myth*, 138.
29. Robert Fisk, *Pity the Nation: The Abduction of Lebanon* (New York: Atheneum, 1990), 78.
30. Follain, *Jackal*, 82; Lucy Szekely, "How Terrorists Entered Unhindered,"

NYT, 22 December 1975; "Terrorist Raid Vienna Oil Parley," *NYT,* 22 December 1975.

31. Yallop, *Tracking the Jackal,* 101.

32. Follain, *Jackal,* 87

33. Clyde H. Farnsworth, "Terrorists Raid OPEC Oil Parley in Vienna, Kill 3," *NYT,* 22 December 1975.

34. Robert D. McFadden, "Terrorists Free All of Hostages, Give Up in Algiers," *NYT,* 23 December 1975.

35. Yallop, *Tracking the Jackal,* 420–23.

36. "Carlos the Jackal to Appeal Against Life Sentence," BBC News, 24 December 1997. In January 2000, a West German court convicted Johannes Weinrich, Carlos' accomplice since the January 1975 Orly airport attacks, for his involvement in the West Berlin bombing of a French cultural center, and sentenced him to life imprisonment. Roger Boyes, "Life Term for Jackal's Deputy," *London Times,* 18 January 2000.

37. Yallop, *Tracking the Jackal,* 316–17.

Chapter 5. We Accept to Live with You in Permanent Peace

1. Fisk, *Pity the Nation,* 7–9; Sayigh, *Armed Struggle,* 372–409.

2. Fisk, *Pity the Nation,* 81.

3. Sayigh, *Armed Struggle,* 395; Iyad and Rouleau, *My Home, My Land,* 189.

4. Gerald Ford, *A Time to Heal,* 377. Ford, who unlike Nixon at least referred to the assassination of U.S. diplomats in the Middle East, nonetheless called the murders one of the "misfortunes" that "plagued our campaign."

5. Ignatius, "The Secret History of U.S.-PLO Terror Talks." A Lebanese court convicted two men for the crimes and sentenced them to death, but both were released in 1996 under the terms of a 1990 amnesty law for crimes committed during the Lebanese civil war. "Lebanon appeals court frees diplomats' killers," CNN.com, 3 March 1996.

6. "Drama in Hijacking of Jet to Uganda: A Long Week of Terror and Tensions," *NYT,* 11 July 1976.

7. "Drama in Hijacking of Jet," *NYT,* 10 July 1976; Follain identifies Bouvier, *Jackal,* 35; Yallop insists that Anton Bouvier, whom he does not identify by name, was in overall command of the mission, and that during the hostage crisis Bouvier, Wadi Haddad himself, and Carlos were present at the airport. *Tracking the Jackal,* 432.

8. "Hijackers Hold 256 Near Plane," *NYT,* 28 June 1976, A1.

9. "Drama in Hijacking of Jet," *NYT,* A16

10. Ibid.

11. Terrence Smith, "Israel, Yielding Tells Hijackers It Will Negotiate," *NYT,* 1 July 1976, A1.

12. "Drama in Hijacking," *NYT,* A10.

13. Ibid.

14. "Text of Rabin Statement to the Israeli Parliament," *NYT,* 4 July 1976, A2.

15. "Egypt Condemns Raid as Aggression," *NYT s,* 4 July 1976; "Statement by Waldheim," *NYT,* 6 July 1976. This was only one reason for Israel's antipathy to the Austrian secretary general. A few years later Israel would produce a photograph of Waldheim dressed in a German uniform in the Balkans belying his claims to have been a university student during the Second World War.

16. "Uganda Bids U.N. Condemn Israel for Airport Raid," *NYT*, 10 July 1976, A1.

17. Sayigh, *Armed Struggle*, 401.

18. Aburish, *Saddam Hussein: The Politics of Revenge* (New York: Bloomsbury, 2000), 95.

19. Seale, *Abu Nidal*, 106; Hart, *Arafat*, 395; Samir al-Khalil, *Republic of Fear: The Inside Story of Saddam's Iraq* (New York: Pantheon, 1989), 13–14.

20. Hart, *Arafat*, 394–97.

21. Sayigh, *Armed Struggle*, 416; Seale, *Abu Nidal*, 106–8. Seale attributes the December 1976 attempt on Khaddam to the Syrian Islamist organization, the Muslim Brotherhood.

22. Jimmy Carter, *Keeping Faith: Memoirs of a President* (New York: Bantam Books, 1982), 276–77; Quandt, *Peace Process*, 255–70.

23. Sayigh, *Armed Struggle*, 420.

24. Segev, *1949: The First Israelis*, 25, 284; Black and Morris, *Israel's Secret Wars*, 37–38; "Menachem Begin—Biography," www.nobel.se

25. Quandt, *Peace Process*, 262.

26. Sayigh, *Armed Struggle*, 420–23.

27. Text available at www.israel-mfa.gov.il

28. Hart, *Arafat*, 435; Sayigh, *Armed Struggle*, 423.

29. Text of Sadat's speech, *www.israel-mfa.gov.il*; Hart, *Arafat*, 397; Iyad and Rouleau, *My Home, My Land*, 203.

30. "Lufthansa 737, October 13, 1977," Special Operations.com; U.S. Department of Defense, Defense Intelligence College, "Counterterrorism Analysis Course, Part 6: Case Studies," Global Security.com

31. Defense Intelligence College, "Counterterrorism Analysis Course."

32. "Hijackers Force West German Airliner to Mid-East, Demanding Freedom for Terrorists in Bonn's Jails," *NYT*, 14 October 1977, A1; "4 Days of Fear, Then 7 Minutes for the Rescue," *NYT*, 18 October 1977, A1.

33. "Hijacked Jet Lands in Southern Yemen; Flies on to Somalia," *NYT*, 17 October 1977, A14.

34. Henry Tanner, "U.S. Woman Says Ruse Saved the Hostages," *NYT*, 20 October 1977, A16.

35. "4 Days of Fear, Then 7 Minutes for the Rescue," A15.

36. "Hostages Describe Hijacker as Fanatical," *NYT*, 18 October 1977, A15.

37. Somali authorities imprisoned Suhaila al-Sayeh, also known as Souhaila Andrawes, for a short time before she disappeared. Norwegian authorities arrested her in 1994 and extradited her to Germany in 1995. In November 1996, a Hamburg court sentenced her to twelve years for the murder of Captain Schumann. "Twelve Years Prison for Aircraft Hijacker Andrawes," *German News* (English Edition), 19 November 1996. Al-Sayeh collapsed when the sentence was read. A German court also convicted a German woman, Monika Haas, for her involvement in the hijacking. According to al-Sayeh's testimony and East German Secret Police files, Haas smuggled the weapons used in the hijacking. "German Woman Guilty of 1977 Hijacking, Murders," *Reuters News Media*, 16 November 1996.

38. Paul Hofmann, "Abducted German Industrialist Found Slain," *NYT*, 20 October 1977, A1; "3 Jailed West German Terrorists Reported Suicides," *NYT*, 19 October 1977, A14.

39. Karmon, "Fatah and the Popular Front for the Liberation of Palestine," 10.

40. Sayigh, *Armed Struggle*, 424–25; Hart, *Arafat*, 436.

41. Hart, *Arafat*, 399; Sayigh, *Armed Struggle*, 425, 431, 435; Seale, *Abu Nidal*, 49. Seale places al-Sibai's assassination on 15 June instead of 15 May. Livingstone and Halevy assert that Abu Nidal murdered Hammami and two other moderates killed in 1980 and 1983, on Arafat's orders; see *Inside the P.L.O.*, 244. The authors' assertion that Abu Nidal "carried out a number of killings at Arafat's behest," differs from the conclusions of most authors, dismisses the enmity between Abu Nidal and Arafat, and seems to reflect their strong opposition to dialogue between the United States and the PLO that began shortly before the publication of their book. With the exception of the PFLP's hijacking of Lufthansa flight 181, Abu Nidal's Fatah-Revolutionary Council was "virtually the only Palestinian organization active in terror," between October 1976 and October 1977. For the next three years, until late 1980, most acts of terror were directed against Palestinians, Egyptians, Syrians, and Iraqis as part of the internal conflict between Fatah and Abu Nidal's organization, or in connection with the Lebanese civil war. See Karmon, "Fatah and the Popular Front for the Liberation of Palestine," 11.

42. Iyad and Rouleau, *My Home, My Land*, 214–16; Sayigh, *Armed Struggle*, 426.

43. Carter, *Keeping Faith*, 304; Quandt, *Peace Process*, 276–83.

44. Ibid., 405.

45. History Channel, "Revenge!"

Chapter 6. We Will Get Slaughtered Down There

1. Gilles Kepel, *Jihad: The Trail of Political Islam* (Cambridge, Mass.: Belknap Press of Harvard University Press, 2002), 109; Robin Wright, *Sacred Rage: The Wrath of Militant Islam* (New York: Simon and Schuster, 1985), 42.

2. Kepel, *Jihad*, 23; Paul Berman, "The Philosopher of Islamic Terror," *New York Times Magazine*, 23 March 2003.

3. Carter, *Keeping Faith*, 457.

4. Maj. C. E. Holzworth, "Operation Eagle Claw: A Catalyst for Change in the American Military" (1997), www.globalsecurity.org

5. See George Crile, *Charlie Wilson's War: The Extraordinary Story of the Largest Covert Operation in History* (New York: Atlantic Monthly Press, 2003); Ahmed Rashid, "Osama Bin Laden: How the U.S. helped Midwife a Terrorist," Center for Public Integrity (13 September 2001), http://www.newhumanist.com/osama.html

6. Yossef Bodansky, *Bin Laden: The Man Who Declared War on America* (Rocklin, Calif.: Forum, 1999), 11–12; John Miller, Michael Stone, and Chris Mitchell, *The Cell: Inside the 9/11 Plot, and Why the FBI and CIA Failed to Stop It* (New York: Hyperion, 2002), 49.

7. See, Edgar O'Balance, *The Gulf War* (London: Brassey's, 1988). The tanker war had direct consequences for the United States. In March 1987, Iraqi war planes attacked the USS *Stark* on patrol in the Persian Gulf with an Exocet missile, killing 37 sailors. In July 1988, the commander of another U.S. warship, the USS *Vincennes*, fearing his ship was coming under attack, ordered the shootdown of an Iranian aircraft that turned out to be a civilian airliner, killing 290 passengers.

8. Aburish, *Saddam Hussein*, 210; Seale, *Abu Nidal*, 123.

9. Text of a confidential memorandum, "Briefing Notes for Rumsfeld Visit to Baghdad," from Lawrence Eagleberger to Ambassador Rumsfeld, reproduced

by the National Security Archives, "Shaking Hands with Saddam Hussein: The U.S. Tilt with Iraq, 1980–1984" (Doc. 28).

10. U.S. Department of Defense, "The Honorable Donald Rumsfeld, Secretary of Defense." The official DOD biography omits any reference to the secretary's mission as special envoy to Iraq.

11. Julian Borger, "Rumsfeld 'Offered to Help Saddam,'" *Guardian*, 21 December 2002. There is evidence that Iraqis used mustard gas, a blistering agent, as early as 1981 and that by early 1983 had introduced Tabun, a nerve agent. This was during the Iran-Iraq War. After the war, Saddam deployed nerve agents, including Sarin, against the Kurds in northern Iraq. See Susan Power, *A Problem from Hell: America and the Age of Genocide* (New York: Basic Books, 2002), chap. 8; National Security Archives, "U.S. Documents Show Embrace of Saddam Hussein in Early 1980s Despite Chemical Weapons, Foreign Aggression, Human Rights Abuses" (Washington, D.C., 25 February 2003).

12. National Security Archives, "Shaking Hands with Saddam Hussein" (Doc. 48).

13. Seale, *Abu Nidal*, 162–75, 178; Sayigh, *Armed Struggle*, 558; Yoram Schweitzer, "Abu Nidal—The Sooner the Better," International Policy Institute for Counter-Terrorism, August 1998.

14. International Policy Institute for Counter-Terrorism, "Fatah-Revolutionary Council (Abu Nidal Organization)," www.ict.org

15. Wright, *Sacred Rage*, 173–84; Jailan Halawi, "Jihad Émigrés Sentenced to Death," *Al-Ahram Weekly* 426 (22–28 April 1999).

16. Douglass Streusand, "What Does Jihad Mean?" *Middle East Quarterly* 4, 3 (September 1997).

17. Another group, Jama'a al-Islamiyya, concentrated on attacking tourists. The group's most lethal attack was the 1997 massacre at the archaeological site in Luxor that killed 4 Egyptians and 58 tourists, 35 of them Swiss. Barbara Plett, "Bin Laden 'Behind Luxor Massacre,'" BBC News Online (13 May 1999).

18. Wright, *Sacred Rage*, 187; Miller et al., *The Cell*, 53–54; Daniel Benjamin and Steven Simon, *The Age of Sacred Terror* (New York: Random House, 2002), 6–7, 76–80; Lawrence Wright, "The Man Behind Bin Laden," *New Yorker* (16 September 2002).

19. Benjamin and Simon, *The Age of Sacred Terror*, 84.

20. Bruce Nelan, "The Dark Side of Islam," Time.com (4 October 1993).

21. Rohan Gunaratna, *Inside al Qaeda: Global Network of Terror* (New York: Berkley Books, 2003), 63.

22. Gunaratna, *Inside al Qaeda*, 34–36; Lawrence, "The Man Behind Bin Laden"; "The Operations Man: Ayman al-Zawahiri," *The Estimate* 13, 17 (21 September 2001); Kareem Fahim, "The Emir and His Lieutenant," *Village Voice* (28 November 28–4 December 2001).

23. Lawrence, "The Man Behind Bin Laden."

24. Jailan Halawi, "Jihad Emigres Sentenced to Death."

25. Interview with *Der Spiegel*, reprinted in Bernard Schechterman and Martin Slann, eds., *Violence and Terrorism, 91/92* (Guilford, Conn.: Dushkin, 1991), 49–50.

26. Sayigh, *Armed Struggle*, 540; Rashid Khalidi, *Under Siege: P.L.O. Decision-Making During the 1982 War* (New York: Cambridge University Press, 1986). The U.S. casualty figure includes 268 Marines and sailors killed during the 18-month deployment of the Marines Amphibious Unit, including the 241 killed in the attack on the Marine Battalion Landing Team headquarters; 17 embassy officials

and CIA agents killed in the April 1983 embassy bombing; 2 Americans killed in the bombing of the U.S. embassy annex bombing; the president of the American University murdered in his office; a hostage murdered during the hijacking of TWA 841 in June 1985; and two hostages, William Buckley and Colonel William Higgins.

27. Ronald Reagan, *An American Life* (New York: Simon and Schuster, 1990), 419.

28. Khalidi, *Under Siege*, 18; Sayigh, *Armed Struggle*, 362.

29. Quandt, *Peace Process*, 342.

30. Reagan, *An American Life*, 427.

31. Yoram Schweitzer, "The Arrest of Mohammed Rashid—Another Point for the Americans," International Policy Institute for Counter-Terrorism (June 1998.); Livingstone and Halevy, *Inside the P.L.O.*, 129. Another of Rashid's accomplices, Adnan Awad, actually carried an explosive device from Lebanon to Geneva later in 1982 at Rashid's behest, but immediately contacted U.S. embassy officials, who defused the bomb in his room in the Geneva Hilton. Adnan later testified against Rashid during a trial in Athens for the Pan Am flight 830 bombing. See, "Opinion in the United States District Court for the Northern District of Mississippi, Eastern Division, *Adnan Awad Plaintiff v. United States of America Defendant*," 2001.

32. Schweitzer, "The Arrest of Mohammed Rashid," 1.

33. Reagan, *An American Life*, 434; "Reagan Peace Proposal," in Carol Goldinger, ed., *Historic Documents of 1982* (Washington, D.C: Congressional Quarterly, 1983), 755–60; Quandt, *Peace Process*, 344–56; Sayigh, *Armed Struggle*, 551–57.

34. Thomas Friedman, *From Beirut to Jerusalem* (New York: Farrar, Straus, Giroux, 1989), 157; Sayigh, *Armed Struggle*, 538.

35. Fisk, *Pity the Nation*, 359–71; Zakaria al-Shaikh, "Sabra and Shatila 1982: Resisting the Massacre," *Journal of Palestine Studies* 14, 1 (Autumn 1984): 57–90; Sayigh, *Armed Struggle*, 539.

36. Fisk, *Pity the Nation*, 398; Reagan wrote in his diary, "the Israelis did nothing to prevent or halt it." *An American Life*, 437.

37. "Commission of Inquiry into the Events at the Refugee Camps in Beirut," in W. Michael Reisman and Chris T. Antoniou, eds., *The Laws of War: A Comprehensive Collection of Primary Documents on International Laws Governing Armed Conflict* (New York: Vintage Books, 1994), 379–80.

38. Khalidi, *Under Siege*, 170–71; Fisk, *Pity the Nation*, 372.

39. "Reagan Statement," in Goldinger, *Historic Documents of 1982*, 784; Reagan, *An American Life*, 466.

40. Benis M. Frank, *The U.S. Marines in Lebanon: 1982–1984* (Washington, D.C.: History and Museums Division Headquarters, U.S. Marine Corps, 1987), 22.

41. Friedman, *From Beirut to Jerusalem*, 135, 191; Reagan, *An American Life*, 461–62; see also John H. Kelly, "Lebanon 1982–1984," in Jeremy R. Asrael and Emil A. Payin, eds., *U.S. and Russian Policymaking with Respect to the Use of Force* (Santa Monica, Calif.: Rand, 1996).

42. Frank, *U.S. Marines in Lebanon*, 172.

43. Ibid., 45–46, 56.

44. Hala Jaber, *Hezbollah: Born with a Vengeance* (New York: Columbia University Press, 1997), 11–74; Wright, *Sacred Rage*, 46–110; Magnus Ranstorp, *Hizb'allah in Lebanon: The Politics of the Western Hostage Crisis* (New York: St. Martin's Press, 1997), 25–60; Kepel, *Jihad*, 123–30.

45. Ranstorp, *Hizb'allah*, 33, 80; Bernard Schechterman and Bradford McGuinn, "Linkages Between Sunni and Shi'i Radical Fundamentalist Organizations: A New Variable in Recent Middle East Politics?" *Political Chronicle* 1, 1 (1989); Joseph Kostiner, "War, Terror, Revolution: The Iran-Iraq Conflict," in Barry Rubin, ed., *The Politics of Terrorism: Terror as a State and Revolutionary Strategy* (Washington, D.C.: Foreign Policy Institute, 1989), 95–128.

46. Terry Anderson, *Den of Lions: Memoirs of Seven Years* (New York: Ballantine, 1993), 59.

47. Quandt, *Peace Process*, 348.

48. Fisk, *Pity the Nation*, 476, 479; Friedman, *From Beirut to Jerusalem*, 198; Frank, *U.S. Marines in Lebanon*, 60.

49. Robert Pape compiled data on suicide attacks since 1980 and found that religion is not the force behind suicide terrorism. "Dying to Kill Us," *NYT*, 22 September 2003, A19. But in Lebanon the suicide terrorists were all Hizb'allah mujahideen. The Palestinians, including those belonging to the secular Fatah movement Al-Aksa Martyrs Brigade, adopted suicide attacks in the later 1990s.

50. Martin Kramer, "The Moral Logic of Hizballah," in Walter Reich, ed., *The Origins of Terrorism: Psychologies, Ideologies, Theologies, States of Mind* (New York: Cambridge University Press, 1990), 131–57.

51. "A martyr's privileges . . . guaranteed by Allah" include immediate forgiveness of sin, intercession on behalf of seventy-two relatives, and marriage to "seventy-two beautiful ones," Rohan Gunaratna, *Inside Al Qaeda*, 9–10.

52. Ranstorp, *Hizb'allah*, 68–69, 91, 93, 98; Jaber, *Hezbollah*, 115; Kramer, "The Moral Logic," 136; Walter Mossberg and Barbara Rosewicz, "Hezbollah Frustrates a Gulliver-Like U.S.," *Wall Street Journal*, 4 August 1989, A4; Kenneth Timmerman, "Likely Mastermind of Tower Attacks: Imad Mugniyah Has Been Murdering Americans and Attacking U.S. Interests for 20 Years," *Insight on the News*, 31 December 2001; Scott Shan, "Failure to Stop Longtime Terrorist Haunts U.S." *Baltimore Sun*, 9 June 2002; "Who Did it? Foreign Report Presents an Alternative View," *Jane's Foreign Report*, 19 September 2001.

53. Wright, *Sacred Rage*, 96; Jaber, *Hezbollah*, 69.

54. Bodansky, *Bin Laden*, 157–58.

55. Shane, "Failure to Stop Longtime Terrorist Haunts U.S."; Timmerman, "Likely Mastermind of Tower Attacks."

56. Frank, *U.S. Marines in Lebanon*, 78.

57. Wright, *Sacred Rage*, 78.

58. Frank, *U.S. Marines in Lebanon*, 51; Friedman, *From Beirut to Jerusalem*, 200–201.

59. Frank, *U.S. Marines in Lebanon*, 167; Reagan, *An American Life*, 446.

60. Reagan, *An American Life*, 452–53; "Interview: Robert McFarlane," PBS documentary *Frontline*: "Target America," PBS.org/Frontline

61. "Adequacy of U.S. Marine Corps Security in Beirut," U.S. House of Representatives, Committee on Armed Services, Ninety-Eighth Congress, First Session.

62. "Estimates by FBI explosives experts who have inspected the scene place the power of the device in the truck at the equivalent of 12,000 pounds of TNT. That was described as a "conservative" estimate. The device is believed to have been comprised of explosives placed around cylinders of gas. The subcommittee was told the gas-enhanced explosion had the effect of increasing the destructive power. The power of the explosion was put at six times that of the car bomb that struck the U.S. embassy in Beirut on 18 April 1983. The power of the explosion

in the atrium of the BLT headquarters was sufficient to drive the floor beneath the truck eight feet down into the earth. That floor was an inch of marble atop a seven-inch base of concrete."

63. Frank, *U.S. Marines in Lebanon*, 98.

64. Ibid., Appendix E, 174.

65. Ibid., 172.

66. Reagan, *An American Life*, 465.

67. Wright, *Sacred Rage*, 112–13.

68. Mahan Abedin, "Hezb al Daawa al-Islmamiyya," *Middle East Intelligence Bulletin* 5, 6 (June 2002); Aburish, *Saddam*, 184–85, 221.

69. Jaber, *Hezbollah*, 82; Shane, "Failure to Stop Longtime Terrorist"; Timmerman, "Likely Mastermind of Tower Attacks."

Chapter 7. America Will Never Make Concessions to Terrorists

1. Anderson, *Den of Lions*, 62.

2. Ranstorp, *Hizb'allah*, 88.

3. Ranstorp, *Hizb'allah*, 92.

4. David Jacobsen and Gerald Astor, *Hostage: My Nightmare in Beirut* (New York: Donald I. Fine, 1991), 5.

5. www.arlingtoncemetery.net

6. Jaber, *Hezbollah*, 118; Ranstorp, *Hizb'allah*, 92.

7. Evan Duncan, "Terrorist Attacks on U.S. Official Personnel Abroad, 1982–1984," U.S. Department of State Bulletin, April 1985; Wright, *Sacred Rage*, 106–10.

8. *Stanford et al., v. Kuwait Airlines Corporation et al.*; Duncan, "Terrorist Attacks on U.S. Official Personnel"; Craig Gilbert, "A Lifetime of Heartache," *Milwaukee Journal Sentinel*, 6 September 2002.

9. Wright, *Sacred Rage*, 133–45.

10. Texts available at www.fas.org/irp/offdocs/nsdd

11. Reagan, *An American Life*, 491.

12. In an interview, Pulitzer Prize-winning journalist Bob Woodward gave credence to the allegation of CIA involvement: "Reagan wanted action. And Casey went off the books on his own, and worked it out with the Saudis. . . . Casey had lunch with Prince Bandar, the Saudi Ambassador to the United States, one of the most powerful figures even today in Washington. And they went for a stroll in the garden and they said, 'We have to go off the books.' And they agreed that the Saudis would put up the money to hire some professionals to try to car bomb Sheik Fadlallah. And it was so off the books, there's no evidence that Reagan knew about it or Weinberger or Schultz. It was Casey on his own, saying, 'I'm going to solve the big problem by essentially getting tougher or as tough as the terrorists in using their weapon'—the car bomb," PBS *Frontline*, "Target America," 4 October 2001; see also Bob Woodward, "CIA Told to Do 'Whatever Necessary' to Kill Bin Laden," *Washington Post*, 21 October 2001; David Silverstein, "Reviving the Assassination Option," American Enterprise Online, December 2001.

13. Anderson, *Den of Lions*, 71

14. Ibid., 86–87; Jacobsen, *Hostage*, 51–53.

15. Ranstorp, *Hizb'allah*, 235; Reagan, *An American Life*, 507. Hizb'allah returned his body in 1991 with that of another American, William Higgins, a Marine lieutenant colonel serving as a UN peacekeeper in southern Lebanon

who Hizb'allah captured and killed in retaliation for the Israeli's abduction of Shi'a leader Sheikh Obied in July 1987.

16. William Smith, "Terror Aboard Flight 847," *Time*, 24 June 1985; ABC News, "17 Days of Terror: The Hijack of TWA 847;" "Terror Aboard TWA 847," terrorismvictims.org; Wright, *Sacred Rage*, 273–78.

17. ABC News, "17 Days of Terror."

18. Final Report of the Independent Counsel for Iran/Contra Matters, vol. 1, Investigations and Prosecutions, Lawrence E. Walsh, Independent Counsel, 4 August 1993. United States Court of Appeals for the District of Columbia Circuit; Part I Iran/Contra: the Underlying Facts; Reagan, *An American Life*, 493–98.

19. Reagan, *An American Life*, 495.

20. ABC News, "17 Days of Terror."

21. Anderson, *Den of Lions*, 103; see also Jeffrey Goldberg, "In the Party of God," *New Yorker*, 28 October 2002.

22. Reagan, *An American Life*, 492.

23. Ibid., 491.

24. Ibid., 504–5.

25. PBS *Frontline*, "The Secret Story of Terry Waite."

26. David Schiller, "A Battlegroup Divided: The Palestinian Fedayen," in *Inside Terrorist Organizations*, ed. David C. Rapoport (New York: Columbia University Press, 2001) 104; Aburish, *Arafat*, 182–83, 190; Sayigh, *Armed Struggle*, 562–73, 585–87.

27. Aburish, *Arafat*, 191; Livingstone and Halevy, *Inside the PLO*, chap. 9.

28. Livingstone and Halevy, *Inside the P.L.O.*, 254.

29. "Informal Exchange with Reporters on the Achille Lauro Hijacking Incident," 10 October 1985, www.reagan.utexas.edu

30. Reagan, *An American Life*, 509. Abu Abbas did not have to hide. After the *Achille Lauro* affair, Abbas resumed his post on the PLO executive committee, a post he held until 1993. Americans did capture him, in Iraq in April 2003, after the invasion that toppled Saddam Hussein. Abbas died in U.S. custody in March 2004.

31. *United States v. Rezaq Omar Mohammed.*

32. "Letter Dated 9 January 1986 from the Acting Permanent Representative of Israel to the United Nations addressed to the Secretary-General," United Nations General Assembly/Security Council A/41/84, S/17728, 10 January 1986. The letter documents a series of terror attacks that killed or injured children of various nationalities dating back to 1968.

33. Chronicles.dickinson.edu/encyclo/b/ed_buonocorej.htm

34. Theodore Draper, *A Very Thin Line: The Iran-Contra Affairs* (New York: Hill and Wang, 1991) chap. 9.

35. Draper, *A Very Thin Line*, 213–14; Final Report of the Independent Counsel.

36. Final Report of the Independent Counsel, vol. 1, part 1; Draper, *A Very Thin Line*, chap. 9.

37. NSDD number 205, Qaddafi's proclamation that the attack was "noble" was more than Reagan needed. Reagan, *An American Life*, 511; Mark Kosnik, "The Military Response to Terrorism," *Navy War College Review* (Spring 2000). The Reagan administration had been sparring with Muammar Qaddafi since Reagan's first months in office. On 19 August 1981, two Navy F-14 Tomcat fighters shot down the two Libyan aircraft over the disputed Gulf of Sidra.

38. Washingtonpost.com, "Bombing of TWA 840"; James Wootten, "Terror-

ist Incidents Involving U.S. Citizens or Property 1981–1989: A Chronology," Congressional Research Service. Greek authorities arrested Rashid for the Pan Am bombing in 1988. A Greek court convicted him in 1992 and sentenced him to fifteen years. He served only four. In 1996 the Greeks released him and Rashid traveled to Cairo. In June 1998, sixteen years after the Pan Am bombing and twelve years after the TWA bombing, Egyptian police arrested him at the behest of the UniTed States.

39. Wootten, "Terrorist Incidents Involving U.S. Citizens or Property."

40. "Operation El Dorado Canyon," www.globalsecurity.org/_military/_ops/_el_dorado_canyon.htm; PBS *Frontline,* "Target America" interviews with Paul Bremer and Robert Oakley.

41. Jacobsen and Astor, *Hostage,* 170; Associated Press, "Profile of the Western Hostages of Lebanon Kidnappers," Congressional Record—Senate, 12 May 1989; Ray Murphy, "The Forgotten Hostage," www.columbia.edu~js322/misc/fpa/history/107-fporgotten.htm

42. PBS *Frontline,* "Target America."

43. Terry Waite, *Taken on Trust* (New York: Harcourt Brace, 1993), 337; PBS *Frontline,* "The Secret Story of Terry Waite."

44. Reagan, *An American Life,* 523; Draper, *A Very Thin Line,* 383.

45. Seale, *Abu Nidal,* 252–53; *United States v. Wadoud Muhammad Hafiz al-Turk et al.*; presentation at sentencing of Zaid Hassan Abd Latif Safarini.

46. "Hijacking of Pan Am flight #73," United States Attorney's Office for the District of Columbia; Terry Frieden and Carol Cratty, "Survivors Condemn Hijacker in Pan Am Massacre," CNN.com, 12 May 2003.

47. Reagan, *An American Life,* 526.

48. Ibid.

49. PBS *Frontline,* "The Secret Story of Terry Waite"; Waite, *Taken on Trust,* 333, 342. Waite mentions meeting David Jacobsen in Beirut in the presence of Oliver North, but not traveling there with the Marine lieutenant colonel. Waite does mention traveling to Cyprus with North and then from Cyprus to Beirut aboard a U.S. military helicopter, but he says the trip occurred in early 1986.

50. PBS, "The Secret Story of Terry Waite"; BBC News, "This Day 1987: Peace Envoy Imprisoned"; "It's Over—Terry Waite Returns Home," BBC.com.uk

51. Reagan Address to the Nation on the Iran Arms and Contra Aid Controversy," 4 March 1987, http://www.reagan.utexas.edu/

52. Executive Summary of the Report of the Independent council for Iran/Contra Matters.

53. National Memorial Institute for the Prevention of Terrorism, MIPT Terrorism Knowledge Base; Seale, *Abu Nidal,* 265–66.

54. Gwen Ackerman, "Barak Assassination of Abu Jihad," Associated Press, 4 July 1997; Livingstone and Halevy, *Inside the PLO,* 36–39.

55. Quandt, *Peace Process,* 367–74.

56. Sayigh, *Armed Struggle,* 624.

57. David Ignatius, "The Secret History of U.S.-P.L.O. Talks," *Washington Post,* 4 December 1988.

58. Sayigh, *Armed Struggle,* 624.

59. Allan Gerson and Jerry Adler, *The Price of Terror: The History-Making Struggle for Justice After Pan Am 103* (New York: Harper Collins, 2001), 3, 281; "Encyclopedia: Pan Am 103," nationmaster.com/encyclopedia/pan-Am-flight-103; "Flash Signaled End of Pan Am 103," BBC News, 4 May 2000.

60. In the High Court of Justiciary at Camp Zeist, Opinion of the Court delivered by Lord Sutherland in causa *Her Majesty's Advocate v. Abdelbaset Ali Mohmed Al-Megrahi and Al-Amin Khalifa Fhimah,* www.ict.org.il/documents/lockerbiejud gement.htm

61. Gerson and Adler, *The Price of Terror,* 66.

62. Central Intelligence Agency, Directorate of Intelligence, Spot Commentary: Pan Am 103: Analysis of Claims, 22 December 1988.

63. Dan and Susan Cohen, *Pan Am 103: The Bombing, The Betrayal and a Bereaved Family's Search for Justice* (New York: New American Library, 2000), 29; Gerson and Adler, *The Price of Terror,* 25–27, 75–78.

64. George Wilson, "Navy Missile Downs Iranian Jetliner on 4th of July," *Washington Post,* 4 July 1988.

65. David Ottaway and Laura Parker, "CIA Confident Iran Behind Jet Bombing," *Washington Post,* 11 May 1989.

66. "Opinion of the Court," paras., 9, 12, 14, 82, 87.

67. Gerson and Adler, *Price of Terror,* 97.

68. Michael Weisskopf and David Zagorin, "Fundraising: How Bush Plays the Game," Time Online Edition, 24 March 2002; U.S. Senate Committee on Banking, Housing and Urban Affairs, Hearing on the Reauthorization of the Iran and Libya Sanctions Act, "Prepared Testimony of Mrs. Stephanie Bernstien, Justice for Pan Am 103," 28 June 2001.

69. BBC, "Blair Hails New Libyan Relations," 25 March 2004.

Chapter 8. The Real Enemy Is America

1. "Genocide in Iraq: The Anfal Campaign Against the Kurds," Human Rights Watch, July 1993; Power, *A Problem from Hell,* 173, 188, 194; Aburish, *Saddam Hussein,* 248.

2. PBS *Frontline,* "The Gulf War," pbs.org/wgbh/pages/frontline/gulf/cron/

3. "Address Before a Joint Session of Congress on the Persian Gulf Crisis and the Federal Budget Deficit," 11 September 1990, Bushlibrary.tamu.edu/_re search/_papers/_1990/_90091101.html

4. Interview, General Wafic al-Sammarai, PBS *Frontline,* "The Gulf War."

5. Michael R. Gordon and Bernard E. Trainor, *Cobra II: The Inside Story of the Invasion and Occupation of Iraq* (New York: Pantheon, 2006), 514. The slaughter of the Shi'a forced Bush to establish a U.S.-patrolled "no-fly zone" over southern Iraq in June 1992. Operation Southern Watch complemented Operation Supply Comfort which Bush established the previous year to protect Iraq's Kurds.

6. Kamal Matinuddin, *The Taliban Phenomenon: Afghanistan, 1994–1997* (London: Oxford University Press, 1999), 9.

7. Steve Coll, *Ghost Wars: The Secret History of the CIA, Afghanistan, and Bin Laden from the Soviet Invasion to September 10, 2001* (New York: Penguin, 2004), 155; Miller, Stone, and Mitchell, *The Cell,* 49; Anonymous, *Through Our Enemy's Eyes: Osama Bin Laden, Radical Islam, and the Future of America* (Washington, D.C.: Brassey's, 2002) 85; Peter L. Bergen, *Holy War, Inc.: Inside the Secret World of Osama Bin Laden* (New York: Free Press, 2001), 52.

8. Gunaratna, *Inside Al Qaeda,* 4; Peter L. Bergen, *The Osama bin Laden I Know: An Oral History of al Qaeda's Leader* (New York: Free Press, 2006), 74, 81; Coll, *Ghost Wars,* 176; Miller et al., *The Cell,* 49; Kepel, *Jihad,* 222.

9. Azzam and bin Laden were being drawn into the factionalism of the Afghan jihad. Azzam was close to Ahmed Shah Massoud, the Tajik commander of the Jamaat-e-Islami, and later, the Northern Alliance. Indeed, Azzam's son-in-law, an Algerian who together with Azzam and bin Laden organized the MAK, recruited Arab fighters for Massoud. Bin Laden drew closer to the Pashtun warlord, Gulbaddin Hekmatyar, whose more radical Islamist Hizb-e-Islami, received the lion's share of the U.S., Saudi, and Pakistani covert funding. Coll, *Ghost Wars*, 164, 202.

10. Coll, *Ghost Wars*, 164.

11. *United States, Appellee, v. Omar Ahmad Ali Abdel Rahman* (2d Cir. 1997).

12. *United States v. Ahmed Abdel Sattar, et al.*, SI 02 Cr. 395 (JGK) ¶ 7 (S.D. N.Y 1996).

13. Abu Ubaidah al-Banjshiri also organized Al Qaeda terrorists in West Africa until he drowned in a ferry accident on Lake Victoria in 1996; his deputy, Abu Hafs al-Masry, who went by the name of Mohammed Atef, was killed by a U.S. air strike in November 2001 in retaliation for the 9/11 attacks; Saif al-Adel, a former colonel in the Egyptian army and once a member of the Egyptian Islamic Jihad, rose to the command of Al Qaeda's military committee after the death of Atef. See Testimony of Jamal Ahmed al-Fadl, Trial Transcript, *United States v. Usama Bin Laden et al.*, S (7) 98 Cr. 1023 (S.D. N.Y. 2001) (hereafter *U.S. v. Bin Laden*, al-Fadl testimony); Coll, *Ghost Wars*, 163–64; Bergen, *The Osama bin Laden I Know*, 81, 114. Bergen insists that bin Laden created Al Qaeda in September 1988 and that he timed the 9/11 attacks to mark the anniversary of its creation. Jamal al-Fadl testified that he was one of the first to join in late in 1989 or early 1990; see also Anonymous, *Through Our Enemy's Eyes*, 100–108; Gunaratna, *Inside Al Qaeda*, 11, 29–31; *Final Report of the National Commission on Terrorist Attacks upon the United States* (New York: Norton, 2002), 56 (hereafter 9/11 Commission Report).

14. Azzam had a host of enemies with motives to kill him. Bergen concludes that Egyptian militants killed Azzam because his interpretation of jihad clashed with their own. Bergen, *The Osama bin Laden I Know*, 92.

15. The History Channel, "History Alive: Targeted: Osama Bin Laden"; Coll, *Ghost Wars*, 212; Bergen, *The Osama bin Laden I Know*, 97–98, 104; Anonymous, *Through Our Enemy's Eyes*, 109.

16. Bergen, *The Osama bin Laden I Know*, 114.

17. According to the 9/11 Commission Report (57), bin Laden left with the help of a dissident member of the royal family; Coll, *Ghost Wars*, 231, writes that bin Laden was expelled, and told the Americans were to blame.

18. Bin Laden was in the region when Massoud's forces took Kabul in February 1992, and even attempted to intercede in the conflict between the two principal Afghan warriors, Ahmed Shah Massoud and Gullbadin Hekmatyar. Coll, *Ghost Wars*, 233; Anonymous, *Through Our Enemy's Eyes*, 121.

19. Kepel, *Jihad*, 176–84.

20. 9/11 Commission Report, 57; Bergen, *The Osama bin Laden I Know*, 120; Coll, *Ghost Wars*, 267–68; *U.S. v. Bin Laden*, al-Fadl testimony.

21. 9/11 Commission Report, 470 n 80.

22. Terrorism Research Center, "Usamah Bin-Laden, the Destruction of the Base," 10 June 1999, www.terrorism.com/terrorism/BinLadenTranscript.shtml

23. 9/11 Commission Report, 58, 60, 468; Bergen, *The Osama bin Laden I Know*, 137.

24. Kenneth Timmerman, "Likely Mastermind of Tower Attacks: Imad Mugniyah," *Insight*, 31 December 2001.

25. *United States v. Ali Mohamed*, S (7) 98 Cr. 1023 (LBS) NY Sup. Ct., 20 (S.D. N.Y. 2000); 9/11 Commission Report, 61.

26. *United States of America, Appellee, v. Mohammed A. Salameh* (2d Cir. 1997).

27. Bergen, *The Osama bin Laden I Know*, 144; 9/11 Commission Report, 73.

28. *United States v. Ramzi Ahmed Yousef*, 925 F. Supp. 1063, 1065–73 (S.D .N.Y. 1996); Bergen, *The Osama bin Laden I know*, 144; Miller et al., *The Cell*, 91; Daniel Benjamin and Steven Simon, *The Age of Sacred Terror* (New York: Random House, 2002), 7–14.

29. Benjamin and Simon, *The Age of Sacred Terror*, 221; Brooke A. Masters and Wendy Melillo, "Kansi Guilty in Slayings Outside CIA," *Washington Post*, 11 November 1997, A01; Tim McGlone, "Execution in Va. Carries Fear of Retaliation," *Virginian-Pilot*, 12 November 2002. Kansi, who was executed fifteen months after the 9/11 attacks, condemned the attack on the World Trade Center, but not on the Pentagon. He expressed no remorse for having attacked the CIA, but he did admit he felt "sorry and sad for the families of the victims . . . I don't say that I feel happy or proud of it."

30. Federal Emergency Management Agency, United States Fire Administration, "The World Trade Center Bombing: Report and Analysis" (1993).

31. *United States v. Ramzi Ahmed Yousef*; Benjamin and Simon, *The Age of Sacred Terror*, 12–13.

32. The American Presidency Project, President William J. Clinton, "The President's Radio Address, February 27, 1993; "Remarks and a Question and Answer Session at the Adult Learning Center in New Brunswick, New Jersey," 1 March 1993.

33. *United States v. Omar Ahmad Ali Abdel Rahman.*

34. Ramzi Yousef told interrogators that Wali Khan told him that al-Khalifa was ready to assist him, but Yousef appears not to have contacted him. Investigators found al-Khalifa's business card in Yousef's Manila apartment in January 1995. *9/11 Commission Report*, 59; Coll, *Ghost Wars*, 272; Bergen, *The Osama bin Laden I Know*, 147; Maria A. Ressa, *Seeds of Terror: An Eyewitness Account of Al-Qaeda's Newest Center of Operations in Southeast Asia* (New York: Free Press, 2003), 10, 19–27; Gunaratna, *Inside Al Qaeda*, xxv.

35. 9/11 Commission Report, 145–50.

36. *United States v. Ramzi Ahmed Yousef et al.*, Indictment S11 Cr. 180 (KTD) (S.D. N.Y. {2001}); *United States of America, Appellee, v. Ramzi Yousef et al.*, 98–1041 L (2d Cir. 2001). In August 2006, authorities in the United Kingdom disrupted a plot to destroy eleven airliners bound for the United States. The plot was substantially the same as Operation Bojinka.

37. 9/11 Commission Report, 147.

38. Coll, *Shadow Wars*, 272–75, Bergen, *The Osama bin Laden I Know*, 144, 147–48.

39. 9/11 Commission Report, 472 n. 10, refers to a CIA analytical report produced by the agency's Counter-Terrorism Center titled "WTC 1993: The Solid Case for al-Qa'eda Involvement," CTC 2002–40084H. In a March 1998 interview with ABC producer John Miller, bin Laden denied knowing Yousef prior to the World Trade Center attack. "Ramzi Yousef, after the World Trade Center bombing became a well known Muslim personality, and all Muslims know him. Unfortunately, I did not know him before the incident. I remember him as a Muslim who defended Islam from American aggression. He took this effort to let the Americans know that their government assaults Muslims to insure Israeli interest, to insure Jews. American will see many youths who will follow Ramzi Yousef," http://www.robert-fisk.com/_usama_interview_john_millerabc.htm

40. Sayigh, *Armed Struggle*, 654; Seal, *Abu Nidal*, 33–35.

41. Aburish, *Arafat*, 231 and 255; Sayigh, *Armed Struggle*, 642, 656.

42. Sayigh, *Armed Struggle*, 659.

43. William J. Clinton, *My Life* (New York: Knopf, 2004), 944.

44. "Report of the Sharm el-Sheikh Fact-Finding Committe" (Mitchell Report), 30 April 2001, http://www.jmcc.org/documents/mitchel.htm

45. 9/11 Commission Report, 491 n.33.

46. Rohan Gunaratna, "Terror from the Sky," *Jane's Intelligence Review*, 24 September 2001; Coll, *Ghost Wars*, 275–76; Anonymous, *Through Our Enemy's Eyes*, 138–41; Institute for Counter-Terrorism, "Suspects in GIA Bombings in Trial in France," 2 June 1999, www.ict.org.il/_spotlight/det.cfm?id=271

47. *United States v. Timothy James McVeigh and Terry Lynn Nicholas*, No. CR 95–110 (W.D. Okla).

48. For speculation about an Al Qaeda connection, see Simon Reeve, *The New Jackals: Ramzi Yousef, Osama bin Laden and the Future of Terrorism* (Boston: Northeastern University Press, 1999), 83–84.

49. Coll, *Ghost Wars*, 278–79.

50. The director of the CIA quoted from a portion of the classified 1995 NIE after the 9/11 attacks. Written Statement for the Record of the Director of Central Intelligence Before the Joint Inquiry Committee, 17 October 2002, www.fas.org/irp/_congress/_2002_hr/_101702tenet.html.

51. Bodansky, *Bin Laden*, 123–33.

52. The CIA analysis, "Usama Bin Laden: Islamic Extremist Financier," was published by the National Security Archive; see www.gwu.edu/~nsarchiv/_NSAEBB/_INSAEBB55/ciaubl.pdf. See also Coll, *Ghost Wars*, 269, 319–20; Bodansky, *Bin Laden*, 120; 9/11 Commission Report, 62; Benjamin and Simon, *The Age of Sacred Terror*, 233–39; Clinton, *My Life*, 797–78.

53. The History Channel, *History Alive* series, "Targeted: Bin Laden"; Anonymous, *Through Our Enemy's Eyes*, 143–44.

54. Combating Terrorism Center, "An Open Letter to King Fahd," www.ctc.usma/_aq/_AFGP-2002–000103-Trans.pdf

55. House National Security Committee, Staff Report, "The Khobar Towers Bombing Incident," 14 August 1996, 5, 9; 9/11 Commission Report, 60.

56. The Office of the Program Manager-Saudi Arabian National Guard incident is described in the report of the House committee that investigated the subsequent Khobar Towers incident. See "The Khobar Towers Bombing Incident," 5; Miller and Stone, *The Cell*, 149–50; Gunaratna, *Inside Al Qaeda*, 190; Bergen, *Holy War, Inc.*, 87.

57. House National Security Committee, "The Khobar Towers Bombing Incident,"9; Department of Defense, "Report to the President and the Congress on the Protection of U.S. Forces Abroad," Annex B, The Downing Report, 15 September 1996, 38–39 (hereafter Downing Report); *United States v. Ahmed al-Mughassil et al.*, Indictment ¶ 30 (E.D. Vir. 2001).

58. National Security Committee, "The Khobar Towers Bombing Incident," 1–2; Downing Report, 1.

59. Miller et al., *The Cell*, 174; Alfred B. Prados, "Saudi Arabia: Current Issues and U.S. Relations" (Library of Congress, Congressional Research Service, 15 September 2003), 6–9.

60. Salah Najm, "Usama Bin Laden and the Destruction of the Base," www.terrorism.com/_modules.php?op=modload&name=News&file=article&sid=12&mode=thread&order=0&thold=0

61. *United States v. Ahmed al-Mughassil et al.*, paras. 1–2, 15, 19, 28.

62. 9/11 Commission Report, 60, 468, "while the evidence of Iranian involvement is strong, there are also signs that al Qaeda played some role, as yet unknown."

63. 9/11 Commission Report, 62; *Through Our Enemy's Eyes*, 141, 185–86.

64. The interview appeared in the British paper, the *Independent*, 10 July 1998; http://_www.pbs.org/wgbh/pages/frontline/shows/binladen/who/edicts.html

65. *Online New Hour*, Bin Laden's Fatwa, www.pbs.org/_newshour/_terrorism/_international/_fatwa_1996.html

Chapter 9. Kill them on the Land, the Sea, and in the Air

1. 9/11 Commission Report, 109; Coll, *Ghost Wars*, 319. The Director of Station Alec was Michael Scheuer, the anonymous author of *Through Our Enemies' Eyes*.

2. 9/11 Commission Report, 109, 479 n. 1; "Usama Bin Laden: Islamic Extremist Fiancier," www.gwu.edu/~nsarchiv/NSAEBB/NSAEBB55/index1.html#docs

3. *United States v. Usama Bin Laden et al.*,, Testimony of Jamal Ahmed al Fadl, 7–8 February, 2001; 9/11 Commission Report, 109.

4. "Enduring anxiety" is from Benjamin and Simon, *The Age of Sacred Terror*, 244, 247. Benjamin served as the senior director for counterterrorism on the NSC staff from 1998 to 1999; Simon was director for counterterrorism during the same period.

5. National Commission on Terrorist Attacks Upon the United States, Eighth Public Hearing, 24 March 2004 (hereafter 9/11 Commission, Public Hearings); 9/11 Commission Report, 109–14; Coll, *Ghost Wars*, 373–79, 391–96.

6. The question was raised repeatedly in questioning by members of the 9/11 Commission. See 9/11 Commission, Eighth Public Hearing, Testimony of George Tenet and Sandy Berger; Coll, *Ghost Wars*, 391.

7. Richard Clarke, *Against All Enemies: Inside America's War on Terror* (New York: Free Press, 2004), 149; Coll, *Ghost Wars*, 396; 9/11 Commission, Eighth Public Hearing, Staff Statement No. 7, Intelligence Policy and Submitted Testimony of Samuel L. Berger,.

8. Anonymous, *Through Our Enemies' Eyes*, 151–56; Coll, *Ghost Wars*, 326–33.

9. Khaled Skeikh Mohammed first proposed the "planes operation" sometime in 1996; Abd al-Rahim al-Nashiri proposed an attack on a U.S. warship to bin Laden in late 1998. See 9/11 Commission Report, 148, 152.

10. *United States v. Usama Bin Laden et al.*, para. 12 (eee); al-Zawahiri circulated a draft as early as 18 January.

11. PBS *Online News Hour*, "Al Qaeda's Fatwa," www.pbs.org/_newshour/_terrorism/_international/_fatwa_1998.html

12. PBS Frontline, "Hunting Bin Laden; Peter Bergen narrates the meeting with Bin Laden." See *Holy War, Inc.*, prologue.

13. PBS, "Al Qaeda's Fatwa." Remarkably, just the day before, Dale Watson, the chief of the FBI International Terrorism section, testified before the Senate Judiciary Committee's subcommittee on Technology, Terrorism, and Government Information, about the lesson of Ramzi Yousef's attack on the World Trade Center more than five years before. "Loosely affiliated groups of like-minded extremists—like the one Ramizi Yousef assembled for the plot against

the World Trade Center—pose a real and significant threat to our security," he said. Watson reported that Hamas, Hizb'allah, and Egyptian al-Jama'a al-Islamiyyah had a presence in the United States, but he made no mention of Al Qaeda. Statement for the Record of Dale Watson, Chief International Terrorism Section, National Security Division, Federal Bureau of Investigation on Foreign Terrorists in America: five years after the World Trade Center, before the Senate Judiciary Committee Subcommittee on Technology, Terrorism, and Government Information, 24 February 1998.

14. Convention on the Prevention and Punishment of the Crime of Genocide, 9 December 1948, preamble and articles 2–3.

15. "Interview of Usama Bin Laden by John Miller—May 1998ABC," www.robert-fisk.com/usama_interview_john_millerabc.htm

16. *United States v. Ahmed Abdel Sattar* (SI 02 Cr. 395) (JGK) ¶ 7, 16–17 (S.D. N.Y. 1996); Bergen, *The Osama bin Laden I Know,* 203.

17. *United States v. Ali Mohamed,* Plea, S (7) 98 Cr. 1023 (LBS) (S.D. N.Y. 2000); Benjamin Weiser and James Risen, "The Masking of a Militant: A Soldier's Shadowy Trail in U.S. and in the Mideast," *New York Times,* 1 December 1988; Lance Williams and Erin McCormick, "Top bin Laden Aide Toured State," *San Francisco Chronicle,* 11 October 2001, A1.

18. *United States v. Wadih El Hage,* 98 Cr. (1023) (S.D. N.Y. 1998); *United States v. Usama Bin Laden,* Indictment, S (10) 98 Cr. 1023 (LBS) ¶ 12 (S.D. N.Y.2001); Bergen, *Holy War, Inc.,* 136–37.

19. Bergen, *Holy War, Inc.,* 107; *United States v. Usama Bin Laden,* ¶ 12 (aaa) and (ggg).

20. The letter can be found at Frontline, "Hunting Bin Laden," pbs.org/wgbh/pages/_frontline/__shows/binladen/bombings/warnings.html.

21. *United States v. Wadih El Hage;* Report of the Accountability Review Boards, "Bombings of the U.S. Embassies in Nairobi, Kenya and Dar es Salaam, Tanzania on August 7, 1998."

22. *United States v. Usama bin Laden;* 9/11 Commission Report, 152.

23. Report of the Accountability Review Boards, "Bombings of the U.S. Embassies in Nairobi, Kenya and Dar es Salaam, Tanzania on August 7, 1998, Executive Overview," 8 January 1999; Bergen, *Holy War, Inc.,* 113. The CIA captured another conspirator, Khalfan Ghailani, in 2003; Ghailani, who forged documents and attended to other logistical matters, was one of the 14 Al Qaeda "Ghost Detainees" whom President Bush revealed had been transferred to Guantanamo Bay on the eve of the fifth anniversary of 9/11. See Jeffrey Smith and Michael Fletcher, "Bush Says Detainees Will Be Tried," *Washington Post,* 7 September 2006.

24. White House, Office of the Press Secretary, Radio address by the President, 8 August 1998.

25. Benjamin and Simon, *The Age of Sacred Terror,* 261.

26. 9/11 Commission, Submitted Testimony of Samuel L. Berger, 24 March 2004; 9/11 Commission, Staff Statement No. 6; Clarke, *Against All Enemies,* 189.

27. 9/11 Commission Staff Statement No. 6, 5.

28. 9/11 Commission, Staff Statement no. 6; Coll, *Ghost Wars,* 449–50; Scheuer's quotation is from Fox News, *Heartland,* September 9, 2001, www.freerepublic.com/focus/f-news/_1698866/_posts; Michael Scheuer, "Bill and Dick, Osama and Sandy," *Washington Times,* 5 July 2006. Scheuer did not elaborate on the ten opportunities to kill bin Laden. The 9/11 Commission discusses only four, including the aborted Tarnak Farms capture operation, the December 1998 and February and May 1999 sightings.

29. Gary Bernstein and Ralph Pezzullo, *Jaw Breaker: The Attack on Bin Laden and Al Qaeda: A Personal Account by the CIA's Key Field Commander* (New York: Crown, 2005); Newsweek Periscope, "Exclusive: CIA Commander: U.S.: Let Bin Laden Slip Away, August 15, 2005; CNN Paula Zahn's *Now* interview with Berstein, aired 6 January 2006.

30. 9/11 Commission Report, 174–75; Coll, *Ghost Wars*, 482.

31. *United States v. Mohtar Haouari*, No 54 00 Cr. 15, 552 (S.D. N.Y. 2001); 9/11 Commission Report, 176–79; Bergen, *Holy War Inc.*, 140.

32. On the USS *Cole* attack, see *United States v. Jamal Ahmed Mohammed Ali Al-Badawi and Fahd Al Quso*, Indictment, S12 98 Cr. 1023 (KTD) (S.D. N.Y.); "The Investigation into the Attack on the U.S.S. *Cole*," House Armed Services Committee Staff, May 2001; Testimony of Gen. Anthony Zinni Before Senate Armed Services Committee on the Attack on the USS *Cole*, 19 October 2000, CNN transcripts.cnn.com/TRANSCRIPTS/0010/19/se.03.html; U.S. Department of State, "Department of Defense Special Briefing on the Cole Commission," usinfo.state.gov/_is/Archive_Index/
DoD_Special_Briefing_on_the_Cole_Commission; 9/11 Commission Report, 190–93.

33. On the *Cole* investigation, see 9/11 Commission Report, 192–93; Miller et al., *The Cell*; Lawrence Wright, *The Looming Tower: Al-Qaeda and the Road to 9/11* (New York?: Knopf, 2006), 323.

Chapter 10. Today, Our Nation Saw Evil

1. 9/11 Commission Report, 148.

2. The material in this entire section is from the following sources: 9/11 Commission Report, 181–82, 192–93, 266–72; "Report of the Joint Inquiry into the Terrorist Attacks of September 11, 2001"; "Report of the Joint Inquiry into the Terrorist Attacks of September 11, 2001"; House Permanent Select Committee on Intelligence and the Senate Select Committee on Intelligence, December 20, 2002 (hereafter Joint Inquiry Report) 131–35, 143–57; Wright, *The Looming Tower*, 310.

3. Wright, *The Looming Tower*, 310; Joint Inquiry Report, 144.

4. Joint Inquiry Report, 154.

5. Although al-Mihdhar and al-Hazmi had now been "definitively" placed "with a known al-Qai'ida operative," the CIA once again did not act to add them to the State Department's watch list. In January 2001, Khalid al-Mihdhar was abroad, his visa had expired, and he would have to clear a watch list check before obtaining a new visa to re-enter the United States. Joint Inquiry Report, 149; 9/11 Commission Report, 266.

6. On Aulaqu, see 9/11 Commission Report, 221.

7. Joint Inquiry Report, 172–75.

8. 9/11 Commission Report, 164.

9. 9/11 Commission Report, 160–67.

10. Dana Priest, "Wrongful Imprisonment: Anatomy of a CIA Mistake," *Washington Post*, 4 December 2005, A1.

11. Jim Popkin, "Video Showing Atta, Bin Laden Is Unearthed," NBC News, 1 October 2006.

12. 9/11 Commission Report, 226.

13. George W. Bush, Inaugural Address, January 20, 2001, http://www_.whitehouse.gov/_news/_inaugural-address.html

14. On Tenet's briefing to Bush, 9/11 Commission Report, 199; Bob Woodward, *Bush at War* (New York: Simon and Schuster, 2002), 39. Here is the full quotation: "There was a significant difference in my attitude after September 11. I was not on point, but I knew he was a menace and I knew he was a problem. I knew he was responsible, we felt he was responsible for the bombings that had killed Americans. And I was prepared to look at a plan that would bring him to justice and would have given the order to do just that. I have no hesitancy about going after him. But I didn't feel the same sense of urgency, and my blood was not boiling."

15. 9/11 Commission, testimony of Condoleezza Rice, 8 April 2004.

16. 9/11 Commission Report, 265.

17. Rice testimony; 9/11 Commission Report, 199; Woodward, *Bush at War*, 34.

18. Clarke's formal title was National Coordinator for Security, Infastructure Protection and Counterterrorism, a position Clinton created in 1998 through Presidential Decision Directive-62, "Protection against Unconventional Threats to the Homeland and Americans Overseas, May 22, 1998"; "Memorandum for Condoleezza Rice," National Security Council, 25 January 2001, emphasis original, www.gwu.edu/_~nsarchiv/_NSAEBB/_NSAEBB147/_index.htm#original_post

19. Ibid.

20. Rice Testimony, 9/11 Commission, Ninth Public Hearing, 8 April 2004; testimony of Thomas J. Pickard, 9/11 Commission Tenth Public Hearing, 13 April 2004; Woodward, *Bush at War*, 116–17.

21. 9/11 Commission Report, 201; Clarke, *Against All Enemies*, 231. The reference to Zero Hour, is from Woodward, *State of Denial: Bush at War, Part III* (New York: Simon and Schuster, 2006), 50.

22. Clarke testimony, 9/11 Commission Eighth Public Hearing, 23–24 March 2004 (hereafter Clarke testimony). On the CIA officials' threat to resign, see Statement of Christopher Kojm, 9/11 Commission deputy director, Eighth Public Hearing, 24 March 2004; 9/11 Commission Report, 259, says "one senior official in the CTC and a colleague." Tenet testimony, 9/11 Commission, Eighth Public Hearing, 23–24 March 2004.

23. 9/11 Commission Report, 237, 255–59; 9/11 Commission, Tenth Public Hearing, 13 April 2004, Pickard and Ashcroft testimony; Coll, *Ghost Wars*, 560; Woodward, *State of Denial*, 51.

24. According to Coll, between January and September the FBI generated more than 200 secret internal reports, six were about attacks at airports or on airplanes; the Department of State circulated 5 reports about threats to aviation; in response, the FAA put out at least 15 notices in the same period. See *Ghost Wars*, 560–62. The 9/11 Commission concluded that the GIA may have intended to blow the plane up in the skies over Paris, not fly it into the Eiffel Tower. See 9/11 Commission Report, 264, 561.

25. www.ntsb.gov/events/EA990/docket/Ex_12A.pdf

26. Lewis Merletti, the former director of the Secret Service, described the videotaped exercise to the author in the fall of 2006. Merletti participated in the exercise as a member of the Presidential Protective Detail. The 9/11 Commission Report (346) confirms that "at least some government agencies were concerned about the hijacking danger and had speculated about various scenarios," but it does not discuss the Secret Service in this context.

27. Joint Inquiry Report, 151, 9/11 Commission Report, 265–72; Wright, *The*

Looming Tower, 341. The Joint Inquiry Report refers to these individuals only by title; the 9/11 Commission Report with pseudonyms. Wright identifies some of them by name and those names are reproduced here. No public source, to the author's knowledge, identifies the CIA analyst who sat through the 11 June meeting without divulging what he knew.

28. Wright, *The Looming Tower,* 343.

29. Joint Inquiry Report, 153. This is the entire quotation: "If al-Midhar is located, the interview must be conducted by an intel [intelligence] agent. A criminal agent CAN NOT be present at the interview. This case, in its entirety, is based on intel. If at such time as information is developed indicating the existence of a substantial federal crime, that information will be passed over the wall." See, also Wright, *The Looming Tower,* 353. George Tenet in his submitted testimony admitted the CIA "made mistakes" like "the failure to watch list al-Hazmi and al-Mihdhar in a timely Manner," but ultimately attributed this to "systemic weaknesses and the lack of redundancy." 9/11 Commission, Tenet testimony, 14 April 2004.

30. 9/11 Commision Report, 258.

31. 9/11 Commission Report, 243–44.

32. Briefing paper is from Eleanor Hill Joint Inquiry Staff Statement, Part I (18 September 2002). Coll says the paper was prepared for presentation to senior administration officials on 10 July. See *Ghost Wars,* 561. Woodward revealed that Tenet and Black visited Rice on that same day. See *State of Denial,* 52. Tenet did not specifically mention the meeting in submitted testimony before the 9/11 Commission, but he stressed that the CIA's "analysis got to [most senior policymakers] in many forms, including daily current intelligence, medium-term assessments, Community papers, and National Estimates," and that "the analysis of the seriousness of the al-Qa'ida threat was a feature of five major Memorandums of Notification that underpinned covert action programs." 9/11 Commission, Tenet testimony, 14 April 2004. In his memoir, published in May 2007, Tenet confirmed the 10 July meeting in Rice's office. With Rice were Steven Hadley, her deputy, and Dick Clarke. Tenet was accompanied by Black and Rich B. (identified only as one of Black's top assistants at the CTC). Tenet reports that Rich B. gave the formal briefing which began with a blunt warning: "There will be a significant terrorist attack in the coming weeks or months." George Tenet and Bill Harlow, *At the Center of the Storm: My Years at the CIA* (New York: HarperCollins, 2007), 145, 150–51.

33. www.thememoryhole.org/911/phoenix-memo/02.htm; see 9/11 Commission Report, 272; Joint Inquiry Report, 325–36. The declassified version of the memo is substantially blacked out. The Joint Inquiry notes that it named ten individuals.

34. Joint Inquiry Report, 333. Sharbi was charged in July 2004 under President Bush's Military Order of 13 November 2001, and is subject to trial by a military commission. See *United States v. Ghassan Abdullah Al Sharbi,* www.defenselink.mil/_news/_Nov2005/_d20051104sharbi.pdf

35. Joint Inquiry Report, 326; 9/11 Commission Report, 521.

36. Joint Inquiry Report, 332.

37. Joint Inquiry Report, 329.

38. 9/11 Commission Report, 247; *United States v. Zacarias Moussaoui,* (E.D. Vir. 2001); Romesh Ratnesar and Michael Weisskopf, "How the FBI Blew the Case," *Time,* 26 May 2002; Coleen Rowley's memo to FBI Director Robert Mueller, dated May 21 2002, www.time.com/_time/_covers/_1101020603/_memo.html

39. Philip Shenon and Mark Mazzeti, "Records Show Tenet Briefed Rice on Al Qaeda Threat," *New York Times*, 2 October 2006.

40. CNN.com, "Genoa braces for G-8 Summit," 17 July 2001; Cole, *Ghost Wars*, 561; 9/11 Commission Report, 256.

41. 9/11 Commission report, 260–62, 534–35 nn 35, 37. "Two CIA analysts involved in preparing this briefing believed it represented an opportunity to communicate their view that the threat of a Bin Laden attack in the United States remained both current and serious."

42. Rice Testimony, 9/11 Commission, Ninth Public Hearing, 8April 2004, 26–28.

43. 9/11 Commission Report, 264–65, 534 n. 37; 9/11 Commission, Testimony of Attorney General John Ashcroft, 13 April 2004.

44. 9/11 Commission Report, 262. Tenet reports that "a few weeks after the August 6 PDB was delivered" he went to Crawford "to make the president stayed current on events." He does not report that the president gave him any specific instructions; instead, Tenet on his own initiative "directed a thorough review of our files to identify potential threats." Tenet and Harlow, *At the Center of the Storm*, 159.

45. Coll, *Ghost Wars*, 562.

46. The information about the 7 February principals meeting to discuss Iraq is from Tenet and Harlow, *At the Center of the Storm*, 303.

47. NSPD-9 remains classified, but in April 2004, in anticipation of the public hearings of the 9/11 Commission, the White House press secretary released this synopsis of the strategy: "The NSPD called on the Secretary of Defense to plan for military options 'against Taliban targets in Afghanistan, including leadership, command-control, air and air defense, ground forces, and logistics.' The NSPD also called for plans 'against al Qaeda and associated terrorist facilities in Afghanistan, including leadership, command-control-communications, training, and logistics facilities,'" Press Briefing by Scott McClellan, 1 April 2004, www.whitehouse.gov/_news/_releases/—2004/04/20040401-4.html#16. See also Federation of American Scientists, National Security Presidential Directives—NSPDS," www.fas.org/_irp/_offdocs/nspd. The president formally signed NSPD-9 on 25 April. Rice testified that NSPD-9, the ninth national security directive, was "the very first major national security policy directive of the Bush administration." The titles of four of those eight previous presidential directives are classified, but according to the Federation of American Scientists, one concerned the United States' nuclear offensive and defensive strategies, another concerned a review of U.S. intelligence.

48. 9/11 Commission Report, 212; Clarke, *Against All Enemies*, 237.

49. The following passages are from the 9/11 Commission Report, chap. 1.

50. "Bin Laden: 'America Filled with Fear,'" CNN, 7 October 2001, http://_archives.cnn.com/__2001/WORLD/asiapcf/central/10/07/ret.binladen.transcript/index.html

51. "Statement by the President in His Address to the Nation," www.whitehouse.gov/_news/_releases/_2001/09/20010911-16.html

Epilogue

1. "Bin Laden: 'America Filled with Fear,'" CNN, 7 October 2001, http://_archives.cnn.com/__2001/WORLD/asiapcf/central/10/07/ret.binladen.transcript/index.html.

2. www.globalsecurity.org/military/library/news/2001/10/mil-011007-usia01.htm.

3. Berstein, *Jawbreaker*, 307; Barton Gellman and Thomas E. Ricks, "U.S. Concludes Bin Laden Escaped at Tora Bora Fight," *Washington Post*, 17 April 2002, A0.

4. news.bbc.co.uk/2/hi/middle_east/2751019.stm.

5. "Evidence from intelligence sources, secret communications, and *statements by people now in custody* reveal that Saddam Hussein aids and protects terrorists, including members of al Qaeda. Secretly, and without fingerprints, he could provide one of his hidden weapons to terrorists, or help them develop their own" (emphasis added), http://_www.whitehouse.gov/_news/_releases/_2003/_01/20030128-19.html Emphasis added. See Ron Suskind, *The One Percent Doctrine: Deep Inside America's Pursuit of Its Enemies Since 9/11* (New York: Simon and Schuster), 75–76.

6. "President Discusses Creation of Military Commission to Try Suspected Terrorists," 6 September 2006, www.whitehouse.gov/news/releases/2006/09/20060906-3.html.

7. Thomas Ricks, *Fiasco: The American Military Adventure in Iraq* (New York: Penguin, 2006), 32.

8. http://www.whitehouse.gov/news/releases/2003/01/20030128–19.html.

9. Tenet and Harlowe, *At the Center of the Storm*, 303.

10. www.globalsecurity.org/intell/library/reports/2006/nie_global-terror-trends_apr2006.htm

Bibliography

Books and Articles

Aburish, Said K. *Arafat: From Defender to Dictator.* New York: Bloomsbury, 1998.
————. *Saddam Hussein: The Politics of Revenge.* New York: Bloomsbury, 2000.
Al-Khalil, Samir. *Republic of Fear: The Inside Story of Saddam's Iraq.* New York: Pantheon, 1989.
Al-Shaikh, Zakuria. "Sabra and Shatila 1982: Resisting the Massacre." *Journal of Palestine Studies* 14 (Winter 1984).
Anderson, Terry. *Den of Lions: Memoirs of Seven Years.* New York: Ballantine, 1993.
Anonymous (Michael Scheuer). *Through Our Enemies' Eyes: Osama Bin Laden, Radical Islam, and the Future of America.* Washington, D.C.: Brassey's, 2002.
Benjamin, Daniel and Steven Simon. *The Age of Sacred Terror.* New York: Random House, 2002.
Bergen, Peter L. *Holy War, Inc.: Inside the Secret World of Osama Bin Laden.* New York: Free Press, 2001.
————. *The Osama bin Laden I Know: An Oral History of al-Qaeda's Leader.* New York: Free Press, 2006.
Bernstein, Gary and Ralph Pezzullo. *Jaw Breaker: The Attack on Bin Laden and Al Qaeda: A Personal Account by the CIA's Key Field Commander.* New York: Crown, 2005.
Black, Ian and Benny Morris. *Israel's Secret Wars: A History of Israel's Intelligence Services.* New York: Grove Press, 1991.
Bodansky, Yossef. *Bin Laden: The Man Who Declared War on America.* Rocklin, Calif.: Forum, 1999.
Calahan, Alexander. "The Israeli Response to the 1972 Munich Olympic Massacre and the Development of Independent Covert Action Teams," Master's thesis, Marine Corps Command and Staff College, 1995.
Clarke, Richard. *Against All Enemies: Inside America's War on Terror.* New York: Free Press, 2004.
Cobban, Helena. *The Palestinian Liberation Organization: People, Power and Politics.* Cambridge: Cambridge University Press, 1984.
Cohen, Dan and Susan Cohen. *Pan Am 103: The Bombing, the Betrayal and a Bereaved Family's Search for Justice.* New York: New American Library, 2000.
Coll, Steve. *Ghost Wars: The Secret History of the CIA, Afghanistan, and Bin Laden, from the Soviet Invasion to September 10, 2001.* New York: Penguin, 2004.
Crile, George. *Charlie Wilson's War: The Extraordinary Story of the Largest Covert Operation in History.* New York: Atlantic Monthly Press, 2003.
Dobson, Christopher. *Black September: Its Short, Violent History.* London: Robert Hale, 1975.
Draper, Theodore. *A Very Thin Line: The Iran-Contra Affairs.* New York: Hill and Wang, 1991.

Frank, Benis M. *The U.S. Marines in Lebanon: 1982–1984*. Washington, D.C.: History and Museum Division Headquarters, U.S. Marine Corps, 1987.

Fisk, Robert. *Pity the Nation: The Abduction of Lebanon*. New York: Atheneum, 1990.

Follain, John. *Jackal: The Complete Story of the Legendary Terrorist, Carlos the Jackal*. New York: Arcade, 1998.

Friedman, Thomas L. *From Beirut to Jerusalem*. New York: Anchor Books, 1990.

Gerson, Allan and Jerry Adler. *The Price of Terror: The History-Making Struggle for Justice After Pan Am 103*. New York: HarperCollins, 2001.

Gordon, Michael R. and Bernard E. Trainor. *Cobra II: The Inside Story of the Invasion and Occupation of Iraq*. New York: Pantheon, 2006.

Gowers, Andrew and Tony Walker. *Behind the Myth: Yasser Arafat and the Palestinian Revolution*. New York: Olive Branch Press, 1992.

Gunaratna, Rohan. *Inside Al Qaeda: Global Network of Terror*. New York: Berkley Books, 2003.

Hart, Alan. *Arafat: A Political Biography*. Bloomington: Indiana University Press, 1989.

Hudson, Rex A. and staff of the Federal Research Division of the Library of Congress. *Who Becomes a Terrorist and Why: The 1999 Government Report on Profiling Terrorists*. Guilford, Conn.: Lyons Press, 1999.

Jaber, Hala. *Hezbollah: Born with a Vengeance*. New York: Columbia University Press, 1997.

Jacobsen, David and Gerald Astor. *Hostage: My Nightmare in Beirut*. New York: Donald I. Fine, 1991.

Jonas, George. *Vengeance: The True Story of an Israeli Counter-Terrorist Team*. New York: Simon and Schuster, 1984.

Karmon, Ely. "Fatah and the Popular Front for the Liberation of Palestine: International Terrorism Strategies (1968–1990)." International Policy Institute for Counter-Terrorism, November 2002.

Kelly, John H. "Lebanon 1982–1984." In Jeremy R. Asrael and Emil A. Payin, eds., *U.S. and Russian Policymaking with Respect to the Use of Force*. Santa Monica, Calif.: Rand, 1996.

Kepel, Gilles. *Jihad: The Trail of Political Islam*. Cambridge, Mass.: Belknap Press of Harvard University Press, 2002.

Khalidi, Rashid. *Under Siege: P.L.O. Decision-Making During the 1982 War*. New York: Cambridge University Press, 1986.

Klein, Aaron J. *Striking Back: The 1972 Munich Olympics Massacre and Israel's Deadly Response*. New York: Random House, 2005.

Korn, David A. *Assassination in Khartoum*. Bloomington: Indiana University Press, 1993.

Kramer, Martin. "The Moral Logic of Hizballah." In Walter Reich, ed., *The Origins of Terrorism: Psychologies, Ideologies, Theologies, States of Mind*. New York: Cambridge University Press, 1990.

Livingstone, Neil C. and David Halevy. *Inside the P.L.O.: Covert Units, Secret Funds, and the War Against Israel and the United States*. New York: William Morrow, 1990.

Matinuddin, Kamal. *The Taliban Phenomenon: Afghanistan, 1994–1997*. London: Oxford University Press, 1999.

Miller, John, Michael Stone, and Chris Mitchell. *The Cell: Inside the 9/11 Plot and Why the FBI and CIA Failed to Stop It*. New York: Hyperion, 2002.

O'Balance, Edgar. *The Gulf War*. London: Brassey's, 1988.

Oren, Michael. *Six Days of War: June 1967 and the Making of the Modern Middle East*. Oxford: Oxford University Press, 2002.

Power, Susan. *A Problem from Hell: America and the Age of Genocide*. New York: Basic Books, 2002.

Quandt, William B. *Peace Process: American Diplomacy and the Arab-Israeli Conflict Since 1967*. Berkeley: University of California Press, 1993.

Ranstorp, Magnus. *Hizb'allah in Lebanon: The Politics of the Western Hostage Crisis*. New York: St. Martin's Press, 1997.

Reeve, Simon. *The New Jackals: Ramzi Yousef, Osama bin Laden and the Future of Terrorism*. Boston: Northeastern University Press, 1999.

————. *One Day in September: The Full Story of the 1972 Munich Olympics Massacre and the Israeli Revenge Operation "Wrath of God"*. New York: Arcade, 2000.

Ressa, Maria A. *Seeds of Terror: An Eyewitness Account of Al-Qaeda's Newest Center of Operations in Southeast Asia*. New York: Free Press, 2003.

Reisman, W. Michael and Chris T. Antoniou, eds. *The Laws of War: A Comprehensive Collection of Primary Documents on International Laws Governing Armed Conflict*. New York: Vintage Books, 1994.

Sayigh, Yezid. *Armed Struggle and the Search for State: The Palestinian National Movement, 1949–1993*. New York: Oxford University Press, 1997.

Schechterman, Bernard and Martin Slann, eds. *Violence and Terrorism, 91/92*. Guilford, Conn.: Dushkin, 1991.

Schiller, David. "A Battlegroup Divided: The Palestinian Fedayen." In David C. Rappoport, ed., *Inside Terrorist Organizations*. New York: Columbia University Press, 2001.

Seale, Patrick. *Abu Nidal: A Gun for Hire*. New York: Random House, 1992.

Segev, Tom. *1949: The First Israelis*. New York: Henry Holt, 1986

St. John, Peter. *Air Piracy, Airport Security, and International Terrorism: Winning the War Against Hijackers*. New York: Quorum Books, 1991.

Tenet George and Bill Harlow. *At the Center of the Storm: My Years at the CIA*. New York: Harper Collins, 2007.

Timmerman, Kenneth. "Likely Mastermind of Tower Attacks: Imad Mugniyah." *Insight*, 31 December 2001.

Waite, Terry. *Taken on Trust*. New York: Harcourt Brace, 1993.

Woodward, Bob. *Bush at War*. New York: Simon and Schuster, 2002.

————. *State of Denial: Bush at War, Part III*. New York: Simon and Schuster, 2006.

Wright, Lawrence. *The Looming Tower: Al-Qaeda and the Road to 9/11*. New York: Knopf, 2006.

Wright, Robin. *Sacred Rage: The Wrath of Militant Islam*. New York: Touchstone, 1985.

Yallop, David. *Tracking the Jackal: The Search for Carlos, the World's Most Wanted Man*. New York: Random House, 1993.

Memoirs

Carter, Jimmy. *Keeping Faith: Memoirs of a President*. New York: Bantam Books, 1982.

Clinton, William J. *My Life*. New York: Knopf, 2004.

Daoud, Abu, with Gilles du Jonchay. *Palestine: de Jérusalem à Munich*. Paris: Carrière, 1999.

Ford, Gerald. *A Time to Heal: The Autobiography of Gerald R. Ford*. New York: Berkley Books, 1980.

Iyad, Abu and Eric Rouleau. *My Home, My Land: A Narrative of the Palestinian Struggle.* New York: Times Books, 1981.

Johnson, Lyndon Baines. *The Vantage Point: Perspectives of the Presidency, 1963–1969.* New York: Holt, Rinehart and Winston, 1971.

Kissinger, Henry. *White House Years.* Boston: Little, Brown, 1979

———. *Years of Upheaval.* Boston: Little, Brown, 1982.

———. *Years of Renewal.* New York: Simon and Schuster, 1999.

Nixon, Richard M. *RN: The Memoirs of Richard Nixon.* New York: Grosset and Dunlap, 1978.

Reagan, Ronald. *An American Life.* New York: Simon and Schuster, 1990.

Government Documents

Accountability Review Boards. "Report of the Accountability Review Boards, Bombings of the U.S. Embassies in Nairobi, Kenya and Dar es Salaam, Tanzania on August 7, 1998." 8 January 1999.

National Commission on Terrorist Attacks upon the United States. *Final Report of the National Commission on Terrorist Attacks upon the United States.* New York: Norton, 2002. (9/11 Commission Report)

National Transportation Safety Board. "Aircraft Accident Report: Trans World Airlines Inc. Boeing 707–331B, N8734 in the Ionian Sea, September 8, 1974." Report NTSB-AAR-75-7.

National Security Council. "Memorandum for Condoleezza Rice." 25 January 2001.

National Security Decision. Directive 205, "Acting Against Libyan Support for International Terrorism." 8 January 1986.

Presidential Decision Directive-62. "Protection Against Unconventional Threats to the Homeland and Americans Overseas." 22 May 1998.

U.S. Court of Appeals for the District of Columbia Circuit. "Final Report of the Independent Counsel for Iran/Contra Matters, vol. 1, Investigations and Prosecutions, Lawrence E. Walsh, Independent Counsel, 4 August 1993. United Part I Iran/Contra: the Underlying Facts."

U.S. Department of Defense. Report to the President and the Congress on the Protection of U.S. Forces Abroad, Annex B, the Downing Report. 15 September 1996.

U.S. House of Representatives, Committee on Armed Services. "Adequacy of U.S. Marine Corps Security in Beirut." Ninety-Eighth Congress, First Session, 18 December 1983.

———. "The Investigation into the Attack on the U.S.S. *Cole.*" May 2001.

U.S. House of Representatives, House National Security Committee. Staff Report, "The Khobar Towers Bombing Incident." 14 August 1996.

U.S. House of Representatives, Permanent Select Committee on Intelligence and the Senate Select Committee on Intelligence. "Report of the Joint Inquiry into the Terrorist Attacks of September 11, 2001." 20 December 2002.

U.S. Senate, Committee on Banking, Housing, and Urban Affairs. "Hearing on the Reauthorization of the Iran and Libya Sanctions Act." 28 June 2001.

U.S. Senate, Judiciary Committee Subcommittee on Technology, Terrorism, and Government Information. "Statement for the Record of Dale Watson, Chief International Terrorism Section, National Security Division, Federal Bureau of Investigation on Foreign Terrorists in America: Five Years After the World Trade Center." 24 February 1998.

Court Cases

Adnan Awad v. United States. U.S. District Court, Northern District of Mississippi. Opinion for the Northern District of Mississippi, Eastern Division, 2001.

Stanford et al. v. Kuwait Airlines Corporation et al. U.S. Court of Appeals for the Second Circuit, Decided 16 July 1996.

United States v. Ahmed Abdel Sattar et al. U.S. District Court, Southern District of New York, Superseding Indictment (SI 02 Cr. 395) (JGK).

United States v. Ahmed al-Mughassil et al. Indictment. U.S. District Court, Eastern District of Virginia, June 2001 Term.

United States v. Ali Mohamed. U.S. District Court, Southern District of New York. S (7) 98 Cr. 1023 (LBS), NY Sup. Ct., 20 Oct. 2000.

United States v. Ali Mohamed. Plea. U.S. District Court, Southern District of New York. S (7) 98 Cr. 1023 (LBS)

United States v. Jamal Ahmed Mohammed Ali Al-Badawi and Fahd Al Quso. Indictment. U.S. District Court, Southern District of New York. S12 98 Cr. 1023 (KTD).

United States, Appellee, v. Mohammed A. Salameh. U.S. Court of Appeals for the Second Circuit, August Term 1997.

United States v. Mohtar Haouari. U.S. District Court, Southern District of New York. 54 00 Cr. 15, 3 July 2001.

United States, Appellee, v. Omar Ahmad Ali Abdel Rahman. U.S. Court of Appeals for the Second Circuit, August Term 1997.

United States v. Ramzi Ahmed Yousef. U.S. District Court, Southern District of New York. 925 F. Supp. 1063, 1065–73, 1996.

United States v. Ramzi Ahmed Yousef et al. Indictment. U.S. District Court, Southern District of New York. S (11) Cr. 180 (KTD).

United States, Appellee, v. Ramzi Yousef et al. U.S. Court of Appeals for the Second Circuit, 98–1041 L, August Term 2001.

United States v. Rezaq Omar Mohammed. U.S. Court of Appeals for the District of Columbia, 6 February 1998.

United States v. Timothy James McVeigh and Terry Lynn Nicholas. U.S. District Court, Western District of Oklahoma. CR 95–110.

United States v. Usama Bin Laden. Indictment. U.S. District Court, Southern District of New York. S (10) 98 Cr. 1023 (LBS).

United States v. Usama Bin Laden et al. U.S. District Court, Southern District of New York. S (7) 98 Cr. 1023, 6 February 2001.

United States v. Wadih El Hage. U.S. District Court, Southern District of New York. 98 Cr. (1023), 17 September 1998.

United States v. Wadoud Muhammad Hafiz al-Turk et al. U.S. District Court, District of Columbia, 28 August 2002.

United States v. Zacarias Moussaoui. U.S. District Court, Eastern District of Virginia. December 2001.

Index

Acknowledgments

So many people have assisted me with this project over the past five years that I cannot mention them all, just as I cannot thank them enough. A few of them deserve special acknowledgment because without them I could not have written the book. But first I should acknowledge that I am solely responsible for any errors of fact or any controversies of interpretation.

The University of Dayton gave me full support and encouragement. In particular, Christopher Duncan, my friend who happens also to be chair of the Department of Political Science, gave me extraordinary latitude and nominated me for the Rev. Roesch Chair in the Social Sciences, believing—correctly—that holding the position would enable me to pursue my research into the intersection of terrorism and human rights. Shawn Robinson in the university's office of media relations has been tenacious in arranging interviews with journalists working for the major news wires or in print and broadcast journalism over the past five years. This has been far more than a matter of publicity: what I have learned in the exchange with journalists has given me deeper insight into war on terrorism.

Countless students assisted me by locating documents, checking facts, and doing other apparently menial tasks that are actually very important to the production of a manuscript. The student assistants for the International Studies and Human Rights program, Adam Ensalaco, my son, and Megan Ware, were especially helpful. Jessica Rapagnani, Ann Marie Edmonds, Michael Soukup, and Jeffrey Pipoli helped with some of the research as they conducted their own independent study projects or Honors theses under my supervision. Special thanks goes to Paula Braley, who even after she was no longer my administrative assistant painstakingly corrected draft after draft and managed the arduous process of putting together the manuscript with consummate professionalism.

I am deeply indebted to Donna Schlagheck, a friend and colleague at nearby Wright State University. Professor Schlagheck scrutinized the manuscript, offered invaluable comments about both substance and style, and endorsed the book at a critical moment when the editorial board of University of Pennsylvania Press was looking for expert confirmation that the book merited the advance contract it offered me.

I am also indebted to Peter Agree, editor-in-chief of the University of Pennsylvania Press. Peter recognized the project's merits when I had only the first few chapters and offered an advance contract that enabled me to focus on the book. Most important, he showed great patience as deadlines came and went, thus affording me the time the make sure that the book met the high standards of both the author and the Press. Alison Anderson, Scott Barker, and Christopher Hu did extraordinary work in editing the manuscript and turning it into a book, something I have always believed is akin to alchemy.

Most important, I wish to acknowledge Sofia, my daughter to whom I dedicate this book, and Maria, my wife, who first suggested that I write it in our backyard on that terrible Tuesday evening in September. Thank you for your infinite patience: ya lo saben.